THE GREAT
TROUBLED FAMILIES
FRAUD

: State Lies & Failed Policies

Professor David P Gregg
(Retired)

THE GREAT TROUBLED FAMILIES FRAUD
Published by Green Man Books
15 Poulton Green Close, Spital, Wirral,
CH63 9FS (davidgregg@talktalk.net)

ISBN 978 – 1543236118

Printed by Create Space
Available from Amazon, the author
And other retail outlets

For my uncle, Newton Worthington, Salvation Army, and his comrades in arms who simply follow the command of their Captain to care for our troubled kindred: no ifs, no buts, no maybes…no moralising, no threats, no sanctions…

CONTENTS

Section 2   An Overview of Family Intervention Projects 1997-2012

Section 3   Commentaries on FIPs & the Causes of Family Dysfunction & ASB

Section 4   Formal Reviews of Government FIP Evaluation Reports 1997-2008

THE TROUBLED 'FAMILIES FROM HELL'

'As hard as it is to accept, the truth is despite our best efforts over many years – and I include myself in that – we just haven't got it right. We haven't succeeded in getting these families to change or in stopping the transmission of problems from generation to generation – we just haven't'

Louise Casey CB, Coalition Troubled Families Tsar
Presentation at Reform, 12.06.14

INTRODUCTION : Why British Society Is Doomed, Doomed !

This book is an account of the latest chapter in the long, sad story of the use of 'moral panics' and the creation of 'folk devils' to justify state interventions against vulnerable and defenceless minorities…those who cost us too much…those the Nazis called the 'useless mouths'. In this instance we will examine the unsuccessful attempts of the last four governments, from 1997 to 2015, to re-programme large numbers of 'dysfunctional' families in the underclass…families supposedly responsible for everything from the 'moral collapse' of Britain to the non-existent tidal wave of crime and anti-social behaviour engulfing us. In fact by 2015 the overall crime rate had been falling steadily for twenty years: since 1995, some two years before Tony Blair came in and invented 'anti-social behaviour', ASBOs and 'families from hell'. These inventions, masterfully deployed, proved very popular with an ill-informed public and became a mainstay of New Labour policy. The Coalition, with their natural authoritarian instincts, built on this base, using fear and disdain for the underclass poor to savagely attack not only the so-called 'troubled families' but also the feckless unemployed, the chronically sick and disabled and the working poor. This is their story and our shame.

This book will examine the 18 year history of state family intervention including the latest Troubled Families Programme. We will show the reader that this intervention programme is fraudulent and abusive.

- In the false characterisation of the families as criminal, addicted and irresponsible, justifying their harsh treatment and a wider attack on welfare benefits for the underclass.
- In attributing the poverty of the families to a feckless reluctance to work and misuse of resources through bad 'lifestyle choices'.

- In ignoring the remarkably high levels of long standing mental and physical illness and disabilities in the families as a key cause of 'problems' (75% of families are affected).
- In subjecting mentally ill and disabled families to a regime of 'tough sanctions' and threats to force co-operation on the grounds that their problems were self-imposed.
- In exaggerating by a factor of at least 3.5 X the cost of the TFP targeted families and implying huge savings could be made to justify the programme (claimed families cost: £9 billion per annum).
- In exaggerating by a factor of 16 X the potential cost reduction accessible by eliminating the 'bad behaviours' and 'lifestyle choices' of the families. Most costs related to poverty and health. (maximum possible saving potential ~£542 million).
- In claiming by 2015 that the TFP had saved £1.2 billion per annum on the basis of small, biased samples of local authority results and in failing to identify this as a *gross* saving before TFP costs.
- In claiming that 99% of the families had been 'turned around', i.e. cured of their dysfunctional behaviour, by the TFP, when the government sponsored National Evaluation (available in 2015) demonstrated **no significant impacts** on family status across *all* outcome performance measures and thus **zero reduction in cost.**

Over **£450 million** was spent on the TFP phase 1 covering 120,000 families with *no* positive impact on them and *no* savings to the state. A further billion is already being spent on phase 2 covering 400,000 similarly vulnerable families. Despite a critical but apparently toothless Parliamentary Public Accounts Committee TFP Inquiry in 2016, phase 2 is going ahead at the cost of ~£1 billion to 2020.

Better investigatory systems for identifying and halting the major misuse of public money are clearly required along with powers of prosecution against gross misconduct in public office and specifically in the making of fraudulent success claims about government spending programmes and policies. Some mechanism is needed completely independent of the Westminster – Whitehall village. Perhaps a new role could be defined for the Serious Fraud Office.

So how did this latest campaign against the feckless, undeserving poor begin? On the 4th of August 2011 the Metropolitan Police shot and killed the young 'black' man, Mark Duggan, in suspicious circumstances made worse by confusion and changes in the police 'story'.

Duggan was unarmed when shot but allegedly a member of a 'criminal gang'. This is still disputed. After some peaceful protests against the police, riots broke out in parts of London and later in several other UK cities. A moral panic and outrage ignited in the political and chattering classes. By the 11th of August David Cameron was addressing the House of Commons in apocalyptic tones. Cameron denied any connection between the death of Duggan and the riots saying

'It is completely wrong to say there is any justifiable link'

Cameron rather, attributed the riots to 'gangs' composed of youths from 'dysfunctional' families who were now responsible for the 'moral collapse' of the UK. By the 15th of August, presumably after consulting colleagues about how the Coalition could respond, Cameron came forward with some well tried, populist favourites. He had instructed police forces, too late, to flood the streets with riot police in order to restore order. The courts would work double shifts to prosecute the rioters who would be shown no mercy. He would move urgently to 'reform' the European Human Rights rules in order to make this easier. He would launch a 'national citizen service' to divert youths from the 'terror gangs'. (This is currently failing).

Finally and predictably, he had been reminded that New Labour had gained popularity by zapping the antisocial, dysfunctional 'families from hell' and their 'menace' children. Gordon Brown's target of reprogramming 50,000 chaotic families would be increased to 120,000 nationwide. The impression was given that this action alone would stop the 'moral collapse' of the country…and future riots. After all as Cameron said

'They [the troubled families] are the source of a large proportion of the problems in society…[These are] people with a twisted moral code…Drug addiction. Alcohol abuse. Crime. A cult of disruption and irresponsibility that cascades through the generations'.

David Cameron speech; December 2011

We will see that this description is *completely false* for the vast majority of the 120,000 families. The descriptor applying to the most families is that '**75%** have a member with a limiting, long standing illness or disability'. The Cameron approach (like that of Blair before him) has a long pedigree. I discussed the issue of 'underclass control' with an ex superintendent friend. He described the '7 Is' of policing: police deal mainly with the idiotic, insane, inadequate, inept, incompetent, incontinent and inebriate.

—

9

My police friend pointed to the long standing history of this issue and to an extensive anthropological research literature. In 'Out Of Care: the Community Support of Juvenile Offenders' (Allen & Unwin, 1980) we learn

'the law is far from being an impartial mediator of social relations... instead *it weighs most heavily upon the most defenceless and is hardly brought to bear against the illegalities of the powerful...*The main target, as it was more explicitly in the nineteenth century, [is] the dangerous classes – unorganized labour, the unemployed, marginal, transient and easily stigmatized groups, the non-respectable workers and the undeserving poor...'

Over centuries the control of the underclass has been justified by generating 'moral panics' about particular classes of crime (or indeed non-crime) directed at 'folk devils' and 'scapegoat' groups. In 'Hooligan: A History of Respectable Fears' (Macmillan,1983) the author traces organized fear of the 'dangerous classes' back to the seventeenth century. We read that it is

'always those crimes that are associated with the *materially disadvantaged underclass* which have provided the continuing thread within this history of respectable fears'

Finally one last item. On the Government National Archive / learning curve website, under 'Crime & Punishment' we read something very familiar

'Vagabonds became the main criminal stereotype of the 16th and 17th centuries. The very existence of such people made the ruling class angry – as can be seen in the language used in some of these [research] sources ...vagabonds [were said] *to choose not to work and were lazy , preferring a life of crime...* Harsh laws were passed against them.'

In this book we will examine what happened next in the Troubled Families Programme but also show that by 2011 the evidence of thirteen years of such intervention projects had demonstrated that these projects achieved very little in terms of sustainably 'turning around' antisocial, chaotic or troubled families. Instead they abused the mentally impaired poor. But before we do this let's look at the evidence that emerged about the *causes* of the Summer Riots which so reinvigorated the state appetite for underclass family intervention and scapegoating.

The LSE, funded by the Joseph Rowntree Foundation, soon published a comprehensive report, 'Reading the Riots', based on interviews with 270 rioters and other data. Let's look at the characteristics of the rioters.

80% of the rioters were male; 30% were aged 10-17 years; 49% were aged 18-25 years; 26% were white; 47% were black; 5% were Asian; 17% were mixed or other ethnicities. Overall 74% were from ethnic minorities. Overall , 59% came from the most deprived 20% of areas in the UK.

Remember the major, knee jerk, role assigned to gang membership by Cameron et al? Well initially the police claimed that 29% of the rioters arrested were gang members! By no means a majority, but still shocking perhaps. On reflection, and no doubt reluctantly, it was admitted only 19% of rioters in London were gang members but nationally the rate was only 13%. Later the independent Riots Panel surveyed 80 local authorities in riot areas and found that only 5% had found an overlap between rioters and families provisionally targeted for the Troubled Families Programme. The 2014 ECORYS troubled family survey suggested that only 7% of families had a member with a gang association.

Already the simple equation, rioters = gang members = dysfunctional families from hell was broken, *but the facts seldom interfere with a moral panic and a populist, political opportunity*. We can describe Cameron's statements as classic 'Fake News'. In fact two characteristics of the rioters stand out. Firstly a large majority were from ethnic minorities. Secondly a large majority were from some of the poorest areas of Britain. Ethnicity and poverty largely defined the rioters.

So what did the rioters themselves say about their motivations?

75% said the Duggan ethnic shooting was an important or very important factor.

85% said 'policing' was an important or very important factor. Many named unfair ethnicity based stop and search practices as an issue, for example.

86% said dissatisfaction with 'poverty' was an important or very important factor. By 2011 austerity had already been biting for three years and youth unemployment had rocketed.

These self-assigned motivations seem to match well with the observed demographics of the rioters. If the 120,000 troubled families were targeted because they were at the root of the riots we might expect some match in their demographics and those of the rioters. In one major respect we will see this is so: the troubled families targeted for reprogramming, like the rioters, were *amongst the poorest in the country*. In other respects it is hard to see any match between the two groups. Consider ethnic mix.

74% of the rioters were non-white and 26% white. In the troubled families 72% were white and 28% non-white. **Only 7% of project families were black compared to the 47% of black rioters.**

We must conclude that the Troubled Families Programme targeted very poor whites in the underclass, not the statistically 'likely' family sources of the rioters. Later as we look closer at the families from hell, we will clearly see another major difference between rioters and the troubled families : *the latter have very high levels of physical and mental health problems and disabilities among both adults and children.* The attempt to justify the Troubled Families Projects via the riots was a cynical political tactic and we will see that the same tactic has been repeatedly deployed since 1997, notably by Tony Blair, et al. These poor and very vulnerable families have been repeatedly branded as the primary source of national crime and antisocial behaviour while receiving very little meaningful help for their multiple, often medical, problems.

This book will attempt to summarise the performance history of organised British State interventions in anti-social, dysfunctional, chaotic, troubled families since 1997 up to the end of 2016.

So far as the author knows this is the first time that a complete performance history based on detailed analyses of successive phases of state intervention, along with commentaries, has been brought together. Over several years students and others have requested parts of this material. Now it is altogether in one place and the author hopes this will aid future researchers in sociology, mental health and criminology in particular. There is also a *slight* chance that a few intelligent, honest, empathic British politicians may find it useful... if there are any.

However he is also confident that lay members of the public will find the information and the arguments about intrusive state intervention, accessible and disturbing. The lay reader will quickly realise that we are not dealing with a 'nanny state' here but a 'wicked stepmother'. The reader may even conclude that the stepmother has a name. If this material reignites compassion for the Troubled Families in one Daily Mail columnist or reader the author will be content.

We will begin with the recent Coalition Troubled Families Programme which set out to process 120,000 of the 'worst' families in 2012. As an illustration, the record of the TF project on the Wirral, the author's own home area, will be analysed in detail based on data obtained by FoIA requests to Wirral Council. Only local authorities, not the Dept. for Communities & Local Government, hold detailed performance and family data, if at all. We will also take a national overview of the characteristics of the families based on an independent 2014 report from ECORYS and the final 2016 TFP National Evaluation. We will show that only a very small proportion of family individuals had histories of crime or anti-social behaviour in contrast to the ongoing government propaganda.

We will find that the families had remarkably high levels of mental and physical health problems. We will show how the project data has been *manipulated*, via dubious success criteria and double counting, to grossly inflate the success in 'turning around' these families. Farcical **99%** 'turn around' rates were claimed for families. 132 local authorities of 152 claimed **exactly 100%** 'turn around' rates by data manipulation and were paid a £4,000 bounty for each family. Yet there is **no** evidence for sustained, positive changes in the families. Supposed family improvements were tracked for only a year, for example. We will also deconstruct the national cost savings claims and show how they have been grossly distorted in content and presentation.

In October 2016 the long suppressed National Evaluation of the TFP phase 1 was published at the insistence of the Parliamentary Public Accounts Select Committee. For the first time the TFP family outcomes were compared with a well matched comparison 'control' group of similar families. This involved using both official national administrative data for the families and a detailed first hand survey of family outcomes and views about TFP changes.

Both exercises showed no statistically significant differences between the reprogrammed TFP families and the control families in all the outcome areas from employment, truancy, crime and ASB through to multiple measures of family health and wellbeing. The TFP had no objective, measurable, attributable effect on the families. It follows that cost savings are not the 2012 claimed £9 billion per annum, nor the mid 2015 claimed £1.2 billion per annum, but ZERO. The promised 'national cost benefit analysis' exercise was quietly cancelled for this reason.

The villains in this story are not the troubled families, nor the many well meaning social workers who administer what help they can in a flawed intervention system, but the politicians who have targeted the troubled families for their 'high cost' in state support while falsely branding them as criminal, degenerate drug addicts and drunks who make deliberate 'antisocial' lifestyle choices on the backs of taxpayers. The other villains are the senior civil servants who have blatantly misused and manipulated data in an astonishing way to support their political masters' claims about the degenerate nature and cost of the families and the savings potential of the TFP. **Their arrogance and contempt for the public is breathtaking and their actions amount to a fraud which should be punished.**

The sad truth is that the substantial support costs to the state of these poor, mainly chronically ill and disabled families could only be eliminated by *eliminating* them. Perhaps a programme of abortion and 'voluntary' sterilisation backed by benefit sanctions? We should recall here that the Nazi Holocaust began with the euthanasia of the German disabled and chronically sick 'useless mouths' justified by their economic burden on the state (see the cover of this book for an example of Nazi 'useless mouth' propaganda). Numbers are uncertain but it is likely that in the Greater Reich between the late 1930s and 1945, ~20,000 disabled children and ~230,000 disabled adults were murdered by the state with the co-operation of *local authority officials*, *doctors* and *care* institutions (10,11). ~370,000 were also sterilised. The pioneering, mass murdering, gassing techniques developed for the 'useless mouths' found other uses of course and 250,000 is a small number compared with 6 million. However while we rightly remember the Jews slaughtered and tell ourselves never again, we forget the chronically ill and disabled innocents who died. They are invisible except to the descendents of their fellow victims who kindly, in their own sorrow, remember them.

In this country we are told in the media that we have 120,000 troubled families *but not* that **75%** have members with 'limiting, long standing illnesses and disabilities.' **52%** have children with SENs or other special needs. **45%** have adults with a mental illness. We are told they are a costly burden on the state because of their 'lifestyle choices'. Even the Nazis did not *blame* the disabled and chronically ill for their conditions.

As Tony Blair famously said in 2006

'There is no point pussyfooting…if we are not prepared to intervene… *pre-birth even*…these kids a few years down the line are going to be a menace to society…'

Prime Minister Tony Blair: On the unborn children of lone mothers.

When senior politicians, whatever their motivations, appeal to our dark angels in such powerful ways *there will be blood*. Later we will examine recent mass benefit sanctions and cuts and increased suicide rates amongst disabled and desperate claimants (Appendix S1).

The second section of the book provides an overview of all the Family Intervention Projects from 1997 to 2010, under New Labour, based on the author's 'FIPs : A Classic Case of Policy Based Evidence', a paper published by the Centre for Crime & Justice Studies in their Evidence Based Policy series; 2011 (see section 2.2). The picture which emerges is very similar to the TFP in terms of the families' health problems and the **very weak evidence** that any sustained improvements resulted from these interventions. The £450 million spent on the TFP phase 1 and the ~ £1 billion to be spent on phase 2 could have been diverted into non-abusive medical/social/education interventions with proven efficacy.

We will then examine the early intervention activities of the Coalition government from 2010 to 2012 noting their extraordinary attempts, by the use of unsustainable and qualitative 'success definitions', to boost claims of project success. They define 10 outcomes and success in any *one* is claimed as an *overall* family success. The TFP plays *the same trick*. In essence black becomes white because the government says so. In successive FIP evaluations from 1999 to 2011 it was clear that the lack of control groups meant that **none** of the claimed improvements in families could be attributed to the projects and those improvements were anyway greatly exaggerated. A *self-sustaining, uncritical, untested myth* emerged that FIPs were a great success and this was propagated from government to government despite clear warnings from the official project evaluators and independent commentators. The TFP was a diluted version of the FIPs.

The third section of the book initially takes a less formal look at the history of the projects with additional commentary on the views of experts in several relevant fields and a look at the nature of those targeted, including the role of neuro-disability in young offenders. This commentary is from my recent book, 'The ASBO Gestapo'. A further commentary from the book looks at the medical evidence for the genetic and environmental basis of supposed 'dysfunctional' behaviour and how it might be tackled by proper medical treatments, remedial education and improved nutrition.

Section four presents four, detailed reviews of the official government FIP evaluation reports over all stages of the New Labour families initiative from the first Dundee Family Project, through the second phase Six Projects, to the roll out of the Fifty Three Projects, main phase.

We will see that the independent, academic research teams who carried out the evaluations for the governments *repeatedly point to the weakness of the data bases used to make public claims of 'success' and to caveats about the unjustified inferences drawn by governments.* In particular none of the projects defined or used control groups; none of the programmes were the subject of randomised controlled trials or the equivalent protocols usually used to assess socio-medical interventions. In strict scientific terms *all the claims are invalid.* Yet in executive summaries and ministerial statements made to the media, *none* of the evaluators' caveats were reported. The family intervention fraud is nearly twenty years old.

These official evaluations also make clear the nature of the families targeted for intervention by New Labour: they are very similar to the 120,000 now targeted by the Troubled Families Programme: very poor, large families, living in social housing, in debt, unemployed, socially inadequate, mentally disordered, physically ill, with learning disabled children with schooling problems. Nothing has been learned in nearly two decades. **Surely this was and is a national scandal**.

Remarkably another common thread runs through the government family interventions under New Labour and the Coalition: the presence of a senior civil servant, **Dame Louise Casey CB**, who was Tony Blair's Rough Sleepers Tsar, ASB Tsar and Respect Tsar before becoming Troubled Families Tsar for David Cameron. She has also been the Victims Tsar and Grand Inquisitor into the Rotherham child sex scandal. We will see that Louise was the 'go to' gun for hire whenever the poor underclass rabble needed another taste of the state lash. That is why this book began with a public statement from Casey confirming the *failure* of eighteen years of state intervention in families with multiple problems. We will see that even so in 2016 Casey was still claiming a great **99%** success rate and **'value for money writ large'** for the TFP, despite all the official contrary evidence, in front of the Public Accounts Committee of Parliament… and getting away with it! She was even given an award !

Readers with an academic background might still be surprised by the weakness of the evidence offered by successive governments for the success of these interventions, *even after* the setting of very weak success criteria and the evidential deck had been stacked. Casey provides an answer. In 2005 she addressed a formal Home Office – ACPO Dinner with her speech 'Research: Help or Hindrance?' Her conclusion was: 'Hindrance thanks very much!' Having extolled to ministers the virtue of 'coming into work pissed' she spoke with passion about New Labour's supposed commitment to evidence based policy.

'If No.10 says bloody evidence based policy to me one more time, I'll deck them one'

So now we know. Shortly after this Blair promoted her. Later she would become Cameron's Troubled Families Tsar and then Victims' Tsar. That says it all about political attitudes to objective evidence analysis in social policy matters.

Some of the arguments in this book are a little technical. The lay reader, if this proves heavy going, may care to simply consider this. The 120,000 family phase of the TF Programme supposedly cost central government ~£448 million with possibly an additional ~£100 million spent by local authorities. We will show that that money achieved very little. Phase 2 at a cost of £1 billion is going ahead despite the clear National Evaluation 2016 findings and the failed 2016 PAC Inquiry.

The author will keep repeating the following statement throughout this book in the light of the obviously limited attention span of politicians who may read it. I ask the normal, alert reader, who can assess evidence without biased, ideological preconceptions, to forgive me for this repetition.

The Public Accounts Committee TF Inquiry, while critical of phase 1, failed to understand that the TFP model is a policy disaster which cannot be redeemed by fiddling around the edges with improved monitoring. The TFP does not address the sources of the TF problems and *structurally* it is incapable of significantly reducing their costs to the state. This book will spell out the truth in language simple enough so that even British MPs can understand the position. But do they care? Will they listen?

The tax payer, seeing the mess which the Troubled Families Programme represents, might also wish to ask themselves these questions.

Is the TFP *atypical* of state programmes in that the targets were in the despised underclass and **a fraudulent waste of ~£1.5 billion** to bully them was worth it for the presumed populist boost it gave the government?

Is the TFP actually *typical* of state programmes, in terms of ineffective, ideologically based policies, incompetently implemented, *whose failures are perfectly predictable from the beginning?*

Is the TFP *typical* in that civil servants find it *easy to mislead* the Public Accounts Committee which oversee major public spending programmes?

Just how much of our tax money is routinely flushed down the drain?

By 2015 Cameron, inspired by the 'triumph' of the TFP initiative, announced that a further 400,000 families from hell would be reprogrammed from 2015 to 2020: estimated extra central government cost alone, around £1 billion. This is your tax money going to support politically motivated, ineffective and abusive, voodoo social engineering at a time when the NHS and mental health services, such as CAMHS in particular, are under severe strain. Yet spending on youth mental health has been shown to be very cost effective in treating the kind of people who are labelled as troubled families as we will see (7). Ironically, as this book was being written, UK mental health trusts reported to the regulator an 8.2% real terms fall in their income from 2010-11 to 2014-15 as mental health referrals increased by 18.5%. This fall in funding amounted to ~£598 million compared with the ~£600 million cost of the TF programme to 2015. Mental health trusts predicted a further 8% real terms fall in income from 2014-15 to 2018-19.Remember these figures as you read on and feel free to get angry. More importantly, for the sake of the vulnerable poor in the 'underclass', don't get fooled again by 'Fake News' and 'Alternative Facts' from governments.

SECTION 1

THE TROUBLED FAMILIES PROGRAMME
PHASE 1 : 2012 - 2015

'As an ever increasing number of families become dysfunctional, an ever increasing supply of socially offensive individuals results'

Frank Field MP DL, Labour Member for Birkenhead.

1.1 Introduction

The aims of the TFP were to 'turn around' the lives of the 120,000 families by getting adults into work, eliminating crime and antisocial behaviour and eliminating child behaviour problems such as truancy. These actions would allegedly greatly reduce the high cost of the families to the state, supposedly some £9 billion per annum, by changing their selfish, feckless life styles and addressing underlying long term problems.

The TFP was supposed to demonstrate that far too much money was spent on 'reactive' policies and support and too little on 'targeted' policies and support. That is a reasonable hypothesis which the TFP tested, possibly unfairly, to destruction. The TFP failed to ask, at the design stage, just how much of the high costs of the troubled families could, *in principle*, be eliminated by family behaviour and lifestyle modification?

Firstly, if most of the costs were *fixed*, because of family size or mental and physical health issues and disabilities and poverty for example, the saving scope would be limited. This turns out to be the case.

Secondly in the limited areas where behaviour modification could affect costs, were the types of TFP interventions intended *actually capable* of changing behaviour? The answer turns out to be no.

The author can hear the DCLG (and perhaps some readers) saying : ah, but hindsight is easy! My point is throughout this book that the history of Family Intervention (government commissioned) evaluations since 1999 onwards had *already answered* these questions. See sections 2,3,4 of this book. The answers were repeatedly ignored by governments and do not seem to have registered with watchdogs such as the Public Accounts Committee. The author hopes this second book on the TF issue finally gets through to honest, intelligent, compassionate politicians.

The Troubled Families Programme was organised on the basis of local authority run or subcontracted projects, under nationally defined rules and a financial framework for the payment of bounty money for each family processed. For simply signing up a family an 'attachment fee' of £3,200 was paid as an inducement. Further bounties were paid for targets allegedly achieved as we will see.

The government *decided* that there were 120,000 troubled families across the country. Local authorities were given an *exact* local TF target number based, supposedly, on a list of 'deprivation' related characteristics. We will see that from the start there was a mismatch between the deprivation selection criteria and the payment by results criteria.

This caused endless mischief and was compounded when LAs were given 'local discretion' on family selection in order to make up the numbers to the DCLG local targets. Each local authority was expected to select families according to the 'rules' we will examine later and to eventually submit evidence about changes in family behaviour as the basis for payments.

It is important to understand that the TFP was not monolithic nor uniform in its design and activities. The ~60 earlier Family Intervention Projects were much more uniform with the template set by the first Dundee Family Project in the late 1990s. The central idea was for an 'assertive' dedicated key worker who rode the families from day to day in a 'non-negotiable' way and (occasionally) provided support and access (occasionally) to additional services. The FIP was described as the 'gold standard' of intervention (but it still failed: see sections 2 and 4). The TFP designers obviously realised that scaling up the FIP design across 132 LAs was not feasible because of cost. The TFP was a pale reflection of the FIPs.

It is also true that many LAs already had some family intervention activities of various types in place. This provided an obvious solution bound to be popular at local level: co-opt these existing activities under the TFP label and provide the LA with cash in the form of bounty money (initially £3,200) for supposedly signing up each family and accepting the new TFP badge. Necessity became a virtue!

Even better, I believe that the DCLG *knew* that family 'turn around', even with creative and flexible definitions of family success, would be difficult … how could they not given the extensive FIP history…so another rationale was invented: never mind turning the families around, we are intent on 'system transformation' in the LAs in how they tackle dysfunctional families. This means that LAs could use the bounty money to set up new internal processes and systems, for example in IT. This 'process' target becomes as important as 'turning around' the families!

The alert reader can surely see the problem here? If the new LA systems and processes *do not lead* to large numbers of 'turned around' families what is the justification for spending the money on them… other than filling the funding gaps caused by government austerity policies? Perhaps that was the point? Everybody wins except the troubled families and the poor bloody, bamboozled tax payer…you and me!

Let's look at the threefold TFP 'delivery model'
(NE Synthesis Report October 2016).

1.   the dedicated team : creating or expanding an existing team.
2.   the hybrid model : combination of new teams and embedding provision within the existing structures or services.
3.   the embedded approach: embed and *transform* the workforce and the way people work.

We are also told that

'a proportion of the TF cohort was supported by existing services or (close to) 'business as usual' *in most LAs*. These families were being *tracked as part* of the TF cohort and *claimed for* under the PbyR based financial framework. Aside from being offered some levels of additional support ....they were distinct from the rest of the cohort...'

   It was this arrangement that led to media accusations that 'data matching' in LA files was being used to claim families as falsely turned around by the TFP. So a range of TFP delivery (or indeed non-delivery) models were in play during phase 1. Just how intensive was the support given to the families overall: that was repeatedly claimed by politicians as the key element of the TFP approach? Section 10 of the NE 2016 synthesis report describes 'families experiences' of the TFP:

Key Worker visit frequency	troubled families support experience
Once a day or more	**3%**
Several times a week	**19**
Every week	37
Every 2 weeks	18
Every month	12
Every 3 months	5
Every 6 months	1

Given the political flim-flam these numbers may surprise the reader as they did the author. We are repeatedly told of the brave key workers, out every day, harrowing the lazy slag, troubled mother into getting the kids up and out to school, smartly dressed, after a hearty middle class, cooked breakfast , etc, etc. Just what does 'intensive' support actually mean? Well only **22%** saw their key worker several times a week. This is the level of intervention familiar from the old FIPs for supposedly 'gripping' ASB families. These proportions alone tell us that 78% of the families *do not* get intensive interventions despite senior ministers' claims of criminal, drug ravaged lifestyles. 36% see somebody every 2 weeks or less frequently. 17% see somebody once a month or less frequently. We are also told that **9%** of the main carers in the families *did not even know the name of their key worker.* Remember the LAs were getting £3,200 for every family they sign up …no questions asked.

Can a 'visit' every 2 weeks or less frequently really 'turn around' the lives of families with multiple, deep seated, problems? Those with 5 out of 7 recognised measures of deprivation? How does a 2 weekly visit address the 45% of families with a mentally ill adult? Or the 33% with a child with mental health issues, or the 39% with an SEN child? Surely we are dealing here with *a cruel fraud and a conspiracy of powerful interests* to the detriment of a vulnerable, powerless minority …*and* the tax payer?

In many respects the TFP was more about cock up than conspiracy. The conspiracy element was in the *deliberate misrepresentation* of the families and in the *manipulation of evidence to claim a 100% family 'turn around' success rate and huge, non-existent cost savings.* Even so the 100% success claims were greeted with immediate derision by knowledgeable observers and we will see that the cost and savings claims are *patently and transparently false.* This did not stop these claims being repeated in the House of Commons as well as in the media. The farce element here is that the architects of this fiasco believed that nobody would notice the crude manipulation of data and evidence, but then the promoters of family intervention projects had gotten away with 'nonsense based evidence' for nearly two decades. Why worry now?

Given the arms length nature of project evaluation (until the final stage), the local authorities held the detailed data on the families and their claims made to the Department for Communities & Local Government were not independently audited. A small number of 'spot checks' were supposedly made.

To understand in detail what happened in the projects it is necessary to look at the local level and apply the Freedom of Information Act to supplement the limited amount of data in the public domain. This has been done for the author's home area of Wirral along with data from similar requests to the DCLG and using the report 'National Evaluation of the Troubled Families Programme' published in 2014 by ECORYS (12), for the government. This did *not* evaluate project effectiveness but provides a good overview of family characteristics from a national sample. Later we will examine in detail the final National Evaluation of phase 1 documents published (a year late after complaints from the Public Accounts Committee) in October 2016.

1.2 Family Selection and Characteristics
   : Myths & Reality

'They [the troubled families] are the source of a large proportion of the problems in society…[These are] people with a twisted moral code…Irresponsibility. Selfishness. Behaving as if your choices have no consequences. Children without fathers. Reward without effort. Rights without responsibilities…Communities without control… Drug addiction. Alcohol abuse. Crime. A cult of disruption and irresponsibility that cascades through the generations'.

David Cameron speeches ; 2011

Cameron also used the familiar tags: 'shameless', 'criminal', 'neighbours from hell'. We will see that for a very large proportion of families these claims are simply lies. Of course most of the families are not involved in crime, nor had addiction problems. We will see that they were merely chronically ill or disabled, socially inadequate, unable to work and poor. An attempt was made to spin the programme as a 'compassionate' one and, as Iain Duncan Smith famously said, we should not let these people 'fester' in worklessness. But Cameron spoiled the story. He also said

'We will not fix these problems without a revolution in responsibility, personal, family, social'

  Yes, if you are sick, disabled, unemployable and socially inadequate you need to show some responsibility, show some backbone and moral fibre! Ironically the new 'family' plan was hailed as part of a major 'family friendly' initiative across government…the election was coming of course.

  In the later sections of this book we will look at the history of family selection for intervention projects. Two characteristics stand out. Firstly the families were carefully selected for their *compliance* with the process. That is, they were those who could be bullied into cooperating by 'assertive, non-negotiable' interventions and threats of 'tough sanctions': benefit cuts, eviction and removal of children into care. Even so large numbers of families typically dropped out. In the TFP 40% of families were sanctioned or threatened with sanctions *during* the programme itself. Secondly those in the FIPs were mainly sick, disabled, poor, socially inadequate and vulnerable. We will see that the Coalition TF programme follows the same pattern. Let us take a quote from the horse's mouth, from the Troubled Families Tsar herself, Dame Louise Casey CB, to give a flavour of the overall approach.

———

'We are not running some cuddly social workers' programme...we should be better at talking about things like shame and guilt...we have lost the ability to be judgemental because we worry about being seen as nasty to poor people'

Many analysts, unfamiliar with the history of state family interventions, were puzzled about the origin of the Coalition's 120,000 troubled families target and understandably confused about selection criteria. Two sets of criteria appeared to be in circulation at the dawn of the TF Programme. Cameron, Eric Pickles and Louise Casey, Troubled Families Tsar, saturated the media with tales of the dark side: of families both lazy and criminal! The official selection criteria were

- One adult in the family on out of work benefits.
- Households with at least one minor with a proven offence or any member of the household subject to an ASB intervention.
- A child in the household with a record of school exclusion and truancy

These should be familiar by now. However the National Audit Office (in December 2013) reported the actual origin of the 120,000 figure and the associated criteria. They came from a report commissioned by the Cabinet Office in 2004, under New Labour: 'The Families and Children Study'. The study looked at families with severe, multiple measures of deprivation.

Here they are:

- no parent in work
- poor quality housing
- **no parent with qualifications**
- **mother with mental health problems**
- **one parent with a long standing illness or disability**
- family on low income
- **family cannot afford some food or clothing items**.

These are not 'families from hell' but 'families in hell'.

We can see that the only overlap between the two criteria sets is worklessness. The 120,000 families estimate was based on families having 5 out of 7 of these measures of deprivation. Please note that there is no mention of school problems, criminality or ASB here. As the NAO drily commented

'There is a *mismatch* between the criteria the DCLG used to calculate the total number of families at which its programme is targeted and the criteria for identifying the families in each local authority and then rewarding positive outcomes.'

This official 2013 assessment seems clear enough but **no** correcting action was taken by government. On the contrary. When commentators pointed out the disconnect and questioned the national families target Eric Pickles dismissed concern as

'a rather silly, academic point'

This is dangerous nonsense: misuse of evidence has consequences. If Pickles and more so Casey, had bothered to look at prominent official information sources including the annual Children & Families Survey from the DWP up to 2007 and the Cabinet Office review of that year they would have found this table.

Family disadvantages	secondary school children	
	In trouble with the police	suspended or excluded
None	1%	1%
1-2	3	4
3-4	5	7
5 or more (our TF cohort)	10%	11%

As disadvantage increases so does the frequency of police and school problems *but* note that even in the families with 5 or more disadvantages only 10% of children are in trouble with police and only 11% in school. **~90% had not been in trouble.** This result is consistent with earlier FIP families going back to 1999 and with *actual*, current measurements on our TFP families as we will see. This anomaly was presented to the PAC Inquiry 2016 as a written submission (13) based on data from the Cabinet Office published in 2008 (14). There is no sign it was registered or acted on, along with the other evidence based, critical submissions.

When we consider the false and damaging denigration of the project families as criminal and antisocial and the massive waste of tax payer money due to TFP mis-targeting, Pickles was surely speaking from another planet. So was Louise Casey, telling the media:

'I think a lot is made of this, in retrospect, which needn't be. The most important thing when I got here in 2011 was if we take that 120,000 figure, give it to LAs, give them the criteria behind troubled families, and they can populate it, which they have done – then I am getting on with the job.'

As a result of this off hand position, which is typical of 'can do' Casey, those targeted were primarily families *in trouble* rather than those *causing trouble*.

The 120,000 figure itself, even if properly applied to families with 5 out of 7 measures of deprivation, is very uncertain since it is based on a small sample. In fact Professor Ruth Levitas (on the Radio 4 More or Less programme in 2012) pointed out that 120,000 is the estimated *central point in a wide range of possible numbers* . If this number is 2% of national families the sampling uncertainty is plus or minus 3%. Insisting that LAs take a *precise* share (based on some other, different again, DCLG deprivation data) of the central estimate and recruit *exactly* that number locally is what is 'silly'. Even so LAs did exactly that. As the DCLG told the media in June 2012

'The 120,000 figure is a widely used and *respected* figure based on government research on families with multiple problems and is a number that is recognised by *all* 152 LAs who have signed up to work with that number of families in their area.'

And we could add : this 'respect' had nothing to do of course with paying each LA £3,200 per family signed up at a time of budget cuts and austerity. Just take the money and run!

What about the other set of criteria for selecting families? That is unemployment, crime, ASB and school attendance problems? Reducing these problems would lead to further payments by results bounties. The framework concentrated on family (mainly youth) crime and school problems. The detailed PbyR criteria were:

'They achieve **all 3** of the education and crime/ASB measures where relevant:

1.   Each child in the family has had fewer than 3 fixed (temporary) exclusions **and** less than 15% of unauthorised absences in the last 3 school terms: **and**

2.   A 60% reduction in ASB across the family in the last 6 months: **and**

3. Offending rate by all minors in the family reduced by at least 33% in the last 6 months.

Bounty paid £700

If they do not enter work but achieve progress to work (one adult has either volunteered for the Work Programme or attached to the European Social Fund provisions in the last 6 months).

Bounty paid £100

OR :

At least one adult in the family has moved off out of work benefits into continuous employment in the last 6 months (and is not on the European Socail Fund or Work Programme to avoid double counting.)

Bounty paid £800

A family was defined as 'turned around' if either the employment or crime/ASB/school targets were met. The reader may feel that the crime/ASB/school target is quite tough at first sight. However we also read

'Note for the crime/ASB/education and 'progress to work' results, if one of the measures is not relevant, the **full** results payment will still be made [and the family defined as turned around overall].'

Note also that a child could be absent from school 1 day in 7 and still be defined as turned around. Minor offending could be at 2 / 3 of the entry level and the family still counted a success. Family ASB could be at 40% of entry level and still the family would be defined as 'turned around'. We will also see that the ASB, even for the small proportion of families involved, was very low level. As was crime. By early 2015 we will see evidence that *even the above loose rules had been relaxed* resulting in 132 LAs claiming a '100% family turn around'.

By signing up a family a LA also received an 'attachment fee' of £3,200 up front, no questions asked. (by 2013/14 the fee had dropped to £2,400 and by 2014/15, £1600.) For the LAs that reward, just for identifying a troubled family, must have been irresistible at a time of severe funding cuts. Many LAs would *know* that getting these families into work or significantly reducing chronic schooling problems and ASB in some recidivist families would not be easy but if they then missed the £800 'turn around' delivery bonus so what? The problem was that the Coalition government had promised to turn around *all* these families. The LAs would be exposed to immense pressures to deliver and when they could not the apparently rigorous rules for claiming success were relaxed in several ways. Meeting 2 or even 1 sub-criterion in the crime/ASB/school target cluster rather than 4 would become acceptable as we will see. For example early on many LAs reported having difficulty finding enough families to meet the PbyR official definition of 'troubled'. In 2013 three London boroughs, Westminster, Kensington & Chelsea and Hammersmith & Fulham, had identified less than 2% of their DCLG defined numbers. The Director of family services at Westminster said:

'The numbers in this cabinet report were *indicative* and we are still waiting on more data from central government to accurately model our eligibility on a local level.'

Inside Housing Friday, May 17 2013.

N.B 'indicative' is civil service speak for 'inaccurate' or 'wrong'. We will see it used often.

This wide spread 'numbers' problem was addressed by inventing 'local discretion' for LAs which in effect gave permission for a free for all and a partial abandonment of the PbyR framework. The top 7 discretionary criteria (of 24) used by councils were

Domestic violence/abuse 68%   safeguarding 65% substance abuse 57%

Mental health   52%   probation / offenders   35%

Child protection issues 33%   housing issues   28%   NEETs 15%

Source : ECORYS 2014 (12)

Note that the top four criteria are medical / social issues and take us a little way back towards the original deprivation based criteria. Although domestic abuse is a commonly cited criterion note that only 0.2% of TF adults had committed a violent offence (NE 2016 administrative data). Note also the housing issues which usually meant poorly maintained or dirty social housing and rent arrears. According to the NAO

'Over 50% of local authorities used domestic violence or abuse, drugs, alcohol or substance abuse, and mental health for their criteria.'

In some councils unambiguous measures of deprivation alone, such as having free school meals or receiving a carers allowance, were used to target families. We will see that in fact issues such as drug and alcohol abuse were at a low frequency but, hey, they helped to get the family numbers up and avoid embarrassment all round.

Other evidence exists of the efforts made to find suitable families matching the PbyR criteria. The phase 1 National Evaluation report 'Final Report on the Family Monitoring Data 2016' provides an analysis of 'issues' experienced by the families. 28 sub-issues are reported in several clusters.

Employment 2   education 6   housing 2   child safeguarding 5

Crime / ASB **8**   police call outs / domestic violence **5**

So 46.4% relate allegedly to crime / ASB, 21.4% relate to education, and 17.9% to child safeguarding. The average number of sub-issues per family was **7** at project entry and **5** at exit. So although **100%** of families were 'turned around', as claimed, it follows that on average 5 out of 7 'long term' problems still continued. **If families still experience 71.4% of serious entry problems can they really be called 'turned around'?** If their 'high costs' to the state are proportional to their problems surely this means that 71.4% of the costs are still there. We will see later that this is roughly so. We can also see that the sub-criteria space is sparsely populated. Fewer than 1% of families had 15 or more sub-problems out of 28. This alone makes a mockery of government claims.

We also see that the deck is stacked : there are *many more ways* to meet the crime / ASB definition than in any other problem area. Does this matter? Well note that at entry 70% of families had 0 or 1 crime / ASB issues and at exit this rose slightly to 89%. *Zero or one out of 13 sub-criteria!* This explains why there is a mismatch between the LA recorded frequency of crime / ASB in the families and that found in the national administrative data base and the family survey database in the final National Evaluation 2016. According to LAs, 48.8% of families had 'any of the crime/ASB criteria' but only 19% of TFP selected families had ASB actions taken against them according to the NE synthesis report. Only 10% of youngsters had been charged by the police. Only 1.7% of families had an adult with a custodial sentence. On Wirral for example only 1.2% of children had an acceptable behaviour contract or an ASBO. We will see in section 4.3 on the earlier evaluation of the 53 phase family intervention projects that the level of crime / ASB was also massively exaggerated. Most ASB was and is trivial but *anything* counts if the government says so.

Here is a simple message for the politicians: please read it carefully.

If you include a long enough list of target sub-criteria you can get any number of families you require. Never mind the quality…feel the width.

If you are then allowed to claim a successful family 'turn around' on just a few sub-criteria met out of many, everybody wins…except the tax payer. The government claims a 99% success rate and the LAs, each pocket another £800 per family bounty.

This kind of intervention programme design is perfectly acceptable to politicians…if it is to be applied to, powerless, underclass 'folk devils' already disdained by an ignorant, brain washed public. However if this cavalier, subjective, sloppy, approach to state intervention design was used in a major public health initiative, say on cancer treatment, the government would be vilified and the public outraged. But who cares about these 'families from hell'? Anything goes. They deserve it…Cameron (and Blair and Brown) said so.

Let's look now at some of the other, widely shared, family characteristics which influenced family selection when the PbyR based LA numbers proved *insufficient* to reach the DCLG set targets. The best sources of data to date on family characteristics are the reports 'National Evaluation of the TF Programme' ECORYS 2014 (12) and the final 'National Evaluation' documents of 2016. We learn that 74% of families are unemployed. 97% are in state supported housing : 70% in housing associations; 18% in private rented accommodation; 9% in temporary accommodation i.e. technically homeless. In addition we learn that 27% are in rent arrears. However the area that stands out is family health. The NE 2016 Synthesis Report tells us that

'75% of families have somebody in the household with a limiting long term illness or disability'

'52% have one or more children with SEN or other special needs'

We learn that families have adult and child problems with the following frequencies (12)

Problem	Adult problems	Child
Mental health	45%	33%

Long standing illness or disability	33	19
Children with SEN statements	-	39
Children in special schools	-	28
Children with school behaviour issues	-	46
Children with safeguarding issues	-	34
Parenting issues (defined by social workers)	- 66% of families	-

German Asylum 1930s : some disabled 'useless mouths' captured by an SS photographer

Let's remind ourselves how Minister Eric Pickles described this situation in June 2012 as he loudly promoted the TFP in the media.

'These families are ruining their own lives, they are ruining their children's lives and they are ruining their neighbours lives'

He added that such families were **'not victims'**. Presumably any family in the UK with a chronic illness or disability are 'not victims' of misfortune but are choosing to 'ruin' their lives and destroy society. There are millions of disabled and chronically ill people in the country: are they all guilty...or is it *only* those also highly dependent on state benefits and without the wits to defend themselves from rabid ministers of the Crown? Do we have evidence for this?

Well, yes: see any speech by Iain Duncan Smith. For example in February 2013 Smith was justifying the throttling of benefits…a cut of £18 billion per annum. He explained why higher benefits 'won't solve child poverty'.

'…it does little more than feed the parents addiction, it may leave the family more dependent, not less, resulting in poor social outcomes and still deeper entrenchment…'

Remember that the government and Cameron, also stressed that in addition to being criminal the troubled families have high levels of drug and alcohol abuse. However we find that only 12% of adults are alcohol dependent and only 13% are dependent on non-prescription drugs (with a significant overlap between them). But only 3% were serious enough cases to receive formal medical treatment (12).

What we actually see are high levels of physical and mental health issues and evidence for a high level of child mental health and learning disability problems resulting in SENs and school behaviour issues. Two thirds of the families are finding it difficult to look after their children. These are families with severe problems, **not** families causing problems…except their high cost. Remember that on Wirral 93.5% of adults and 89.6% of children were **not** involved in ASB and crime. Only 1.2% of children had an ASBO or ABC. What successive governments call 'irresponsibility' is a reflection of socially inadequate, sick parents failing to cope with disabled children and not moral degeneracy requiring state bullying, sanctions and invitations from senior ministers and civil servants for the families to feel 'guilt' and 'shame'. Why not just gas them?

We can look at this another way which may give some insight into the families' condition. The 120,000 represent 0.65% of the 18.6 million families nationally. We know the families are at the bottom of society financially and most are mentally disordered and cognitively inadequate in one way or another. Let's consider IQ, a parameter not unfortunately, explicitly measured in the projects. The standardised IQ distribution is normally distributed with a mean of 100 points and a standard deviation of 15 points. An interesting question is what is the upper IQ threshold for the lowest 0.65% of the population? Consulting standard tables we find an IQ of ~ 63.

If societal and economic 'performance' correlated perfectly with IQ *all* our families would have *IQs less than 63*. That is in the moderate learning difficulties to severe learning difficulties range. In civilised democracies the cut off for adult 'legal responsibility' is an IQ of 70.

The author suggests that it is not surprising that some of our project families (11% on the Wirral) fall foul of the law. Later we will examine how this happens. In section three we will also look at the interplay of genetics, environmental deprivation and epigenetics in determining the IQs of our troubled families. The good news is that there are interventions in education and nutrition that can help. The bad news is such interventions have no appeal to populist politicians…they don't create useful folk devils to look down on and vilify and they don't attract votes.

We will see in later sections that this pattern of gross family mislabelling has been repeated by governments since 1998. We will also see that only a small proportion of troubled families with mental disorders and learning disabilities get professional help. This is a scandal since study after study shows that investment in mental health and family therapies and the Children & Adolescent Mental Health Services in particular, pay large, proven dividends...unlike the TFP and its siblings. To take one recent example: the Centre for Mental Health in February 2015 found that primary school based behaviour programmes aimed at 'conduct disorders' cost ~£108 per child but produced behavioural and later outcome benefits of nearly £3,000 per child. Tackling aggressive adolescents returned ~£ 27,700 per child for an intervention cost of £1,260 per child. Cognitive behaviour therapy for school children suffering from anxiety and depression yielded a benefit : cost ratio of ~31 : 1 (7). These results and others, often based on randomised controlled trials, or equivalents, *far outperform the doubtful claims of the Troubled Families Programme,* examined below, and its politically motivated forerunners.

The TFP selection farce continues. By 2014 phase 2 of the programme was announced which would involve a further 400,000 troubled families. Naturally there was some interest in how this 400,000 figure was derived. Stephen Crossley, then of Sheffield University, made a FoIA request to the DCLG for details of the criteria and methodology used in selecting the 400,000 new families to be targeted by the Coalition (6). *His request was denied and the Information Commissioner's office supported the refusal.* The reasons given are very informative. Apparently the issue would 'attract a high degree of public and media attention' which

'would be harmful as it would give the public and local authorities …*a potentially inaccurate and misleading impression*…about the design of the [phase 2] programme'

Could it be that this was another Dame Louise Casey numerical 'cock up' exercise, like the 120,000 number, which would reveal that the families were again to be targeted for disability, economic and social deprivation, and cost to the state, not ASB and crime? Or did they simply toss a coin? Numbers matter. Take the cost of our TFs to the state. We will see that in 2012 the government claim was that the 120,000 families cost us £9 billion per annum. But by 2014 we were told that there were actually 520,000 TFs ! Did the £9 billion actually result from this larger cohort or some even bigger fraction of the feckless underclass? If so the phase 1 families cost us at most £2.1 billion. This is much closer to the eventual number emerging from local authority sampling of real families and the final Eric Pickles claim that £1.2 billion had (potentially) been saved by reprogramming the 120,000. In fact we will show that **the £9 billion was a fantasy figure** in the first place based on that favourite word of the TFP bureaucrats, 'indicative' and also the phrase 'informed and conservative judgments'. Indicative means 'we know the number is incorrect... but what the hell.' and this 'judgment' business means 'we guessed and we *are* the experts ...and besides the Conservative PM told us the answer to look for'. The £1.2 billion saving claim also proved to be an unsupportable fantasy only finally abandoned , under MP pressure, during the Public Accounts Select Committee Inquiry in 2016 as we will see.

1.3   The Fiscal Case For the TFP : 'Fake News'

'We have sometimes run away from categorising, stigmatising, laying blame...It's time to wake up to that ...to realise the state is no longer willing to subsidise a life of complete non-fulfilment on just about every level'

DCLG Minister Eric Pickles 2014

1.3.1   Introduction to the Methodology

This FC report was issued by the DCLG in February 2013 (8). Its objective was to underpin the case for the TFP by highlighting the allegedly huge amounts of money spent in supporting or containing the 120,000 troubled families targeted in phase one. The report split spending, with some difficulty, into 'targeted spend' or supposedly preventative spend and 'reactive spend', or that spending resulting from the bad and dysfunctional behaviour of our families. Targeted spend was calculated as £1.05 billion per annum and reactive spend at £7.98 billion per annum giving the £9 billion total spend which was fed to the media. Since reactive spend is much greater than targeted spend the inference appears to have been crudely drawn in the DCLG that reactive spend could be greatly reduced by increasing targeted spend i.e. on schemes like the Troubled Families

Programme: QED. The impression was given to the public that all or a goodly part of £9 billion would be saved as a result. This inference does not appear to have been tested *against the facts then available* including the failure of the previous 'gold standard' Family Intervention Projects since 1999, brought to the attention of New Labour and Coalition governments by this author, directly and in published papers (see sections 2 and 4 references). Given the cognitive limitations and lack of numeracy of leading politicians this is not too surprising. It is surprising, given also the blatantly poor quality of the fiscal analysis, *that senior civil servants did not sound a warning note.* Cameron got the 'story' he wanted but it was bound to unravel under formal, independent examination …which is what happened. Unfortunately the Public Accounts Committee, in two TFP Inquiries, failed to understand what the objective evidence was telling them…or worse.

The success of such a preventative intervention policy would depend on two factors: the composition of targeted spend and the scale and proportion of the areas where spending was implicitly irreducible and the sensitivity of the areas where spending *could* potentially be reduced due to the *kinds* of interventions proposed for the TFP scheme. For example the costs, including benefits and health, associated with the chronic illness and disability applying to a large proportion of the families *would not be cut* unless the TFP could miraculously engineer cures. If most so-called reactive spend was essentially fixed or if interventions turned out to be ineffective, few cost savings would be made. This turned out to be the case.

There is also the basic question of the accuracy of the costs attributed to our 120,000 troubled families. We will see that many of these costs appear to be based on unsupportable assumptions and guess work. The DCLG approached other government departments for help in estimating the costs of the troubled families and it appears from the content of the Fiscal Case report, which is highly recommended reading, that the quality of response varied markedly. Some departments such as Work and Pensions made a good attempt; others such as the Home Office and Justice juggled assumptions with alacrity but by the end of the exercise a grossly distorted estimate emerged for the cost of crime. Who is responsible, the Home Office or the DCLG, is not clear. What is clear is that a variety of different approaches to estimating costs were applied by various departments. The DCLG Fiscal Case report, which is remarkably short for such an important document, gives the impression that memos received on the fly from other departments were simply stapled together. It looks like a rush job. In most government departmental areas genuine direct costs associated with our actual 120,000 troubled families were *not available.*

35

"Last year the state spent £9 billion on just 120,000 troubled families...that is around £75,000 per family"

David Cameron PM 2011

"This disabled person costs the state 60,000 Reichsmarks.
Citizens this is your money too"

Office of Racepolitics NSDAP

Think about this for a moment. LAs had been told exactly how many troubled families they had and the recruitment criteria. By 2013 many had supposedly already been recruited, providing a large potential sample. Would not the LAs themselves be the best source of information about the *actual* costs of the *real* families? (Later, but too late, costs were calculated for 7 'exemplar' LAs which led to the Pickles claim of £1.2 billion saving versus the initial £9 billion discussed here. Even this new number proved fallacious. Later still the DCLG tried again with partial data collected from 67 LAs.)

Well of course LA data was preferable (properly used), but Cameron wanted some big numbers to throw to the media and parliament about his grand scheme to save us from national moral collapse …and suppose the *actual* costs turned out to be modest and irreducible?

In fact what happened instead is that the **Fiscal Case report costs became definitive 'gospel' and were used to power official cost calculators**, such as that of the Department for Education, which LAs eventually were encouraged to apply to *their real families* to calculate how much had been saved *locally*. The official cost calculators propagated fantasy numbers across the country! LAs, such as the Wirral, if challenged, simply said: look we are using the approved national cost calculator, don't blame us.

Given that direct (real) family costs were said not to be available, indirect estimates were made in the following way:

'To estimate the amount spent just on troubled families, we looked at the groups of people that each service reached and the proportion of them that *was likely* to be troubled families. In cases where the department was unable to identify the proportion of its spend reaching troubled families, information on the *characteristics* of troubled families from *several sources* was used to estimate this spend. This included

* looking at how many individuals nationally were treated by *or eligible* for each policy.

* considering the prevalence among troubled families of the *eligibility criteria*, and,

* calculating the number of individuals in these families the policy *would be reaching.'*

There is nothing intrinsically wrong with this multi-step procedure.

The problems come from the sequence of assumptions which must be made and in particular the questions of *family characteristics and eligibility criteria*. We have seen that the official selection criteria for PbyR focussed on crime, ASB and school behaviour while 'local discretion' used a much wider range of criteria including health issues. Note also that *eligibility* for a policy intervention or service does *not* mean that such service was *receiv*ed. We will often see that a family is *'affected'* by a service. Often this seems to mean 'eligible for' not 'in receipt of'. This inevitably leads to *overestimates* for family costs …sometimes gross ones.

The several sources of information used to populate this scheme included

- The Families and Child Study carried out under New Labour in 2004 which looked at seven measures of deprivation centred on poverty, and worklessness due to poor health …not crime.

This was the source of the infamous 120,000 families target based on families having 5 out of 7 measures of deprivation. We will see that the DfE further separated out 50,000 families with children supposedly having multiple 'extreme behaviour' problems for 'extra' costs. The author could not match this number to the real family characteristics in any way.

- The National Centre for Social Research report 'Monitoring and evaluation of family intervention services and projects between February 2007 and March 2011'; Dept. for Education.

These FIPs included families who had serious mental and physical health problems *but* the focus was on supposedly attacking families high levels of ASB and crime. Qualitatively many of the same issues were in play in these two studies but what we need for cost saving calculations are *good quantitative matches to the actual families selected for the TFP.* We do not have that, which explains the emerging problems below. For example the NCSR report says 85% of their families had 'engaged in some form of AS or criminal behaviour' but in our TFP families only ~19% had been in trouble with the police and 16% had ASB reports. Fewer than 10% had convictions for anything.

Yet other sources of information were also used to supposedly 'cross-check' the DCLG analysis, no doubt adding more apples to the main pears.

- the Department for Education's C4EO cost calculator.

- Evaluation evidence on Intensive Intervention Projects from the DfE. These projects focussed on young people with the most challenging behaviour. Only a small minority of our TFP children met this definition.
- evaluation evidence on the family and Young Carer Pathfinders Programme , DfE.
- research on different local approaches to families with multiple problems, DfE
- emerging results from the 16 Community Budgets wave 1 pilots.

We will see later the meticulous statistical work carried out in the TFP National Evaluation 2016 analyses to *carefully match* the characteristics of the TFP families and the comparison control group of similar but unprocessed families. No such careful matching appears to have happened in using all the above information sources to generate the Fiscal Case £9 billion potential cost saving estimate. We have instead a mix of apples, pears, sprouts and clairvoyance. In some places we are told that 'informed and conservative judgements had to be used'. In other words they guessed the numbers and it shows. It is very curious that *nearly all* the assumptions and guesses lead to errors in the *upwards* direction.

Let's look at the detailed cost categories. Total targeted spend on the 120,000 TFs was calculated as **£1.05 billion per annum** over several areas.

- Education/early years : Sure Start and work with young people including youth work, positive activities, information , advice and guidance (DfE) **Cost £440 million per annum.**

- Child Protection: family intervention and targeted protection work (DfE) **Cost £250 million per annum.**

- Health : mental health, drug and substance misuse programmes, early years food & milk, teen pregnancy nurses and health visitors (Dept. of Health) Cost £250 million per annum.

- Welfare: some of the Work Programme, European Social Fund provision for families with complex needs (Dept. for Work & Pensions) Cost £80 million per annum.

- Crime: parenting orders and preventing teenage knife/gun/gang violence (Home Office & Min. of Justice) Cost £30 million per annum.

The total reactive spend is said to be **£7.98 billion** consisting of

- Education/early years: fixed term and excluded pupils, pupils in receipt of behavioural and emotional support (DfE) **Cost £390 million per annum.**

- Child protection: looked after children or children in care, social care and child support (DfE) **Cost £3,490 million per annum.**

- Health: alcohol & drug dependence, dealing with mental health problems (excluding A&E or GP costs) (Dept. of Health) Cost £780 million per annum.

- Welfare: benefits (excluding child benefit or child/working tax credits) (Dept. for Work & Pensions) Cost £ 750 million per annum.

- Crime & Justice: police, courts, custody, other costs of serious crime like burglary, criminal damage, assault, drug related offences but excluding ASB. (Home Office/Min. of Justice) **Cost £2,570 million per annum.**

Note that the biggest players in the game are the DfE with a total alleged cost burden of **£4,570 million per annum** and Crime/Justice with a cost burden of **£2,600 million per annum,** together representing **79.7%** of the alleged total cost of 120,000 troubled families. Welfare (allegedly due to lazy worklessness) costs amount to just 9.2% of the total. We can see why the TFP PbyR criteria focussed on crime, ASB and education targets and *why it was important* to be able to claim 89% of families turned around under this criterion. A genuine 89% turn around on the Fiscal Case data should have yielded savings of **£6,381 million** compared with the final (disputed and still gross) claim of **£1,200 million over ALL areas of spending.**

We can also see why much of the families source information and the official cost calculators derive from the DfE : it had the biggest dog in the fight and a huge budget to defend. It is clearly *critical* that the costs of the DfE and Crime/Justice assigned to the 120,000 troubled families were accurate since they *essentially justified* the TFP fiscally. Clearly something went badly wrong. We look now at each spending area estimate in detail and suggest corrected costings.

We also ask what proportion of the family costs were *open in principle* to reduction and what even smaller proportion was likely to be affected by TFP type interventions. *The numbers are disappointing and could have been quite well predicted at the inception of the TFP from previous FIP evaluations.*

1.3.2 Education/early years costs

Targeted Spend

Targeted spend on Sure Start.

The DfE had no data so assumed a proportion based on families with multiple problems eligible for the Pupil Premium. This led to an estimate that 20% of Sure Start money went to troubled families. The total SS budget was £1000 million giving the cost of TFs as £200 million.

In 2012 2.08 million pupils received the PP in England. Their claim is that 67% of troubled families were eligible for PP (and thence SS) or 0.67 x 3.07 x 120,000 = 241,200 children. This gives the TF proportion as 0.241 / 2.08 = 0.116 not 0.2. The cost of TF children must be 0.116 x 1000 = £116 million. This is a maximum estimate since *eligibility does not equate to access to services.* The average take up was ~60% giving us **£69.6 million.**

In the long and contentious debate about the effectiveness of Sure Start one issue was clear. Evaluations showed that SS was quickly colonised by more well off working families and 'aspiring immigrant' families and did not reach the poorest families, the supposed SS target, as successfully (33,34). So what is the true SS TF cost? £50 million? £30 million?

Targeted Services to Young People.

The total cost of these services is given as £370 million. The estimation of the share of cost to the TFs is said to be 'difficult' and therefore the DfE made 'informed and conservative judgements'. That is they guessed the answer was 56%. Let's see if we can do better.

The services are said to cover youth work, positive activities, information, advice & guidance, substance misuse services and teenage pregnancy support services. We look at NEETS, offenders, drug abuse children and pregnancy rates in the TFs and split the costs across the above service categories. 23% of families had a NEET and there were 843,000 (16-24) NEETS; 6% of TFs had a youth with a caution or conviction

41

(NE 2016) and in England in 2015 there were 94,960 (10-17) youth arrests; 2% of TF children under 18 fell pregnant and in 2013 there were 24000 such pregnancies in England (NSO); 5% of TF children were said to be near the drug 'edge of treatment' criteria and 3% of TF adults actually received specialist treatment (Ecorys report 2014) while in total 25,000 received specialist treatment in England (NHS); I make an 'informed judgement' that none of our 'criminal and antisocial' TF youths volunteered or undertook youth work during the TFP: the National Citizen Service flopped for example. With this data we can work out rough proportions of service costs attributable to our TF youths.

Substance misuse 4,896 / 25,000 = 0.196

Pregnancy 360,000 x 0.4 x 0.02 / 24,000 = 0.12

Crime 360,000 x 0.06 / 94,960 = 0.227

NEETS 27,600 / 843,000 = 0.033

Total share of service cost is (0 + 0 + 0.196 + 0.12 + 0.227 + 0.033) / 6 = 0.096. The TF cost estimate is 0.096 x 370 = **35.5 million** compared with the DFE guess of £207 million. This is 5.8 X my estimate. The author makes no claim for accuracy in his estimate but has confidence that it is better than guessing.

Other DfE targeted spend

This item covered several sub-items but the primary element was the Children & Family Court Advisory & Support Service. The cost is given as £130 million and 30% is assumed to be down to our TFs giving us £39 million. We are not told whence came the 30% assumption. We know that 6% of TF children were cautioned or convicted and that there were 94,960 10-17 arrests in total. Let us assume the arrest proportion was reflected in court related activity giving : 0.06 x 360,000 / 94960 = 0.227 and a TF cost share of 0.227 x 130 = **25.1 million** versus the DfE estimate of £39 million. This time the ratio is only 1.6X.

So for DfE targeted spend our new estimate is **130.2 million** against the claimed **446 million**, or some 70% smaller.

 DfE Reactive Spend

Pupil Referral Units / Exclusions

There are around 400 units covering ~19,000 children with numbers varying over the past ten years. The units cover pupils excluded, SEN pupils, the long term ill, teen pregnancies and mothers and kids having no school place. Note that many of these children are troubled rather than causing trouble. The total cost of PRUs is given as £310 million with 58% of the cost going to TF children, or £180 million. This was obtained by reference to (unidentified) 'family intervention data' suggesting that 11% of children with 'additional needs' related to behaviour had attended a PRU with similar exclusion rates. The DfE defined 50,000 families of the 120,000 with such special children of whom 32% required special support. This gave 50,000 x 3.07 x 0.32 x (0.11+0.11) = 10,806 children. Then 10,806 / 19,000 = 0.569 or 57% versus the claimed 58%. However the NE 2016 administrative data tells us that 2.4% of TFs had a child in a PRU or 2880 children and 1.5% in alternative provision or 1800 children. This suggests a TF share of 2880 / 19000 to 4680 / 19000 or 15.1% to 24.6% with costs of £46.8 million to £76.2 million compared to the claimed £180 million. How can the DfE numbers be so wrong?

A key question is how reliable is the DfE 50,000 families estimate since this affects several education cost estimates. We are referred to Annex B where the 50,000 is explained. These are families with the usual 5 of 7 areas of deprivation AND children with multiple behavioural problems. This is *clearly* defined as children having

'*all* of the following characteristics : being in trouble with the police, having run away from home; having been expelled or suspended from school; having an SEN statement.'

So let us calculate the numbers under each sub-criterion from the actual TF characteristics.

19% of families have a child who had been in trouble with the police (NE 2016). 7% of children have been permanently excluded from school (Ecorys report 2014) involving 13% of families and 3.9% of families have a child in PRUs or alternative provision. 39% of families have a child with an SEN statement.

The 50,000 special families number implies that 41.7% of TFs meet *all* the above sub-criteria. However the prevalence of problems is sparsely scattered across the families as described earlier with some expected correlation between police problems and school exclusion. The DfE appear to have taken the highest common factor, SEN prevalence, to determine their 50,000 number contrary to their own definition.

That requires using the lowest common factor which is school exclusion involving 13% of families. Their own rules then give us 0.13 x 120,000 = 15,000 families not 50,000. This yields a PRU cost of **£54 million** not £ 180 million …keeping the other DfE assumptions. This is now in line with our new £ 46 – 76 million estimate using *actual* PRU rates. Confusing logical OR with logical AND in setting and applying criteria seems to be a universal problem in the DfE and the DCLG. Or is the assumption that nobody will notice the sleights of hand in the many pages of analysis and technical appendixes? After all, few people seem to read past the press releases and executive summaries of government documents…*even* parliamentary select committees, our supposed watchdogs.

Behavioural & Emotional Support

This is said to be £240 million per annum nationally. BES costs apply to the 50,000 families with 'additional' needs or 31% of the total, £74.4 million. There is no other detail on the DfE origin of the 31%.
We argued above that the upper bound of this group was actually15,000. On this basis the TF spend must be (15 / 50) x 0 .31 = 0.093 or 9.3%. The TF cost is then 240 x 0.093 = **£22.3 million** not £74.4 million.

Pupil Premium

The total cost is said to be £490 million per annum and the TF share 20% giving TF cost as £98 million. Eligibility depends on receiving any benefit such as income support, JSA, ESA, pension credit, child or working tax credit. The NE 2016 family survey tells us that during the TFP 42% of adults were employed and 11% were claiming JSA. 19% of adults were claiming ESA / incapacity benefit. There is little detail on the DfE origin of the 20% estimate.

   We must look elsewhere in government statistics for answers. The number of pupils on the premium was 2.08 million in 2012. The DfE told us that 67% of families with multiple problems get the PP based on 'family intervention data'. This presumably refers to the earlier FIP families. These families supposedly represent 29% of all children with PP. Hence the share 0.67 x 0.29 = 0.195 or 20% given above. However this also gives us 120,000 x 3.07 x 0.67 = 246,800 TF children of all ages. But 25% of TF families have a child/children under 5 according the NE 2016. This gives overall eligible children per family as 0.75 x 3 + 0.25 x 2 = 2.75 at most and 2.5 at least giving a total eligible as 21700. TF cost is then (0.217 / 2.08) x 490 = **£ 51.1 million** not £ 98 million.

Early years reactive spend

The total cost is £440 million. The TF share is said to be 9% giving their cost as £39.6 million per annum. No other information is provided. Let us try with accessible government data. In 2011 there were 1.32 million 3-4 year olds in England and 0.157 million 2 year olds ('Provision for children under 5',SFR 20/2015). In the TFs 25% had a child under 5 years, giving us 30,000 children. Ecorys 2014 data gives us (21.8+14.4+3.6) thousand for under 5s or 39.6 thousand. We then have 39,600 / 1,480,000 = 0.0267 or 2.67%. However we have data on the take up of 'early years' services. It was 72% in Q1 income families and 54.3% in Q5. For our very poor TFs this gives us 2.67 x 0.63 = 1.69%. The 30,000 estimate gives us1.3% not 9%. So taking the higher figure the TF cost share is **£7.4 million** not £39.6 million.

Overall our new estimate of TF reactive DfE spend is **£134.8 million** per annum not **£390 million;** or 34.5% of the DfE estimate.

Just as interesting is the spending make up: Pupil referral units / exclusion £54m; Behaviour and emotional support £22.3m; Pupil premium £51.1m; Early years 7.4m. Note that the Pupil Premium and Sure Start services are provided purely because of family poverty.

Behavioural and emotional support are required because 52% of TF children are SEN or have other special needs. 33% of families have children with mental health problems and the families are dysfunctional with 45% having adults with mental health problems. We can say that 22.3 + 51.1 + 7.4 = £80.8 million of DfE TF costs relate to poverty and mental health problems not trouble making, feckless families.

We also saw that children referred to PRUs included those with SENs or long standing illnesses or exclusions. But we know that ~ 2/3 of exclusions relate to children with learning disabilities and mental health problems (16), say 0.67 x 54 = £36.2 million of the PRU cost. 19% of families had children with long standing illnesses. So overall at least £117 million of £134.8 million reactive spend, or 86.8 %, relates to mental health / disability and poverty NOT 'bad' behaviour. The poverty element also relates to *inability* to work since 75 % of the TFs had someone with a 'limiting long standing illness or disability'.

If most of the TF cost in this area is health related how did the TFP do on health issues? As we saw it did little in practice and the national administrative data and family survey data both show **no** impact on health. This is a repeat of the FIP situation.

The failure of the TFP was built in at the design stage. Many of the TF costs could never be reduced except by euthanasia and sterilisation of the families.

Taking education targeted and reactive spend the **total cost** of the TFs is **£265 million** per annum not the claimed **£830 million.** The difference is a factor of 3.1 X in the overestimate direction. Within this, 87% of the reactive spend (£119.8 million) was health related and not accessible to the TFP interventions.

This leaves the so-called targeted spend of £130.2 million of which £70 million maximum could be assigned to our TFs and Sure Start. These families certainly needed support to improve their lot and ability to cope. Three evaluations showed that in anecdotal terms, the families 'felt' better about their condition (15). However Sure Start was aimed at *concrete targets* like getting young children 'school ready', and improving school performance. The first evaluation found no evidence for significant impacts on such targets and naturally the New Labour government dismissed it. The second evaluation was more cautious and convoluted and therefore more acceptable. The third, like the Troubled Families NE 2016 reports, found no improvements relative to comparable control groups in the *primary* targets for improvement…although, just like the troubled families, the SS families subjectively, 'felt better'. This is an expensive way to improve mood. There was no change in 'school readiness' and subsequent child performance in school.

The TF cost (£35.5 million) of 'targeted services to young people' split is also informative. Remember only 2% of children fell pregnant; only 6% of families had a child conviction; only 3% of children had drug treatment, while 23% had a NEET. We see the biggest problem is economic and related to illness / disability /low IQ. Crime is infrequent as is pregnancy and serious drug use. We can say that pregnancy and drug use are purely social / health problems.

Altogether 61% of this cost is definitely health / social issue related and 39 % is 'crime' related. However youths with mental health issues and learning disability are disproportionately represented in the criminal justice system. 75% of adult prisoners have a mental health problem or disability. 85% of youths in custody have two or more mental health problems (17). 60% of young people in court for antisocial behaviour had *diagnosed* mental health problems (Cabinet Office paper 2002, 18).

We might reasonably conclude that 80% of the 'crime' costs are mental health related in which case 92% of the targeted youth service cost is health / social related. It is unclear to the author how handing out leaflets, pep talks and so on can impact these health problems.

The other DfE targeted services related to Children / Family Court advisory services and we can argue as above that 60 to 80% of the costs of £ 25.1 million are mental health / learning disability related. How much does it cost to refer a mentally vulnerable child to a qualified consultant? The rest is spinning wheels, going nowhere. Surely spending all this money on directed mental health support would take us further? We need early diversions from the CJS.

If we add together the targeted DfE spend I estimate that 112.7 / 130.2 = 0.865 or **86.5%** is related to mental health /social inadequacy/low IQ issues in the families. Targeted spend has been demonstrably ineffective because it is largely directed at the wrong issues yet the TFP was predicated on the assumption that (current) targeted interventions were good and we needed more of the same. This is folly built on folly and the DfE is not alone as we will see.

1.3.3 Protecting Children

Child protection is the biggest single area of spending with the claim that **£3,730 million per annum** is spent on our TFs or 41.4% of the total £9 billion TF cost. We will see that this is grossly exaggerated.

Targeted Spend on Protection

Intensive Family Interventions

This is said to be £60 million in total and all the cost is assigned to our 120,000 families with no justification. It covers a family having access to a dedicated 'practitioner' or an LA putting a support / care plan in place. Two issues are worth noting. Firstly only 34% of current TFs have 'safeguarding issues' (NE 2016) similar to the historical position in the earlier FIPs. In which case only 0.34 x 60 = £20.4 million should be assigned to the TFP phase 1. Secondly in 2014 Cameron announced that, sorry, actually there were an additional 400,000 TFs with multiple problems who would be processed in the TFP phase 2. Assuming the 400,000 have always been there we can say that the £60 million must have supported (120,000 + 400,000) = 520,000 families.

The TFP phase 1 families share of cost must be 120 / 520 = 0.23. On this basis phase 1 families cost £ 20.4 x 0.23 = **£4.7 million**, not £60 million. These are rough estimates but one thing is certain: to load *all* the cost onto our 120,000 families is arbitrary and unsupportable.

£180 million was also spent by LAs on 'functions in relation to child protection'. The cost includes that of 'local safeguarding children boards' which in the author's experience means producing strategy and policy documents and having lots of liaison meetings i.e. LA , 'lets look busy' bureaucracy. Other 'discretionary spending' is not identified. Why all this is described as 'targeted' is difficult to say. Still, the cost has to be assigned somewhere but why only to our 120,000 families? I suggest that we can legitimately use the same reasoning as above and assign only 0.34 x 0.23 x 180 = **£14.1 million** to the TFP phase 1.

 Note also that the ratio of 'hands on support' to 'LA functions' / bureaucracy is 60 / 180 or 0.333…75% of spending is *not* in front line child / family support.

 Overall I suggest that the child protection targeted spend specifically on our 120,000 families is **£18.8 million per annum** not the crudely assigned, **£240 million.**

 Looking at the Fiscal Case document the DfE costings are the weakest and least detailed, which is troubling since the DfE cost calculator was the definitive 'official' tool used by LAs during the TFP.

Reactive Spend on Protection

The claimed cost of our families is a huge £3,490 million per annum of which £ 2,660 million relates to removing children from families.

Child Removal Costs.

This includes: residential care £920m ; fostering £1,280m ; leaving care support £230 ; adoption services £230m. Remarkably the DfE tells us that 86% of these costs can be assigned to our 120,000 TFs in TFP phase 1. Lets see if we can reproduce this estimate.

The HoC Library briefing paper 'Children In Care', October 2015 tell us there were 67,070 children in care in 2012 including 42,030 on care orders. 75% were in foster care. Around 30,000 enter and leave care every year giving an average residence time of 2.23 years. The Profile of Families, (Table 3.8), in the NE Synthesis Report 2016 tells us that 'at least one child was living with neither parent' in 5% of TF low intensity services support and 13% in high intensity support. 22% of families were classed as high intensity. The mean figure is then $0.78 \times 5 + 0.22 \times 13 = 6.8\%$. Now some of these children will be with relatives such as grandparents. We also know (NE Table 4.9) that an average of 3.95% TF families (TFP and control group) had a child in care 12 months after project entry. This information gives us $120,000 \times 0.0395 = 4,740$ children minimum and 8,160 maximum. We will take a mid value of 6,400 children. This suggests the share of children in care attributable to our 120,000 phase 1 families is $6,400 / 67,070 = 0.095$, or 9.5%. It is difficult to reconcile this with the 86% of all care related costs assigned to our TFs by the DfE. This is a huge difference, some 9.05 X. For families with care characteristics like ours the DfE estimates would relate to ~58,000 children and 1.1 million troubled families. It is surprising given the 60 or so FIPs in play before the TFP that the DfE did not consult the evaluation reports for data on children in care etc. They would see that 86% was something of an overestimate.

The probable care cost of the phase 1 TFs was in the region of $(9.5 / 86) \times 2660 =$ **£293 .8 million per annum** not **£2,660 million.** The remaining reactive costs were 'commissioning and social work' and 'other costs'. Commissioning was £1,480 million in total and 'other' £900 million. There are ~16 million families in England and 2% were said to have 5 out of 7 indicators of deprivation by the Families and Children Study of 2004…one source for the TFP numbers. This gives us $16 \times 0.02 = 0.32$ million families who could receive such services. We also know that Cameron now says there are 520,000 families in the TFP phase 1 and 2 cohort. If we take the 320,000 estimate the share of commissioning costs would be $120,000 / 320,000 = 0.375$ and for 520,000 families $120 / 520 = 0.23$ with an average of 0.303. The DfE estimate was 0.33 so it is for once in the correct ball park. If we take the probable 0.23 the TF phase 1 cost of commissioning would be £340.4 million per annum.

£900 million in total went on 'other support' costs with 79% assigned to the 120,000 TFs. A footnote tells us these estimates assumed '*all* troubled families were accessing these services including past cohorts of children from these families that are currently in care'. Well *all* troubled families should refer to the 320,000 'Families and Children' study estimate or Cameron's new 520,000 TFs in phase 1 and phase 2. The claimed 79% cost share is therefore a mystery. If we apply $120 / 520 = 0.23$ as above we get a TF phase 1 cost of £207 million not £711 million.

We conclude that reactive spend on child protection for the 120,000 TFs must be around **£841.2 million per annum** and not the claimed **£3,490 million.** This is a factor of 4.15 X different.

Our estimate of the total TF phase 1 cost for child protection is **£860 million per annum** not the claimed **£3,730 million.** We have an overestimate of TF phase 1 costs of 4.34 X.

1.3.4 Crime/Justice costs

Targeted Spend

Targeted spend on our 120,000 TFs on crime and justice matters was a surprisingly small £30 million per annum (or £250 per family) given their supposed high criminality. The total national component costs include parenting orders at £32.3m per annum which applied to 48,500 families. We are told the Ministry of Justice 'assumed' the whole 32.2 million was spent on *troubled families.* This was based on the various qualitative selection criteria for TFs....Cameron said they must *all* be in trouble with the police and so on. The DfE assumption that 50,000 families had children with 'additional' behavioural problems, which we demolished earlier, was said to confirm this. This all demonstrates a remarkably sloppy, hand waving, cost estimation approach. The Min. of Justice must have been aware of the 60 or so FIPs which had been largely targeted at families with supposedly high levels of crime and ASB. Read carelessly one might believe that ~ 80% of families were criminal but a closer read shows low level ASB at worst (see section 4.5).

  The TFP NE 2016 shows that 17% of children had been in trouble with the police. 3.9% had been convicted of a crime. On the Wirral remember just 1.2% of children had an acceptable behaviour contract or an ASBO. If one child per family was in trouble this means 0.17 x 120,000 = 20,400 families at most had conditions attracting a parenting order, or at a minimum 0.039 x 120,000 = 4,680. The parenting order share of TFs must be between 9.6% and 42% if we just assume that there are only 120,000 TFs in the country ...but Cameron's estimate is now 520,000. Surely the 48,500 parenting orders must draw from this total i.e. *all* TFs, not 120,000. On this basis surely the phase 1 TF share must be only 120 / 520 = 0.23, or 23% of our 9.6 – 42% range or 2.2 – 9.7% of £30 million. Let's be generous and say phase 1 share of parenting order cost was **£2.9 million per annum versus the £30 million claimed.**

The crime and justice section of the Fiscal Case report tells us that 'any overestimate' in the parenting order cost is 'mitigated' because none of the £9 million per year spent on 'Projects against Knife, Gang and Gun Violence' was included. Clearly somebody was unhappy with the parenting order estimate. We are told it was likely that a 'proportion' of the gang spending would reach the troubled families. The numbers are small but this reasoning is interesting. The Riots Panel in 2012 covering 80 LAs found only a 5% overlap between rioters and families targeted for the TFP while nationally ~13 % of rioters were gang members. We can conclude that teenage gang activity is low. What about violence levels in the TFs? Well only 0.2% of TF adults had a conviction for a violent offence and only 3.9% of TF children had a conviction for anything. Also of course we now are told there are 520,000 TFs not 120,000. Shall we say the TF phase 1 share of the prevention project cost was 0.1 x 0.23 = 0.023 or 2.3% and **£207,000** not £9 million. This does *not* mitigate the gross overestimate of the parenting order cost of the TFs. These analyses are best described as feeble.

Reactive Spend

We are told that a number of attempts have been made to estimate reactive spend but the final costs are claimed to be underestimates. The reader may conclude otherwise. The analyses were confined to 'offences that are likely to be recorded by the police and if caught attract some sort of formal sanction'. This is said to cover ~20 core offence types. This does not include homicides. It does include burglary, vehicle theft, theft from the person, violent robbery, business robbery, assault, drug selling …The reader may wonder how many 10 – 18 year olds get involved in much of this. In the TFP (NE 2016) we noted that even for the adults only 0.2% committed a violent offence, 0.4% committed theft or fraud and only 3.9% of children were convicted of any offence.

The analysis looks at estimates of the number of offences by 10-18 year old males and females according to various characteristics, primarily the recent offending record and truanting record. This data is drawn from the annual 'Offending, Crime & Justice Survey' for England and Wales. The other basic parameter is the unit cost of a crime, said to be £496. This is from 'Estimates of the economic and social costs of crime in England and Wales: costs of crime against individuals and households, 2003/4', Home Office. The costs were adjusted for inflation to 2011/12 prices. The number of males and females in the TFs was also calculated.

There is nothing wrong with such an approach providing great care is taken in making key assumptions and in reporting.

We end up with a table which gives the 'implied number of crimes *that might be committed* by the 302,000 young persons *assumed* to be in the TFP, by *different characteristics*'. The key requirement is to match these characteristic categories to the real families. If this is not done carefully we get nonsense.

The base data for the calculation appears in Annex C of the Fiscal Case report. Table C1 shows the 'mean number of crimes in 12 month follow-up period for young persons aged 10 to 18 by differing offending and educational histories'. The author has no basis for questioning these numbers but a few comments are worth making. The range of crime rates is wide. For example the male range is 1.4 – to 14.4 crimes (expected in the next 12 months) from those who have not truanted or offended to those who have done both. The table provides an entry for all children aged 10-18 which gives us the following crime rates.

Offended in last year	Truanted in last year		crime rate
no	no		0.8
no	yes		5.2
		Mean	1.3
yes	no		6.9
yes	yes		13.3
		Mean	8.5

These figures are interesting for several reasons. There is a large multiplier between those with no offending history who have not and have truanted, a ratio of 6.5 X. However for those who have offended the influence of truanting is smaller, some 1.9 X. For those who have truanted the ratio of crime rate for non-offenders to offenders is 2.5 X. One can see why governments claim truancy leads on to crime but perhaps the causative effect has been overplayed. The figures also hide the relative prevalence of problems. For non-offenders the mean rate of 1.3 allows us to calculate that 88.6% had also not truanted. Similarly for offenders we can use the mean rate of 8.5 to show that 75% had not truanted.

For our TF families we know that 11% of youngsters had a police charge or caution. We also know that 10.3% of families had an under 18 year old with a proven offence in the last year NE 2016, administrative data).

We do not know what proportion would be defined as 'serious' i.e. being one of the 20 serious crime categories. We do know that only 3.9% of TFs had a child with a conviction. Custodial sentences ran at 0.4% of families. We can estimate the **maximum** crime rate as roughly 0.103 x 8.5 + 0.897 x 1.3 = 2.04 crimes per year, in total 616,180 crimes. It could be lower based on 'serious' crime, say 0.04 x 8.5 + 0.96 x 1.3 = 1.6 crimes per head.

Annex C calculates that there are 302,000 young people in the TFs aged between 10 and 18 years. This is based on FIP data claiming that 49.7% of all persons were 10 to 18 years old. The cost of crime attributed to the TFs is then 302,000 x 496 x 2.04 = 305.6 millions per annum. They also give the NHS cost of a crime as £149 and so the health cost is 2.04 x 149 x 302,000 = £91.8 million per annum. So the total reactive cost of crime is **£397.4 million per annum.**

Comments on Crime Costs

The Fiscal Case report gives the cost of crime as **£2,579 million per annum** some 6.5 X greater. How can this be? The surprising answer is found on page 28 in a summary table based on the earlier offence/ truancy profiles. This gives

Profile	total crimes (millions)	total cost (millions)
Previous truant and offender	4.0	2,579
Previous offender No truancy	2.06	1,327
Previous truancy No offence	2.15	1,384

Note that the table does not give the fourth profile category: no offence / no truancy: the great majority of 10 – 18 year olds. Let's add it in.

No offence No truancy	0.31	200

Allowing for the 89% not offending our crime total was 616,180, closer to the zero offence/ truancy case than the previous offender/ truant case. So why was the latter profile cost reported as definitive? Well page 28 tells us

'This implies that the total cost of crime to the Exchequer **could be as much as** £2.6 billion per annum…'

But only if you assert that all the TFP children offended and truanted which was far from the truth. Previous Family Intervention data is widely quoted in the Fiscal Review so the Home Office / Justice Ministry could have checked the offending rates. They did not and by the time cross departmental costs were added up the £2,579 million had become the definitive gospel with no sign of a caveat.

The author as a student of the Family Intervention saga is used to such sleights of hand with indefensible claims but this is the most *blatant* and disgraceful one he has encountered.

On their own data, the reactive cost of TF children is exaggerated by a factor of 6.5 X.

But governments *knew* the cost of these 'criminal' families was high, Cameron, Brown and Blair had said so for years. There were no prizes for small costs estimates...call them all criminal, nobody will mind. The Civil Service obliged, just as it did in the education / child protection sector.

For crime / justice in total we have a *maximum* of **£400.5 million per annum** compared with the published cost of **£2,609 million per annum.**

1.3.5 Health

The cost of our 120,000 TFs is said to be £1,030 million per annum with 25% of this on targeted spend. Given that 75% of our families have a 'limiting long standing illness or disability' we might feel that a higher proportion on targeted spend would be justified since we saw that much spending in other areas like education and crime/ justice was health related …and particularly to mental health and disability.

Targeted Spend

No fewer than 12 areas of targeted spend are said to be relevant to our families. In several areas of health support we actually have numbers of individuals nationally 'affected' by individual services. This is very helpful compared to other government departments although we note that there is a difference between 'eligible for' and 'receiving' a service.

Attempts are made to also calculate the actual numbers of TFs 'affected' by each service. In principle this is a direct way of proportioning the total budget for each service.

Primary care

This calculation is convoluted being based on 104 new GP practices in the 'most deprived areas' serving on average 1,500 patients. The DoH says that 80% of multiply deprived families lived in these areas and 10% 'benefitted from closer GP provision'. We appear to be looking at a marginal gain here for deprived families from the new services. What this has to do with the experiences of TFs in general is mute. They then say we have 10,000 TFs and 43,000 individuals benefitting. The sequence is 120,000 x 0.8 x 0.1 = 9,600 families with 1.36 adults and 3.07 children giving 41,528 individuals. The TFP cost share is then 41,528 / (104 x 1500) = 0.266 or 26.6% of £110 million or £29.3 million but the average family cost 110,000,000 / 156,000 = £705 and our families treated as average, £84.6 million…er? Perhaps we should try another way?

In 2013/14 8,060 GP practices cost £7.6 billion per annum and on average £136 per patient (Health & Social Services Information Centre, Feb 2015). Our 120,000 TFs considered as 'normal' patients should have cost **£72.3 million** but perhaps this is too simple? It does not capture 'targeted spend' which was the aim. However the other health items examined do this so let's keep the real GP cost and add the 'specials' on.

Health Visitors.

They work from the 41,000 births involving teenage mothers in England in 2009 since all such mothers would have a health visitor. Using Family Intervention data (presumably from the FIPs, but the author does not recognise this number) we are told there was a 14% family incidence of teenage mothers. They estimate 16,800 TFs are affected giving 16800 / 41000 = 0.41, 41% of the total £140 million cost or £57.4 million per annum to the TFs (rounded up to £60 million in the report).

However under 18 conceptions affect just 2% of the TFP girls or 120,000 x 1.5 x 0.02 = 3600. We also have 5% of families with an under age pregnancy (Ecorys 2014) suggesting 6,000 pregnancies.
The difference may reflect pregnancies terminated. Half of under 18 pregnancies were terminated around 2010. We will take 4,800 births as an estimate. This gives a share of 4800 / 41000 = 0.117 or 11.7% and a TF cost of **£16.4 million** per annum not **£57.4 million**.

Family –Nurse Partnerships

The work with 35,000 first time mothers and a total cost of £40 million per annum. They assume a 41% share as above. If we take 4,800 new mothers from the TFs the share is 0.117 and the TF cost **4.7 million** not **£20 million.**

Welfare Food : Healthy Start.
Welfare Food: Nursery Milk.
School Fruit and vegetables.

Nationally HS cost £120 million for 1,050,000 children under 5. Nursery milk cost £60 million for 1.5 million under fives. F&V cost £20 million for 2,1 million primary school kids. The Dept. of Health assumed every TF child in primary education or benefitted from Healthy Start and the other services. This is reasonable. Then things go wrong.

The report says 35% of the HS budget goes to TF children. This implies 367,500 TF children benefitted, but this is **all** TF children. From the NE 2016 we know that around 23% are under 5 and 32% of primary school age. So the real number of HS kids is 120,000 x 3.07 x 0.32 = 117,888 and the cost share 11.2%. Cost is **£13.4 million** not **£ 42 million**. This is careless to say the least.

For nursery milk we have 23% of TF children under 5 or 84,732 children maximum. The share is 84,732 / 1,500,000 = 0.056 or 5.6% and **£3.4 million** not the claimed **£10 million**. The error here was to use primary school, not under 5, numbers in the TFs.

The number of TF primary school kids getting F&V must be 117,888 and the cost share 117,888 / 2,100,000 = 0.056, 5.6% again. The F&V TF cost must be **£1.12 million per annum** not the claimed **£10 million**.

I suggest it is legitimate to describe this analysis as *negligent and sloppy*. Amusingly, footnote 46 in small print, tells us that 'this [cost] has proved to be an overestimate.' But it and other 'overestimates', are *still included* in the Fiscal Case executive summary …and of course in the media spin.

Drug Intervention Programme

Nationally 210,815 individuals are treated at a cost of £60 million. The Family Intervention (earlier FIP) data 2011 is used to say that 33% of families with multiple problems 'had a drug or substance misuse problem'.

This was equated with *receiving treatment*. However form the author's FIP analyses those receiving treatment in the FIPs was much lower at ~11%. (see all section 4 reports).The FIP evaluation reports were readily available in 2011 and still are. 17% of TF reported that a youngster had taken a non-prescription drug in the past 3 months and 9% of adults. The ECORYS 2014 report on the TFs tells us that actually only 3% of individual adults were receiving non-prescription drug treatment and 6% of children met the criterion triggering treatment…not actually receiving it. Let's say 5% of individuals are getting treatment. The share of treatment cost is 18,000 / 210,815 = 0.085 or 8.5% and the TF cost **£5.1 million per annum** not the claimed **£20 million**.

Pooled drug treatment budget.

This covered the same population as above and cost £100 million per annum. Reasoning as above the TF share is 8.5% and **£8.5 million** not the claimed **£30 million**.

Mental Health Liaison and Diversion Services.

Nationally 1.027 million people access this service at a cost of £30 million per annum. The Family Intervention 2011 report based on the FIPs gave 39% of adults and 10% of children from multiple problems families having a mental health issue. That was translated into 47,000 TF adults and 5,000 children accessing the service or a 5.1% share of the national cost or £1.8 million reported as 'less than £10 million'. Let's look at the actual TF data. 45% of families have an adult with mental health problems. 33% of families had a child with mental health problems (ECORYS 2014).
It is probable that there is considerable overlap between these conditions. Take the total as 120,000 x 0.45 = 54,000 individuals and *assuming all get access to the service* this gives a cost share of 54000 / 1027000 = 0.043 or 4.3% and a cost of 0.043 x 30 = **£1.3 million** compared with **£1.8 million** reported as '**less than £10 million**. We are at least in the right ball park here.

Talking Therapies Children.
Talking Therapies Adults.

163,800 children are 'affected' (eligible or actually seen?) by this service at a cost of £10 million per annum. This is just £61 / head. For a MH specialist getting £50,000 per annum this equates to 3 hours of therapy …very impressive! 452,400 adults are 'affected' at a cost of £280 million or £619 per head. This equates to 31 hours of therapy. 33% of TFs with a child affected gives us 39,600 children.

The analysis tells us that 60% of those contacting GPs on mental health go on to talking therapy giving 23,760 children and a cost share of 23760 / 163800 = 0.14 or 14% giving us £1.4 million. 45% of families with adult mental health problems gives 54,000 individuals (assuming 1 per family) eligible and 0.6 x 54000 = 32,640 getting help. The share is 32640 / 452400 = 0.072 or 7.2% and a cost of £ 20.2 million.

The total TF therapy cost is **£21.6 million** compared with the FC estimate of **£50 million** despite the higher frequency of TF child mental health. This assumes 60% of individuals got help. In the earlier FIP evaluations it was found that ~12% of families actually received professional treatment giving 120,000 x (1.36 x 0.45 + 3.07 x 0.33) = 195,012 individuals eligible and 23,401 in treatment. The share is 23,401 / (163800 + 452400) = 0.038 or 3.8% and the total TF cost (10 + 280) x 0.038 = **£11.02 million.** This estimate based on actual FIP / TF treatment data should be more accurate.

Multi-systemic Therapy.

We are told after a convoluted calculation, not actual numbers, that 1,200 families *nationally* received MST. Given that clinical trials show that MST is cost effective this level of service is deeply disappointing. It is assumed that all these people come from troubled families. Yet our FIP data suggests that only 12% of troubled families get any MH treatment. This is 14,400 families. Few TFs are being helped. We know from the NE 2016 that there was no difference in a range of health outcomes between our processed TFs and a matched control group. Mental health problems are not confined to the 120,000 TFs to which the fiscal costs are supposed to apply. We are now told that 520,000 families are troubled nationally and recent selection emphasises mental health and parenting issues. These families did not just spring into existence. If they were always out there and we drew families at random from that total, the service share of our phase 1 TFs would be 120 / 520 = 0.23 or 23%. But one in four families has a mental health problem at some point and the divorce rate is 42%. 25% of children now live in lone parent families. 66% are working. Are we saying that all these people, often with greater intellectual resources than our TFs, are not able to access MST or other therapies? 23% of the service going to TFs is surely an overestimate. 23% gives a cost of 10 x 0.23 = **£2.3 million** not the claimed **£ 10 million.**

Youth Justice Liaison and Diversion.

They estimate that 4,400 referrals per annum at 37 YJL&D pathfinders cost 37 x £65000 = £2.405 million.

We are then told that 'we assumed that *all TFs would be eligible* for these services' and so assigned all the cost to them. Apparently they took Cameron's word that there were exactly 120,000 TFs and no more. But we know now that 520,000 were lurking out there …Cameron says so! So at most 23% of cost should go to our phase 1 families or **£0.55 million per annum** not **£2.4 million and not the reported 'under £10 million'**. The author would bet that even this is an overestimate.

The reader may say: look these health service costs are small numbers anyway, a few millions to a few tens of millions…why worry? Well small numbers add up. More to the point we have several extremely offhand assignment of costs to our TFs which simply take the *politically defined position* that the TFs are responsible for everything! That is an extremely dangerous attitude development in government department civil servants. It is a poison which must be stamped out. Political and ideological myths about vulnerable minorities, becoming accepted facts in the machinery of government, and in the public mind, take us on the road to Auschwitz.

The total cost of targeted health spending reasonably assigned to the 120,000 TFs is at most **£140.1 million per annum** and not the claimed **£268 million.** £72.3 million, 52%, is simply the normal cost of a family attending their GP service. I suggest the true **targeted** cost is **£67.8 million.**

Health Reactive Spend

Reactive spend is intended to represent the costs due to 'bad' behaviour by the TFs. It includes healthcare costs of alcohol / drug misuse and mental health problems in children and adults. Alcohol / drug abuse is arguably a lifestyle choice …up to a point. Genetic predisposition and addictive personalities are recognised as innate and hardly lifestyle choices. The remaining mental health problems are presumably not lifestyle choice related in our TFs… or any more so than in the general population.

Alcohol and Drug Misuse costs.

The total budget applying to alcohol / drug abuse is given as £1,700 million per annum and relates to 143,000 individuals.
    The analysis uses both the DfE 50,000 families with 'additional child problems' and the Family Intervention 2011 report that 30% of these families have drug and alcohol problems. This supposedly leads to 17% of the budget going to our TFs. This implies 24,300 adults. However using their numbers I get (50,000 x 1.36) x 0.3 = 20,400.

However for the actual TFs we know that 3% of adults received 'structured treatment' for alcohol dependency and 3% for drug dependency (ECORYS 2014). This gives (120,000 x 1.36) x 0.03 = 4,896 adults. So at most, if drug and alcohol treatments were for different people we have 9,792 adults. However these problems frequently go together. For a 50% overlap we would have 7,344 TF adults in treatment. The TF share is then 7344 / 143,114 = 0.051 or 5.1%. The cost would be **£86.7 million per annum** compared with the indirect claim of **£290 million**.

Mental Health Spending: Children.

273,000 are treated nationally at a cost of £1,690 million per annum. The Cost of our TFs is said to be £101.4 million or 6%. This is derived from the estimates described earlier. We noted instead 12% families getting formal MH treatment and that ~33% of children had mental health problems. So we have 120,000 x 0.12 / 273,000 = 0.053 or 5.3% share. The TF cost is **£89.6 million** per annum not **£101.4 million**. This is fairly close for once.

Mental Health Spending: Adults.

754,000 adults were treated at a cost of £4,670 million per annum. 8.3% of the cost is assigned to our TFs or a reported £390 million. Taking the 45% rate of families with adult MH problems gives us (120,000 x 1.36) x 0.45 = 73,440 adults but 12% receive treatment giving 8,813. The share is 8813 / 754000 = 0.0117 or 1.17% and a cost of **£54.6 million per annum** not the claimed **£390 million**.

The total cost of reactive spend on the TFs amounts to **£230.9 million per annum** versus the claimed **£780 million.**

The overall health cost of the TFs is £230.9 million plus £140.1 million (including 'normal GP' costs of £72 million) = **£371 million per annum** versus the claimed **£1,040 million**. Our family health costs are exaggerated by a factor of at least 2.8 X.

Comments on Health Cost Causation

But remember that these still considerable costs are attributed by Cameron et al to the results of lifestyle choices and bad behaviour. Is this true? Taking so-called targeted spend £13.6 million goes on drugs and youth justice liaison.; £21.1 million goes on under 18 pregnancies. We could say these lifestyle choices (of vulnerable children) lead to £34.7 million avoidable costs.

A further £17.9 million on food goes to children of impoverished families. Successive governments from New Labour to the Cameron Conservatives have told us that poverty is simply caused by laziness, on which basis benefits have been cut and a harsh sanctions regime introduced. However we noted in the NE 2016 that 75% of our TFs had 'a member with a limiting, long standing illness or disability'. These families are poor because they cannot work due to high levels on illness.

So of the £140.1 million targeted health spend we calculated was spent on our TFs, only a maximum of £34.7 million could be claimed to be 'lifestyle' based. This is 24.7%. It is a long way from the £260 million claimed in the Fiscal Case Report. If the bad behaviour of the TFs could be totally turned around the savings would be 34.7 / 260 = 0.133 or **13.3%** of claimed targeted health costs of the troubled families.

The reactive health TF spend was calculated as £231 million. Of this £86.7 million was drug / alcohol related. The rest was spending on mental health…not a lifestyle choice. So 37.5% could in principle be saved by completely eliminating substance misuse. Given the NE 2016 finding that the TFP did not improve TF mental health the remaining £144.3 million could not. The earlier Family Intervention Projects came to the same conclusions on health. In fact taking the Fiscal Case TF reactive spend estimate of £780 million the realistic scope for saving is 86.7 / 780 = 0.111 or **11.1%.**

So the realistic health saving potential for turning around our TFs is no more than ~12% or ~£120 million. **Health is the worst area for exaggerating TF costs and saving potential.**

1.3.6 Welfare

Welfare is also split into targeted and reactive spending. Reactive spending includes all benefits except child benefit or child and working tax credit presumably on the grounds that including these would look like attacks on children and smack of eugenics. These costs could only be reduced by eliminating children (TF average 3.07 children).

Welfare Targeted Spend

Targeted spend includes the cost of 'some' of the Work Programme and European Social Fund provision for families with 'complex needs'.

UK Work Programme & European Social Fund.

We are not given the cost of the programme just the numbers of TFs projected to be 'affected' and their cost : 21,000 and £30 million per annum so the cost per head was £1,428. Only 'some' WP costs are included. All the estimates are said to be based on the numbers claiming benefits (at some time) in the 2004 Families and Children Study. (We can do better by consulting government statistics sites. The Work Programme cost £2.2 billion over 2012-2015 or £628.6 million per annum but numbers 'affected' could not be found.) Using these numbers suggests that the projected TFs were only 30 / 628.6 = 0.048 or 4.8% of the service.
In the TFP NE 2016 we learned that ~10% of TFs 'made progress to work' through the WP or ESF. This is 120,000 x 0.1 = ~12,000 families and adults. For the ESF we are told 50,000 TFs are 'affected' at a cost of £50 million or £1,000 per head. 50,000 coincides with the DfE 'families with additional needs' estimate. It was wrong. (Searching government statistics tells us that in 2012 78,700 households supported cost £357 million per annum or £4,530 per head.

Exp. Official Statistics, DWP, July 2015). Does 'affected' actually mean eligible rather than expected to be processed? If so we can reconcile the costs. The 12,000 families who definitely attended the ESF (**or** WP) scheme would cost 12,000 x 4,530 = £ 54.4 million (maximum) compared with £50 million ESF estimate. If 12,000 is correct the 21,000 WP estimate is wrong and we are double counting. We can go no further here. I take the new higher ESF estimate as the actually experienced overall cost : **£ 54.4 million per annum**.

Welfare Reactive Spend

Incapacity Benefit / Employment Support Allowance

13,000 families are said to be 'affected' at a cost of £70 million per annum. The NE 2016 tells us that 19% of families received benefit for an average of 13 weeks over 18 months. Assuming 1 adult affected per family we have (13 / 78) x 0.19 x 120,000 = 3,807 equivalent families. In 2012 IB was ~ £94 per person per week. The cost is then 94 x 52 x 3807 = **£18.6 million.** Many people receiving IB and now in the ESA 'work related' group are not permanently impaired.

Income Support

89,000 TFs are said to receive IS at a cost of £440 million per annum.

74% are in poverty and on out of work benefits. IS was 73.1 per week for a lone parent and £114.85 for a couple in 2016. The average TF has 1.36 adults
or 36% with 2 adults and 64% with 1. This gives us 0.36 x 114.85 + 0.64 x 73.1 = £88 per week average and adjusting back to 2012 say £81. The annual cost is £4,212 compared with £4,944. The cost is therefore 89,000 x 4212 = **£374.9 million per annum**. The DWP estimate is close.

Job Seekers Allowance

It is said that 4,000 families are 'affected' at a cost of £10 million. This appears surprisingly low given the claimed 74% out of work. However this number appears to take into account duration of unemployment in some way. We can do this for the TFP families using the NE 2016 data. Taking an 18 month period 11% of families were unemployed for an average period of 9 weeks. This gives (9 / 78) x 0.11 x 120,000 x 1.36 = 2,071 equivalent families. At ~ £65 per week in 2012/13 this gives **£7 million per annum.** The Fiscal Case estimate was £10 million.

Council Tax Benefit

We are told that 99,000 TFs were 'affected' by council tax benefit at a cost of £100 million per annum. This is 82.5% of families.
In 2012 the Institute of Fiscal Studies estimated £5 billion for 5.9 million families or £847.5 per family. This gives us 99,000 x 847 = **£83.9 million per annum** compared with **£100 million**.

Housing Benefit

106,000 families are said to be 'affected' at a cost of **£120 million per annum.** This is £1132 per family. Looking at the government expenditure records for 2012 standard housing benefit was ~£89 per week and £4628 per annum. This leaves us with something of a puzzle, possibly involving interference between benefit claims, which I cannot resolve. I have to accept their estimate here.

Comments on Welfare

The total cost of TF welfare was given as £820 million with £80 million spent on targeted programmes to encourage work. This £80 million would supposedly allow ~12,000 (or 10% of our current TFs) families to make 'progress to work'. In the TFP PbyR rules 'progress towards work' receives 1 / 8 the bounty for actually getting a job. The reader can consider whether 'targeted' work programmes are good value for money.

The author's estimate of total TF welfare cost came to **£659 million per annum** using actual TF characteristics data, compared with the Fiscal Case report cost of **£820 million** based on projections from previous intervention / family characteristics studies. The difference is a factor of 1.24 X. I must congratulate the DWP on the most realistic cost estimates of all the government areas considered. One assumes this is because benefits are tightly defined by written rules and numbers tracked over time in government statistics. This is **not** the case elsewhere.

The costs highlight other interesting issues. The *direct* cost of 'high' unemployment is relatively low because our families spend a good fraction of time in jobs. Taking the Fiscal Case's own figures JSA is under 2% of reactive spend. Similarly because many IB / ESA (work related group) claimants get better or work periodically, 'disability' cost is only 9.5% of reactive spend. These people are at the bottom of the stack in the job market. They are the casual, part time workers on zero hour contracts and minimum wage, in and out of work; some in and out of chronic illness. They are the people we sanction with benefit removal for breaking the Byzantine benefits rules they cannot follow and who end up in B&Bs with their children and in Food Banks or the morgue (see App 1 on benefit sanctions).

So where do their huge costs to the state come from if not feckless laziness? The biggest welfare item is Income Support at £440 million per annum, 59.5% of reactive welfare spend. The next item is Housing Benefit at £120 million per annum or 16.2% of reactive spend. These are the people in poor social housing or rented accommodation ripped off by landlords and blamed by the state. The government's answer? Cap benefits to £23K in London and £20K elsewhere…that will teach them! These families are costly, *even though many work*, because they otherwise would starve. Be clear :

The families are costly because they are structurally poor – not because of their lifestyle choices.

So far, we as a society quietly decline to let the children starve but if they are all antisocial hooligans, who will only breed more of the same… as Tony Blair, a 21st century British prime minister assured us…well why not let them starve? That is the dark path down which government lies and misrepresentation of the poor, exemplified by the TFP policy, take us.

1.3.7 The Real Fiscal Case for the TFP Phase 1

We can now compare the new cost estimates based on real TF data and other historical departmental costs publically available, with the Fiscal Case costs supposedly based on historical family intervention data and the Families & Children Study of 2004.

	New Estimate (£ millions)	Fiscal Case	Factor
Education / early years	265	840	3.2 X
Child Protection	860	3,730	4.3 X
Crime/Justice	401	2,609	6.5 X
Health	371	1,040	2.8 X
Welfare	659	820	1.2 X
Total Spend	**2,556**	**9,039**	**3.54 X**
Spend per TF per annum	21.3 K	75.3 K	

The overall overestimate factor is 3.5 X with the top prizes going to crime / justice (6.5 X) and the DfE (4.1 X). We looked in detail at how these overestimates arose in each area. In general we have two problems.

Firstly *quantitative* information on TF characteristics is drawn from several sources. The Families and Children Study 2004 features frequently as does the Intervention Projects data of the NCSR 2011 report. But as has been widely pointed out these studies are looking at very different families in terms of the quantitative frequency of their (qualitatively similar) problems. TF ASB and crime levels in particular are grossly over claimed in the Fiscal Case report. To assign costs we need quantitative statistics. Recall that Dame Louise Casey and minister Eric Pickles dismissed the chaos over family selection criteria as 'a silly academic point'. Now we see the consequences of that arrogant attitude. **It reflects either a negligent ignorance of fiscal consequences or a deliberate fraud.**

Secondly we also see major incompetence or deliberate sleight of hand in some areas in proportioning costs to the specific 120,000 families cohort.

On occasion *all* costs are simply assumed to be due to this group. In others 120,000 TFs are assumed to be the total of *all* TFs in the country as the basis for further calculation. But Cameron told us that there are (at least) 520,000 families who he defines as troubled and who will be reprogrammed in TFP phases 1 & 2. This alone gives us an overestimate of 4.3 X. Please remember also that the 120,000 number of TFs was the mid point of a range subject to a large error, calculated from a small sample of TFs. The upper bound was ~16,000000 x (0.2 +0.3) = ~800,000 families. That would give us a 6.7 X error in cost assignment to TFP phase 1 families.

Occasionally the sleight of hand is blatant. In the crime area what appear to be good basic data on costs for four categories children with different offending / truancy profiles produce a very wide range of possible TF costs which includes the probable real number. The analysis then chooses the *extreme case where all children* have an offending / truancy record ignoring the actual family profile of low offending (which could have been found in previous Family Intervention Project reports going back to 1999 (see sections 2 and 4 for the history). We are given a figure of '*up to £2.6 billion per annum*' in an Annexe which then becomes the *actual* claimed cost in the main report....hence the over claim of 6.5 X.

The cost of services analysis whether the Fiscal Case version or the author's, also highlights another issue: **what proportion of TF costs, could in principle be eliminated by changing family behaviour?** Costs are supposedly due to bad behaviour and lifestyle choices. Remember the proposition is that assertive intervention can slash costs...up to £9 billion per annum if we took the Cameron / Pickles 2012 spin seriously.

We take each area of spend in turn:

Education:

Behaviour costs relate to under18 pregnancy and youth crime liaison. However 85% of young offenders have 2 or more mental health conditions and low IQs. Then 0.85 x 25.1 m = £ 21.3 m of the youth crime cost is health related. We also know that many pupil referral children are SEN or have long standing illnesses. 33% of our TF families have SEN children and 52% overall have an SEN or other special needs. 19% of families have children with physical problems. Let's say half the PRU cost is due to such children or 54 x 0.5 = £27 m. In all 'behaviour' cost that cannot be linked closely to health issues is not £114 m but **£57.4 m.** This means **£207.6 m** costs come under the poverty / health heading or 78.3%.

Only 21.7% of cost is open to 'behaviour modification' of the assertive, non-negotiable, sanctions based, TFP kind. The rest requires medical intervention or poverty reduction. This is a general pattern as we will see.

Child Protection : £860 m (Fiscal Case £3,490m).

Most of the cost relates to taking children into state care. 34% of our TFs are said to have 'safeguarding issues'. Why is this? Well we know that 75% have a member with a 'limiting long standing health issue or disability' (NE 2016). 45% of families have an adult with mental health problems. 33% of families have a child with mental health problems (ECORYS 2014). 39% have an SEN statement. IQs are low: we estimated < 63. Most are very poor. (Even so only 3.9% have a child in care). We may conclude that the families are both inadequate and under stress.
Are we dealing here with innate bad 'behaviour' problems or a medical / social problem? How does a TFP type assertive, sanctions based, intervention address this? Can parenting lessons cure illness and disability? I suggest that a very small proportion of the £860 million cost is actually accessible to reduction. Being generous, say the 25% of families without major health / disability issues.

Crime / Justice: £400.5 m.

Crime / ASB is behaviour unacceptable to society. This estimate takes into account the actual (low) levels of crime in TF members. It is 6.5 X smaller than the Fiscal Case estimate for reasons explained above but may still be an overestimate because most TF crime / ASB was low level. We can say again that much crime is carried out by people with mental health problems and such problems are very common in our TF families (see above).
 The prevalence of learning disabilities in young offenders is 9.2 X that in the general population; the prevalence of autistic spectrum disorders is 16.6 X normal ; the prevalence of communication disorders is 12.5 X normal (see section 3.2).

  We may conclude that 'getting into trouble' over ASB is easier for such youths and they lack the cognitive agility to defend themselves. The data suggest a youth with a mental disorder or disability is 12.8 X more likely to end in court than a normal person. 60% of young people appearing in court on ASB charges had a diagnosed mental health problem (section 3.2). We can conclude that 60 to 90% of youth ASB etc is related to health conditions. The issue then is how much these behaviours (and costs) are amenable to TFP type interventions? The historical evidence back to 1999 says very little. The NE 2016 administrative data and family survey data comparisons of our TFs with a matched control group say **zero.**

Medical interventions and even better nutrition, might make a difference (see section 3.3). Let's say 80% of ASB is mental health /disability related.

Health : £371m.

We calculated that £34.7 m of targeted spending was directed to under 18 pregnancies and drug misuse in our TFs. A further £86.7 m was spent on drug related fallout. The total 'lifestyle' and 'bad' behaviour cost was £121.4 million at most. Some would see drug addiction as a bad initial choice magnified in some by an innate addictive tendency. This is 32.7% of the health total spend accessible in principle to reduction if treated as a medical / social problem. Whatever the TFP did the NE 2016 shows it had no impact at all on our families in comparison with matched control groups. When will the lesson be learned.

Welfare : £ 659 m. (Fiscal Case £820 m)

The direct cost of JSA and IB / ESA (worklessness) was only ~12% of the total reactive spend according to the Fiscal Case analysis. Recall that 26% of our TFs were in continuous employment anyway. By far the biggest spend was income support at £375m in my estimate or 57% of total welfare spend (£440 m and 53.7% in the Fiscal Case). What we appear to have here is a reflection of very poor families working when they can in part time lowly paid (minimum wage, zero time contract?) jobs despite illness and disabilities. This is not the picture put out by successive government spin doctors. The second biggest spend is housing benefit at £120 m or 20% of reactive spend. We have nearly all TFs in social housing (housing associations) or private rented accommodation. The families have no control over rents charged.

How could these costs be reduced? If our families had full time jobs it would eliminate £7 – 10 million JSA. Curing all illness and disabilities would save £19 – 70 million. The total is £26 to £80 million or 4% to 9.8% of total welfare spend. These families are **structurally poor** and it is hard to see how being in the TFP could change the situation.

What about the other welfare costs? Income Support and housing benefit are income determined. If our families are employed won't these also be eliminated? Let's try a rough estimate. In our Wirral example 43% of the families lived in the top 5% most deprived areas of the country. 75% lived in the top 20% most deprived areas.

According to the ONS (2105) before benefits and taxes, the poorest national quintile average income was 6,100 per annum compared with the top quintile at £83,800. After benefits and taxes the figures became £16,500 and £62,500. This suggests that our troubled families would still be eligible for large benefits even if they were all employed. Using the Fiscal Case estimates the welfare cost per family is 820m / 120,000 = £6,833 per annum. Using my estimates it is £5,492.

Using the Fiscal Case data, the remaining benefits (after JSA / IB removal) are £740 million and the remaining benefit fraction ~90%. In both estimates most (~90%) of the welfare cost of the TFs is irreducible even if the TFP had 'turned around' 100% into employment. It managed 11%...not attributable to the programme based on control group comparison. Recall also the Fiscal Case Welfare definition *did not include* child and child working tax credits. These benefits are also not susceptible to the TFP, unless later phases include euthanasia.

Conclusion

Having looked at all areas of spend and the above evidence we can now estimate the proportion depending on family lifestyle choices and bad behaviour and so, in principle, accessible to TFP or similar reprogramming. We split the costs into 'lifestyle' and 'health / poverty' categories. These estimates *cannot* be precise but the main result are the large differences our analyses lead to in comparison with the original £9 billion per annum costs of Cameron's 120,000 TFs.

Spending Area	'Behaviour/ lifestyle' Costs	'Health / Poverty' Costs
Education	£58m	£207m
Child Protection	215m	645m
Crime / Justice	82m	321m
Health	121m	250m
Welfare	66m	593m
Total	**542m**	**2016m**

Our total spend is £2.56 billion compared with the Cameron / Pickles £9 billion per annum for the 120,000 families cohort.

This is **28.4%** of the £9 billion claim. The cost is £21,317 per family per annum compared with the original £75,000 per family per annum claim.

Using our £2.56 billion estimate the proportion of total spend which is reasonably attributed to bad behaviour / lifestyle is 542 / 2558 = 0.211 or **21%.** That £542m is *in principle accessible* to reduction by interventions …possibly TFP style interventions. It is just 542 / 9000 = 0.06 or **6%** of the original £9 billion cost estimate. This is £4,517 per family per annum. That is the saving which could be made by eliminating **all** family 'bad' behaviour. But we know from the NE 2016 that **no** changes resulted in crime, child protection and health areas and the small gain in employment and reduction in truanting could **not** be attributed to the TFP.

The author suggests that by looking more carefully at family characteristics based on the earlier Family Intervention Project studies and published government cost statistics and by partitioning out health and poverty factors, the real and small *order of saving* from the TFP could have been predicted in 2012.

Since nothing has changed in the family 'processing' content of the TFP phase 2 it is unlikely a different outcome from the above will result at its conclusion. There is no shift in emphasis towards treating family health and poverty issues.

We can predict now that phase 2 will be a washout. Let the Public Accounts Committee note this now at the start of 2017. The author and others will hold them to account in 2020.

1.4   The Wirral TFP

1.4.1 Introduction

 In this section we will look at the Wirral project claimed family outcomes as an example of LA behaviour. Later the national results will reflect such behaviour across 152 LAs. Cross checks of family characteristics with national data suggest that it is not untypical of other areas, including in the creative and imaginative use of results data by Wirral Council. The Wirral is a long peninsula of land some 15 miles by 7 miles, sandwiched between the Dee to the west and the Mersey to the east. The east coast facing the city of Liverpool, is heavily urbanised down its whole length. The west of the peninsula is rural with farm land and small, affluent towns. The total population is ~320,000 with two thirds of the population in the eastern urban strip. Birkenhead is the main conurbation opposite Liverpool. The town was once the centre for industry, hosting the famous Cammel –Laird shipbuilding site. Further south there are still some light industrial companies in the Bromborough area.

Today much of the old industry and the need for skilled and unskilled manual workers, is gone. Some 0.3% of the local economy is agriculture, 25% industrial and 74.7% is service based. The eastern urban areas and in particular, Birkenhead, have significant areas of deprivation. **55%** of Birkenhead working age adults (16-64 years) subsist on out of work benefits. Frank Field, the local MP, has described his constituency in 2014 as 'becoming like Beirut'. **30%** of the population are in the most deprived quintile of people in the UK. **50%** are in the two most deprived quintiles. 16,000 children are living in poverty.

Wirral Council published a review of their TFP (called the IFIP) in 2015 containing 28 pages (19). 27 pages detailed the wonderful IFIP results based on multiple, anecdotal case studies. One page briefly summarised outcomes and remarkable 'money saved' claims which we will examine later. We simply note now that at the beginning Wirral expected the family cost to be £75 K per family per annum, exactly as the government claimed in 2012, and at the end in 2015, sure enough, the savings were claimed to be £76 K per family. *This is a miraculous result!* It is even stranger since by mid 2015 minister Eric Pickles was only claiming £26.5 K per family…and this was a gross cost. Wirral tax payers might well wonder what was going on and we will tell them later. The report also provided more on the deprived nature of the families worth noting here.

35.1% of the troubled families were living in one of the top 3% most deprived areas of the country; 43% in the top 5% most deprived areas; 75.1% in the top 20% most deprived areas.

The difference in male life expectancy between the poorest areas of Birkenhead and the wealthiest areas on Wirral is **14.6 years.** The small suburban area around Bebington, post code CH63, in the south, was recently defined as the best place to live in England on a range of criteria. The author is privileged to live there. Politically, three constituencies were held by Labour and one by the Conservatives until 2015. At the general election Conservative Esther McVey, Coalition Employment Minster and former Disability Minister, was thrown out against the national swing to the Conservatives. McVey's support for Iain Duncan Smith's rabid attacks on the sick and disabled poor and the huge growth in Wirral food banks, had presumably touched some consciences.

In summary the Birkenhead conurbation provides plenty of deprived families with 'multiple problems' for the Troubled Families initiative and the food banks. This is not new. The Labour council ASBO team was highly active during the mid 2000s, hunting mentally disordered and inadequate families under the prize winning, sadly accurate slogan

'ABUSE YOUR RIGHTS: LOOSE YOUR RIGHTS'

The Troubled Families Programme is based on the ASB Family Intervention Projects introduced by Tony Blair to combat the antisocial behaviour attributed to the 'menace' children of irresponsible 'lone mothers'. The FIPs actually targeted deprivation and health problems as we will see, but even Blair was reluctant to admit it. Today the government still stresses criminality and anti-social behaviour, along with school attendance problems and worklessness, as the key criteria for targeting Troubled Families. However most of the families targeted for nearly eighteen years were not involved in crime or antisocial behaviour. In the case of the Wirral troubled families only 1.2% of the children have an ASBO or Acceptable behaviour Contract. Only 13% of the children had three or more temporary exclusions from school.

There was and is a long standing tradition of making misleading, premature, and exaggerated claims for the success of these projects as we will see. Wirral Council continues that proud tradition. What follows is taken from the TFP 'evaluation report' which the author received after he requested the *detailed* cost-benefit analysis promised in 2012 (19).

'Intensive Family Intervention Programme October 2012 – March 2015'

This 'evaluation' consisted of 28 pages of family anecdotes and TFP self-congratulation and 1 page of summarised behaviour and 'cost / benefit' outcomes. The anecdotes tell us nothing about the effectiveness of the IFIP but are enlightening. We seem to have full or sample entries for 7 families. This is a sample of 7 out of 910 families or 0.77%.We do not know how these families were selected…they do not appear to be randomly chosen. Even if we considered qualitative evidence as useful this scale of sample is meaningless. The families chosen are large and display high levels of anti-social and criminal behaviour including domestic abuse. The anecdotes list the problems and the IFIP responses : 'what was done' One other thing stands out: 5 of the 7 anecdotes mention health problems including:

A child with autism :
no mention of medical treatment as a result of the IFIP.

A child mental health issue:
no mention of medical treatment.

A mum with stress and depression; child with ADHD :
no mention of medical treatment.

A mum long term alcohol abuse; child violent with ASB (mentally ill?)
: no mention of medical treatment; child was imprisoned.

An adult perennial drug addict :
no mention of medical treatment; adult was jailed for possession.

We will see that the incidence of offending / ASB is actually very low
(~8-15% depending on the measures considered) so this family sample
is clearly **biased and untypical**. The sample **is typical** in the health area.
We see that 71% have health issues but this is unsurprising. The National
Evaluation 2016 reports that 75% of families have one or more members
with a 'limiting, long standing illness or disability'. 52% of families have a
child with an SEN or other special needs. 45% of families have an adult
with a mental health issue. *Mental health is clearly a key determinant
of the inability of the families to cope and to meet the behavioural
expectations of society.* We know that the prevalence of learning
disabilities in young 'offenders' is 9.2X to 16.6X that in the 'normal'
population (see section 3.2).

Health is supposed to be one of the key targets for the TFP but it appears
that Wirral has not registered that fact like many other LAs. The emphasis
is on control of 'bad' behaviour whatever its source. Like many LAs
Wirral has a history in the ASB Family Intervention Projects and later we
will see that here the emphasis was on 'tough sanctions' and threats of
sanctions. In the 'helpful, kindly' TFP 40% of the families had such
'assertive' interventions. The NE 2016 will confirm that across the
country the impact of the TF projects on family health and wellbeing
was **zero**.

The one page report of quantitative Wirral results confirm that the results
refer only to 'the families receiving intensive support from an IFIP
key worker'. But we know from the national data that on average only
22% of TFP families received intensive intervention of this kind. Wirral is
reporting results for only ~20% of its families. The families described are
not typical of ~80% of the Wirral families in the scheme.

Such reporting is a common problem across LAs, encouraged by the centre to reinforce Cameron's 2012 highly misleading description of troubled families.

On March 25th 2015, a conference to 'celebrate' the Wirral TFP was held at the New Brighton Floral Pavilion. The project was described as a 'remarkable success' in 'turning around' the lives of the families. One claim reported that '67% of [project] participants re-engaged with or stayed in employment, education or training in 2013-14' (1, 2). Clearly those who 'stayed in' work etc, were **not** turned around by the project. They may have continued in work anyway as the national evidence will show us later. Public claims across all LAs emphasise the *final* family figures without stating the entry figures on problems or providing *any evidence* that any net change was due to the TFP interventions.

In this way we will find 132 LAs claiming a 100% success in 'turning around' families. Wirral only claimed a modest 98.9% turn around rate! We will look in detail at the Wirral claims but please remember that *none* of the improvements claimed can be objectively attributed to the IFIP actions according to the National Evaluation reports 2016. However analysis gives an insight into how data can be selected and misleadingly presented. We will see that this was endemic in the TFP across the country and in the centre.

So how successful was the project in getting the 74% of workless households at entry, into work? At the end of 2014 the Wirral entry on the DCLG database told us that just 2.6% of households got a job …possibly as a result of the project intervention but objectively we cannot say. There was no control group to compare. By mid 2015 this had miraculously risen to 7.14%. The 2015 report tells us

'56% of adults had engaged in training, learning, volunteering or employment opportunities.'

Well again we do not know how many were 'engaged' before the project in these activities but ~26% of families already had one or more members in work at entry, remember. There are 1.36 adults per family on average so actually ~41.2% of families achieved the above claim. 10.6% had a member who had 'made progress to work' by the end. That meant attending the state Work Programme, not getting a job. The bounty for getting a job was £800, that for making progress to work, £100. We must assume the latter is equivalent to 1 / 8th of a job in the state's eyes. So we have 41.2 – 7.14 – 10.6 = 23.5% compared with the ~26% of families having an adult in work at entry…close enough.

There is little room for training, learning or volunteering. This is padding. Note again that there is no evidence that the 7.14% of families getting an adult into a job resulted from TFP action. Later national employment comparisons with a control group will confirm this.

We also see that

'90% of childrens' school attendance had increased to over 85%.'

However below we will see that 58% of children were not involved in truancy at project entry. Nationally only 20.3% of families had a child with less than 85% attendance. The misleading data continue. We learn that

'70% of families with substance misuse issues received support to address their problem.'

However the national data tells us that only 9% of adults had taken non-prescription drugs (in the previous 3 months). 7% had a diagnosed dependence on alcohol (ECORYS 2014). Only 3% of adults had received medical treatment for substance abuse.

We learn that on Wirral

'67% of families were *supported to register* with a GP and/or dentist.'

However the national data tell us that *only* 4% of troubled families had any member NOT registered with a local GP and *only* 10% with a member NOT registered with a local dentist. This creative style of outcome reporting was adopted across LAs with the tone set by the DCLG and as we will see, 132 of 152 LAs reported a totally false 100% success rate in 'turning around' their families.

Back on Wirral we are also told (2) of a

'95% reduction of ASB across **all** families engaged with the service'

However the mid 2015 report also says

'74% of families with a history of crime / ASB had stopped offending.'

These are truly a remarkable claims since we will see that only 6.5% of adults and 10.4% of children had reports of incidents of ASB at project entry.

Recall also that the national data shows us that 70% of families at entry had either 0 or 1 ASB issues out of a possible 13 issues…hardly a crime wave. We also learn that

'92% of families self-assessed that their parenting skills had improved… 84% of families reported improved mental health…59% with a history of domestic abuse had issues resolved.'

It is worth noting that in the final NE synthesis report the family survey data showed *no evidence* for improvements here in comparison (for the first time) with a matched control group of similar but un-processed families. Please note that parenting issues and within family abuse were often reasons for targeting these families for 'intensive intervention' and 'tough sanctions'.

A number of commentators have pointed out that self-reported and assessed results like these are collected under conditions amounting to duress. Admitting no subjective improvement surely invites further 'interventions'. If this seems speculative note that 40% of TFP families were threatened with or received sanctions during the projects. Dame Louise Casey ran into similar trouble in 2012… when she interviewed 16 troubled families who were reported to be so grateful to the TFP and Saint Louise. It was pointed out that the ethical rules for carrying out social research without the (unforced) permission of the subject had been breached (20). The DCLG simply replied that this was an 'informal / dipstick' exercise by Casey and therefore not covered by the ethical rules! In this arena we see, repeatedly, policy evaluation by 'dipstick'!

All the Wirral material is not untypical of other LA and government national claims and *represents incredibly sloppy reporting or an attempt to deliberately mislead the public.* The reader can decide. We will see much more as we proceed. Caveat emptor.

1.4.2   The 'CRIME / ASB / EDUCATION' Target

Warning : none of the data used by the DCLG to make these 'success' claims is defined as 'official government statistics' …for good reason.

Note also that the published changes in family behaviour claimed by Wirral, the other LAs and the government cannot be attributed to TFP interactions. Objectively there is **no** evidence of causation. For example a family member may have found a job anyway through other means. We will see later in the National Evaluation 2016 studies that administrative data and family survey data both show that there is **no** difference in outcomes between a large sample of the 120,000 families and a carefully matched control group of similar but unprocessed families. The purpose of the current analyses is to demonstrate the gross public exaggeration of the claimed outcomes, however caused. The 'outcome' deck was deliberately stacked in a variety of ways approved by the DCLG.

The DCLG Troubled Families financial framework paid a bounty for 'success' in three areas.

1. 'Crime / ASB / Education'   £700 per family 'turned around'.

2. An adult gaining continuous employment for 6 months.   £800 per head.

3. An adult making 'progress to work'   £100 per head.
   (i.e. Joining the government Work Programme)

Each family listed for the project attracts an 'attachment fee' or bounty, of £3200 (3).

On Wirral the record shows that by end 2014 2.6% of families met the employment target and by March 2015 this increased to 7.14%. (83% were on out of work benefits at entry). A further 10.6% joined the government 'Work Programme' so, allegedly, making progress to work. The bounty here is just £100 compared with £800 for getting into employment. Clearly the relative bounty size shows how little the 'progress' really amounts too.

In this section we will examine the claims for success in the 'crime/ ASB / education' target which nationally and locally are both stressed in the media and exaggerated in a grossly misleading way. Firstly, by lumping together crime, anti-social behaviour and educational issues and reporting an overall success rate the public is misled about where the families have been 'turned around'.

Clearly there is a very big difference between reduction in criminal activities by adults and reduction in truanting by children. Secondly by not telling the media and public about the levels of criminality and ASB in the families **at project entry** the government narrative that the families are highly criminal and anti-social is preserved and the implied scale of success in this area is exaggerated. Thirdly the thresholds in the criteria for success are set surprisingly low. For example, youth offending in minors need only fall by 33% for this to be counted a successful turn around.

77

Fourthly it is important to stress that the various improvements in family behaviour need only be sustained for short periods for the families to be judged 'turned around'. This period is six months for four criteria and a year for one criterion. Given that we are told that all the families were targeted for having multiple, *long standing* 'problems', this provides little evidence for a permanent 'turn around' once close project supervision is removed.

We will see that in the case of the earlier FIPs, monitoring for about fourteen months after exit showed, for example, a decline from 85% of families with significantly reduced ASB claimed, down to at most 35% over this period and possibly ~23% (4). At best this is a re-offending rate of ~59 % per annum compared with a national current youth re-offending rate of 37% in a year and ~65% in the medium term.

We will now explore these issues using data from my FoIA requests, the DCLG website databases and the ECORYS 2014 report on family profiles. These are the detailed success criteria for payments under the TFP financial framework :

They [a family] achieve **all** 3 of the education / crime / ASB measures set out below

1. Each child in the family has had fewer than 3 fixed term exclusions **and** less than **15%** of unauthorised absences in the last 3 school terms; **and**

2. A **60%** reduction in anti-social behaviour [incidents] across the family in the last 6 months; **and**

3. Offending rate by all minors in the family reduced by at least **33%** in the last 6 months.

At first sight the overall success requirements look tough. However the government bounty is paid even if only 2 out of the 3 criteria above are relevant and met. Were 'local discretion' criteria were applied by a LA in family selection 1 criterion (or sub-criterion) met is sufficient to claim a 'turn around'. In the Wirral results database we find that 100% of families are claimed as having a 'local discretion' origin. Despite the above criterion definitions the headline public figure for project success is often apparently obtained by **adding together** numbers of successful families under each sub-criterion. Since we are told that these families have been selected for having multiple problems and that we might expect correlation between the occurrence of criminal and ASB, this procedure must lead to double counting.

The author suspects that as the finish date for TFP phase 1 approached, at the end of 2014, the word went out that the centre would take a favourable view of a relaxed interpretation of the claiming rules for 'crime/ASB/education' under PbyR and that 100% family 'turn around' figures would not be questioned. Since employment achieved numbers were small and could not be fiddled, this meant that the 'crime/ASB /education' results had to carry the success claim load…anything goes!

In fact we will see that media stories emerged that some success claims were based on 'data matching' in LA files. That is, locate families known to the council for say, ASB issues in the past, who had ceased offending at some time during the TFP phase 1 period and claim these families as 'turned around' by the TFP. This procedure was perhaps occasionally semi-legitimate because of the diversity of ways in which local TFPs were implemented. In some places money was funnelled into existing intervention initiatives. We will see later (in looking at the Public Accounts Committee Inquiry) it was admitted that success rate was also 'enhanced' by counting successes for families **not** in the LAs TFP phase 1 cohort. The most generous thing we could say about all this is that the TFP implementation and monitoring was a disastrous shambles rather than a well organised conspiracy to protect a key, failed, government social policy. In fact it was both, but the conspiracy element was laughably inept.

We will now look at each crime/ASB/education sub-criterion in turn for the Wirral.

1A. Fixed Term [temporary] Exclusions from School.

35% of families had a child with 3 or more fixed exclusions. 65% of families had no exclusions. This issue involved just 13% of all children in the project. Note that 87% had not been excluded. However we know from other work that nationally ~2 / 3 of children excluded from school had mental health issues or learning disabilities (16).

In October 2013 Department of Education statistics showed that overall 1.4% of school children had been excluded in 2011 / 2012. However 8.2% of SEN children had been excluded; 9.5% with School Action Plus status and 4.6% with School Action status, the lower tier 'SEN' categories. This means an SEN child was **6X** more likely than a 'normal' child to be excluded. Most SEN exclusions were for disruptive behaviour and resisting teachers but SEN pupils were *far less* likely to be excluded for bullying, theft, drug and alcohol abuse, sexual misconduct or physical assault on other pupils. In other words, teachers could simply not cope with learning disabilities and mental illnesses in the SEN children.

In spring 2014 the charity 'Ambitious About Autism' found that four in ten autistic children had at some time been 'informally excluded' from school on a temporary basis. Two fifths of the parents had been told to collect their children early without prior warning. Three in ten had been asked to keep their child home. These practices are **strictly illegal.** Would they be tolerated in the case of normal children? Parents of disabled children soon realize that they are second class citizens in such circumstances. But what can they do when the school involved does not have staff trained to cope with learning disabilities?

Back to the Wirral troubled family project. At project conclusion the claim is that 94% of families had children with fewer than 3 exclusions. At entry 65% of the families *already met* the criterion so the claimed improvement over the project is 94 – 65 = 29%. We give this number to show the distortion in success reporting but please note that there is *no evidence* that even this modest fall in exclusions is due to project interventions. Note that the 'successful' families could have experienced 2 exclusions per child and **still** met the criterion.

The exclusion rate could **still** be 2 / 3 of that at project entry. Note that this improvement was while the families were under close supervision by a 'key worker'. What happened a year or two years after the project ended? We do not know since the TF projects, like the Family Intervention Projects before them, are not monitored long term. However the arguments that these projects will save the state money depend on sustained savings over many years having 'cured' the families once and for all. Official, government assigned, academic project evaluation teams have been calling for long term family monitoring since 2000 as we will see.

1B. Unauthorised Absences from School.

At project entry 52% of the Wirral families had 15% or more unauthorised absences in 3 terms. This involved 42% of the children in the project, a high number. But a majority, 58% were not involved in truancy. At project exit it is claimed that again 94% of families had all children with less than 15% absences so the improvement was in 94 – 48 = 46% of families. It is also claimed that 90% of children had met the attendance criterion. On the basis of children the change was 90 – 58 = 32%.

This reduction in unauthorised absence must be welcomed however it *cannot* objectively be attributed to the TFP intervention. We will see from the National Evaluation analysis that 80% of troubled families met the unauthorised absence criterion *but* so did 79% of families in a matched control group who had no interventions. The difference of 1% is not statistically significant.

We should also consider the causes of absence. The government attributes absence to feckless parents and badly behaved, out of control truants who rampage around the community. Is this true? Note that the project families are among the poorest in the country even though 26% had an adult in a job at some point. Some absences will involve parents removing children to take much cheaper holidays in term time. Not ideal, but perhaps understandable and particularly so if parents have correctly deduced that education will not help their children get better jobs in our post-industrial economy. The marginal value of GCSEs to a shelf stacker on a zero hours contract is negligible. We will also see below that these families have remarkably high levels of adult and child physical and mental health problems and disabilities. Nationally **39%** of the families had SEN children. **52%** had one or more children with an SEN statement or other recognised special needs. This may be pertinent to absence frequency.

Given the high levels of 'long standing' mental and physical illness (in **75%** of families) and the high number of children (average 3.07) it is also interesting to consider another factor. The Carers Trust notes that there are 700,000 young carers (16-24) in the UK. In January 2017 a CT survey to mark 'Young Carers Day' found that **73%** of young carers 'took time off learning while a **third** admitted *skipping school* most weeks'. 53% admitted to having problems coping with school work while 60% said they struggled to meet deadlines. 42% of our Wirral children met the TFP unauthorised absence criterion of > 15% and nationally 36% of TFP families had a 15-16 year old. How many of our 'fiendish' TF youths are 'skipping school' to care for their sick mothers and siblings? Health and Care minister, David Mowat said on the day that a national carers strategy would be launched this year.

'It will recognise that truly effective support can only happen when we reach beyond health and care services into schools, workplaces and community centres.'

Super! But how about ending the hounding of young carers in troubled families for 'skipping school' in the mean time? We can go on and on. In the first, Dundee Family Project which set the pattern for later interventions, 70% of the family children had been bullied (5).

Mencap repeatedly shows us that ~80% of learning disabled adults suffer regular verbal or physical abuse in the community. Note again that the school absence 'improvement' was monitored only while the families were under close supervision. We do not know what happened over one or two or more years, never mind the long term.

By the way, 'successes' in exclusions and absences *included* truanting children who simply reached school leaving age during the project. Out of sight out of mind but *in* the success statistics. This is relevant because of the high proportion of families selected *because* they had 15-16 year old children at entry. 36% of children were 15 or 16 years old according to the 'Fiscal Case for Working with TFs', DCLG, Feb. 2013. 78% were in the 10-18 year age range. These kids must be criminal louts and rioters all, surely? Actually not, as we will now see.

2. Reduction in Family ASB.

At project entry 11% of the Wirral families had an adult with reports of ASB. We learn that 6.5% of adults had such reports. **93.5%** of adults had **no ASB.** 26% of families at entry had one or more children with reports of ASB. This involved just 10.4% of all children. **89.6%** of the children had **no ASB.** This seems a long way from the impression given to the public that the troubled families are heavily involved in ASB. Nobody in the media it seems, bothers to check.

Also by reporting headline results at the family level the prevalence of ASB and other problems is magnified and the public misled. This trick has been used since the beginning of the intervention projects under New Labour. As in those projects we have no published data on the *severity or frequency* of the ASB individuals were allegedly involved in. However for Wirral we know that only 1.2% of the project children had an ASBO or Acceptable Behaviour Contract. This is even lower than the 3-6% typically seen in the New Labour and earlier Coalition FIPs. We will see later in the earlier FIP analyses of similar families that the level of most LA claimed ASB was trivial (section 4.5). For example although councils reported 62% of families for 'rowdy' behaviour only 1% had a fixed penalty notice for disorder. Note also that the average TFP family had 4.43 members so the actual 'rowdy' behaviour claim could relate to only 21% of individuals.

The ASB success criterion required a 60% reduction in ASB incidents across the family over the 'last 6 months'. It is claimed that 87% of the Wirral families achieved this. Clearly if that is reported without context it is very misleading. Recall that in fact the local media were told of a

'95% reduction of ASB across **all** families engaged in the service'

In fact success occurred in just 11x 0.87 = 9.57% of all families based on adult ASB or 26 x 0.87 = 22.6% based on child ASB.

Note that in 'turned around' families ASB incidents are **still** occurring at up to 40% of the project entry rate. This criterion uses a rather low threshold to claim success and is not known to the public at large who are told ASB has been eliminated. In fact Cameron famously said at the start of the TF programme that **no** bounties would be paid unless

'anti-social behaviour stops completely, and I mean completely'.

So much for politicians promises. Yet again we have no information on the longer term sustainability of these improvements beyond 6 months. As usual there is no evidence that any change in ASB was caused by project intervention …there was no control group.

3. Minor Offending Rate.

At project entry 31% of families had one or more minors with an 'offence' as defined by the TFP. 69% of families had no minors offending. Nationally just 16% of minors in the projects had 'offended'. 84% had not offended. An 'offence' is defined as 'a formal court or out of court disposal'. These include reprimands, warnings, cautions, penalty notices, fines and custody. This is a very wide net in terms of implied severity of offence. We had no published information on severity to assess this but recall that only 1.2% of the Wirral project children had received ASBOs or ABCs. The author made a FoIA request to Wirral Council requesting details of the more serious minor offending 'disposals'. The answer was

'This information is not available as we did not record a breakdown of sentences or fines. Children were identified through having an offence as defined by the TFP financial framework'

In other words a box was ticked somewhere : severity evidence was not recorded…the payment system did not require it. In fact such evidence might undermine the DCLG claims about the high criminality of the families and children. What fraction of the 16% of all minors recorded as 'offenders' received custody, the most serious justice intervention? Nobody knew until the NE of October 2016 a year *after the end* of TFP phase1. In the national administrative database 0.4% of children received a custodial sentence.

Only 3.9% of children were convicted of an offence. Clearly many 'offences' were trivial with few leading to conviction. But Cameron, Pickles, et al told us repeatedly of families and youths leading a life of crime. A FoIA request to government in 2015 confirmed that

'Details of sentencing are not available through the Family Monitoring Data'

The minor offending success criterion called for a 33% fall in offending rate by all minors in the family over 6 months. It is claimed that 82% achieved this. This implies that 31 x 0.82 = 25.4% of families were 'turned around', perhaps 13.2% of project children. Perhaps there were 3.9 x (1-0.82) = 0.7% fewer child convictions. On Wirral this would be ~19 minor convictions. Note that in the 'successful' families minor offending rates could **still** be up to 67% of the entry level. Yet again the improvement was only monitored over a 6 month period. What happened after close supervision and support ended? The Ministry of Justice tells us that the current youth re-offending rate amounts to 36.7% in a year and ~66% over a longer period. The Wirral outcomes 2015 document also claims that

'74% of families with a history of crime and/or ASB had stopped offending.'

Considering this claim in respect to crime it is important to note that according the data in the National Evaluation Synthesis Report 2016, adult conviction rate was 7.1% of individuals and child conviction rate 3.9%. Adult custodial sentence rate was 1.7% and child custodial rate 0.4%. If we assume the 74% Wirral claim applied to criminal individuals this means that offending ceased in 0.74 x 7.1 = 5.2% of adults and 0.74 x 3.9 = 2.9% of children. We have on average nationally 1.36 adults per family and 3.07 children so in family terms the improvements would be 3.8% and 0.95%. Either way the crime claims by Wirral, other LAs, the DCLG and ministers are *incompetently and grossly misleading* at best. **At worst we are dealing with a deliberate fraud on the public.** The reader can judge which when we consider the conclusions of the Public Accounts Committee Inquiry on the TFP.

1.4.3 The WIRRAL Overall TFP Success Claims

According to the DCLG data base at the end of 2014, 77.2% of Wirral project families had been 'turned around' in the 'crime / ASB / education' area and 2.6% had an adult entering employment. By March 2015 the database showed employment risen to 7.14% and crime/ASB/education turn around to 91.65%...a total, remarkable turnaround rate of **98.8%.**

Nationally the figure was 98.93% and 132 of 152 LAs declared a precise and miraculous 100% family success rate! As a member of the PAC TFP Inquiry drily commented, this was so spectacular that Dame Louise Casey's DCLG team should be 'put in charge of all government policy implementation.' How was this miracle achieved?

We may assume that the 7.14% Wirral employment gained figure and the other LA figures are reasonably accurate since these numbers are readily audited. But what about the 91.65% crime claim? It was 77.2% at the end of 2014. The crime/ASB/education turn around claims suddenly jumped upwards in all LA areas in early 2015. It is as though the rules of the TFP game changed. How might we explain this? Consider the Wirral claims for each of the sub-criteria.

1a). fixed school exclusions: 29% of families changed between entry and exit.

1b). unauthorised absence: 46% of families improved.

2. 60% reduction in family ASB: 9.6% of families based on adults. 22.6% based on children.

3. 33% reduction in minor offending: 25.4% of families turned around.

We do not know the distribution of these improvements across the families but we know that the 'worst' families have multiple problems. We might expect high correlations between exclusions and unauthorised absences and between family ASB and minor offending. If **all** sub-criteria must be met to define a family as turned around (as in the original PbyR scheme) and these families exhibit all these problems, then the turnaround figure would be controlled by the lowest rate or 9.6% for adult ASB, not the claimed 77.2% or the later 91.65%. If we concentrate on minors and just the lowest rate in each of the 3 sub-criteria we can get 29+22.6+25.4 = 77%, the early 2015 claim. However if LAs claim family selection by local discretion, meeting any one criterion is sufficient to claim a family is turned around. Applying this rule to the school sub-criteria gives us 46% instead of 29% and in total 46+22.6+25.4 = 94% compared with the final 91.65% claimed. A slight change or relaxation in the PbyR rules yields a wide range of possible crime/ASB/education turnaround results. If we took the 94% and added the 7.14% employment figure we get 101.4% turnaround which is clearly impossible. The scope for fine tuning (while conforming to the rules of course) is remarkable and repeated in all 152 LAs.

A further FoIA request to Wirral in 2016 provided additional information on the claimed outcomes in documents said to have 'underpinned' the local evaluation of the TFP and DCLG PbyR claims. It took the author two attempts to obtain the data. The first response from the senior manager of Targeted Services (responsible for what is now the Wirral Family Intervention Service) was

'I am not able to provide a location for the detailed IFIP outcome / cost-benefit evaluation report as this was not published locally.'

Does this imply that the data collation and processing for the PbyR claims to the DCLG were done by a third party? Across the country a number of private firms were offering TFP support services to LAs including expertise in the Department for Education Troubled Family 'cost calculator' which we will see has a lot to answer for when it comes to the 'fantasy' savings claims by LAs.

After a second FoIA request three data files turned up but not the detailed evaluation report promised in the previously published council documents. The Wirral 'eligibility' and 'outcomes' data file provides 0,1, codes for school attendance, youth crime & ASB, out of work benefits, local discretion, family crime & ASB, continuous employment and progress to work criteria for all 910 families. The proportion of families continuously employed works out at 7.14% and progress to work as 10.6% as previously reported.

The other criteria claims were interesting. Eligibility for claiming out of work benefit results was 80.3% compared with families gaining employment at 7.14% and making progress to work at 10.6%. All 910 families are recorded as being eligible for a 'local discretion' selection claim. Readers will recall this has the effect of allowing a family to be defined as 'turned around' even if only one of the crime/ASB/education sub-criteria are met.

The claimed success eligibility under the crime/ASB/education criterion is 91.65% which is identical to the figure in the final DCLG outcome tables for LAs. However the proportion of families meeting the crime/ASB /education criterion in the Wirral local data base is only 44.6%. How do we get 91.65% for the overall claim? Well the proportion meeting the school attendance eligibility requirement is reported as 99%. It appears that a positive result on attendance defines the overall crime/ASB /education result as we surmised earlier …presumably allowed because we are told that 100% of Wirral families also meet the 'local discretion' criterion.

But as we saw 48% of families met the school attendance criterion *at project entry.*

It is clear that the claims data submitted by Wirral Council (or its agents?) were not validity checked by the DCLG. This appears to be the case generally. But there is more to consider. The Wirral 'distance travelled' outcome file reports the views of the families about improvements achieved in the project. One assumes that the families would be keen to agree that they had improved to avoid further 'interventions' and 'tough sanctions'. We find that only 89.5% of families report *any* improvement in school attendance in comparison with the 99% reported by the council as meeting the tougher PbyR attendance criterion.

Similarly the proportion of families reporting *any* reduction in crime and ASB is 80.3% versus the official council claim of 91.65%. But recall also that at entry 89% of Wirral families had **no** adult with ASB reports (or 93.5% of individuals) and 74% of families had **no** children with ASB reports (or 89.6% of individuals). At project entry 69% of families had **no** minor offending ...or up to 90% of individual minors. How can we explain theses inconsistencies? Either we have a high level of negligence and incompetence in the submission of official data upon which public tax money will be handed over to the council ...or this council and many others have been *instructed* by the centre that 'anything goes'.

How can we tell which hypothesis holds? Well we can look at the summary results for a range of councils and the reader can decide. For the moment note that the 2016 National Evaluation Synthesis Report highlights the disconnect between the prevalence of family problem issues according to LAs, in comparison with prevalence recorded in the (independent) national administrative data base and the (independent) family survey data base. The two *independent* data sets are in close agreement. The council data show much higher levels of ASB and crime than the NE reports. While the NE data show ~10% of families as criminal-ASB the councils (allegedly) report ~49%. Remember on Wirral only 7 to 10% of individuals were involved in ASB at project entry. Somehow ASB has multiplied five fold along the data pipeline.

Let's look at the overall LA results. It is surely remarkable that the DCLG March 2015 outcome tables show that 132 of the 152 LAs in the TFP claim exactly 100% of families successfully 'turned around' with on average 10.1% gaining an adult in employment and 88.8% meeting the crime/ASB/education criterion. The lowest overall turn around rate was 97.8% in the south west region.

Many knowledgeable commentators pointed out that a 99% or indeed 100% success rate in a state social intervention policy was unprecedented *…and incredible.*

Jonathan Portes views, for example, are worth considering here for two reasons. Firstly he is a (recent) former head of the respected National Institute of Economic and Social Research and a former senior civil servant familiar with the mandarin approach to evidence analysis and presentation. Secondly he was called in 2015 to oversee the preparation of the final National Evaluation reports for the Troubled Families Programme phase 1. The NIESR was one of the ECORYS academic syndicate who carried out the 2016 National Evaluation for the government. We may consider him an expert witness who knows how and where the bodies are buried.

'The DCLG told Manchester it had 2385 troubled families. Amazingly Manchester found exactly that number. Ditto, Leeds, Liverpool and so on… I doubt the North Korean statistical office would have the cheek. *Frankly this whole episode is disgraceful… deliberately misleading the public is not public service.'*

We will hear from Portes and the NIESR again in discussing the Public Accounts Committee TFP Inquiry. But could it be that the 100% success claims merely reflect excellent work by the LAs? Let's look at the results claimed by some of the largest LAs as reported in the DCLG database 'TFP progress information and families turned around as at May 2015'

Local authority	family numbers	crime/ASB/ education	employment	total
Manchester	2385	95.3%	4.7%	100%
Liverpool	2105	92.87	7.13	100
Leeds	2190	86.48	13.52	100
Kent	2560	84.84	15.16	100
Sheffield	1680	96.02	3.99	100
Hampshire	1590	88.62	11.38	100

The employment success rate varies from 3.99% to 15.16%. We can assume these numbers are fairly accurate. Remarkably in these LAs (and 126 others) the crime/ASB/education success claim is *exactly sufficient* to to yield a 100% family 'turn around' outcome in each case.

This is a statistical miracle. Not only are exactly 100% of families turned around in 132 LAs …a phenomenal achievement by Dame Louise's team… but the laws of probability have been overturned!

Truly Dame Louise Casey is a chosen one! It finally becomes clear to mere mortals like the author why successive prime ministers, Blair, Brown and Cameron turned to her repeatedly for deliverance in tricky policy implementations. Or perhaps it was *not* a miracle. We noted earlier the inconsistencies in key numbers and the shifting quick sands of project success criteria. Could it be that many LAs, with a limited grasp of logic and statistics, started with the answer, 100%, and worked backwards to the *required* crime/ASB /education success rate? But would they have done this without tacit agreement from the DCLG? Even the PAC Inquiry members were suspicious (see also section 1.7).

Q67 : Meg Hillier (Chair)

'You had a nearly 100% success rate.'

Melanie Dawes (DCLG Permanent Secretary):

'In fact *we never said that.* LAs worked with more families than that…'

Melanie has forgotten the press releases and TFP outcome tables published on the DCLG website which show a 99% turn around rate and the formal HoC statement by her minister, Mr. (now Sir) Eric Pickles in March 2015, bragging of his TFP success.

We also note Q104 from a puzzled Mr. Chris Evans MP.

'I am looking at para. 1.21 which says "a total of 116,654 families eligible for the programme had met the criterion" of reducing crime…that seems a massive figure. You have helped 116,654 out of 117,910 families you identified [98.93%]. Where does that figure come from? To be honest if that is what you have turned around, *you should be running every single government department.'*

Note the rather dry final comment. The answer from Dame Louise Casey CB was :

'It was suggested in the financial framework that that local authorities reached more families, although we would not pay for them, in order both to reach that and as part of a system of change… our sense is that people did more in order to meet that…We need to be clear: we know that 116,654 families basically had their lives changed by the programme according to the payment by results system. That is a **99%** success rate.'

So Dame Louise is contradicting her then boss, Melanie Dawes, and still claiming a 99% turn around success rate based on the miraculous PbyR data. Casey presumably calculated that the PAC would not have the time or skills to take apart the PbyR data (given that they only received the 7 National Evaluation 2016 documents consisting of several hundred pages two days before the Inquiry). She was correct.

The author suggests again that at some point after the end of 2014 the word went out to that LAs that the rules for claiming crime/ASB/education 'turn around' could be greatly relaxed in the ways we have examined and that families turned around beyond the initially set LA phase 1 targets from the DCLG could also be counted, but not claimed for in terms of a bounty (outcome fee). The press had also claimed that LAs used 'data matching' for families on file, but not part of TFP processing, who had ceased offending or got into work, to claim additional 'turn rounds'(21). Whistleblowers confirmed this (22).

Nevertheless it was surely remarkably stupid of Casey and her team to believe that the 99% (or 100% in 132 LAs) turn around claim would go unchallenged by independent observers with a knowledge of government policy implementation and basic statistics. Such a level of arrogant hubris and incompetence in senior civil servants is astounding and troubling. One cannot expect much from the current generation of politicians and ministers but where was the fabled intelligence, wisdom and common sense of the Civil Service? Sadly gone, after years of battering by the likes of Tony Blair. We must also not forget that the extremely doubtful claims of success for state family intervention schemes have been going on for 18 years without successful challenge despite attempts to do so. The author regrets deeply that he was such a failed independent challenger over the last decade or so along with just a few outspoken academics such as Stephen Crossley. Given this history, the arrogance of many of our current politicians and their disdain for the intelligence of voters, perhaps Casey's hubris is understandable.

Perhaps finally, given the 2016 National Evaluation, the truth is out : on this performance the DCLG is dysfunctional, not fit for purpose, and needs a clear out intellectually and managerially.

As Ms Bridget Phillipson MP noted in the PAC Inquiry, Q109

'Doesn't making grandiose claims about the effectiveness of programmes undermine the whole concept of some of this work?...if ministers go out there claiming it saves £1.2 billion and clearly that cannot be evidenced, that undermines the whole basis of that social policy intervention.'

Ms Phillipson is absolutely correct. The permanent secretary replied

'I am confident that the department's report was as Joe [Tuke] described...Then there is *just the question of how those results are expressed*...and I think the caveats were there.'

Perhaps so, but there were **no** caveats in the DCLG press releases and executive summaries nor in the pompous HoC and media statements of minister Eric Pickles in 2015. At that point the draft National Evaluation was already pointing to the truth about the TFP.

Why weren't the damaging 'grandiose claims' about 100% success rates and vast fantasy sums saved not corrected by Dawes or Casey before release? Did they warn Pickles he was headed for disaster? Well Casey was *still* claiming a 99% 'turn around' at the PAC inquiry. Perhaps all this is because Dame Louise has an interesting attitude to objective evidence in social policy arenas. As she said in her infamous HO / ACPO after dinner speech in 2005

'Topic for tonight: Research : Help or Hindrance?...hindrance thanks very much...If No 10 says bloody evidence based policy to me one more time I'll deck them one...I say to ministers come into work pissed in the morning, you might cope better love.'

1.5 A Commentary on the 'National Evaluation of the First TFP' (DCLG, 17th October 16)

> '...our analysis found no impact on these outcomes attributable to the programme...There were no [significant] impacts identified for housing, employment and job-seeking, antisocial behaviour and crime, school behaviour and attendance, health, drug or alcohol abuse, family dynamics or wellbeing.'
>
> **Synthesis Report section 4.3.1**

1.5.1   Introduction: How the emperor lost his clothes

Since the first Dundee Family Intervention Project evaluation in 1999 several academic evaluation teams have been hired by successive governments. Some have gone along with their masters in an unfortunate way, failing to question ridiculous criteria of success or warn the public of false conclusions drawn. But most have honestly reported serious caveats about monitoring data quality and the objective limits to making claims for such interventions: but unfortunately only in the technical analyses reports and not in executive summaries or media releases. Data quality was often poor and samples ridiculously small. These issues are reviewed in detail in sections 2 and 4. Apart from data issues there were two other key problems:

1.   Claimed changes in the families re-programmed were not compared with changes (due to other causes) experienced by a matched control group of similar families not subject to intervention.

2.   Claimed changes in family behaviour were only observed for short post-intervention periods (in which close supervision had ended) but the families had multiple, *long standing* problems often health related.

   The various evaluators called for the use of control groups and longer term post project observation periods. We still only have short term observations for the TFP phase 1 evaluation but *for the first time* careful efforts were made to provide a control group for some large family samples. Ironically the short observation period has been grasped by the DCLG as a lifeline: if only we wait the families will suddenly change for the better...sometime down the road! We will demolish this nonsense by reference to the FIP history which shows family deterioration over time.

   The NE 2016 is by far the most comprehensive evaluation of intervention projects and deserves careful attention. Its conclusions are so clear that we will see every (feeble) effort was made by the DCLG to muddy the waters, deny conclusions, denigrate outspoken members of the evaluation team and delay publication...to the extent that the Parliamentary Public Accounts Committee TFP Inquiry *forced* publication only two days before the start of their inquiry.

This author is still mystified how the NE 2016 even came about given that it included a matched control group. It should have been obvious to senior civil servants with any knowledge of family intervention history that putting into place a powerful and respected evaluation team and a family control group was dangerous to their position. Perhaps there was a secret fifth columnist at large who persuaded the Pickles! If so tax payers should award him or her, a medal. It was certainly not the Casey whose negative views on 'research' are infamous. Somehow she took her eye off the ball and in January 2013 the ECORYS consortium was appointed by the DCLG to carry out the phase 1 evaluation. ECORYS included

Clarissa White Research (who in an earlier incarnation was involved in detailed FIP evaluations).

Bryson Purdon Social research.

The National Institute of Economic and Social Research (whose former director, Jonathan Portes was heavily involved in the later NE report stages and who blew the whistle on the DCLG).

Ipsos MORI.

Thomas Coram Research Unit, UCL Institute of Education.

That Casey was not central to the 'nemesis' appointment of ECORYS can be seen from her input to the earlier Parliamentary PAC TFP Inquiry under Margaret Hodge MP in 2014. As she said then

'We have let a huge, in my view, evaluation contract to a consortium called ICARUS [sic]…I can't remember who they are, but they are *terribly good* at their job. There are other people but we have got *the best…*'

She does not even recall their name correctly. In the second PAC Inquiry in October 2016 the 'best' according to Casey had suddenly become the 'organisation [that] had put through data that was flawed' and caused the reporting delay; the organisation who 'misrepresented their own results' and made false claims about what the DCLG 'cannot prove' and so on, as we will see later…. along with devastating replies from the 'accused', NIESR and Jonathan Portes.

1.5.2 National Evaluation Methodology and Reports

The methodology is summarised in the Synthesis Report and described in detail in several technical reports. The SR also describes the main outcomes in 'summated' form. The SR is

'based on triangulated evidence from across all strands of the evaluation informing the final report series, which include:

- quasi-experimental research using outcomes data from national administrative datasets, and a large-scale face-to-face survey of families, comparing families going through the programme with a matched comparison group.
- Qualitative case study research with a purposive sample of 20 local authorities conducted longitudinally, and
- Snapshot qualitative telephone interviews with a further 50 local authorities.

We will later hear that the SR took considerable negotiation to finalise between the ECORYS academics and the DCLG civil servants. The reader may decide like this author that the ponderous DCLG 'speak' is quite easy to spot in the mix. Look out for words like 'summated', 'triangulated', 'strands' and 'indicative'. Please do not be put off by the language of the SR. Once into the meat, the language is normal and the technical work good and clearly explained without pomposity or verbiage. We are also told that

'The report also draws selectively on monitoring data collected on a self-report basis from 143 LAs at three points in time during the evaluation, and a quantitative survey of LAs conducted during the early stages of the programme to map the broad characteristics of local TF programmes.'

The author has carefully checked the SR and the technical reports to check that the outcome results in particular are correctly reported: they are, with results tables carefully transferred from the technical reports. However added comments on the results in the SR (favourable to the TFP) could be easily attributed to a 'different hand' so to speak. Caveats are clear in the technical reports (although Casey denied this in the media and PAC) but some of these are grasped in the SR as loopholes to excuse TFP failure. These will be pointed out to the reader and deconstructed. The SR is clearly a 'committee' job with interjections from a 'nervous' client. Dr. Pangloss is alive and well and employed in Whitehall as we will see when discussing the Public Accounts Committee TFP Inquiry.

Given the above comments the interested reader is urged to at least scan the various technical reports which hide many gems of information and insights. They also, pre-empting published Casey false claims that results were distorted and caveats hidden, thoroughly discuss key issues like data limitations. Here are all the TFP 2016 national evaluation reports available on the DCLG website:

Final Synthesis Report : ISBN 978-4098-4912-4 PDF; 86 pages.

Process Evaluation Final Report : ISBN 978-1-4098- 4910-0 PDF; 98 pages.

Families' Experiences and Outcomes: ISBN 978-1-4098-4907-0 PDF; 68 pages

Family Survey Technical Report: ISBN 978-1-4098-4911-7 PDF; 76 pages

Annex to Family Survey Technical Report: ISBN 978-1-4098-4913-1 PDF; 83 pages

National Impact Study Report : ISBN 978-1-4098-4909-4 PDF; 273 pages

Final Report on the Family Monitoring Data: ISBN 978-1-4098-4098-7 PDF; 81 pages

These formed the *independent* basis of the evaluation. This is 689 pages of dense material given to the Public Accounts Committee TFP Inquiry only two days before it started. We will see that the PAC was not amused but, incredibly, went ahead with the inquiry anyway. The reader may well ask how the PAC could even flip through all this evidence, never mind subject it to careful analysis (It took the author, who is used to such analyses, several weeks to absorb). The tax payer may conclude that PAC inquiries are only intended to be *superficial and decorative* (see their tiny final report) but I could not possibly comment.

In addition the DCLG itself put out two other 'documents'

The First TFP 2012 / 2015: an overview.

TFP: local authority costs.

You may take it that these should be read with caution. The overview is about what one would expect from Dr Pangloss. We will dissect the LA cost report later. The most important report is the *national impact evaluation* based as it is on comparison of outcomes for the TFP families and a matched (non-processed) control group of families. The meticulous matching process and caveats are described in family monitoring data technical report. The equally important report is that on the *survey on family experiences and outcomes*. This is important because it *confirms the results* of the analyses in the impact evaluation based on the national administrative data. This latter report by the NIESR was vigorously attacked by Dame Louise Casey at the PAC Inquiry. Casey appeared to ignore the close agreement of the survey data and NIESR analysis on TFP impact…**essentially it was zero in both independent analysis cases.**

1.5.3   National Evaluation 2016 Impacts

A. Claimed Process Related 'Achievements'

The process evaluation final report looks in detail at how the TFP impacted on LA systems and practices. 'System transformation' was stressed in the SR to counter balance the zero family impacts conclusion. The fact that all this wonderful 'transformation' and money spending failed to actually transform the troubled families in any measurable way is not commented upon …for some reason.

The SR lists seven classes of systems change supposedly achieved:

Scaling up provision   Mainstreaming whole-family approaches

Driving innovation   Stimulating multiagency working

Improving the capacity to capture and measure outcomes

Enhancing family intervention practice

Improving the responsiveness of employability support

Section 5.1 of the NE synthesis reports positively on six classes of local authority self-reported achievements in the process transformation arena. In a *separate* later section it then discusses a long list of caveats which seem to largely disassemble the earlier positive claims: the 'committee' strikes again! Below I merge both sets of comments.

1. The TFP national policy 'spotlight' was said to have 'helped raise the

profile of family intervention'. This is certainly true *but* the TFP did not deliver any impacts on the troubled families. We can argue that this much spun programme has in reality brought large scale state social intervention into disrepute as suggested later by several Public Accounts Committee Inquiry members.

2. Local services and systems were allegedly 'transformed' because of the injection of TFP bounty payments at a time 'when budgets were undergoing retraction'. This is true at £3,200 to £4,000 per family processed but where is the value added? We read that 'the payment by results framework and targets were *contentious* in many areas and were thought to have resulted in *certain perverse incentives'*. Despite supposed 'system transformation' the evaluation also found *'wide variation in local practice'*.

3. The programme 'played a key role in boosting local capacity for family intervention and expanding the work force'. Money again. But we then read that *'it is questionable whether deep and sustained improvements were achieved in partnership working at local level'*. Strategic (political) agreements on multi-agency collaboration *'had not always translated into benefits at the local level'* **but** 'gripping the agencies', enabling or forcing multi-agency working was a key objective of the TFP.

4. The programme allegedly 'played a key role in raising the quality and capacity of local data management systems'. *But TFP data quality* was poor and *cover* was still patchy. We know because the PAC inquiry was told that they received the NE reports at the last minute, after a year's delay, amongst other things, because of *ongoing data problems*. Improving local IT systems is fine for the LAs but that was *not* the objective of the TFP investment and the IT improvements did *not* improve data collection and analysis.

5. The 'Development Agreement between DCLG and DWP had accelerated the employability dimensions of the programme …paving the way for better joint working with Jobcentre Plus at a local level'. Fine…*but* only 11% of families gained an adult with a job and that could not be attributed to the TFP. Worklessness was a major target of the TFP. With 57% of families receiving disability related benefits and 75% having a member with a 'limiting, long standing illness or disability' a 'Development Agreement' with the NHS might have been more productive (see below).

6. The evaluation found 'beacons of good practice' but *'wide variations in*

local practice' and 'a stark contrast in how local teams recruited and trained workers, set case load sizes, and exited their families'. This is interesting since the senior DCLG civil servants reassured the PAC Inquiry that *all* the LAs had been trained using the experiences and lessons from past family intervention projects back to the first, Dundee Family Project which started in the mid 1990s.

In considering 'processes' the evaluators also made particular note of the

'limited evidence for the efficacy of the interventions offered to families'

Surely this opinion is of central importance given that according to the DCLG

'99% of the families were turned around' and

'£1.2 billion per annum was saved'

In practice the 'therapeutic dimensions' of the programme (mental health, DA / DV and parenting) were 'not always clearly defined'. They add

'there appeared to be little progress in addressing the health issues for families'

Given the high levels of mental and physical illness and disability in adults and children this is alarming but not surprising. **The 2016 family survey technical report tells us that 75% of the TFs have at least one member with a serious long term illness or disability. 52% have one or more children with SEN statements or other special needs.**

This is a key issue which has been *loudly reported* in all previous family intervention scheme evaluations and ignored by successive governments over 18 years. **It is the key reason for the failure of these interventions.** Treating mental illness and learning disability in particular are expensive …but often effective. Mental health services have long been in decline in this country …why waste resources on 'families from hell'? It is superficially cheaper to talk of 'irresponsible life style choices' and 'shame and guilt' and 'bad parenting' and 'tough sanctions' …it is popular with a misinformed public: the modern equivalent of stoning to cast out devils. The reader may conclude with the author, reading this section, that the local authorities and civil servants have concentrated, largely ineffectively, on their 'processes' and 'system transformation' and lost sight of delivery and the core reasons for the families' troubles. So what was actually delivered?

98

B. TFP Family Impact Results.

The key statement of the synthesis report is on the front page of this commentary.

There were no impacts attributable to the TFP in any of the key target areas or the secondary areas of the programme.

At this point we could simply stop the analysis. This author's strong suspicions about zero delivery over 18 years of intervention projects are completely vindicated. In fact even this old cynic is stunned by the *total lack of impact* on such a wide range of outcome measures for the families. This is a sad and discouraging result and a tragedy for our vulnerable families…and for the tax payer during a period of overstretched public services. However looking further at the non-impact results is informative: that is the *small, non-statistically significant differences between TFP families and the control group families* teach us important lessons.

It was interesting that senior civil servants at the PAC inquiry attempted to maintain that the inability to 'attribute' the 'monumental' changes in the families was some obscure, unimportant technical point. This displays an arrogant and alarming lack of understanding of the importance of evidence in assessing state policy effectiveness…or something worse.

Let's consider a more familiar example. To test the efficacy of a new, expensive cancer drug the originators would be required by the state to carry out an extensive clinical trial. We give the drug to say a thousand cancer patients. We select a matched group of patients of the same size and monitor them, but do not give them the new drug. After some agreed time we check the survival rates of both groups. The result is conclusive: the survival rates are almost the same and the difference is *small and not statistically significant.* The expensive new drug has had no objective impact and will not be approved by NICE for general use in the NHS.

Why should a costly state family 'intervention' treatment, aimed now at a further 400,000 vulnerable families, be assessed in some other, non-objective and indeed non-rational way?

Listen to Dame Louise Casey in her PAC Inquiry interrogation

'Lots of comments made by those closely involved in the evaluation have been unedifying…*the impact on these families was monumental.*

99

…what the research says we can't prove is that we can attribute them to the TFP…we haven't had the chance to set the record straight.'

On the other hand we have the very direct view of the expert Casey criticised, Jonathan Portes, head of the respected NIESR team and co-author of the impact studies widely quoted in the official, government, NE synthesis report (23).

'[the TFP] was a perfect case study of how the manipulation and misrepresentation of statistics by politicians and civil servants −from the Prime Minister downwards- led directly to bad policy and, frankly, to the wasting of hundreds of millions of pounds of tax payers' money.'

So who is correct Casey or Portes? Let us call Casey's bluff and look more closely at the impact data…'to set the record straight'. I have high lighted the following important statement to aid politician readers with poor eyesight and short attention spans so they do not miss it again:

The key point is: we will see that **the differences in outcomes** between the TFP families and the control group families, **relate to only very small percentages of families,** *even if* **we were to accept the differences as statistically significant** *and* **attributable to the TFP.**

Casey's PAC and media objection is crude, diversionary bluster and shows no respect for the PAC, parliament or the educated public. This is disgraceful behaviour from a senior civil servant. *Unless that is, she really cannot understand what the data is saying.* In which case she is not fit to advise ministers on important policy matters. The same comments apply to her civil service and nominal political masters. But we know Casey has little respect for them. As she said in her famous HO – ACPO after dinner speech

'The first time I met a minister it was like something from Acorn Antiques …I say to ministers, come into work pissed, you might cope better love…'

She also said in a widely reported interview in 2006

'If it is the Home Office I say 'enforcement', if it is the Dept. of Health I say 'support', and to the DCLG I say 'empowering' …you have to play this game across Whitehall.'

And what do you say Louise, as an unelected civil servant, if it is our elected parliament's Public Accounts Committee? We will look at the disturbing answer in section 1.7.

The bounty money paid to the Local Authorities depended on producing measurable changes in employment, crime & ASB and school absence and exclusion rates so we will begin our look at the synthesis report in these areas. Then we will look at health, housing, wellbeing and at the changes in family benefit claiming which should equate to the £1.2 billion cost savings claimed by Eric Pickles and the DCLG. **It does not**.

Employment and Jobseeking Impacts

The evaluation used the administrative database to identify adult employment rates 18 months after programme entry.

	TFP families	Control group families	TFP impact%
% employed	40.7	43.6	-2.9
Weeks in Employment	26.3	27.8	-1.5

Base 11,807 adults.

The differences are not statistically significant but notice that they are also small... just a few %. This is typical of the impact results. We see no 'monumental' changes here. If we take Casey's view that any changes *must* be real and *attributable* to the TFP we note that the control group has *better employment statistics* than the reprogrammed TFP families. So TFP participation *reduces* employment outcomes. It would follow that employment benefits for the TFP families would have increased! The evaluation also looked at employment expectations and intentions.

	TFP families%	Control group families %	TFP impact%
Respondent expects themselves or partners to be working in the next year	59	61	-2
Partner in work or Job-seeking	87	88	-1

These differences are not statistically significant and are very small in addition.

But if, like Casey, we took them seriously, we would conclude that the TFP families had *lower expectations* than the control group on future employment intentions.

Crime and ASB Impacts

Reduction of these behaviours is a key government TFP objective and 'high' levels of criminality have been used to sell the TFP to a trusting and gullible public. Often data in this arena has been poor and deliberately misrepresented. We showed in section 1.2 that ASB and crime was absent from the vast majority of families. In the author's area (Wirral) 93.5% of adults and 89.6% of children had no reports of ASB at project entry. Nationally 84% of TFP minors had not 'offended'. The new NE report has finally clarified the position on more serious issues using the Police National Computer offending database. The evaluators found no statistically significant impact on crime outcomes. The detailed data was again informative.

Adults	TFP families	Control group families	TFP impact %
% with an offence resulting in a caution or conviction	8.7	7.8	+1.0
% with an offence resulting in a custodial sentence	1.7	1.5	+0.2

Note that the frequency of adult crime is low. The frequency of families with an adult with a custodial sentence is very low at ~1.6% for both of these groups selected for TFP 'reprogramming', we were told, because of high levels of criminality. These groups bear no resemblance to David Cameron's 'criminal' families from hell. We have a scandalous and damaging misrepresentation of the families here. The differences between the TFP families and the control group families are small at <1% and not significant. But if we accept Casey's view that TFP impacts are real we would conclude that TFP participation *increased* offending by 1.0 x 100 / 7.8 = 12.8% and custodial sentences by 0.2 x 100 / 1.5 = 13.3% relative to the control group! We would conclude that the TFP promotes adult offending. What about the children?

Children	TFP families	Control group families	TFP impact %
% with an offence resulting in a caution or conviction	5.8	5.7	+0.1
% with an offence resulting in a custodial or community sentence	3.4	2.6	+0.8

The frequency of offending in children is low in both groups selected for TFP intervention. We see no juvenile crime wave here. The differences are not significant and are again small. Taking the Casey 'impacts are real' position we would conclude that the TFP *'caused'* a 31% increase in custodial sentences relative to the control group! Now that is what I call an 'impact'.

Using cross checked survey data the evaluators also looked at lower level ASB issues over a previous 3 month period using ASB actions and at police contact.

	TFP families	Control group	TFP Impact%
No ASB actions against family members.	84 (16)	86 (14)	-2
No family problem contact with police	78 (22)	82 (18)	-4
No police actions against a young person	77 (23)	80 (20)	-3
Young person not in trouble with police	85	85	0

These differences are not statistically significant and are small. In both groups 85% of youngsters are not in trouble with the police. Note that, in both groups, police contact and ASB actions (numbers in brackets) occur at only low frequency in the families. If we take the differences as real we would conclude that TFP participation *increases* police contact and ASB frequency.

We are often told that police contact is high and expensive in the TFP families. But here we see that family contact *increases* by 4 x 100 / 18 = 22.2% and ASB actions by 14.3% in TFP reprogrammed families in comparison with the control group…if the effects are real. On the Casey position we must conclude that the TFP *increases ASB and costly police actions*.

The technical family survey report also looks at the impacts for the group which received high intensity intervention. We know that 22% of the families had contact with their key worker 'once a day or more' or 'several times a week'. Across all categories of impact examined the evaluators found no significant differences in outcomes for the intensive group compared with the whole cohort. However, remarkably, there are significant differences in the crime area.

	TFP group	matched control Group	difference	P-value
No ASB actions used against family	76%	86%	-10	0.01
No trouble with police by family members	73%	83%	-10	0.046

The differences here are highly statistically significant. Taking them at face value they tell us for the intensive intervention families, TFP reprogramming **increases** the prevalence of ASB and police trouble by 71.4% and 58.8% respectively, relative to the general control group families. Now that is an impact! However the survey report 'interpretation' section suggests that perhaps the intensive intervention group was more involved in ASB and so on at project entry and therefore it is a harder nut to crack.

This is surprising because Table 3.8 of the report presents **all** those characteristics in which the intensive treatment group is *statistically significantly different* from the low intensity treatment TFP group. Note that ASB and police contact measures do not appear: there is no significant difference between high and low intensity treatment families here. The significant results are worth considering briefly:

Characteristic	Problem incidence in High Intensity Intervention Families	Prevalence relative to Low Intensity Intervention Families

104

Three or more children	15%	2.14 X
Ex-partner with a Criminal record	15	2.14 X
Oldest child 15/16	49	1.48 X
Adult domestic abuse	43	1.43 X
At least one child with SEN statement	57	1.24 X
Family member with long standing illness or disability	78	1.1 X

This table exposes the thinking behind selecting families for high intensity intervention. Large families and *previous* association with a criminal partner are strong selectors even though the frequency of these 'problems' is low. Having a 15 / 16 year old (who must be trouble re. riots, truancy and so on !) and adult domestic abuse are also strongly targeted. There is weaker selection for SEN children / chronic illness / disability since a very high proportion of *all* the families have these problems. Clearly the focus of intensive intervention is not therapeutic but based on (supposedly) modifying bad behaviour…and support costs.

Please note that 'ASB actions' and 'trouble with the police' measures *do not* appear in the table. On these measures at least, the intensive treatment families were no different from the rest of the TFP families at entry. Recall that ASB and police contact also *increased* for the total TFP family cohort although the increases were not significant and smaller. **Overall it is legitimate to conclude that the intervention received by the high intensity treatment families resulted in a higher proportion of families getting into (low level) trouble with the law.** Perhaps such mentally impaired families respond badly to intensive bullying. Threats and sanctions are not part of any mental health or disability therapeutic treatments familiar to the author.

School Attendance and Welfare Impacts

Attendance was assessed using both administrative and family survey data. Both data sets showed no statistical differences between TFP families and the control group families.

Attendance	TFP families	Control group families	TFP impact
% of time absent from school after 3 terms in project	9.6	9.9	-0.3
% of children absent from school for 15% or more of the time	20.3	21.2	-0.9

Notice that only a small % of families selected for the TFP (in both groups) have children with unacceptable unauthorised attendance levels. If we treated the differences as real in this case we would claim a small impact in favour of the TFP group but across the TFP families it would amount to just 3% with absence reduction relative to the control group. It is difficult to imagine that this materially reduces the 'misery' these children are said to cause in their communities. We noted earlier that unauthorised absence in all these families may reflect the high levels of child and adult chronic illness and disability. Recall that 45% of families have adults with mental illness; 39% of the families have children with special educational needs statements and 28% have children in special schools.

The evaluators did not look at fixed term (temporary) exclusions from school, the other component in the PbyR educational bounty criterion. We noted from earlier data that 87% of TFP children at entry had *not* been excluded from school. Also DFE statistics showed an average a 1.4% national exclusion rate in 2011/12 whereas 8.2% of SEN children had been excluded along with 9.5% with School Action Plus status and 4.6% with School Action status …in total 22.3% or 16 X the national average exclusion rate. This may help explain the 13% of TFP children with 3 or more exclusions (see also 16).

Child 'welfare' was assessed using the National Pupil database and applied two measures: the proportion of children classed as in need, CIN, or in care 12 months after programme entry. Reduction in CIN status or children in care would allegedly lead to reductions in the cost of the families to the state. The evaluators in discussing child welfare considered 'ambiguity' and whether reducing children taken into care or with CIN status was *'incontrovertibly beneficial to the child'*. I leave that to the experts to debate. I will only say that the record of the state in looking after children in care is abysmal considering the outcomes for the children as young adults and beyond. 'Handle With Care'(24) paints a dreadful picture of care leavers fate : 50% unemployment; 20% homeless; 35% pregnant or unmarried mothers; 25 X normal rate of going to prison. These figures reflect the mental impairment and inadequacy of the children : just like our TFP children. The NE team's 'ambiguity' is understandable.

Welfare	TFP families	Control group families	TFP impact
% of children with CIN status	40.1	36.7	+3.3
% of children In care	3.1	4.8	-1.7

These are some of the few impact measures where the differences are statistically significant. However note again that they are small. The % of CIN children is higher but the % of children in care is lower for the TFP families in comparison with the control group. If we accept the fall for 'in care' numbers it affects just 1.7% of children in the ~120,000 TFP families cohort. On the other hand the proportion of children with CIN status is 3.3% higher in the TFP families group. The evaluators try to explain this result by suggesting poor matching of the groups in this case. Some 'matching methods' gave non-significant differences. In terms of cost saving implications the impacts are in opposite directions. What is the net cost effect? We do not know.

Other Impacts

Now we turn to the family characteristics not part of the 'payment by results framework' but which certainly influenced the selection of TFP families: housing status, health and wellbeing, financial status and subjective family attitudes and outlooks.

Housing Impacts

The evaluation survey used a standard template to enquire after housing issues and stability over a three month test period. None of the differences between TFP families and the control group were statistically significant and the differences are tiny.

	TFP families	Control group families	TFP impact
Families with no housing issues	75	73	+2

No rent arrears	71	71	-1
No notices served to leave property	99	99	0
No evictions	98	97	+1
No possession orders	96	95	+1
NO ASB Complaints	94	93	+1
No bailiff warrant issued	95	97	-2
No warning letter issued	90	89	+1

The TFP reprogrammed families and the new entry control group are statistically identical. There is no TFP impact on housing issues. However all these families are described by politicians as bringing 'misery to their communities'. Yet the proportion of families receiving serious housing interventions is on average ~4% and only 6-7% have generated complaints of ASB. Some 9-10% have received warning letters but 29% of the families are in rent arrears. No doubt the warnings mainly relate to this for the 25% having housing issues. The housing data confirms what we learned from the crime and ASB data : such issues affect only a small proportion of TFP selected families, the biggest issue is debt, and the TFP reprogramming did nothing to change the situation.

Family Health & Wellbeing Impacts

The evaluation surveyed a wide range of 'secondary outcome measures' related to health and NHS support including :

1. Alcohol use in the previous 3 months by the respondent and young person interviewed and reports on partners.

2. Use of non-prescription drugs by respondent and young person interviewed.

3. Wellbeing (Short Warwick – Edinburgh mental wellbeing scale) and depression (Malaise scale) of the main carer responding.

4. 'Life satisfaction' of the respondent and young person interviewed.

5. GP and A&E visits in the previous 3 months.

6. Self reported general health of respondent, young person and partner.

The evaluators also looked at 'how well the parents got on in the family' and reports of 'physical, verbal, emotional and sexual domestic violence.' **The analysis found no statistically significant differences between TFP families and the control group on all these measures.** Life satisfaction was not impacted which is hardly surprising given the problems the families face.

Given the high levels of mental and physical illnesses and disabilities in the targeted families the negative results are disappointing but not surprising. It matches the pattern of 18 years of previous intervention schemes. Recall that 57% of TFP households were in receipt of 'disability related benefits' a year before the survey; 39% of the families had at least one child with a statement of Special Educational Needs; 45% of adults had mental health issues and 33% had long standing illness or disabilities; 48% were on JSA. We noted above that few had received 'therapeutic' help for health conditions from NHS services. The TFP did not successfully 'engage' those services. **Without tackling long term, underlying health and wellbeing problems in these families, long term costs to the state will not be reduced.** Recall that for the 120,000 families £2 billion per annum is related to health / poverty costs versus £0.54 billion nominally linked to 'bad behaviour' and 'lifestyle choices'. But on the latter sum remember that such 'behaviour' is often a function of untreated mental health and disability issues.

Financial Management Impacts

'[Locally] some scallywags were choosing not the feed their children…'

Frank Field MP, TFP debate, HoC.
10th March 2015

The TFP families have been repeatedly criticised by politicians for mismanaging their finances to the point where their children go hungry while they waste money 'irresponsibly' and indulge in alcohol and drugs....a cause for 'guilt' and 'shame'. This alleged situation has been promoted as a justification for reducing state benefits which they will 'only waste' and for redefining relative poverty to downplay low income as a cause of poverty. The TFP was part of a *wider* political strategy to attack benefits. Iain Duncan Smith was a prominent leader in this movement. In a widely reported speech on why higher benefits won't stop child poverty (30.01.2013) he claimed that parents wasting benefits on alcohol and drug addiction was the problem.

'Parental addiction not income is the reason for child poverty…even an extra pound could push families further into difficulties…If it does little more than feed the parent's addiction it may leave the family more dependent, not less, resulting in poor social outcomes and still deeper entrenchment.'

IDS

Recall that only ~3% of our TFP families had received medical treatment for addictions. Besides, IDS also claimed income based poverty measures are intrinsically wrong.

'The current child poverty measure – defined as 60% of median income – is considered to be deeply flawed and a poor test of whether children's lives are genuinely improving.'

DWP site, Poverty and Social Justice section, 1st July 2015

Redirecting state benefit funding to re-programme families via schemes like the TFP was supposed to deal with multi-generational family 'irresponsibility', the 'real' cause of poverty. Apparently the welfare state

'encourages individuals, not unreasonably, to try to ensure they qualify under this guise. It therefore pays to lie about one's earnings, to cheat or to be inactive. The worst side of human nature is encouraged…Benefits rot the soul.'

Frank Field MP, Cameron Poverty Tsar

'We recommend that schools should …refer such chaotic families to their local Troubled Families project whose success can be measured in the number of families they have 'turned around' to be functioning in a normal way.'

Frank Field MP, 'Feeding Britain' APPG, Dec. 2014

110

It is interesting in this light that the national evaluation team surveyed the views of the families themselves on financial issues (and below, on wider competence and confidence issues) to see if any positive TFP impacts had emerged.

	TFP families	Control group Families	TFP impact
Kept up with bills in the last 3 months	79	79	0
Managing finances Well	69	59	+10
Managing better than a year ago	26	19	+7

The difference on debt is zero. Both groups report exactly the same high proportion keeping up with bills. Sadly 21% of both groups are not. TFP participation has had no concrete impact here. However there is a statistically significant increase in the proportion of families who **feel** they are managing well financially. 10% more families **feel** they are managing well than in the control group. The reasons for this are not explored. Note that the difference between keeping up with bills and managing well is 79 – 69 = 10% for the TFP families and for the control group, 20%. What is influencing TFP families? 26% of the TFP families **feel** they are managing better than a year ago compared with 19% in the control group. Why? The TFP families were helped with debt, benefit and finance issues in the programme. This training appears to have increased family *declared* confidence. However it has *not* had a concrete impact on 'keeping up with bills'. We also saw that 29% of both groups (from the survey data) were in rent arrears and that the proportion out of work was 45.3% in both groups. The income and debt data show no sign of objective reasons for the declared improved confidence of the TFP families. However we must recall that families were targeted for financial and social 'irresponsibility'. After the 'assertive' reprogramming it might be wise for them to say, when asked, 'yes we are managing better now financially' in order to escape more 'non-negotiable' intervention and 'tough sanctions'. The issue of opinions given under 'duress' has been noted in all previous family intervention schemes. This brings us to the wider family survey results on declared attitudes on coping and confidence.

Family Perceptions on Competence Impacts

The synthesis report tells us that the TFP families reported statistically significant better perceptions about 'how they were doing' than the matched control group which could legitimately be attributed to the TFP in : keeping family on track; feeling in control; feeling positive about the future; belief that their worst problems were behind them. It is this material which encourages the TFP civil servants to claim that the families 'liked' the programme and found it useful. An increase in confidence must surely be welcomed. **However such a subjective perception is only of real significance if it leads to better family outcomes in reality and over the longer term.** This is worth exploring in more detail.

Carer agrees that they	TFP families	Control group	TFP impact
know how to keep my family on the right track	96	91	+5
feel in control	69	60	+9
feel positive about the future	69	61	+8
are confident that the worst problems are behind them	68	52	+17

This data is very enlightening. 91% of the control group families felt that they knew how to keep their families on the right track *despite being selected for the TFP because they could not, according to the state, having multiple serious problems.* An additional 5%, or 96% in total, of TFP reprogrammed families also felt able to keep on track. Has another 5% of the families been given *false confidence* by the TFP training? Most families still have multiple problems, most seriously in health and wellbeing. Their health problems have not changed in drugs, alcohol, life satisfaction, family relationships, GP and A&E attendance and domestic violence. Employment 18 months after project start up was actually lower at 40.7% for the TFP families than in the control group at 43.6%, as was number of weeks employed. Are the TFP families now in control as 69% **feel**? 60% of the matched control group **felt** in control before TFP entry but the state disagreed. 68 – 69% of the retrained TFP families felt positive and that their worst problems lay behind them. This compares with 52- 61% of the control families.

There is a 17% increase in TFP families **feeling** that their worst problems are behind them compared with the controls *despite no material changes* across a whole range of problems, most notably in health, wellbeing and family relationships. Did most families decide it would be wisest to tell the TFP monitors that everything was rosy in order to avoid further 'assertive, non-negotiable interventions'?

Two, what we might call instrumental, measures related to family competence were also assessed but showed no statistically significant impacts. They are, though, also interesting.

Families agreed that they	TFP families	Control group	TFP impact%
know where to seek outside help	80	76	+4
can count on family support	73	72	0

The programme has (perhaps) slightly increased the proportion of families who know where to look for outside help but it is interesting that 76-80% of both groups of families *know where* to seek help. Of course from the zero TFP impacts in many areas like health and wellbeing, knowing *where* to physically go for help is not the same as receiving help. It is notable that of those who know where to seek help (76-80%), a very large proportion, 72-73% can 'count on' extended family support. We might conclude that the family is *where* they go. It would have been most valuable to have asked the families whether they could similarly 'count on state support' before and after the programme.

Overall the national evaluation synthesis report has been generous in *avoiding* a forensic analysis of the results here and in describing the TFP impact on family confidence and competence as a success. A less generous interpretation looking within and across group data is that 'reprogramming' had a modest effect on confidence and outlook in a *small proportion* of families but that this was not reflected in delivered family changes. It can also be reasonably argued, and some observers have, that family opinions in such surveys were also effectively *given under duress*. Remember, as Casey told the press repeatedly

'We are not running some cuddly social workers programme.'

And as Eric Pickles said, defending a tougher, less understanding, approach

'We have sometimes run away from categorising, stigmatising, laying blame.'

This might be considered by some merely as empty, populist rhetoric. However the DCLG technical report on 'impact evaluation using survey data' actually documents *enforcement actions* taken against the families *during* the TFP itself. We learn that 40% of families had been sanctioned including 13% of families evicted or formally threatened with eviction, 12% with benefit cuts or threats, 5% with injunctions or ASBOs and 15% with child care orders. Such a programme ideological ethos plus the threat and delivery of 'sanctions' and further 'assertive' interventions hardly constitutes a neutral platform for eliciting family views critical of the TFP. **Surely we cannot safely take the family declared attitudes to the TFP intervention at face value.**

Family Benefit Claiming

We showed in section 1.3 that the £21K per annum average cost of a troubled family could be largely explained in terms of legitimate claims related to health, family demographics (large families) , out of work and incapacity benefits, housing and disabled child support. A key aim of the TFP was to reduce the 'high cost' to the state in supporting these families. This is the bottom line. The NE synthesis report looks in detail at work related benefits based on the DWP Longitudinal Study tracking families at 18 months after project entry. They looked at both the fraction of families claiming out of work benefits and at duration of benefit claims for both the TFP families and the control group families.

	TFP families	Control group	TFP Impact %
% claiming OOW benefits	45.3	45.3	0
Number of weeks on OOW benefits	33.8	34.6	-0.8
% on incapacity benefits	18.6	19.3	-0.7

114

Number of weeks on incap. Benefits	12.8	13.8	-1.1
% claiming JSA	10.9	11.6	-0.6
Number of weeks claiming JSA	8.6	9.0	-0.5

All these TFP impact differences are statistically insignificant and note that *the differences are very small.* The difference in families claiming OOW benefits is zero. The differences in numbers of weeks on OOW, % on incapacity benefits and number of weeks on incapacity benefits are at least in the right direction …but sadly insignificant. Recall that according to the National Evaluation 2016, 75% of families have one or more members with a long standing illness or disability. The (statistically insignificant) fall in families on incapacity benefits relative to the control group was 0.7%. *TFP assertive threats of sanctions do not appear to cure chronic mental and physical illnesses nor disabilities.* This is a simple and obvious lesson which one would hope, after 18 years, could be understood by moralising politicians who keep telling us these families will be healthier if they only 'gerra job'. Iain Duncan Smith et al, please note. Nor does the TFP approach build 'moral fibre' and 'save the souls' of vulnerable families. Frank Field et al, take note.

Earlier we looked at % in employment and also noted no significant difference between the TFP and control group families. Overall we must conclude that there is no evidence in support of any impact of the TFP on employment and incapacity associated benefit claims among programme adults. The latter point is consistent with the finding of no TFP impact on the health and wellbeing of the families, adults or children. Nor is any evidence presented for changes in social care support costs and we saw earlier that there were only small, contrary TFP impacts on child welfare issues. The evaluation reports that 57% of families were receiving disability related benefits at entry. No impacts recorded in these areas tells us that there can have been no reduction in the high costs related to these typically large, unemployed families with disabled children.

We saw that there were no differences in the 97% of families living in social housing and that 29% were in rent arrears in TFP and control groups. 75% reported no other housing problems in both groups. There is nothing to suggest that housing related benefit claiming changed.

We noted that only a small minority of TFP families were involved in ASB and crime at project entry (78% of families had no police problem contact in the 3 month survey period; 85% of children had no police contact; only 7.1% of adults had a conviction; only 0.9% of adults had an ASBO or similar order). The evaluation found no significant difference between TFP and control families. ASB and crime levels were small anyway and there is no evidence of any significant changes that might have reduced the supposedly high police and criminal justice costs attributable to the families.

Considering all this evidence and the payment by results data we explored earlier, the only 'clear' change in benefit and support costs is the PbyR system claim that ~11% of families gained an adult in employment. This, if correct, must have led to a small change in the total support cost of the ~120,000 families in phase 1. **But that small cost saving cannot be attributed to the TFP.** It is therefore still unclear how the official, highly publicised, £1.2 billion per annum saving estimate was derived from the 7 LAs used as an 'exemplar' sample....just 4.6% of the LAs involved in the TFP. We have no information on how the DCLG checked that their small sample was representative of all the 152 LAs in the TFP (see section 1.6 for an attempt to fathom what went on). Clearly some doubtful assumptions must have been made in deriving the £1.2 billion delivered savings claim repeatedly made by Eric Pickles, DCLG minister.

In the HoC PAC inquiry on the TFP held on the 19th of October 2016 (just 2 days after the NE reports became available to the PAC and public) Melanie Dawes, the senior civil servant at the DCLG, when pressed, told the committee that the TFP had achieved

'some really good results'

Adding, far too late

'...but we don't want to over claim it...*We are certainly not claiming any definitive cost savings from the programme.*'

Er? Where is the £9 billion potential savings used by Eric Pickles and PM Cameron (along with an end to rioting, gangs and British moral decay) to justify the TFP phase 1 in 2012? Where is the £1.2 billion delivered 'savings' reported by Pickles to the HoC on 10th March 2015? How can we account for Louise Casey's remarkable claim at the PAC inquiry that

'[The TFP is] value for money writ large...'

In reality several hundreds of millions of pounds have been spent on a purely politically motivated project, sold on the basis of a gross misrepresentation of the target families while ignoring the several, accumulated official evaluations on such failed intervention schemes, followed by denial of definitive, objective evaluation evidence and a delaying, rear guard action during which a further £900 million plus has been committed to yet another TFP phase which demonstrably cannot deliver.

The author spent several decades leading a mathematical and statistical development and analysis team, helping to optimise business policies up to the strategic level in a major multinational company.

If a 'TFP like' fiasco happened in such a major private sector project, senior heads would roll and the fraud squad would be called in to protect the reputation of the business and restore the confidence of the shareholders. It should be no different in the public sector.

The NE Synthesis Report 'Concluding Thoughts and Lessons'

We have seen herein a bleak litany of zero, statistically non-significant, family impacts attributable to the TFP. Equally important, where *any* differences occurred between the TFP family group and the matched control group they were typically small, *affecting only a small percentage of families.* Government and DCLG TFP apologists are still claiming that the evaluation team was merely unable to formally 'attribute' the 'monumental' family changes achieved, to the TFP. One assumes these 'monumental' changes also refer to the 'claims' made under the PbyR scheme but the official synthesis report itself says

'However the evaluation sounds *a cautionary note for relying on PbyR data to inform assessments about the added value of policy intervention* and highlights the importance of applying a suitable counterfactual.'

Casey et al tried to give the impression to the media (and the PAC) that this 'attribution' business was merely some nit picking, academic point to be dismissed. This ignores the *small differences* in the proportions of TFP families compared to control families who experienced *any* changes. If we took those small numbers of families seriously, often the *direction of change* was **not** in favour of the TFP's supposed reprogramming effects. The TFP often made things worse. In the intensive intervention group the TFP statistically significantly increased family police contact and ASB compared with the control group.

We also showed earlier in detailed analysis of the payment by results data (up to mid 2015) that the claimed changes were reported in a way that greatly exaggerated the impact of the programme. The 'claimed' changes in employment and other targets could also not be attributed to the TFP. The ongoing denial by some senior civil servants in the face of such clear evidence is astonishing and must be challenged and openly condemned.

The synthesis report attempts to soften the blow of the zero delivered impact results by reporting 'process' achievements claimed by the local authorities. These boil down to: the TFP bounty money came in useful at a time of budget cuts; we got to improve our IT systems (money again); we got a lot of good publicity for family intervention; we had top level inter-agency meetings and wrote strategic agreement papers; we all felt better.

The synthesis report describes these claims with a straight face. It then later presents a *separate* section analysing very serious ongoing 'process' problems at the coal face. In this commentary we merged both sections. The author contends that the key TFP strategic aim of 'gripping the agencies' and enabling 'system transformation' in local authority family intervention was clearly not achieved. It is clear that all the lessons and experiences from the previous stages of family intervention schemes back to ~1999, were not successfully transmitted via staff training, nor acted upon, despite ongoing senior DCLG civil servant claims to the contrary, as in the PAC inquiry meeting.

The synthesis report provides a second line of defence in support of the TFP. Various excuses for the lack of 'impact' are rehearsed. Data quality issues have always been a problem in such intervention schemes but this has never stopped politicians from successive governments claiming outrageous levels of success. However if 'data' is such an issue this also means that claims such as '99% of families are turned around' are also invalid. A third line of defence is the several aspects of variability within the programme: variation in how the families were selected; variations in the severity of family problems; local variations in the approach taken to 're-programming' the families; variations in detailed intervention practice; the disjunction between the wider family problems experienced and the narrow focus of the PbyR framework which only looked at ASB, minor offending and school attendance.

This author can only see these excuses for lack of impact as a confirmation that the TFP implementation was chaotic: the local agencies were not 'gripped'. A key strategic TFP aim was not met despite the repeated spin.

The evaluators also highlight the issues of TFP scale up and speed of implementation of the programme in causing problems. Of course the TFP apologists might claim that their brilliant social engineering vision was spoiled by local incompetence: that if properly implemented, next time around, all would be well. This has been the argument since ~1999. However the evaluators make comments which suggest that, local variability or no, the basic assertive, intensive, non-negotiable, sanctions based, ignore the deep causes, intervention model is flawed. Critically, they found **no** *relationship between the intensity of intervention and family outcomes.* As they say

'It would seem surprising that *no direct correlation* was found between service intensity and impacts given that the 'high intensity' variants of family intervention were often more strongly associated with FIP provision (and might therefore offer a good proxy for a strong and well developed model of family intervention).'

Remember that the FIP model has been in use since the first Dundee project began in 1995 and then in about sixty formal projects around Britain before the TFP. The formal FIP is supposed to be the gold standard. We saw in police contact / ASB the TFP actually (statistically significantly) *increased* problems in the high intensity group and (directionally in the) low intensity group. The TFP evaluators (or somebody else) fall back again on issues of variability to explain this lack of correlation. They also say

'But other possible explanations include this group of families simply having more entrenched problems and hence it being harder to change outcomes within the evaluation time scale.'

For ASB we saw this excuse did not hold. In the previous FIP schemes this excuse was also used to 'explain' the lack of impact on the families. But under the 'family characteristics' report section the evaluators tell us in **bold** type that

'The Family Monitoring Database shows that the typical family composition of the Troubled Families group was ...similar to those supported by previous family intervention programmes.'

The author from many years of study of these programmes can confirm this in terms of poverty, unemployment, ill-health and disability as well as family size.

So let us now look at the question of the length of observation of the TFP families also used to excuse lack of impact. Clutching at straws the evaluators (or somebody else) comment

'The evaluation does not rule out the possibility that impacts from the phase one programme *may* occur further downstream......it was possible that the observation was too soon to provide firm conclusions.'

Is there any evidence for this? And why is it assumed *a priori* that any emerging impacts would be *positive* ones, once intensive project supervision and support is removed? The evaluators tell us that the slightly increased 'levels of confidence and optimism' amongst TFP families in comparison with the control group

'imply that changes in outcomes may be occurring in these families'

It shows no such thing. Recall that 91% of control (untreated) families felt they already 'know how to keep my family on the right track' despite being selected for the TFP *precisely because they did not know*. 96% of the post treatment families also felt they knew how to keep on track, an increase of 5% of families. If this translated miraculously into real impacts 'downstream', as claimed, it would affect only a very small proportion of families anyway. We noted that objectively the condition of the families in key areas like poverty, debt, family health and wellbeing had *not* changed despite apparent small increases in confidence. We also noted that it was in the interest of the families to 'agree strongly or tend to agree' that TFP participation had improved their competence and outlook. Anything said by the families could be claimed to be made under duress. The evaluators (or somebody else) are clutching at very weak straws here.

Fortunately if we turn to the sixty pre-TFP intervention projects there is direct evidence on 'downstream', late developing impacts. The author deconstructed the report 'Longer Term Outcomes for Families who had worked with Intensive Family Support Projects', DCLG, 2008. Let us consider ASB since this is still a key target for the TFP. The families were assessed fourteen months after project exit. The tracking sample data suggests that 31.5% of families had greatly reduced levels of ASB (relative to entry). However at project *exit* it had been claimed that 85% of families had ceased or greatly reduced their ASB. In a year or so the tracking data tells us that behaviour had decayed in 53.5% of families. If decay continued all families would be offending in another year. This result is hardly surprising since 'intensive' supervision and support had largely ceased at project exit. Other impact measures such as housing status also exhibit decay.

By last interview we also learn that 36% of families had suffered family breakdown with children taken into care or custody. But at project *referral*, 38% had a child at risk of being taken into care. A year after exit that prediction had sadly become fact. Intensive FIP reprogramming had no effect on family stability. The LTO report evaluators honestly concluded the following on impact 'sustainability' problems

'it also reflects the fact that the families often had deep rooted problems, suffered from multiple deprivations and were therefore likely to continue to be vulnerable to external influences.'

The 53 project FIP phase (under Casey's Respect programme) evaluated by the NCSR, ('Family Intervention Projects'; NCSR, 2008) came to similar conclusions

'FIP families by their very nature tend to have entrenched and complex problems which can take time to reveal themselves, *let alone start to be resolved.*'

This was true for the intensive FIP programmes and for the TFP where we saw there were no impacts on poverty, health, wellbeing and depression, alcohol and drug problems, family cohesion, domestic abuse or life satisfaction. *The fundamental underlying problems of the families have not been addressed or changed by the TFP.* The idea of positive impacts mysteriously emerging 'downstream' is not supported by the extensive evidence. The evidence points rather to decay. It is pure wishful thinking and does the evaluators (or whoever insisted on inserting this nonsense in the Synthesis Report) no credit.

The evaluation team, like all those before them, conclude with a plea for a 'further wave of impact analysis…repeating the analysis after 24 or 36 months…'. This author would agree with that plea (for the phase1 families cohort *while halting further spending*) if only to nail the lack of TFP impact once and for all in an open forum…*although the zero impact results already established in the synthesis report are very clear and strongly supported by the evaluations of the previous FIP schemes back to 1999.*

There is already sufficient evidence that the TFP intervention model is irredeemably flawed and of no objective value.

Any similar, future schemes will also fail since they begin with the *flawed ideological assumption* that troubled family behaviour is rooted in 'irresponsibility', 'poor parenting' and 'bad lifestyle choices' rather than poverty, mental and physical chronic illness and disability, social inadequacy and low IQ. **We have exhaustively tried 21st century, state sponsored, 'stoning to cast out devils' and it has repeatedly failed. Surely it is time to cry stop?**

1.5.3 Anecdotal Family Experiences & Outcomes

Throughout the history of chaotic, anti-social, dysfunctional, troubled family initiatives great emphasis has always been placed on qualitative analysis: anecdotal stories of the families' lives, their interactions with state agencies and their (genuine) gratitude for a little help. As evidence of intervention efficacy these exercises have no value. However any student of the field should immerse himself or herself in the descriptions of the lives of the families. If a student comes away from this exercise unmoved and not determined to challenge the state failure to help these families …if only to stop misguided, political state interference…find another arena for study. The student will also see the heroic efforts often made by workers at the coal face and by the families themselves, to 'turn around' their sad lives.

The problem is that the road to hell is paved with good intentions. Well meaning people in local authorities, and certainly the front line workers, are mostly happy to quietly go along with ideology based models of the causes of troubled families and outrageous political objectives, such as reducing already starvation level benefits, in order to secure funding so they can 'help' locally. It is a devil's bargain. The impulse is to help the families, hands on, under any circumstances. The problem is then being unable to *enforce access* to the services families *really* need : most prominently medical treatments and *real* remedial education, rather than containment. Various anecdotal studies make this clear but the messages taken out seem to focus on TFP procedural matters and key worker 'style' issues. If only workers followed the official model and stopped 'colluding' with the families. The fundamental limitations of the TFP model are never questioned. In the hands of DCLG civil servants the emphasis becomes the bad lifestyles of the families themselves which need 'gripping': we just need to teach them how a (mythical healthy, well off, middle class, exemplar) family behaves and all will be well in society.

It is worth looking at some of these exercises including the 'Families Experiences & Outcomes' report of the National Evaluation 2016.

122

But first we consider the work of that great humanitarian and research analyst, Dame Louise Casey CB. As Eric Pickles pointed out in 2012 his people were not just sitting in offices but getting out there to study the families and providing 'real insights into these families' lives'…or arguably not. Casey's report was misleadingly called

'Listening to Troubled Families' DCLG, July 2012.

Her study involved recorded interviews with 16 families from 6 LAs who had participated in recent Family Intervention Projects. The LAs were asked to provide the families who 'agreed' to be interviewed. We are not told how the families were selected other than they had multiple problems. The interviews make harrowing reading with domestic abuse and chaotic instability commonplace along with children with schooling / behaviour problems. Crime also features, often emerging from the general chaos rather than criminal enterprises. The author would say these are the kind of families who are singled out for intensive 'core unit', ASB Sin Bin intervention in the FIPs and the intensive 22% group in the TFP. As such *they are not typical* of the FIP or TFP families. Nevertheless they teach valuable lessons about the sources of the family problems and the vacuity of the TFP intervention model.

The author went through the 16 interviews carefully. Only 2 family descriptions failed to mention health problems. The author recorded the following conditions in adults and children: ADHD, a mental health problem, ADHD, post natal depression, PTSD, drug addiction, adult reading age 7, cannabis use, learning difficulties, speech difficulties, depression, cancer, ADHD, alcohol abuse, learning difficulties, nervous breakdown, 3 children with serious physical health problems, depression, drug addiction, ADHD, schizophrenia, personality disorder, cancer, cannabis misuse, deafness, depression, learning difficulties, drug addiction, dyslexic, learning difficulties, substance abuse, anorexia, self harming.

That is 36 health conditions across 14 families. Health is an issue for 87% of the families. 31 conditions, or 86% were mental health / disability issues affecting ~12 families or 75%. These figures are comparable with the TFP NE 2016 finding of 75% with a 'limiting, long standing illness or disability' and the 52% of families with a child 'having SEN or other special needs' and 45% having an adult with mental illness. One assumes that even the Casey would not argue that this level of ill heath was a 'lifestyle choice'. Are there links to the families' other problems such as antisocial behaviour and 'bad' school behaviour and truanting, the key targets of the TFP PbyR scheme?

Well yes, actually. Recall that the prevalence of youngsters with an autistic spectrum disorder among young offenders is 16.6X that of normal people. The prevalence of youngsters with any learning disability among young offenders is 9.2X that of normal people (See: 'Nobody Made the Connection'; Children's Commissioner for England, October 2012). Recall that Mind / Mencap find ~80% of mentally disordered people are subject to regular verbal and physical abuse in the community. 60% of the FIP families had experienced such hate crime and some responded badly. Recall that 2 / 3 of children excluded from school had a mental health or disability problem (16).

Reading the Casey interviews one can see these strong links clearly. Did Casey? No, because Casey knew the answers already. She describes them in the report section

'What the interviews tell us'

Her headings are: intergenerational transmission, large numbers of children; shifting family makeup; dysfunctional relationships; anti-social families & friends; domestic abuse; institutional care; teenage mothers; violence; early signs of poor behaviour; school difficulties; ASB; mental health – depression; drugs & alcohol.

We appear to have a close correspondence here with Cameron's 2012 media characterisation of the families. Casey gives us a list of symptoms and bad behaviours but no deep analysis of causes although depression is mentioned as another symptomatic behaviour along with drug and alcohol abuse. The probable causative links between mental health and disability and undesirable behaviours and social inadequacy are not recognised. So what incisive conclusion does her 'research' make? We are told at the end that

'At the most *fundamental* level is an absence of *basic family functioning* which must be restored…'

Her 'fundamental level' is a trite, superficial listing of symptoms obvious at the beginning of the exercise. Is this what passes for analysis in the DCLG? Anyway, she already knows how to 'restore' proper functioning: 'grip' the family with 'assertive non-negotiable' intervention and 'tough sanctions' until they straighten out. And that's not all. The damn social workers just need to get their act together! How hard can it be? Hold on, says the fair minded reader, surely there is more to the TFP model than that?

Well consider Casey's famous speech at the annual Local Government Conference in Manchester (the favoured 'exemplar' TFP council) in 2013 (25). Here are some of the views she expressed:

'This time around we [social workers, et al] *cannot collude* with parents to find excuses for failure...there is a lack of decision making, things are open-ended, there are lots of meetings, lots of discussions, but nothing's closed down...You are in a meeting and everyone wants to be nice to each other...Well I'm saying I don't really mind whether you're nice or not. ...So *if you are not doing your job* you need to be challenged on it....It's the same with families who need to be told the honest truth...[TFP] co-ordinators crack on....they are tougher... they get on with the job...Family intervention is about getting in there and saying : actually you know, your kids are going to be taken away...'

Such statements are not a momentary lapse. Casey has also told the media that in her intervention model

'We are not running some cuddly social workers programme...we should be talking about things like guilt and shame...we have lost the ability to be judgemental because we worry about being seen as nasty to poor people.'

Casey has been as good as her word. Indeed 40% of TFP families were sanctioned or threatened with sanctions. Who knows, perhaps crude threats of eviction, benefit cuts and child removal are just the therapy a clinically depressed mother with a couple of SEN children needs to get herself 'turned around'. You know, a kind of Casey electro-convulsive therapy without anaesthesia. Except of course the National Evaluation 2016 showed **zero** impact on family outcomes in all outcome areas measured including family health and wellbeing. The evaluation also found **no** significant impacts on

'how well the parents got on within the family and of physical, verbal, emotional and sexual domestic violence.'

So Casey's 'fundamental' issue, basic family functioning, had **not** been improved by her TFP intervention model. We are told in the NE family survey report that the main carer reported subjective improvements in a positive feeling of confidence and control and there were statistically significant differences here to the control group carers. But alas when we look at the numbers affected we are talking about ~5% of the TFP families reporting a difference. The expressions of confidence and control were high in *both groups* : ~95% despite the fact the families were selected because the state said they could not cope.

Why? Well this result raises another issue about interview based anecdotal research. The families are not free agents. They were put into the FIPs and the TFP by the state and sanctioned or threatened to force compliance. To avoid further sanctions and more interventions would not sensible families say, yes, we are feeling much better thanks. Aren't the family views obtained under duress? Is this unethical as well as being misleading?

Consider the views of Nick Bailey, senior lecturer in Urban Studies at the University of Glasgow. Bailey used the FoIA to approach the DCLG for the ethics application form for Casey's study' necessary under government guidance on social research. He was told no such ethical clearance was necessary because the study was 'not research'…despite what Eric Pickles said loudly in public. Bailey tried again and received this remarkable reply from the head of profession for the GSR at the DCLG (26)

'Having considered these guidance notes, their definitions of social research and the report in question, I can confirm that *I do not consider 'Listening to Families' as being within the definition of government social research* and thus the scope of the guidance. My rationale for this is that *this report falls more properly under the description "dipstick / informal information gathering."*'

But Casey's 'research' was given high prominence in the media as such. It was used to promote the supposed scientific basis of the TFP policy. In reality we have not 'evidence based policy' but *'policy by dipstick'*. Bailey reminds us the government social research guidance sets out 5 ethical principles. He concludes that Casey breeched 3.

1. **Free and informed consent of the subjects.** But the TFP families were under threat of sanctions. *Particular consideration* to consent must be given if the subjects are vulnerable. See the list of health conditions above.

2. **Confidentiality and non-disclosure**. The families are anonymous. However they are highly distinctive and details are provided of numbers, ages and genders of children and adults, medical conditions and intimate details of family relations.

3. **Sound and appropriate methods and interpretation of findings.** The research cannot provide reliable conclusions because the sample is clearly biased. The families are not representative of the TFP cohort…so what is the purpose of the research? For example family sizes are often much larger than the 3 children TFP average. There is no analysis of causes, merely a list of symptoms.

Bailey suggests that the report should be withdrawn. The author disagrees. It is a useful contribution to understanding *the pathology underpinning the TFP and the dangerous behaviour of the DCLG and its agents.* In the arena of government intervention in the lives of 'undeserving' poor and vulnerable families it provides another piece of damning evidence in establishing 'a course of conduct': in the same sense as building a legal case against a person accused of harassment or stalking. The mentally vulnerable at the bottom of society, 'the useless mouths' have long suffered such harassment but in Britain, rabidly so since the first New Labour government (27).

The TFP story goes on and on! Part of the NE 2016 was the report

'Family Experiences & Outcomes'

We are assured that *this time* proper informed consent was obtained from the families ...but the issue of co-operation under fear of further 'interventions'...given the wrong answers, still exists. Other problems are still with us. The report looks at just 22 families: some 62 individuals from 10 LAs. So our sample is 0.018% of TFP families from just 6.6% of the TFP LAs. We have a sample of 0.012% of TFP individuals. It is difficult to understand what we are expected to conclude from such tiny samples. The family descriptions are familiar, involving

'commonly, combinations of physical and mental ill health, drug & alcohol misuse, educational and behavioural problems affecting children...often compounded by living in poor quality conditions and managing on a low income.'

We are told also

'A few families also presented issues related to crime and ASB.'

A few families out of 22 is 9% to 13% which corresponds closely to the overall frequency of such behaviours found in the national administration data and the family survey data we examined earlier. We are also given reasons for the sample family referrals including: school related (behaviour / learning) difficulties; autism; ADHD & learning difficulties, ADHD & Aspergers Syndrome, autism, SEN twice, speech problems, post traumatic stress disorder three times. The similarity to the health issues prominent in the Casey 'research' families and the Wirral family anecdotes is clear.

However all is still not what is seems! As we read on we find that of the 22 families only **8** had data for *both* the baseline (pre-treatment) *and* the project exit time periods. 7 had baseline data only. 7 had exit data only. So our 'before *and* after sample' is only 1 in 15,000 families. It is difficult to know what to say. The report is a masterpiece of understatement

'[The results] cannot be generalised to the programme level.'

So what are we about here? The report adds that the results are 'illustrative' only. Illustrative of what? Other comments are also helpful.

'[The sample] was considered to be the more intensive cases.'

And yet only 'a few' were involved in crime and ASB. That tells the reader a great deal about the government denigrating lies vilifying these families for 18 years, up to and including Cameron. It also explains why the supposed cost of 'troubled families' was massively exaggerated. It was based on very extreme cases. We also learn that

'These families were wary of professional help because they had been let down in the past.'

That is hardly surprising. No doubt the 40% receiving TFP sanctions and threats were still glad that things had changed for the better.

So what is claimed? Anecdotes are said to support self-reported family improvements in 6 areas.

- Improved coping skills & resilience.
- Improved financial circumstances
- Improved parental confidence
- Improved social confidence
- Improved crisis avoidance
- Better access to entitlements & specialist support.

It would be wonderful indeed if the above was true. Remember 'before and after data' covers just 8 families. We are, to be fair, warned that these results *cannot be extrapolated* to the full national level. That is a wise caveat since the impact evaluation we examined in detail, using national administration and family survey data for large samples shows impact differences in subjective 'confidence' measures for only ~5% of families relative to the control group. Financial and employment circumstances had not improved. The outcome differences between the TFP processed families and the control group involved only a small percentage of families and most were also statistically insignificant.

Perhaps some families learned to make better benefit claims…one hopes so. But if 'specialist support' means medical treatment there were **no** resulting improvements in family health and wellbeing in the NE data.

The author has reported these hopeless anecdotal results for two reasons. Firstly to show the consistent qualitative picture of the high levels of health problems in the TFP families. Secondly because Casey et al *fall back* on such studies when in trouble. In looking at the NE 2016 in the PAC Inquiry we will see that she attempted to downplay the NIESR impact report, since it showed **zero** impact, by saying well, it was only one of 7 reports in the evaluation. But the above anecdotal family experiences report cannot contradict the NIESR analysis. It cannot make any TFP national level claims at all. She also failed to point out to the PAC that the *independent* family survey study agreed with the NIESR findings. The other NE 2016 reports are technical reports and annexes. The NIESR and the family survey reports are the only ones with reliable information on outcomes. We have yet more bluster and misdirection from Louise and we will see more in the PAC Inquiry section.

However since Casey regularly adduces anecdotal evidence, the author will follow her lead just this once. The Centre for Crime & Justice Studies is a reputable think tank with a long interest in studying state family intervention. In February 2016 as the TFP claims reached new and creative heights the CCJS published a commentary by a 'front line social worker' who had a 'strong need to air my frustration and flesh out the *growing incredulity* in policy circles from a front line perspective' (28).
Our whistleblower than goes to town.

'My observations on the delivery of the programme so far are:

*   There is no qualitative evidence that the TFP is actually responsible for 'turning around' the families it comes into contact with. *It is claimed[in the profession] that many of the positive outcomes are a result of pre-existing multi-agency partnerships.*

*   This is all the more troubling because many families are assessed based on information which is between one and four years old. *Most have therefore resolved their issues with the help of other organisations or through their own accord.* In this case *those involved in the TF management simply 'map' this progress, despite the fact that these*

outcomes cannot be attributed to the work done by the TFP itself.

* *Much of the basis for the 'independent evaluation' of the TFP is on cases which are deemed high risk.* This means they will be dealt with by a 'flagship' TF team, which has a smaller case load and subsequently is able to meet with families a number of times a week. *This practice is unsustainable if applied to the programme at large and yet it is used as the basis for evaluation of the entire programme.*

* The programme is also used as a means to bridge the hole created by cuts in LG funding. *Refusal to engage in this programme is therefore not accepted by TF process managers, who encourage staff to use 'creative' tactics to make up [family] numbers. This has led to disadvantaged families being coerced into joining the programme through intimidating and potentially harmful 'hard sells'.*

* The TFP has used established referral processes in order to continue the expansion of the policy. *This means that staff may have cases suddenly re-classified as TF cases, or be forced to nominate cases against their better judgment and ethics.*

The management of the TFP is therefore questionable and *its continuation is best explained by the revenue stream it provides for local government funding rather than its actual results.*

The public has been misled by suggestions that this programme is astoundingly successful and worth the large investments it has received when in fact it is a waste of public funds.'

The alert reader will note that many of these front line observations were picked up independently in our earlier, detailed technical analyses of the evaluation results. The situation on the ground is even more dire than the author believed. Particularly troubling is the potential harm done to vulnerable families forced into the TFP meat grinder to satisfy DCLG 'targets' or to 'fill' local authority funding gaps. This is a truly dreadful situation.

The 'dipstick' approach to social research such as the misuse of biased sampling and anecdotal evidence to support political preconceptions about minority groups and policies is *extremely dangerous* to the health of the state. How widespread is it? In the DCLG it appears to be endemic. We spoke earlier of repeated incidents of 'misbehaviour' being used to establish a 'course of conduct' for presentation in court.

Let us take one last example of another dangerous situation which required very careful but honest handling. In 2014 Eric Pickles commissioned Louise Casey to look into the functioning of Rotherham Council in the areas of governance and children and young people. This of course related to child sexual exploitation in a Pakistani taxi driver ring. Casey did her 'investigation' and condemned the local social services team. There was also a great deal of press speculation about the role of Labour party influenced political correctness preventing the fingering of an ethnic minority group but that is the responsibility of local councillors not the social workers. Social work academics considered the report and cried foul. Community Care (29) issued a piece called

'Louise Casey report into CSE represents a missed opportunity for children'

After a review the six authors concluded that

'There are troubling aspects of the report. Firstly the process by which it was prepared, in particular *the lack of rigor and transparency in the methods used to gather and analyse data.* Secondly its *failure* to connect what happened in Rotherham with *the current model of child protection* that dominate services and *the need for change* in this respect.

This gap [in methodology] in the report should concern us as it goes to the heart of issues of accuracy, transparency and rigor.'

It would seem we have another piece of Casey 'dipstick' non-research here. How much damage can one, unelected civil servant be allowed to do?

1.6 TROUBLED FAMILIES 'COST SAVING' CLAIMS

Warning : the data used by the DCLG to support these national cost saving claims are not accepted as 'official government statistics'

1.6.1 The National 'Cost Saving' History

At the inception of the TFP in December 2011 David Cameron was keen to stress the outrageous financial burden that the bad behaviour of the TFs imposed on the state.

We've always known that these families cost an extraordinary amount of money... but now we've come up with the *actual figures*. Last year the state spent an estimated £9 billion on just 120,000 families ...that is around £75,000 per family... £8 billion was spent purely reacting to their problems.'

The impression was given that the TFP would zap these reactive costs of £66,666 per family and indeed eliminate them, for a modest investment of £3,733 per family (or £448 million in total). We saw in section 1.3 that this was always a false expectation because of the small proportion of cost which could be attributed to 'bad behaviour' and 'lifestyle choices' and the large proportion of cost related to health and poverty issues which (on the copious historical evidence) would not be addressed by TFP style interventions.

'Assertive non-negotiable' interventions backed by 'tough sanctions' were unlikely to impact positively on chronic illness and disability. Remember **40%** of the families were sanctioned or threatened with sanctions during the local projects. Few received help with help long standing health problems.

In section 1.3.7 we calculated that the actual cost of the real families was £2.56 billion not £9 billion and therefore £21,317 per family not £75,000. We also estimated that bad behaviour and lifestyle choices (ASB, crime, alcohol and drug abuse, under 18 pregnancies...) cost at most £542 million per annum. In principle this amount might be accessible to TFP interventions...if effective. This potential savings amount is 21% of the author's cost estimate and just **6% of Cameron's £9 billion per annum.** (and 6.8% of his reactive spend claim). No *formal* target for cost saving was promoted by the DCLG in the early days but behind the scenes it would appear that more realistic estimates were made.

The NAO report

'Programmes to help families facing multiple challenges'
HC 878 2013 -14, December 2013

contains the original DCLG business case *reactive spend saving* estimate of £ 2.9 billion per annum which later became £2.7 billion. This compares with the author's independent estimate of the *total cost* of £2.56 billion for the 120,000 families based on the real proportions of families with particular problem sets. These could also be estimated from a detailed look at the earlier Family Intervention Projects data.

The business case still overestimates the *real potential saving* available from eliminating all bad behaviour and lifestyles by a factor of 5X. As the programme progressed further attempts were made to estimate accurate cost savings based on samples of LA results to date. These include

'The Benefits of the TFP to the Taxpayer'; DCLG, March 2015

'LA data on the Costs & Fiscal Benefits of the TFP'; DCLG, October 2016

The original promised National Evaluation plan also called for a full cost / benefit analysis based on all LA results. By mid 2015 this had been dropped from the NE scheme…presumably because by then the national administrative data and the family survey impact analyses demonstrated **no** significant (and indeed numerically tiny) differences in family outcomes relative to the matched control groups.

Zero impacts on outcomes means zero savings from the programme. Nevertheless we will look at the official savings claims even though they are all invalid. We do this to shine a spotlight on the chaos and bad practice in the TFP and the DCLG. After all, following the zero impact outcome results all that could be claimed, falsely, was positive 'transformation' of LA 'systems' and procedures.

By early 2015 105,000 families had allegedly been 'turned around'. The March 2015 savings report was based on results from 7 'exemplar' LAs. It is unclear how these LAs were selected or how representative they are of the 152 LAs in the TFP phase 1. The analyses relied on data presented and processed through the official online 'cost savings calculator' (see below). The 7 LA (4.6%) sample may simply reflect an early uptake and supposed (judged by the DCLG) competence in the use of this calculator. This was not universal as we will see later. The data is interesting for several reasons including its marked variability.

Local Authority	Average cost per family in the 12 months before TFP intervention
Bristol	£26,095
Derbyshire	13,235
Manchester	
Year 1	58,238
Year 2	37,075
Year 3	27,793
Redcar & Cleveland	31,132

133

Salford	33,456
Staffordshire	
Year 1	53,810
Year 2	48,362
London – Wandsworth	17,895
LA Average	**30,562**

Local Authority	Average saving per family in the 12 months after TFP intervention
Bristol	£6,339
Derbyshire	4,740
Manchester	
Year 1	6,240
Year 2	7,632
Year 3	9,530
Redcar & Cleveland	6,164
Salford	17,897
Staffordshire	
Year 1	48,724
Year 2	42,486
London – Wandsworth	6,528
LA Average	**13,583**

Just to be clear: all these cost estimates are based on the same *unit costs per 'issue'* in the official cost calculator. They are hypothetical costs we found wanting in section 1.3.

The huge range of costs and indeed savings reflect a very wide range of alleged family characteristics despite the DCLG view that clear, standard selection criteria were applied by all LAs. The cost ranges confirm this is rubbish. The average cost of a family varies from £13K per annum in Derbyshire to £58K in Manchester. The savings vary from £4.7K in Derbyshire to £48.7K in Staffordshire. The latter is claiming to remove ~90% of its families' costs. Frankly, looking at our earlier analyses, this is not credible in any way. This may be why Staffordshire 'disappears' from the finally released average cost calculation (see below).

That varying family composition is an issue is confirmed by looking at Manchester. They took a deliberate strategy of beginning with the 'hardest' families in year 1. Costs fall from £52.8K in year 1 to £27.8K in year 3. The latter is still close to the final 7 LA average implying more challenging families in Manchester. Derbyshire's cost is only 47% of Manchester's lowest cost. Manchester teaches another lesson if we accept at least the relative numbers as correct. The percentage savings from year 1 to 3 are 10.7, 20.6, 34.3%. It is easier to reduce costs as the initial 'difficulty' level of the families' decreases.

Several reasons are given in the report for the variability of the results: access to the necessary data; sample size; delivery strategy time varying; and different family 'types' in the sample. For example LAs collected data on 22 to 29 of the 39 family problem indicators. One local authority reported just 14 of the 39 required. Clearly the LAs have not been 'gripped' or brought into line with the DCLG evaluation mechanisms.

We also have just this 4.6% sample of LAs. Given the very wide range of family costs and savings any extrapolation of the results to the national level was extremely uncertain. Yet we were told confidently in March 2015 that the saving was £11.2K per family and the total saving 11,200 x 105,671 = £1.184 billion per annum …rounded up by Pickles to £1.2 billion. As the NAO pointed out, a bit too politely, this claim was a gross estimate before allowing for the cost of intervention. They also pointed out, but the media ignored them, that the cost saving did not take into account changes that 'would have happened without intervention'. Indeed, by March 2015 the draft National Evaluation results were available to the DCLG and *they knew* that two independent lines of analysis demonstrated that, relative to matched control groups, the TFP outcomes impact was **zero.**

Going back to the 7 LA sample the average family cost before intervention is £30.56K (as opposed to Cameron's £75K) but the reported average was £26.2K and the average saving £13.6K not £11.2K. Why the differences? The author struggled to reconcile these numbers, particularly since they were more favourable to the TFP case. Only by rejecting the incredible Staffordshire numbers and using the year2 Manchester data can we obtain an average cost of £26.5K…not far off that announced. How many other embarrassing LA results in the 152 would need to be rejected if we looked closely? What about savings? If we leave out Staffordshire we get £8.22K savings not £11.2K so how was it obtained? We do not know. The DCLG also claimed in its press releases that the 'worst families' cost an 'average' of £44K per annum.

This appears to be a rough average of Staffordshire and Manchester, the highest cost LAs, since (41 + 51) / 2 = 46K….based on just two extreme outlier LAs in 152… including the rejected Staffordshire results! With the DCLG anything goes.

I ask the reader: would you say that the DCLG use of the word 'exemplar' to describe this sampling exercise is accurate or misleading? Are we supposed to read 'exemplary'? Are Number 10's psychological 'nudging' experts at it again? Yet again pompous language is being misused to give credibility to unjustified conclusions drawn from highly doubtful data and analysis. They should have used their other favourite bureaucratic standby, 'indicative', which we decided earlier means 'we know it's wrong but we can't say that'.

The DCLG also declared that the average cost of intervention was £5,214 per family. If so the total cost at that time was 5,214 x 105,671 = £551 million versus the original £448 million. That would have given us £3,730 cost per family. (A £3,200 sign up bounty and £4,000 for a 'turn around' gives us an average of £3,600). If we take their number seriously this implies that 551 – 448 = £103 million was spent locally on LA budgets.

If we accepted gross savings of £8,220 (the 7 LAs less Staffordshire) the nett savings become 8.22 – 5.214 = £3K or £318 million to March 2015. This is 27% of Pickles £1.2 billion and **3.5%** of Cameron's 'cost to the state' of £9 billion per annum. The reader may reasonably ask again : *at what point does the usual political hyperbole and misdirection become fraudulent?*

The great TFP saga rolled on! Within a few months in mid 2015 families processed had suddenly jumped to a total of 117,910 with 116,654 or **98.9%** 'turned around' based on the PbyR LA claims. Surely the DCLG and our LAs are miracle workers? Have we not already seen that, pulling together, they can even suspend the laws of probability? Congratulations all round! All went quiet for a while (since the National Evaluation results already available, were in effect *suppressed*). But behind the scenes the independent evaluators were battling with the DCLG to agree the wording of the devastating TFP negative results and the great 'cost savings calculator' was churning on. Only in October 2016 was the final report on LA costs and savings (completed during 2015) slipped out *separately* from the NE documents. That is

'LA data on the Costs and Fiscal Benefits of the TFP'

The exercise now involved 67 LA data sets, a 44% sample of the 152 LAs, covering 16,820 families. N.B : this is only a **14%** sample of the families in the TFP. This is still rather small to extrapolate to the national level. In fact, the report if read through carefully, warns us that the

'benefits cannot be scaled up to the national level'

By August 2015 100 LAs had submitted data to the mighty cost savings calculator. Recall the calculator worked by using 'unit costs' for a wide set of family bad behaviours, 39 in all. The unit costs came from the 'New Economy Manchester's Unit Cost Database'. (Manchester looms large in the TFP adventure for several reasons. Its families in year 1 had the distinction of being the 'worst' and most costly in Britain. It is the favoured LA in government propaganda on TFP success. Its evidence was prominent in the written submissions to the PAC Inquiry and it was 1 of only 7 LAs to submit evidence out of 152 : clearly an exemplar among exemplars. Manchester was also a leader in the FIPs and in applying the ASBO to mentally impaired youngsters under Blair's ASBO Jihad. It had the distinction of the highest ASBO breach rate in Britain: 90%. It obviously believes in vigorous state social interventions whatever the evidence says.)

Typically LAs could provide data for only half of the needed 39 costing outcomes. This partial data was used to reconstruct a hypothetical 'average family' for overall cost estimation. The error implicit in this process must be large. Data gaps were also filled by using key worker anecdotal records. Of the 100 LA data submissions only 67 provided an allegedly random sample of families; 20 provided data for all families; 8 supplied data for only their 'high intensity' treatment families; 5 provided data for only their 'turned around' families. (The Wirral data appears to be in this latter class, only more biased, and was *not* used in computing the sample 'national' cost estimate …for good reason.)

As usual if we read carefully we *are* warned that attribution of cost changes before and after TFP reprogramming, *cannot be attributed* to the TFP and that there was 'a lack of uniformity in LA sources and methods'. All this is in contrast to the claims in the National Evaluation 2016 headlines that LAs had been brought into line through 'system transformation'.

Only the 67 'random' data sets were used. We are not told if a standard, statistically valid, random sampling process was recommended to the LAs by the DCLG et al, or if they were left to improvise. If the latter we must not expect much. In the author's experience LAs find it difficult to count consistently never mind understanding the rules of random sampling.

We are not told if any checks of this LA data were made. We *are* told that a 'quality assurance' exercise found that only 80 LAs used 'consistent methods with the cost calculator'. Let us hope the 67 LAs adopted for analysis were also in this group.

Given all the above factors the author suggests that the 'new' national cost / benefit estimates be taken with a large pinch of salt. The new estimate for the average cost of a TF before reprogramming is £26.7K (compared with the earlier £26.2K: *surprisingly* close given all the issues and a tenfold increase in sample size! Truly the DCLG *can* suspend the laws of probability). This is £3.2 billion per annum for our phase 1 families compared with Cameron's £9 billion in 2012.

The after treatment cost of a family was now said to be £19.6K per annum. The mean cost to an LA is £3,350 with the upper quartile at £4,600 and lower quartile £2,150. Months earlier the mean cost was £5,200. The basic attachment fee for signing up a family was initially £3,200 (80% of total bounty falling to 60 and finally 40%) but a ¼ of LAs averaged £2,150 (equivalent to an initial fee of £1,350) indicating later sign up of families. The maximum bounty for early sign ups was £4,000. The upper quartile LAs must have spent on average another £600 per family of local money or 15%. The average spend of £3,350 implies most families were signed up fairly early since the equivalent attachment fee must be (3350 – 800) / 3350 = 0.76 or 76% of total bounty which initially was 80%.

The gross (un-attributable) savings are now 26,700 – 19,650 = £7,050 per family per annum compare with the claimed slightly earlier £11,200. The TFP gross saving then becomes £831 million compared with Pickles £1,200 million…a fall of 31% in less than half a year. As our LA sample increases the gross savings fall sharply!

The author stresses this result to highlight the issue of using small sample sizes and lack of randomness (possibly accidental) in family selection in calculating **false claims** of national scale costs and savings. This is quite apart from the other severe problems in the DCLG / LA approach to evidence.

Taking the new £7,050 gross 'saving' estimate this gives us a net saving of 7,050 – 3,350 = £3,700 per family per annum. Six months before it was said to be £6,000. Our savings estimate has fallen by 38%. The overall net savings from the TFP (ignoring the attribution issues and zero impact results) now become 117,910 x 3,700 = £436 million per annum, or 36%

138

of Pickles £1.2 billion and **4.8%** of Cameron's £9 billion families cost in 2012. **Even if attribution to the TFP was valid the % of troubled family cost saved would be trivial and savings less than the overall cost of £448 million minimum said to have been invested.**

One can see why this latest Fiscal Benefits report was *suppressed* for a year along with the National Evaluation reports which additionally *proved* that The TFP had **zero impact** statistically **and** in terms of the **tiny measured differences, even if treated as significant** in comparison with matched control groups as we saw in section 1.5 One can only assume the PAC Inquiry members *missed* the above savings report which on the DCLG webpage is not identified as part of the National Evaluation.

If the 120,000 troubled families really do cost the state £9 billion per annum it should now be blindingly clear from this evidence that the TFP model, even ignoring the impact statistics, can remove at best ~5% of the TF costs.

Despite the 99% 'turn around' claim by the DCLG and its senior civil servants at least 95% of the troubled family costs remain in place. In objective, evidence based, terms it is 100%.

Surely even a committee of MPs can see the extreme disconnect here? *It cannot be talked away. It cannot rationally be ignored.* Can the claims made before, during and after the TFP be seen as anything other than **fraudulent**? If not deliberately fraudulent they surely must reflect **an extraordinary level of incompetence and culpable negligence in the DCLG.** Surely there should be blood on the floor?

How does the final savings claim compare with the author's blind estimate of section 1.3 (which he carried out before deconstructing the emerging detailed claims)? His estimate was made by considering the detailed characteristics of the dysfunctional families in the 60 Family Intervention Projects from 1997 to 2011 (see sections 2 and 4). This involved looking at issues such as *actual* family offending and its severity. The FIP numbers are close to the real TFP family characteristics he also used. The detailed, accumulated FIP data *could have been used in 2012* to get close to the real costs...but that would have sunk Cameron's Crusade.

We calculated a total cost (reactive + targeted) of 120,000 families as £2.56 billion per annum compared with Cameron's £9 billion. This is £21,330 per family compared with the latest DCLG £26,700 estimate. Of this 21% could be *generously* attributed to bad behaviour and lifestyle choices or £542 million (£4,157 per family). This is the *saving potential* for removing *all* 'bad behaviour'. It is **5%** of Cameron's £9 billion. It compares with the latest £7,050 gross savings claim and the £3,700 net savings claim. We are finally at least in the right ballpark. The £7K gross savings estimate is still inflated I believe, based on experience of the cost assumptions used in the first £9 billion exercise which went on to 'inform' the official cost calculators.

If we take the author's potential saving of ~£4.16K and the average LA cost we get 4.16 – 3.35 = **£0.81K** per family or saving of £95.5 million per annum compared with Pickles £1.2 billion claim to the House of Commons in March 2015.That is **8%** of his claim. As Pickles said then, measuring outcomes is 'notoriously difficult' and we can sympathise …but an error factor of 12.7 X? You have to work at it to be so wrong.

But the *evidence based* (and tiny) family changes and savings *attributable* to the TFP are **zero** according to the National Evaluation 2016. After 18 years of state TFP style intervention projects the failure is proven.

Meanwhile another 1£ billion is being spent from 2015 to 2020 on more of the same medicine. In the name of God why?

The outcome of TFP phase 2 cannot be any better because the basic model is fundamentally flawed.

'Bad behaviour' and 'lifestyle choices' are problems for a small proportion of these families and may respond to threats and sanctions (while the families are under close supervision but not later). Perhaps 3% will again get treatment for drug and alcohol misuse which is welcome.

But 75% of the families have a member with a limiting, long standing illness or disability and the evidence clearly says this will not be addressed in TF projects. What about the 52% of families with SEN or other special needs children? Or the 45% of families with an adult having a mental illness?

Is it really so difficult to see the blindingly, bloody obvious? The key issue is mental and physical health, low IQ and consequent social inadequacy and limited employability. Any effective state intervention must start from here.

But then the author is merely an old scientist, not a sophisticated Westminster politician who is able to see the 'bigger picture'…and loose sight of the bloody obvious.

Daily this disabled man costs the state 5.50 RM.
A healthy family could live for a day on that !

(N.B. I have fallen into bad language on the grounds that swearing seems to help Dame Louise Casey CB, communicate successfully with, and beguile, senior politicians.)

1.6.2 The WIRRAL Cost Saving Miracle

We have examined the national savings claims over time from 2012 to 2016 and probed the very large and continuing variability in LA results. We also noted the use of the official 'cost calculator' based on standard unit costs per 'issue' to supposedly impose uniformity in LA cost estimation and reporting. Clearly for several reasons uniformity was not achieved. We know family selection was a shambolic free for all and central monitoring of LA actions and interpretation of the 'rules' non-existent.

Ideally if one could dissect the behaviour and data of all 152 LAs many lessons could be learned. The author lacks the resources to do this but he can continue his dissection of his local council TFP project in the Wirral to highlight at least some of the problems.

This is a small but random sample selected simply because the author lives there. Let us begin with the council document

'Project Initiation Document.

Children & Young People's Department

February 20th 2012.

Project Title : Intensive Family Intervention Programme.'

This is a brief two page document outlining the Coalition Government's TF initiative and how the Wirral will join in via an 'interagency approach'. The paper promises that

'there will be an evaluation to establish the impact of the approach on this on reducing the level of [family] needs.'

As to financial implications we are told that for each family

'the cost to society is *at least* £75K per year and in some cases rising to *several hundreds of thousands of pounds*.'

This statement is an exaggeration of the already false DCLG claims. We are also told

'The *government* estimates that Wirral has 900 families who meet the referral criteria.'

This estimate is not discussed nor questioned. Then we read

'*It can be suggested* that 900 families with multiple issues cost Wirral upwards of £60 million per year.'

Note the passive voice...already somebody is uneasy! As we saw in the last section the claimed national cost of the TFs continued to evolve from the £9 billion figure. By December 2013 the NAO was reporting a £2.7 billion cost or £22.5K per family. By early 2015 the DCLG was giving £26.7K and claiming £1.2 billion saved. By mid 2015 the saving based on the 67 LA sample was £7K and net saving £3.7K. This is £436 million per annum. It appears that all this material somehow passed the Wirral TFP team by as we will now see.

So how did the Wirral calculate and report its TFP success? We looked at the propaganda reports and TFP impact claims in section 1.4. The detailed project evaluation report was requested by the author in 2015. He received reference to a 28 page document which mainly consisted of anecdotes about 'turned around' families. There was **no** evaluation of the project, merely a list of ambiguous outcomes for the sub-group of families who had received *'intensive support from an IFIP key worker'*. But nationally we saw that *only* 22% of TFs on average had received such intensive support. We saw that the claimed Wirral results do not cover the whole 910 families processed and give a misleading picture of outcomes. The short 'cost benefit analysis' section says just this

'Using the Department for Education Family Savings calculator the average *saving* for a family engaging in IFIP is **£76,125** with the lowest saving at £3,453 and the highest at £152,726. Average savings across agencies can be broken down as follows…'

Costs follow for the LA, society (?), social services, health, police, criminal justice, YOT and other. The highest sub-cost item is police at £12,827 per family. The inference is that this is the average saving for all the Wirral 910 families.

This is truly remarkable. The IFIP inception document gave the (government derived) **cost** of a Wirral troubled family as **£75,000** and three years and 910 families later we find Wirral has **saved £76,125** per family. They have achieved what no other LA in the country has achieved: **They have eliminated all of the claimed cost of a typical troubled family!** Even the DCLG did not claim to have *saved* the whole £75,000. By early 2015 they were merely claiming £11,200 gross and by mid 2015 (quietly) a net saving of £3,700 per family per annum. Wirral did **21X** better than this!

But there is more to this miracle. The savings range is from £3.4K to £153K for a 20% sample of Wirral families yet somehow the *average* saving is within 1.5% of the £75,000 cost Cameron claimed in 2012. The probability of this match by occurring by chance is negligible.

What is going on here? The author requested the detailed cost / benefit analysis for the Wirral IFIP for the second time…under the FoIA. You will recall that the senior manager of the project (now senior manager of something called targeted services) did not possess a copy of the evaluation report and could not supply it since it was done elsewhere. My request did eventually result in three data files which had provided the input to the Wirral PbyR claims to the DCLG.

Document 1: Wirral Family Outcomes and Eligibility Tables
           [for the PbyR scheme]

Document 2: Distance Travelled Table
           [families own views on outcomes]

Document 3: Cost / Benefit Results
           [For 180 of the 910 families, a 20% sample]

We looked at D1 and D2 in section 1.4. Document 3 looks at claimed savings under the headings listed earlier by family. We are assured that the family sample size was approved by the DCLG TFP 'guidance board'. Nothing is said about *how* the families were selected. However by mid 2015 the cost / benefit team analysing the 67 LA results sample was emphasising the critical importance of providing *random samples* of families. Was this true of the earlier 7 'exemplar' LAs exercise?

Was it emphasised before LAs began to use the 'cost savings calculator'? We don't know. Wirral is silent on the matter. Clearly a non-random sample will lead to a biased estimate of outcomes and savings. Looking at the Wirral eligibility and cost for their **180** family sample is most enlightening. We find that **179** families meet the crime, police and youth justice success criteria and have substantial crime related costs (police average £12,827; crime and justice average just £1,586. Given the claimed high criminality of the families the latter is surprisingly small. Few appear to be getting to court. Is the police cost reflecting call outs to family domestics rather than crime and community ASB?). Note that only 1 family in the sample has **no** crime related costs.

This is puzzle. We know that on Wirral only 1.2% of TF children have an ABC or ASBO. 6.5% of adults had reports of ASB and 10.4% of children. As little as 10% of minors had offended. A random sample of families should reflect this low frequency of criminality and police involvement ...shall we say **10%** of families with associated costs? Yet in the sample submitted for PbyR analysis **99 %** of families have such costs....and they are substantial. We must infer that the sample submitted was *hopelessly biased and not representative of Wirral TFs.*

We might assume that Wirral (or their unidentified, sub-contracted agents) had *accidentally* misconstrued the TFP 'governance board' rules for submission... if they existed at the end of 2014. By mistake did they submit *only* those families with high crime and possibly other costs?

Let's look at the bigger mystery. They say the 'average saving' for those 'engaging' with the IFIP is £76,125 per family. Their project inception document noted the Cameron cost as £75,000 as fiscal justification. The early 2015 DCLG figure was 9 B / 117,910 = £76,300. The range of Wirral cost *'savings'* was from £3,453 to £152,726 yet somehow our *biased*, 20% family sample average is within 1.5% the original government *cost* estimate and within 0.2% of the nominal early 2015 national estimate of *cost* (not saving).

Truly, some LAs, inspired by Dame Louise Casey and the TFP Jihad, are able to *suspend the laws of probability* and perform miracles! In addition Wirral achieved a **98.9%** family turn around rate and *eliminated all of their costs* to the state. Surely all concerned should receive a medal for services to the tax payer? After all the DCLG is quietly now only claiming gross savings of £7K per family and net savings of £3.7K. Wirral has achieved 11X the national gross saving or 21X the national net savings level. No wonder Louise Casey, the TF Tsar, congratulated the Wirral Chief Executive as early as 2013 on

'a fantastic performance…you have a tremendous team.'

Well yes, they did *exactly* what the government told them to do…but unfortunately perhaps, became carried away. The reader may feel, seeing the above analysis, that 'fantastic' is the appropriate description of Wirral's TFP achievement claims. And remember there were 151 other LAs out there trying to be 'helpful' to the government …having taken large sums of public bounty money. But are we dealing here with conspiracy or cock up? I suspect largely a creeping cock up. The Wirral TFP team did not seem to notice that the government cost and savings estimates changed over time. They were stuck in 2012 in terms of *what they thought was expected of them.* Unless of course they chose to be out of date to save problems with explaining the fiscal disjunction to the Wirral Council members and tax payers. Wirral has an unfortunate recent history of scandals and inter party warfare over misuse of money. Anyway, perhaps nobody would notice? Alas, somebody did.

The IFIP team somehow confused the original £75K total troubled family *'cost'* with a *'savings'* target and allegedly *met it.* The incredibly close 'savings' estimate of £76.1K to the £75K 'cost' estimate of 2012 cannot be attributed to chance. It remains a deep mystery. The reader may see a solution but I could not possibly comment.

Does all this matter? Well yes it does.

There are 152 LAs out there presumably doing similar things with the tacit encouragement of the DCLG. Locally the public claims made and the outcomes document, completely mislead the tax payers to a huge degree. The total cost of the TFs has supposedly been removed which is equivalent to £67.5 million per year 'savings'. But the National Evaluation 2016 demonstrates that the actual savings nationally and locally are **zero.** The author is aware of no correction or apology in the local media for all these totally false claims.

More to the fiscal point in January 2015 the Wirral Childrens' Trust Board was briefed on the IFIP update and the TFP phase 2. From 2015 – 2020 Wirral will work with 3010 troubled families. At the new bounty levels the central cost will be 3010 x 1800 = £5.42 million. From phase 1 experience I estimate that the average council will spend an additional 15 – 25%. In Wirral's case say £1.1 million. The total cost to the tax payer will be ~£7.24 million. If we scaled up the Wirral phase 1 savings claims this would result in savings of £229 million locally! The actual savings on the phase 1 evidence will be **zero.**

The Wirral CTB document also assures us that the DCLG 'principles' for phase 2 projects will be followed rigorously. These include, trust, transformation and transparency. Trust involves

'flexibility to work with the families of greatest concern and to shape outcomes achieved locally.'

What the hell does this statement have to do with trust? The issue is whether tax payers can *trust* the claims of their local authority and central government servants. We don't want LAs to 'shape outcomes' but report honestly. Any tax payer who now 'trusts' the DCLG or LAs like Wirral deserves to be ripped off.

Transformation involves

'ambitious service transformation goals to embed integrated, whole family approaches.'

Fine but the current 'whole family approaches' have been proven to be totally ineffective and a waste of money.

Transparency involves all TAs in the

'introduction of a model of *transparent local accountability* for the success of the programme as a tool to drive greater service transformation, using streamlined data collection tools.'

What? This sounds a little like: deliver or else. Surely the important issue, given what we have seen, is *transparency* about the assumptions made in any data analysis and the opening of those analyses to *public scrutiny*. It is not good enough for LAs to say: er, we don't have a copy of the cost – benefit analysis …somebody else did it for us using a cost model we don't understand.

The author is unaccountably reminded in these policy statements of North Korean propaganda banners or Orwell's 'Ministry of Truth' pronouncements. Who is paid to write this stuff? As for trust and transparency in the TFP phase 2, the author will also keep an eye out for porcine aerial perambulations : or in Old Speak, flying pigs.

We will look at the phase 2 details later. I note now that crime, school attendance and worklessness are still being targeted along with domestic abuse and families with health problems. This is a finally recognition of the actual TFP problem composition experienced in phase 1. However the priorities are interesting.

- Families who are **a high cost to the public purse.**

- Ability to **get families to resolve low level health issues independently.**

- Knowledge of how to **access local health services for high level needs.**

The high cost to the state is still a priority. Families with low level health problems are on their own. 'Knowledge' of how to access high level health needs is not the issue based on 18 years of intervention projects : **actually getting treatment for mentally ill and disabled children and adults is**. The intervention projects have failed to do this repeatedly despite innovations such as attaching a medical 'liaison' practitioner to the FIP teams in one phase. Unless this problem is seen as central, phase 2 will fail as phase 1 did. Don't hold your breath fellow tax payers.

The Wirral is one of 152 TFP LAs. Let us hope that it is not typical. Its data was *not* used in the 7 'exemplar' LA exercise *nor* in the 67 LAs cost / benefit study *but* it did count in the overall DCLG success claims tables.

However even without the ludicrous gross errors (being generous) of the Wirral case we noted many other problems in the exemplar studies. How many other LAs are as 'error' (being generous) prone as Wirral?

1.7   The Public Accounts Committee TFP Inquiries
: Exercises In 'Alternative Facts'

'[The PAC] is the queen of select committees…[which] by its very existence exerted a *cleansing effect* in all government departments.'

Lord Hennessy

1.7.1   Introduction

The TFP has been 'investigated' twice since its inception in 2012. Both inquiries are worthy of comment for several reasons. But first the basic facts about the PAC. It was founded in 1857 and it is the *oldest* select committee in the House of Commons.

 It has evolved over its 150 years and its influence we are told has steadily increased. In 1983 the National Audit Act founded the National Audit Office whose head, the Comptroller & Auditor General, attends the PAC hearings and 'assists' it as we will see.

Today the PAC has 15 members one of whom is the Financial Secretary to the Treasury …but he or she *does not* attend hearings. The reader may conclude that here we have a most powerful committee of MPs which is deeply embedded in the Westminster-Whitehall *'system'*. The reader may also wish to ponder the implications of this in considering what follows in the TFP case.

 We are also told on the PAC official site that

'As the collection and spending of public money present new challenges *the work of the committee is vital to protecting the interests of the tax payer.'*

 The author could not agree more.

So let us consider the work load of this 'vital' committee. In the 2010-2015 parliament the PAC held 276 evidence sessions and published 244 *'unanimous'* reports including 1,338 recommendations. The reader might wish consider such unanimity as impressive for a variety of reasons. The committee is cross party which makes the 'unanimous' reports interesting. Could we be talking about a long standing 'non-aggression pact'? In the last parliament the PAC produced an average of **41.7** reports per annum following **46** hearings per annum. That is an impressive work rate. However taking the TFP Inquiry of October 2016, the National Evaluation documentation amounted to nearly 700 pages and was only available to the PAC two days before the TFP hearing.

The evidence also demanded *a careful consideration of logical and statistical arguments* as we have seen. Perhaps the TFP case was unusual but how can a lay committee like the PAC possibly dissect **46** such issues per annum? Even if ably assisted, presumably, by the NAO? Could it be that the PAC in fact *is not expected to do anything other than pass lightly across spending items?* Perhaps 'its very existence exerts a cleansing effect on departments' as Lord Hennessy suggested? Or perhaps not. See what you think.

We are told also that

'As proof of *how seriously* government takes the committee's work 88% of the recommendations are accepted by departments.'

The reader might feel that the significance of this claim rather depends on the strength of the recommendations. How many policies have been flagged up as *failures* and how many programmes have been *stopped* for example? In the case of the TFP, *with the clearest possible technical evidence of programme failure and wasted money,* the phase 2 programme was allowed by the PAC to go ahead. **Surely the only valid evidence based recommendation would be to cancel it?** Another billion pounds is being spent on a programme **with a predictable zero impact and saving**… surely this is not supportable? What is going on? But then the author is not a politician. More importantly, what does the reader and tax payer think? We have two PAC interventions to consider.

1.7.2 The 2014 PAC TFP Inquiry

A year after the start of the TFP phase 1 early results began to appear. The DCLG released data that showed that 35,618 families had been 'worked with' between April 2012 and March 2013. This was 6,217 shy of the planned first year target, but not too bad. It did though leave 70% to be processed in the final two years.

The LAs had also identified 66,470 of the total target of 118,082 families to be re-programmed in the 3 year programme. This seems rather slow if the troubled families were so obvious and commonplace. Were they not wrecking communities? However in the first year 1,675 families had been turned around or 4.7% of those worked with. Was this the low hanging fruit? Did this mean that in 3 years, in that first group, 14% would be turned around? Minister Eric (Pangloss) Pickles was not worried, describing the first year progress as 'remarkable'. He added

'This programme is not only transforming the lives of families …but it will deliver considerable savings to the tax payer by reducing their demand for services…'

Well we know what happened…**zero** savings. The LGA rallied around with its chairman, Sir Merrick Cockell opining

'The rapid progress being made by LAs vindicates the government's decision to put councils at the centre of this programme…'

And we could add, paying councils a £4,000 bounty for every family processed. By July 2013 the DCLG found new, more promising results. 80,011 families had been identified and 13,999 of the first cohort turned around, or 26.7%. 660 nationally had found work, or 1.3%. Given the centrality of getting 'lazy' families off out of work benefits this is not impressive is it? 13,339 had met the 'crime/ ASB/ education' target or 25.4% but as we saw this is primarily about reduction in truanting.

Overall in the media, the Pickles spin was not swallowed. This may be why by 2014 the Public Accounts Committee first became engaged. The PAC site reported its April 2014 hearing under the title

'Troubled families targets may be missed unless delivery speeds up'

The committee simultaneously reviewed parallel programmes run by our DCLG friends and the DWP programme aimed specifically at increasing employment in families 'facing multiple challenges'. The PAC site quotes the summary remarks of the Rt. Hon Margaret Hodge MP, chair of the committee.

'We welcome the commitment shown by both departments involved in delivering the programmes.'

We will see how well this 'commitment' was rewarded a little later.

'However we are concerned that the Government is on course to miss its targets of 'turning around' the lives of 120,000 troubled families...By October 2013 it had achieved lasting [?] improvements in the lives of 22,000 families leaving a further 98,000 to be turned around by May 2015....More worryingly DWP's programme had achieved only 720 sustained [?] employment outcomes by September 2013, just 4% of expected performance...another challenge has been the departments' reliance on individual LAs and *private providers* to deliver outcomes ...there have been big variations in performance...The departments must ensure that *performance in each LA and by each contractor is scrutinised ...imposing sanctions where necessary*...We now need to see clear improvements in performance against targets and *real cash savings* made from these programmes. These actions are essential not only to turn around the lives of the troubled families involved, but also to deliver savings and *demonstrate value for money.*'

This seems clear enough and the PAC are on the job, are they not? Well the author has read through the transcript of the oral evidence. It includes a bravura performance by Louise Casey who swamps every question with 'honest to God' anecdotes and local detail. It is truly impressive filibuster and committee members, ordinary constituency MPs, do not stand a chance in most cases! Please remember also that these MPs are sitting in judgement on the work of 152 LAs which overlap with their own constituencies. There is a saying about not crapping on your own doorstep which should perhaps be remembered. Lets take a few excerpts of the testimony to give a flavour.

There was considerable debate about cross department sharing sensitive data on individual families and issues of confidentiality and data safety. Some agencies like police and the NHS appear nervous which is reassuring.

Q92 Mr. Bacon: 'You will recognise this quote : "We need to find out what is happening to all of the data. *I don't think that is about somebody's civil rights.* I think it's about their right to get help and *the system's right to challenge them to take it.*" You are saying that unless you have all of that [data], the system cannot operate as effectively as it should...'

Louise Casey: Are you quoting me, just so I know? That's me is it?'

Mr. Bacon: Yes.

Louise Casey : 'Well, I was right...'

This is interesting in the light of Casey's similar off hand approach to the question of informed consent and questioning of families under duress which we examined in section 1.5.3.

Q111 : **Meg** Hiller MP [future PAC chair in the second inquiry] : I want to raise one practical thing…How does the data move?

Louise Casey : 'I would feel nervous about being too know-it-all about that **Meg** but my sense is …it would not be a problem…'

Note the use of Ms. Hillier's first name. Familiarity happens several times during the hearing. Consider Casey and the Auditor General. Ms Hillier was interested in how best practice was being propagated.

Q116 Meg Hillier: And best value for money practice as well?

Louise Casey : 'Yes we did a costing of the troubled families, nine moths to 12 months ago…we are now putting together *this thing called a cost calculator*… three LAs [of 152] that have gone into this with us in a lot of detail **know the costs**…the treasury is happy what we are doing on the calculator…

The NAO report is absolutely right to say – I will not even look at **Amyas** [NAO head and Auditor General] because he is probably thinking that I am overstepping the mark – that *we do not have a fiscal analysis* and that we have one coming through the evaluation…'

If so Sir **Amyas** Morse's telepathic scepticism was correct. Notice that Casey is relying on costs estimated by just 3 local authorities. The 2015 national evaluation showed **zero** cost saving and we showed forensically that very limited saving *was predictable at the start of the programme.* We also see from this first name familiarity how well Casey was embedded in the Westminster - Whitehall system.

One member was unable to contain himself in the face of the Casey's, not Tsar like but Svengali like, charismatic onslaught and gave the underlying PAC attitude away.

Q150: Mr Chris Heaton-Harris : 'First to Louise Casey: thank you. I love you. You're brilliant. Every [government] department should have one of you.'

No, dear reader, this was not sarcasm but adoration!

It is difficult to understand since Mr. Heaton-Harris was chair of the APPG on learning disability. Any familiarity with the selection process of the TFP families would clearly show the targeting and abuse of the mentally disordered. Mr. Heaton-Harris became a Conservative Party whip and resigned as the APPG chair.

Just a moment, says the fair minded reader, one sycophantic outburst cannot characterise the opinion of the whole committee…and they were critical of the TFP weren't they? Well let's move forward a year as Pickles declared the TFP triumph and the mythical £1.2 billion saving. The TFP was on a roll! Civil Service World on the 24th of March 2015 put out the ultimate hagiographical profile.

'Speaking Truth to Power : CSW interviews Troubled Families Tsar Louise Casey'

We can safely skip much of the biography. Let's move on to 2014.

'Described by Public Accounts Committee chair Margaret Hodge as "a bloody good thing for the civil service", Casey was awarded the PAC award at last years Civil Service Awards, making it a double whammy for the Troubled Families team who also won the policy award.'

'Presenting Casey with her award, **Hodge** joked that while Casey has never managed not to swear during a select committee hearing, **she " has support across the political system".'**

Isn't this cosy? According to CSW

'[Casey] says she always bases her recommendations on evidence, and isn't trying to go out of her way to be difficult. **"Uncomfortable truths are still true"** she adds.'

What does the reader of this book think?

So Casey and her team, win the PAC annual awards despite the apparent PAC 'concerns' about TFP delivery 'falling behind schedule' and 'lack of cost saving evidence' just months before. Does the reader feel confident that the PAC is on the ball? Even the Casey was surprised.

'That was extraordinary wasn't it? We didn't think we were going to win **the policy award** and we **bloody** did, didn't we?

...and then for me to win the PAC award, that was extraordinary, very emotional. Who would have thought?'

Extraordinary indeed but of course David Cameron had flagged the Troubled Families Programme as *the flagship political response to the Summer Riots ...and the justification for severe benefit cuts...* it had to be seen to be successful... never mind the evidence. But then, according to Hodge, Casey also has 'support across the political system'.

Remember Hilary Benn, on behalf of Labour, standing to congratulate Pickles *and* Casey in the House of Commons in March 2015 ...and to remind them that Family Intervention was *invented* by New Labour. Many MPs also rose to puff their local authorities and their inspiring visits to 'brilliant' projects. Alas it was all a remarkable mirage, the emperor had no clothes on, and the National Evaluation, published finally in 2016 but *available in early 2015*, provided **'uncomfortable truths' ...which were still true: no evidence of changes to the families on all measured outcomes attributable to the TFP... and zero cost savings.**

Surely the PAC 'attitudinal' tide was bound to turn in line with the objective evidence as we reached the end of the TFP phase 1?

1.7.3   The PAC TFP Inquiry 2016

'Politics is the art of looking for trouble, finding it everywhere, diagnosing it incorrectly and applying the wrong remedies'

Sir Ernest Benn

We have noted the presentation of the TFP as a 'remarkable' success in the House of Commons and the media in March 2015 by DCLG Minister Eric Pickles. Let's take one more statement from him.

'I am genuinely honoured to have led this remarkable life-changing programme ...and why I am delighted it is being expanded to help more troubled families...**The figures we are publishing today prove beyond doubt that the approach is working....**'

Pickles then gives data for **4 LAs out of 152** as his evidence. We looked at this problematic material earlier in section 1.6.1. We noted other MPs rising to take a slice of the 'credit.' Hilary Benn added

'We support the programme precisely because LAs that are implementing it on the ground are convinced it makes a difference…We support this important work……*the Labour Government started the family intervention project and a future Labour government would want it to go from strength to strength*…It is not often in this House that we pay tribute to public servants…so I would like to thank Louise Casey for the leadership she has shown…'

Benn seems unaware that the positive 'conviction' of the LAs may not be unconnected to their mouths 'having been stuffed with gold' as one of his Old Labour forerunners once remarked to explain a policy success. Others were equally complementary and indeed on the edge of ecstatic hallucination. Since we looked earlier at the author's area of Wirral let us take a typical, hyperbolic input from Frank Field, MP for Birkenhead.

'I congratulate the Secretary of State, Louise Casey and the families who have turned their lives around. **On behalf of my constituents, many of whom now have a more peaceful existence**, may I also, through him, thank the front line workers who brought about these changes? In 'Feeding Britain' …although we drew attention to those families who did not have enough money to feed their children, *there were other scallywags who could not be bothered to feed their children.*'

These scallywags presumably are among the 'undeserving' troubled families who also 'destroy' communities. We should repeat again that none of the family intervention project evaluations nor the TFP evaluation demonstrated *any* impacts on the wider community in terms of crime and anti-social behaviour. The National Evaluation 2016, completed in early 2015, showed no *statistically significant differences* in outcomes between the TFP families and the matched control group. In fact if we *accepted* the small differences between the groups as real, *the level of crime and ASB was significantly higher in the TFP reprogrammed families.* Yet somehow Mr. Field's constituents can now thank the TFP 'for a more peaceful existence'. Is there no end to the TFP miracle?

In fact Mr. Field has long believed in the TFP message: all the problems of the families are largely the result of lifestyle choices, weak 'character' 'lack of responsibility' and the want of 'a substitute' for Evangelical Christianity. There is no recognition of mental incapacity and disability in considering causation. The reader is recommended to read Mr. Field's master work 'Neighbours From Hell' wherein much will be familiar (30). Remember that Frank was Tony Blair's Welfare Guru and Cameron's Poverty Tsar. His 'unthinkable' policy ideas were quietly 'put away' but are still influential behind the scenes. For a deconstruction of Frank's views see this author's long essay 'Politicians From Hell' (31). The essay also explains the hysterical origin of the ASBO Jihad and the FIPs and the targeting of mentally impaired youngsters.

The bubble of delusion, misdirection and self congratulation was bound to burst eventually. Enough is enough. Independent observers Stephen Crossley of Durham University and Jonathan Portes then head of the NIESR published scathing commentaries on the DCLG claims (23). This author published his book 'Troubled Families' which analysed results of state intervention schemes from 1999 up to March 2015 and sent it to many MPs in the appropriate parliamentary committees and the press ....with no result whatsoever. Crossley wrote a number of critical pieces the most comprehensive, published by the CCJS in late 2015 (32).

'The TFP : the Perfect Social Policy?'

As more claims continued to emerge he wrote in June 2015

'The TFP has apparently achieved a 100% success rate…It is …staggering that work with some of the most disadvantaged families who have allegedly been immune to all previous policy interventions and whose 'troubles' have existed 'for generations' has been so successful…'

'Manchester have identified, worked with and turned around a staggering 2,385 [the exact DCLG set target] 'troubled families'. Not one has slipped through the net or refused to engage. Leeds and Liverpool have a perfect success rate…By my reckoning over 50 other LAs [eventually 132] …have been similarly 'perfect' in their TF work. Not one single case amongst those councils where more TFs were identified or where a TF has failed to have been turned around.'

Portes was equally forthright in a number of critical pieces including the excellent and incredulous (23)

'A Troubling Attitude to Statistics'

'Last week a government press release …claimed:

"More than 105,000 TFs turned around saving taxpayers an Estimated £1.2 billion."

Much of the press was too supine and lazy to bother to question this… But the headline is untrue.

…The £1.2 billion is pure, unadulterated fiction…Why?...Well there are obvious problems with [LA] sample size, selection bias and the fact that the LAs get paid according to the number of families they have supposedly 'turned around'…there is no counterfactual and hence there can be by definition no estimate of "taxpayer savings".'

'So are the DCLG officials stupid of ignorant? Of course not. Do they not understand the basic principles of programme evaluation? Of course they do. Buried in a 'methodology' report on the DCLG web site –not even referenced, let alone reflected in the press release:

"…however it is likely that some improvements in outcomes would have happened in the absence of intervention…[Also] however, in the report all the figures provided are gross."

In other words civil servants knew the truth. And still they allowed the publication of a press release which in *bold type headline*, deliberately and successively sought to mislead the press and the public.'

'…I doubt the North Korean Statistical Office would have the cheek…'

'Frankly this whole episode is disgraceful. Of course it reflects badly on ministers – and not just Eric Pickles but Danny Alexander…they are making claims that are not true. That's politics although I don't much like it and I don't think we should stand for it.

But it reflects far worse on the civil servants whose professional duty it was to stop them. Deliberately misleading the public is not public service.'

Cameron remember was gung ho about the TFP PbyR scheme and wanted to see it become the norm across government. Also in June 2015, by coincidence, Sir Amyas Morse, who we met in the PAC 2014 TFP Inquiry, head of the National Audit Office, urged caution on whether PbyR offered value for money.

'PbyR potentially offers benefits such as innovative solutions to intractable problems. If it can deliver these benefits, then the increased risk and cost may be justified. *Without such evidence commissioners may be using this mechanism in circumstances to which it is ill-suited, to the detriment of value for money.'*

Which major programme, currently the subject of a loud dispute, could he have been talking about do you think?

Well in the PAC (in public) he remained neutral. We will see the PAC, in the end, and presumably lacking technical guidance, simply go along with the views of the DCLG civil servants.

Dissent rumbled on. On August 8th 2016 BBC's Newsnight attacked the TFP and claimed that it had achieved **'approximately nothing'** based on 'leaks' from the upcoming TFP National Evaluation, with particular attention to the NIESR impact results (21). The leak was an accurate summary of the final report. It would appear that someone finally got fed up sitting on results which had been available in essence, a year before but were suppressed. The BBC claimed, based on a civil service 'source', that if the results had been favourable it would have been published earlier. A DCLG source was reported as saying

'there were several strands to the evaluation work commissioned by the last government and there is not yet a final report.'

We will see that this was economical with the truth to say the least. It was also claimed on the programme that there were large discrepancies between LA figures for families worked with and the figures published by the DCLG. This is hardly surprising given the chaos of data collection and manipulation we examined earlier.

Finally in October 2016 the Public Accounts Committee got around to the TFP again… they could hardly ignore the bad press. A call went out for written submissions to the Inquiry under the usual rules.

Meg Hiller who we met in 2014 and now the chair of the PAC approached the DCLG for a copy of the final National Evaluation documents. These were delivered *2 days before* the PAC Inquiry hearing held on the 19th of October. There were 7 reports in all and 689 pages (plus 2 other, off the books, DCLG reports on the NE website page). There were also 22 written submissions. Nevertheless the Inquiry went ahead. This is deeply disturbing.

A comment on the PAC submission policy may be helpful here. The PAC recommend papers of no more than 3,000 words. There should be an executive summary and each paragraph should be numbered (as in Hansard). Well the PAC members are busy, important people, we should make their lives as easy as possible: I mean, you can learn a lot about complex policy matters from an executive summary …if it is honestly written. The 22 written submissions added at least another 200 pages of bumf to read (based on the rules). Truly, the PAC members must have a phenomenal attention span and power of concentration to absorb all this material, never mind draw meaningful conclusions from it!

Let us look briefly at the submissions. They came in four categories: LAs and LA lobby groups; companies and charities touting for business; academic analysts; government agencies.

Local Authorities.

The LAs support the TFP as expected but some comments are interesting.

London Borough of Enfield : begins with a twitter exchange on the need to consider case studies *not numbers*; one case study described; They claim 149 of 877 families turned around: 16%. Yes, these *numbers* can be tricky.

Greater Manchester : stresses the importance of 'system transformation' as an outcome *not* the PbyR 'turn around', in their case 100%. Given Manchester's prominence as a DCLG costing pathfinder and 'exemplar' this is rather surprising.

Brighton and Hove City Council : they say they achieved a 75% turn around by March 2015 but claimed 100% in reporting to the DCLG; provided one case study as evidence.

Dorset County Council : Report 80% crime / ASB / education turn around and 16% gaining employment; 3 case studies; saving per family £2,964.

Hampshire County Council : Report 87.9% *reduction in prevalence* of families with a child persistently absent from school. Other similar 'prevalence' claims. These are for *families having the problem, not all families.* We have the same misleading reporting as in Wirral and elsewhere. We are told 'costs avoided' were £1,509 per family.

Kirklees County Council : A 92.6% turn around total with 2.9% gaining employment. Family health was poor with 60% unemployed as a result; Two case studies presented.

Doncaster County Council : 100% successful turnaround *but* some problems with definitions; 1576 families worked with under phase 1 and 914 turned around or 58% not 100%. We see here again, as in Wirral, why the DCLG performance claims are extremely doubtful.

London Councils group : the TFP is excellent; opinion only , no evidence.

Local Government Association : The LGA describes itself as 'a politically led, cross-party organisation' whose members have received up to £4K bounty per family in TFP phase 1 and are already engaged in phase 2. The bounty is also 'cross party'. Their views are business like and not unexpected : the TFP claims good outcomes and useful service transformation. Enough said.

Society of Local Authority Chief Executives : they say the TFP has 'delivered positive outcomes for many families' and led to 'improved working practices'. But 'the definition of turn around creates unrealistic expectations'. No it does not: shifting definitions and the encouragement to make false claims creates total disbelief in the results. SOLACE see hard metrics as 'potentially unhelpful'. This is true if LA people get caught and burned at the stake by angry tax payers…look, just give us the money and trust us!

  Note that only a few of the 152 LAs offered a view even though 132 had reported a 100% family 'turn around' in claiming the £4,000 bounty money and the rest above 98%. Above we have 16,58,75,92.6, 96 and 100% turn around claims: mean 71.3%. The DCLG average is 99%. Where family savings are given they are £1.5K – 3K, not the DCLG £26.7K or £75K. Interesting? The reader can decide if this small, keen LA sample backs up our earlier analyses of the TFP.

Companies & Charities

These submissions are essentially about touting for business.

New Philanthropy Capital : This is a think tank on the charity sector. They are selling their model of a 'Theory of Change', concluding that the PbyR commissioning model may not be the best model. 100% success claim 'is indicative of an unhelpful evaluation model'. 100% turn around claim is 'too good to be true' and 'unhelpful to learning'. If success is 100% nothing needs to change does it? These are valid points.

Family Action : TFP suppliers to 7 LAs. They prefer a 'more nuanced' analysis of performance. We can bet they do. Their evaluation focuses on the visual 'family star' which uses subjective scales for several family factors. They provide 1 case study as an example. They tell us that 'the journey towards improvement is just as important as the end result'. No, it is not if the 'journey' ends in failure and a waste of money.

Joseph Rowntree Foundation : JRF have an impressive history including studies of poverty and the criminal justice system approach to the underclass and dysfunctional families. They call for an independent evaluation of the TFP (presumably being sceptical of any evaluation commissioned by government; the National Evaluation 2016 should reassure them). They support the basic TFP model : the key worker, the whole family approach, etc. They also suggest that the role of poverty should be properly addressed. Hear, hear! No doubt JRF would be happy to supply evaluation services to TFP phase 2.

Tavistock Relationships : They are plugging their services in training project key workers in 'couple' counselling on the grounds that relationship breakdown is a prominent feature of TF histories. Fair comment. No evidence given of efficacy.

Power To Change : This is a charity supporting community businesses. It believes the current measures of TFP impact are deeply flawed. It is offering a cheap system for small businesses (and LAs?) 'for providing reliable, transparent and comparable data'.

Academic Submissions

These are from people who have made formal studies of the TFP or related approaches to dysfunctional families. They include three inputs to the PAC from this author. He declared in his submission a personal interest: he is sole carer for his learning disabled son and stroke disabled wife and became interested in state interventions on vulnerable people because of direct experiences of the mistreatment of his son and of learning disabled and mentally ill friends.

City University of London :
(Dr. Matthew Barnes; Dept of Sociology; Mr. Andy Ross; Quant, Social Research & Consultancy)

Barnes and Ross look at the origin of the TF criteria in the Social Exclusion Task Force using the Families and Children Survey. This led to the infamous 120,000 TFs estimate. They note Cameron's equation of these families with criminal, ASB, work shy, rioters. Most importantly they demonstrate that as early as 2007 the Cabinet Office knew that youth crime and deprivation are only weakly linked. Only 10% of the 'multiply deprived' (TFP) family children were in trouble with the police or had been suspended or excluded from school.

The reader will recall my analyses of FIPs back to 1999 showed the same pattern and the NE 2016 confirmed it. Did the PAC understand this critical point? There is no sign of it.

Professor (retired) David Gregg : Before the 2016 PAC Inquiry this author wrote to the chair, Ms. Hillier, summarising the FIP -TFP failure evidence and enclosing his book 'Troubled Families', Green Man Books, 2015. As a result he was invited to make his short PAC submission. This was an early version of section 1.4 on the Wirral impacts and a summary of his FIP studies from 1999 to 2011. He concluded that all the FIPs and the TFP were ineffective, abusive and a waste of money.

After the PAC hearing in November 2016 he submitted a draft version of section 1.5 on his analysis of the National Evaluation 2016 impact results. This long piece was circulated to PAC members as 'background' according to the committee clerk, but not entered into the written record. It made the critical observation *that even if* the differences between TFP processed families and the matched control group *had* been statistically significant *only **a small percentage** of families showed any 'improvements' and on several measures, like crime /ASB, the results were **worse** for the TFP families.* If you accepted the Casey position that the programme impacts were real, the TFP made behaviour worse for some families.

Mr. Stephen Crossley :
(University of Durham/ University of Northumbria)

Crossley presented evidence from close observations of the TFP undertaken for his PhD project including work with LAs. He reviews the whole sad history of issues: the 120,000 families origins fiasco; the non-links to the 2011 riots; misrepresenting of the evidence supporting the FIP (TFP) model, ethical issues to family evidence collection in Casey's 'Listening To Families'; the falsity of the 'turn around' phrase; the misrepresentation of the families : health not crime dominates; discussions with LAs: misgivings on the TFP; 'data matching' to claim families turned around; pressure applied to LA officers on success, etc'; the suppression of the TFP National Evaluation from 2015. This is a very useful, compact, roundup which should have been as gold dust to the PAC.

Mr. Michael Lambert :
(University of Lancaster)

Lambert reviewed the long history of concepts equivalent to 'troubled families' and their treatment by state interventions.

He looks at 'problem families' from 1945 – 1974 and demonstrates remarkable similarities and state arguments to the TFs. These approaches were not evidence based. Outcomes historically were measured if at all, by small qualitative studies. The supposed family problems are painfully familiar: criminality, juvenile delinquency, truancy, illegitimate children, worklessness, *'subnormality'*, substance and alcohol abuse, low income …Interventions were focussed on 'tough love' including 'rehabilitation centres'. (This author adds, that these were revisited in the ASB FIP core units or 'ASBO Sin Bins' under Blair and the proposed centres for unmarried, under age, pregnant benefit recipients: Brown's 'Slag Hostels'.) After reviewing familiar interventions Lambert concludes **'The TFP has exactly repeated the failed steps of the past'**. So we know that the PAC *received written evidence of similar intervention failure* for the periods 1945 to 1974 and 1999 to 2011 in addition to the new NE 2016 material. The evidence appears to have had no substantive effect on the PAC.

Government Agencies

The National Audit Office : The NAO provided a purely factual description of the TFP and a useful, key events diary for the programme. It summarised for example the results for the 7 LA 'exemplar' study of cost savings which we analysed earlier. Given the NAO legislated role in 'advising' the PAC, as an expert group of analysts, it is surprising that **no** comments are made on the TFP and **no** opinions offered as to its value even though it also reviews the history, post the PAC 2014 Inquiry. It ends by commenting drily that the promised NE 2016 'has not been shared with the NAO'. The front page of the report carries the standard NAO mission statement:

'Our vision is to help the nation spend wisely'

The reader may feel there is a disconnect between the vision and delivery in the TFP fiasco.

The Youth Justice Board : They admit that they are 'not in a position to state whether the TFP is effective or not in meeting its aims'. They then tell us that some YOTs have received 'extra funding for prevention and diversion activities'. If the TFP was stopped some YOTs 'would suffer' as a result. This is at least an honest position: one of few in this scandal.

  Later in October 2016 two further written submissions were made by Jonathan Portes and the NIESR as responses to critical claims on their behaviour and professional conduct made by Dame Louise Casey at the hearing. We will examine them in context.

Written evidence from Jonathan Portes (in a personal capacity) ;
27th October 2016.

Written evidence from the National Institute of Economic & Social
Research; 26th October 2016.

Oral Evidence

Oral evidence was presented on 19th October 2016 by :

Dame Louise Casey CB , Director General, Casey Review Team,
DCLG.

Melanie Dawes CB, Permanent Secretary, DCLG.

Joe Tuke, Director, Troubled Families & Public Service Reform.

Despite the centrality of the TFP to the government's social policy to stop future riots, save communities devastated by 'neighbours from hell', to stop national moral decay, get the undeserving poor back into work...and reduce support costs by up to £9 billion, *no member of the government was called to the hearing or volunteered to appear.*

Where was the Eric Pickles, minister responsible for the TFP until the Cameron reshuffle? Where was Lord Bourne the current minister? He was busy telling the media online, a few days before the hearing, that

'We know that more than 116,000 of the families who participated in the first phase of the programme have seen significant improvements in their lives with children back in school, reduced youth crime and ASB , and adults holding down a job...we believe this programme has transformed the lives of thousands of families. The councils and front line staff who have put it into practice should be pleased with the work they have done. ...[I am] confident that the programme will save money for the tax payer.'

Did he *not know* that the independent NE 2016 had found *no significant and consistent impacts attributable to the TFP at all?* Had he not been briefed by his civil servants? His statement is straight from the Casey DCLG spin handbook. Perhaps his absence was wise. Westminster denial was rampant. A 'spokeswoman' for Theresa May allegedly said

'The work that's been done by the Government to look at the impact of the programme shows that these families have seen significant improvements in their lives.'

No it did not : it showed **zero impact** in all outcome areas as we examined in detail earlier. **Clearly the DCLG is not under the control of ministers but vice versa.** As we proceed the reader should also note the pernicious effect of there being no balancing voices in the hearing to respond, on the spot, to the false claims and evasions of the civil servants. The reader may also wonder *why* the National Evaluation team was not present to give evidence. Surely they are the experts? Or does the PAC consider such experts as mere hired hands? Or was there a fear that the experts might be able to *counter* the statements made by the civil service team? That might be embarrassing and the PAC could hardly ignore it…if it was on the record. Let's see how the PAC (mis)read the copious evidence of TFP failure.

1.7.4 PAC Conclusions & Commentary

The interested tax payer is recommended to read the full Inquiry text which is available on the PAC site. The exchanges between PAC members and the civil servants are very enlightening as the latter struggle to defend and sometimes abandon their former public positions on the TFP. Of particular note is the performance of Louise Casey who gives little ground despite the National Evaluation evidence and accuses various parties of misleading the media and the PAC. The reader will enjoy the accuseds' robust responses which decimate Casey's testimony. **Just imagine if this evidence had been given at the hearing itself!** Sadly these late inputs seem to have had no effect on the PAC who seem to accept her misdirection sufficiently *to leave open the question* of the TFP's value for money: the case is just not proven yet, OK? Watch out also for the civil servants subtly shifting blame for some of the excesses of TFP presentation onto the notably absent and defunct politicians including Pickles and Cameron.

Conclusion 1 : The DCLG's delayed publication of the evaluation of The TFP was unacceptable.

The committee point out forcefully that the original publication date for the evaluation was 2014 but the PAC only received the report (after strong lobbying) on 17th October 2016. The delay 'gave a bad impression' of the DCLG's 'openness.' The committee spent much time focussing on why 'they' had been so inconvenienced, in fact via 35 questions. After all this questioning the chair was not sanguine.

Q35 Meg Hillier: 'OK. We're not going to get very far…Your answers have been, I have to say, *a bit evasive*, so I wonder who you are protecting from all this…are you protecting your Department or your Minister?'

Melanie Dawes (Permanent Secretary, DCLG) : 'No, I don't think so. I'm sure Louise will want to come in...'

Dame Louise Casey : 'The process was...that they [the NISER] had to take the [LA] information in-house...when they looked at the information they found things like they had put three LA's flawed data through their system. They accepted it: the department did not. They ended up having to go to the University of Cambridge ...and say is this OK? ...a lot of comment and extraordinary negative publicity in the last few days has been based on that one report.'...one element of a 700 page report says the TFP has no impact. I for one do not believe that is true...'

Q37 Chair : 'Were you trying to suppress that element of the report?

Melanie Dawes : No, we weren't...

Of course the NIESR impact study on the administrative study along with the *independent study* on the family survey data *was the heart of the evaluation*: the other reports were either technical adjuncts or presented anecdotal and subjective evidence. Casey with Dawes approval, is blaming the NIESR and *their professional failure* for the publication delay...*and so undermining their results.* The NIESR October 26th 2016 PAC submission answers these charges definitively. Here is a summary:

1. LA data cleaning commenced in January 2015. A full draft report went to the DCLG on 28th July 2015.*The main findings have not changed since that draft.*

2. In response to DCLG queries they reworked the results excluding data from 3 suspect LAs. *Their key finding of a lack of significant and systematic impact of the TFP **did not change before or after** this data removal.*

3. The *evaluation team suggested to the DCLG sending the report for external review* in Spring 2016 for reassurance on the data and analysis. Cambridge and Surrey were approached by the DCLG. They confirmed that the methodology and analysis 'was sound'. Partial data was a concern but not the analysis. *The review did not change the analysis nor the key findings of the findings.*

4. A near final draft was sent to the DCLG in June 2016. The report emphasised that while the data was imperfect *there was no reason to believe the results were statistically biased. They passed various*

reliability checks. The results agree closely with the independent
family survey data analysis.

The reader can see that Casey's charges are unfounded. The submission also points out that Casey's claim (Q52 and Q127) that the NIESR 'had not put out any caveats in the public domain' and 'misrepresented their own research' is false. They attach their press release (Annex A) issued as the report was published. It includes the caveats also in the Executive Summary of the NE report. *This text had been explicitly agreed with the DCLG.* Jonathan Portes separately provided written evidence that he had also put clear caveats in the blog criticised by Casey.

The attempt by Dawes and Casey to shift the blame for the NE publishing delay is surely unacceptable. **Yes, the reports were suppressed**.

Conclusion 2: The Department's evaluation of the TFP was unable to find consistent evidence that it had any significant impact AT THIS STAGE.

One suspects that the committee has been successfully sidetracked here into criticising the evaluation methodology instead of acting on its clear results (via the testimony of Casey et al). They begin their conclusion by accepting the DCLG and LAs argument that the claimed successful spreading of 'good practice' and 'transformed' ways of working was a preeminent result. *They fail to comment on the NE Synthesis Report negative comments on this*. Next they report on the claim that the 'confidence and attitudes' of the families had significantly improved. This is true but only for ~5% of families as we showed and it was based on *subjective* views of the families *under conditions of duress*. The author's November PAC submission circulated to the committee, stressed these points. The **zero impact** on families over the full range of government target outcomes is *relegated to third place and posed as a methodology issue*. Where did these views come from? Casey's response to Q146 and Dawes response to Q147.

Dame Louise Casey : 'Did we oversell and under-deliver? …no. Did we change the lives of 116,000 families? Yes, we did. …*LAs and their colleagues across the country sorted them out…nobody disputes the fact that, actually, the impact on those families was monumental*…what we can't prove is that the NIESR research says that you can't attribute all of those things to the TFP – *you can't not attribute them, either*…'

Actually the 116,000, 99% family turn around is strongly disputed …and doubted by the PAC itself…and the impacts are **zero** in both the NIESR

and family survey analyses: and the last sentence is nonsense.
The chair then calls on Melanie Dawes.

Q147 : 'Ms Dawes on the basis of the evaluations and everything you have seen, should the programme continue?'

Melanie Dawes : ' Yes, I believe it should. ...the evaluation is very clear about the *transformation that has already been achieved in how local authorities ...are working.* It is clear there are *statistically significant improvements in how families feel about their circumstances...*
Those things for me are very compelling results to have achieved *in addition to the outcomes that have come through the PbyR mechanism* ...Do we need to improve and adapt? Yes we do...'

PAC Conclusion 2 follows *exactly* this pattern of views: the value is in LA practices, subjective family feelings, things will improve...next time we will prove it works. The astonishing thing is the bloody obvious point that LA 'system transformation' and 'feeling better' is nice, but **demonstrably ineffective** for the purposes of eliminating actual deep seated family problems ...and support costs.

The PAC appears to have downgraded the central, government outcome objectives for the TFP in judging it.

Having huffed and puffed a bit, its conclusions seem to simply follow, *exactly*, the DCLG Permanent Secretary's view. Is this acceptable?

The author is surprised that having finally reviewed the National Evaluation 2016 the NAO analysts ***did not correct*** the committees misunderstanding (or arguably, misrepresentation) of the findings. The committee appears to be bending over backwards to find reasons for phase 2 to continue. This misdirection of the committee was helped by the DCLG's clever position that they would not be able to 'evidence a statistically significant impact of the programme in future'...so that doesn't matter really, surely? This is *not* a methodology issue, but rather that the clear evidence shows *there is no impact*. Notice the words in the conclusion : *'at this stage'*. The committee's assumption appears to be that somehow phase 2 will be better. **It will not be. It cannot be.**

Conclusion 3 : The PbyR framework led to some councils attempting to move families through the programme quickly, potentially at the expense of reduced quality of support.

The committee realised that council actions were driven by the bounty system to recruit families and get the money in. There was a further incentive to claim the turn around bonus as quickly as possible and move on. They recognised that some LAs *falsely* used data mapping to identify families already turned around by other means, who could be claimed under the TFP scheme. This is surely a case of *fraudulent misuse of public funds* but it is not stressed in the above conclusion 3 summary.

Should not the guilty LAs be pursued legally? Should there not be a **public inquiry** into what instructions from the DCLG allowed a large deviation from the initial success criteria rules in the PbyR scheme? As we saw this is the only way to explain the 132 out of 152 LA 100% turn around claims. The PAC should also have noted that in 2014, the first PAC Inquiry instruction not to miss the government 'turn around' target may have had unforeseen consequences: fraud.

Conclusion 4: the terminology used by the Department overstated the success of the TFP in transforming the lives of families.

They conclude the 99% turn around claim was unsupportable. The committee note that 'the implication of turn around was misleading as the term was only indicative of achieving short-term outcomes under the programme rather than representing long-term sustainable change...' This is perfectly true. However it (accidentally?) misses the point that duration of improvement is not the only or the key issue. **The key government targets were missed**. Only 11% of families gained an adult in employment according to the DCLG statistics. ~80% were on out of work benefits at the start. The claimed 89% national turn around in crime / ASB / education is simply false. Most improvement related to *reduced truancy* not reduced crime. To see the falsity of the claim simply note again that ~ 90% of family individuals were not involved in crime or ASB at project entry. *If the committee had read my October submission this would be obvious.* Perhaps they did.

The PAC members did get to the bottom of how the 100% turn around claim arose. It is worth repeating.

Q67 : Meg Hillier (Chair)

'You had a nearly 100% success rate.'

Melanie Dawes (DCLG Permanent Secretary):

'In fact *we never said that.* LAs worked with more families than that…'

Melanie has forgotten the press releases and TFP outcome tables published on the DCLG website which show a 99% turn around rate and the formal HoC statement by her minister, Mr.(now Sir) Eric Pickles in March 2015, bragging of his TFP success. We also note **Q104** from a puzzled Mr. Chris Evans MP.

'I am looking at para. 1.21 which says "a total of 116,654 families eligible for the programme had met the criterion" of reducing crime…that seems a massive figure. You have helped 116,654 out of 117,910 families you identified [98.93%]. Where does that figure come from? To be honest if that is what you have turned around, you should be running every single government department.'

Note the rather dry final comment. The answer from Dame Louise Casey CB was :

'It was suggested in the financial framework that that local authorities reached more families, although we would not pay for them, in order both to reach that and as part of a system of change… our sense is that people did more in order to meet that…We need to be clear: we know that 116,654 families basically had their lives changed by the programme according to the payment by results system. That is a **99%** success rate.'

So Dame Louise is contradicting her then boss, Melanie Dawes, and still claiming a 99% turn around success rate based on the miraculous PbyR data which as we saw defies the laws of probability.

More importantly, the NE 2016 NIESR analysis of the administrative data *and* the family survey data showed clearly **no significant differences** in crime and employment outcomes for the TFP processed families and the control group. Also, significant or not, **the differences were tiny,** in most cases, of the order of a few percent of families. This is obvious from the National Evaluation 2016 Synthesis Report and was highlighted in the author's November PAC submission circulated to the committee as 'background' material.

The chair obviously also did not understand the issue of control groups.

Q149 : 'How realistic was it to secure a proper realistic comparative group? Given that …most of them will be having some intervention, even if just through the GP or whatever? Was that a big issue in measuring it?'

Committee members had obviously not had the time to read the technical appendices and had to rely on Dawes since no NE experts were called.

Melanie Dawes: '*We did not have a control group*…we looked at the *national administrative work*. The researchers looked at families who had similar characteristics to those who were in the TFP, but it was an estimate, so it was subject to *that level of uncertainty*…I think the problem will be with us throughout this work.'

This is both roughly true and deeply misleading. Dawes is cleverly casting doubt on work she signed off on. There *was* a control group: a matched comparison group. The technical matching of the comparison group in the NIESR analysis was immaculate, thorough and fully reported. The analysts computed and reported the level of uncertainty for each of the estimates of difference between the TFP families and the matched comparison group. We have pointed out repeatedly that *the differences (even if significant), positive and negative, were small* : of the order of a few percent of families.

If the differences had been much bigger and in one direction, say the positive direction, there would be room for debate. They were not. Dawes repeatedly gave the impression that this kind of control group procedure was an innovation in policy assessment. As commentators such as Portes and the NIESR pointed out, the randomised controlled trial is the long recognised standard approach to such analysis.

Q143 Dawes : 'So the TFP tried to measure itself by a much higher bar than is usual in social policy…What we are not able to say definitively, with statistical certainty, is that it [a positive improvement] would not have happened anyway. *No other programme has asked itself that question, of course: we haven't been able to answer it either.*'

This is nonsense…the question *has* been answered for the TFP. The NIESR submission to the PAC of 26th October 2016 answers the other false claims robustly.

'**This is incorrect**…The question of whether a programme has achieved a statistically significant, robust net impact with respect to the *counterfactual is the* **standard question** *that almost any quantitative evaluation of a social policy programme asks.*'

The author refers the reader to section 2 and 4 where successive FIP evaluation teams plead with successive governments to set up control groups and pursue long term longitudinal studies.

The NIESR then continues.

'For example the early evaluation of the labour market impacts of Universal Credit adopted a very similar (propensity score matching) methodology to that used in the TFP evaluation and found (a small but significant) positive net or "attributable" impact. There are numerous similar examples across the social policy field, showing both positive net impacts and, *as with this evaluation, no net impact.*'

The *net zero impact is just that*, not a limitation of a familiar, standard methodology. Dawes also surely deliberately failed to mention the independent family survey analysis which reported the same *zero impact* results as the NIESR.

The NIESR submission also points out that the original plan for a total programme cost-benefit analysis was dropped when the *zero impact* results emerged. The 67 LA sample analysis *had already showed how small the net savings were,* even bending over backwards with the data, even if those savings *had been attributable* to the TFP. **Dawes failed to remind the committee of this critical material.** It was **not** in the NE 2016 package.

Failing PAC recognition of all of the above issues the NAO advisors *must* have understood the Synthesis Report and technical report results. Why did they not explain their significance to the PAC? *If they did why is it not reflected in the PAC conclusions? There were **two months** to correct any committee misconceptions about the evidence before the PAC response was published.*

In conclusion 4 the PAC focuses on the *misdemeanou*r of 'misleading terminology' and ignores the *major felony* of the totally false 99% claim and the attempted cover up and fudging of TFP failure to deliver the key government targets under the PbyR scheme *and* on all the other family outcomes including health, wellbeing and family stability.

Conclusion 5: the Department has not demonstrated that the Programme has provided genuine financial savings.

They conclude the £1.2 billion savings claim is 'an overestimate'. This is true. It 'does not take into the account' the cost of delivering the TFP. This is also true. The committee also (I think) acknowledges that the Pickles number did not take into account 'what could be attributed' to the TFP. This presumably is referring indirectly to the NE 2016 finding of **zero**

impact on family outcomes which directly translates into **zero savings** attributable to the TFP…but for some reason this is not stated explicitly. Surely this is the key point: **if there are no savings why proceed with TFP phase 2 at a cost of a further ~£1 billion up to 2020?**

Under questioning Dawes claimed

'some really good results' adding, far too late (**Q107**)

'…but we don't want to over claim it…**We are certainly not claiming any definitive cost savings from the programme.'**

Er? Where is the £9 billion potential savings used by Eric Pickles and PM Cameron (along with an end to rioting, gangs and British moral decay) to justify the TFP phase 1 in 2012? Where is the **£1.2 billion** delivered 'savings' reported by Pickles to the HoC on 10th March 2015? How can we account for Louise Casey's remarkable claim at the PAC inquiry that (**Q100**)

'But it [The TFP] is value for money writ large, Chairman.'

Despite all this the PAC conclusion 5 *mildly* describes DCLG claims as an 'overestimate'. **Why conclude this when Dawes now says the DCLG 'are not claiming ANY definitive savings' from the TFP?**

The PAC accepts that the DCLG is 'working' to improve its cost saving *estimation* methods so *assuming* that another method may be able to find '*a better approximation* of its financial benefits'. **A better approximation of zero is still zero.** The PAC position is nonsense.

The PAC seems to have accepted the Casey, hand waving, anecdotal assurance that the TFP is 'honest to God', 'value for money writ large' and it's just a matter of finding the evidence. This cannot be the right position can it? Well conclusion 5 ends with

'Although these claimed net savings cannot be attributed to the programme directly, *it also cannot be proven* that the programme has had no financial benefit.'

This is rubbish. **Zero impact means zero benefit**. It is difficult to know where to start. The PAC position is logically identical to the argument that says equal time should be given in school science classes to creationism and evolution.

One is based on subjective faith, fanaticism and misdirection and the other on objective scientific evidence. Faith, while deserving respect, should have no place in the science classroom *nor in state policy evaluation.*

The author would add that control groups are central to clinical trials of new medical treatments. If NICE sees a statistically insignificant *and tiny difference* between the treatment group and control group in patient outcomes **it rejects the treatment**. It does not say to the Big Pharma company pushing a scandalously expensive *and* useless nostrum: Oh well, never mind, *we accept also that the trial cannot prove that your treatment has no benefit so we will approve it...*maybe it will work next time! This is what the PAC is saying to Big Government about the TFP.

We are repeatedly told that modern government is committed to evidence based policy' (while Casey detests it). So we finally get *definitive evidence* in the NE 2016 on a key social policy and *it is rejected by the parliamentary watchdog!* **One last time**: the essence of the national evaluation is that the family impact assessment based on national administrative data and the *independent* family survey data shows four things.

1. Most of the differences between the TFP processed families and the matched control groups families, across all the outcomes defined by the DCLG as relevant, are not statistically significant. This means that in these cases *those differences cannot be attributed to the TFP interventions*. That is certain.

2. Most of the differences both positive and negative are tiny anyway. They typically involve less than **10%** of families. Even if all the *positive* differences and none of the *negative* differences were attributable to the TFP they could save very little money.

3. A few differences *are* significant, notably in a few measures of family attitudes and confidence from the family survey, something the PAC highlighted as important. However they are tiny. Take an example from section 1.5.2: 'I know how to keep my family on track'. The subjective view of processed TFP family carers was that 96% of them agreed. The subjective view of the unprocessed control group carers was that 91% of them agreed with the above. The positive difference you *could* attribute to the TFP was in just **5%** of families. However it was in the *interest* of both groups to claim to be in control to avoid more intervention in the already processed TFP families and to avoid future intervention in the control group (already under the attention of the authorities).

The opinions were given under duress. Just as significant and absolutely clear from the NE: there were **no** differences in control related outcomes on objective measures like being in debt, managing rent arrears, being workless, health problems, family relationships, etc, etc…

The author went into these arguments carefully in his November 2016 submission to the PAC analysing all the National Evaluation impact results and explaining the implications.

4. Suppose further refinements of the impact measurement and savings estimation systems are made. What could be the impact? Let's take crime reduction, a key TFP target. The NE looked at 'adults with an offence resulting in a caution or conviction'. It found non-significant but measurable differences between TFP families and the control group. Let's assume the DCLG improved system, the PAC wants, makes these differences significant. The TFP processed group had 8.7% of families with an offence. The control group had 7.8% of families with an offence. We would conclude that *crime had increased as a result of the TFP* in 0.9% of families! The TFP causes crime. There are other 'bad' results of this kind.

More to the point in countering the PAC position, notice for example that **92%** of *all* of these targeted 'troubled families' have *not* committed an offence. The *maximum potential* for reducing the costs of crime is small from the beginning and the *claimed* impact of the TFP is a smaller proportion still.

The PAC says that with current evidence it *'cannot be proven that TFP has no financial benefit'*. If the above evidence is insufficient let us turn to the most recent DCLG savings estimation exercise *which for some reason the PAC Inquiry has not taken into account.*

In section 1.6 we analysed the results from 'LA Data on Costs & Fiscal Benefits of the TFP' based on a sample of 67 LAs. It was based on up to mid 2015 data but not released until October 2016. **It is referenced on the DCLG website alongside the National Evaluation 2016 reports.** Should not this have been pointed out to the PAC? Or did they know? The 67 LA exercise was also reported in the excellent history of the TFP published by the HoC Library (CBP 07585, 9th of August 2016).

We learn that the gross saving per family is £7.05K per annum. The net saving is £3.7K. For 117,910 families processed in phase 1 this is £436 million per annum. This is 36% of Pickles announced saving. But the cost of the TFP officially was £448 million (although actual cost is likely over £500 million). **So we see that the cost was at minimum £448 million and the benefit at most £436 million.** Forgive this naïve old scientist but isn't the cost of the TFP larger than the benefit? (There is no evidence that such a gross saving will be sustained over time. The FIP evidence speaks for rapid decay. Recall also that in reality the evidence actually shows a zero impact and therefore zero saving.)

Isn't the benefit / cost ratio **0.97** at best? The idea that 'more work' with the LAs will make the result better is *fantasy*. Every successive LA exercise has led to a lower net cost saving estimate despite the 100% turn around claim.

The author also looked at troubled families costs and his detailed analysis estimated that the *removal of all bad behaviour and lifestyle choices could **in principle** save gross £542 million per annum or £4,157 per family* . This compares with the official TFP cost for a turned around family of £4K and the probable total cost of £4,600. However if we take off the *claimed* average LA cost of £3.35K this leaves a net saving of 4,157 – 3,350 = £807 per family. The benefit / cost ratio is then **0.24**. But the NE 2016 showed no impact on 'bad' behaviours like crime and the 11% gaining a job *cannot be attributed* to the TFP anyway so this is an *upper* limit.

The PAC already has the answer on fiscal benefit : it is less than the TFP cost on the DCLG's own data and latest analysis and strictly speaking zero. Why then is the TFP phase 2 being allowed to proceed with the agreement of the PAC?

The PAC was quick to put a tough spin on its Inquiry Report in the media. Meg Hillier sounded suitably harsh

'Government officials might be inclined to consider our comments on the *delay* in publishing its troubled families evaluation as a slap on the wrist about Whitehall bureaucracy. Let me assure them that given the ambitions for this programme, the implications for families and the significant sums of money invested, it is far more serious than that. *The Department has undermined any achievements the Government might legitimately claim for its overall work in this area...*

But it is particularly important with *a new initiative* that there is transparency so that the government can *learn and adapt the programme*….a tick in a box to meet a prime ministerial target is no substitute for a lasting solution to difficulties that may take years to properly address…we would also question the suitability of the PbyR model which similarly risks incentivising quantity over quality.'

Notice that the TFP is described as a *'new initiative'* despite 15 years of ~60 very similar, organisationally superior, FIPs, which also failed. The PAC is also *assuming* that there *are* achievements 'to legitimately claim'…its just that the Department messed up in its reporting.

The PAC conclusion is that there is still scope for the programme to *'learn and adapt'*. If the PAC had understood the evidence they would know **there is not**. So what is their answer?

'The Department has now committed to providing parliament with an annual report of progress with the TFP starting in March next year. For this to be meaningful *government must be far clearer about the benefits that can be directly attributed to the public investment in it.* **Only then can parliament and others properly assess the value-for-money of this programme** and its merits as a model to bring about lasting change in the lives of those families it is intended to support.'

This statement confirms that the PAC has not understood the evidence. They also ignore what Dawes told them explicitly at **Q149.**

'I think the problem [of proving attribution] will be with us throughout this work.'

Reporting annually with data that **will not,** according to Dawes, prove attributable results is surely useless? If so, *given the massive evidence of failure on all levels,* why proceed with phase 2 at the further cost of ~1£ billion to 2020? God knows.

But the alert reader might recall the MPs from all parties leaping to their feet in March 2015, as Pickles puffed his 'remarkable success', to claim some of the credit for the TFP. As Hilary Benn said: we [New Labour] invented family intervention. Going back a year the reader may also recall Margaret Hodge (Labour), PAC chair, awarding Louise Casey and the TFP team their civil service awards for best policy, etc. As Hodge said :

'she[Casey] has support across the political system.'

The whole of the Westminster club **backed** the TFP on flimsy, over blown evidence and rhetoric. The reader might conclude that politically it was too embarrassing, cross-party, to admit a monumental mistake and stop the phase 2 programme. Better to waste another 1£ billion. Besides if we try to take the committed money off the LAs now we might have a rebellion...they might start telling the media the *whole* truth about the TFP and the DCLG! That we must avoid...for the greater good.

The reader may feel, considering all the evidence we have examined together, that what is needed is a Public Inquiry to fathom just what is going on here. The author can only agree.

1.8   CONCLUSIONS & RECCOMMENDATIONS

' If the misery of the poor is caused not by the laws of nature but by our institutions, great is our sin.'

Charles Darwin

1.8.1 Summary

Very briefly: we have showed the reader that this family intervention programme is **fraudulent and abusive** on every level.

- In the false characterisation of the families as criminal, addicted and irresponsible, justifying their harsh treatment and a wider government attack on welfare benefits for the underclass.

- In attributing the poverty of the families to a feckless reluctance to work and misuse of resources through bad 'lifestyle choices'.

- In ignoring the remarkably high levels of 'limiting, long standing mental and physical illness and disabilities' in the families as a key cause of 'problems'.75% of families are affected. 52% of the families have children who are SEN or have other special needs. 45% of the families have an adult with a mental illness...and so on.

- In subjecting mentally and physically ill and disabled families to a regime of 'tough sanctions' and threats to force co-operation on the grounds that their problems were self-imposed and that such 'support' will help them 'turn their lives around'.

- In exaggerating by a factor of at least **3.5 X** the cost of the TFP targeted families and implying huge savings could be made to justify the programme. It was claimed families cost: £9 billion per annum by Eric Pickles, David Cameron, et al in 2011.

- In 2013 a larger sample of LAs showed the gross cost was ~£2.7 billion per annum. The author's blind estimate based on earlier FIP family data and TFP 2013 data but DCLG claimed unit costs found a maximum possible cost of £2.56 billion gross.

- In exaggerating by a factor of **16 X** the *potential* cost reduction accessible by eliminating the 'bad behaviours' and 'lifestyle choices' of the families. Most costs related to poverty and health. The maximum possible saving potential was ~£542 million gross based on government data and assumptions available in 2011.

- In claiming by 2015 that the TFP had 'saved' **£1.2 billion** per annum on the basis of small, *biased* samples of local authority results and in failing to identify this as a *gross saving before TFP costs*. The public claim was made when it was already known that the (suppressed) National Evaluation had proved **zero** family outcomes impact attributable to the TFP.

- In not drawing attention of parliament to then available savings exercises which contradicted the above DCLG claims. The author calculated a total cost (reactive + targeted) of 120,000 families as £2.56 billion per annum compared with Cameron's £9 billion. This is £21,330 per family compared with the latest LA data £26,700 estimate. Of this 21% could be generously attributed to 'bad behaviour and lifestyle choices' or £542 million (**£4,157 per family**). This is the *saving potential for* removing *all* family 'bad behaviour'. It is **6%** of Cameron's £9 billion. It compares with the latest **£7,050** DCLG gross savings claim and the **£3,700 net savings claim.** The £7K gross savings estimate is still inflated I believe, based on experience of the cost assumptions used in the first £9 billion exercise which went on to 'inform' the official cost calculators.

- If we take the author's potential saving of ~£4.16K and the official average LA cost we get 4.16 – 3.35 = **£0.81K** per family or a saving of **£95.5 million** per annum compared with Pickles **£1.2 billion** claim to the House of Commons in March 2015. That is **8%** of his claim. As Pickles said then, measuring outcomes is 'notoriously difficult' and we can sympathise…but an error factor of 12.6 X? You have to work hard at it to be so wrong.

- In claiming that **99%** of the families had been 'turned around', i.e. cured of their dysfunctional behaviour, by the TFP, when the government sponsored National Evaluation (available in 2015) had demonstrated **no statistically significant impacts** on family status across *all* outcome performance measures including the PbyR outcomes. The measured differences between the TFP families and a matched control group, significant or not, affected typically *a few percent of families.* The national 99% claim was based on an unacceptable manipulation of LA results by relaxing the original success criteria and rules and by including families treated by other means outside the TFP phase 1 scheme. 132 LAs out of 152 claimed perfect , 100% family 'turn rounds'. This was achieved by taking the (difficult to fiddle) gains in employment (~11 % on average but very variable across LAs) and subtracting from 100% to get the local 'crime/ ASB /education' turn round number submitted to the DCLG for bounty payment. Other wise we must assume **a statistical miracle** to explain the 132 LA, 100% results! Even stranger the National Evaluation tells us that on various measures *~90% of TFs were not involved in crime or ASB at project entry.* The 89% 'crime' turn around claim really is a miracle!

Strictly speaking even the above recent, much smaller cost savings claimed from the 67 LA data exercise and the even smaller savings estimated by the author, cannot be attributed to the TFP interventions.

The bottom line is that the TFP phase 2 outcome will be the same as phase 1…zero. It should be stopped now, including spending on LA 'systems transformation', and the money transferred immediately into intensive, targeted medical support for the 75% of families who need it plus additional spending in school mental health support for the 52% of families with SEN and other special needs children. We should do this because the families are in need.

Any ministerial spin that this will make the families 'less dysfunctional' or less costly to society should be punished severely. The small percentage of families who are a danger to the public should be dealt with through the NHS psychiatric services and / or the criminal justice system.

- So we come to the guardians of the public purse, *'the queen of select committees'* : the Public Accounts Committee. We examined the TFP Inquiries of 2014 and 2016.

- In 2014 the PAC expressed concern that the TFP phase 1 was falling behind schedule and must speed up. It was on first name terms with Dame Louise Casey who gave her usual barnstorming presentation. Things could not have been too bad though since in 2015 the PAC chair, Margaret Hodge MP, personally awarded Casey the PAC civil service prize for 2015. Her TFP team also won a policy prize. Hodge noted that Casey 'has support across the political system' so setting the context for the 2016 PAC Inquiry.

- In October 2016 the PAC led by Meg Hillier MP grilled Louise Casey and Melanie Dawes, Permanent Secretary at the DCLG. **No minister was present. Nobody from the National Evaluation team was called to give evidence.** After the hearing Jonathan Portes and the NIESR made written submissions which strongly refuted the Casey –Dawes evidence. This author in November submitted a detailed commentary explaining the implications of the impact analyses in the Synthesis Report to counter Casey's grossly misleading Inquiry claims. It was circulated to the committee but not listed as written evidence. I gave a voluntary undertaking not to publish my analyses until after the PAC report was published.

The Inquiry was called because media leaks of the long delayed TFP National Evaluation written in 2015 claimed (correctly) that the TFP had achieved *no significant impacts on the families*. The committee had just two days to absorb over 700 pages and 7 NE reports. There were also many pages of written submissions from other interested parties provided in the few weeks before the inquiry. The PAC were critical of several aspects of the programme but nevertheless they allowed TFP phase 2 to continue at a cost of ~1£ billion (2015 – 2020).

The author concluded that they had not had time to absorb and understand the technical evidence before the hearing and had been misled by the civil service testimony which was not balanced by other views. We can only sympathise. ***The result was that the PAC closely followed the civil service interpretation of the situation.*** However the head of the National Audit Office is a permanent member of the PAC. There was a two month period after the hearings and before the PAC report was issued. The NAO presumably has the technical skills to correct misunderstanding of the evidence by committee members. *Either* this did not happen *or* political considerations trumped the facts. We saw that the TFP (and Casey) had strong cross-party support.

To stop phase 2 would surely be embarrassing… and dangerous if the 152 LAs, already receiving funding, cried foul.

The TFP national evaluation involved a number of technical and statistical issues clearly unfamiliar to the PAC but now standard in socio-medical intervention policy evaluation . Such issues will become more and more common place in policy assessment. The reader may feel after reviewing all we have considered here that the time has come to take **investigations** of major, costly social policy interventions out of the hands of MPs deeply embedded in the Westminster –Whitehall system.

Surely an independent major programme evaluation system is long overdue? We do not have and could not have a committee of MPs playing the investigatory role now played by NICE in medical treatment evaluation. Nobody would accept that. Why accept such a set up for major social intervention programmes?

We need a system outside the Westminster-Whitehall village staffed with the appropriate experts familiar with modern evaluation practice and reporting back transparently to parliament AND the public, openly and simultaneously.

Final spending decisions, contrary to the independent analysis and evidence, should be justified by a designated minister, formally and in a way easily accessible to the public.

Just consider for a moment : the PAC, according to their own web page, holds an average of 46 hearings per annum and publishes ~42 reports. We are talking about typically complex programmes costing billions of pounds. Can the PAC really do an in depth job at a rate of 0.9 hearings per week? Or 1.05 per week allowing for holidays? *Or perhaps an 'in depth job' is not the aim?* After all the site tells us proudly that, according to Lord Hennessy, the PAC

'by its very existence exerted a cleansing effect on government departments.'

Well that may have been true in 1857 but now, in 2016? For a start the scale of Whitehall bureaucracy and the range and complexity of state spending has hugely expanded. The author suggests we are in the same position here as we were over MPs expenses. Who will guard us from the guardians?

In the TFP case we also appear to be dealing with huge sums of public money disappearing into the void under false pretences. The fact that spending departments are allowed to make their own rules and bend them is not an excuse when the public is repeatedly misled. **Surely there needs to be the possibility of legal redress for serious misconduct in public office?** The author suggests that this will never happen under the current 'embedded system' run by MPs.

1.8.2 Helping The Troubled Families: It's Health Stupid!

The author was originally motivated to get involved in these issues by the state neglect and active mistreatment of those called 'Dysfunctional' or 'Antisocial' or 'Chaotic' or 'Troubled' families. The author is not a Christian, despite the dedication of this book, but looking at the treatment of the poor, chronically ill and disabled in this country it is hard not to believe in Evil. As the sole carer for a learning disabled son, now nearing forty, and having helped his disabled friends from time to time, and having seen the distress of mentally impaired friends trying to get meaningful help from the state…while being pursued by the DWP and other agencies such as the criminal justice system…he has seen the Noonday Devil face to face …like many family carers.

If the reader, particularly the politician or civil servant, thinks this is overly melodramatic consider this fact : *one in four of us will experience a serious mental health issue at some point* .For the average size family it is only a matter of time. Think about that.

The middle class reader may think he is immune from state abuse. I sincerely hope that he never has to test that false assumption. But imagine how much worse it is for a mentally ill or low IQ mother, struggling with disabled children and subsisting on state benefits. She is told by British Prime Ministers that her children are 'menaces to

183

society' and that she is a drug crazed, antisocial criminal, ruining her community. If you live on ESA, income support, housing benefit, etc; if you cannot work for a good reason, that is what your country thinks of you: in fact you are a 'useless mouth'. We pretend that disability and poverty are 'lifestyle choices'. *Great* Britain will not gas you or sterilise your children, well not yet, but it will despise, denigrate and humiliate you. It will make you suffer for your benefits and drive some of you to suicide…the final solution for state cost saving. If the reader thinks I am exaggerating please scan through Appendix S1.

But every social intervention based on the 'useless mouth', moral degeneracy model, *which is not challenged* , brings us closer to the next Holocaust. The author has studied the lead up to that last eugenic abomination. What is striking is that the Nazi race politics rhetoric seems *less denigrating* of the disabled 'useless mouths' than that used by current British politicians. Hitler, like most of Europe and the USA, initially favoured sterilisation. The Nazi focus was on the *waste* of Reich economic resources and eventually gassing the disabled was cheaper. There was nothing personal in it. The real venom and studied cruelty was reserved for the Jews and political enemies.

Very well, if the TFP has failed what can we do? My outline answer was given above: divert the money to deal with the real issue: treating mental and physical illness and disability via specialist medical support and remedial schooling. Also look very closely at what we do with the lowest IQ quintile of the population in a post – industrial world requiring fewer low skilled workers and increasing automation. The question is much wider than the 'bottom' 120,000 troubled families. Whatever you do, do not *expect* to save money: expect, perhaps, to relieve some suffering and distress.

The author is not a politician so he cannot claim to be able to 'magic' a detailed Panglossian solution out of thin air... the best of all possible policies with a miraculous 100% 'turn around'. If the reader wants to know more of what lies behind his outline proposal, please go on and read section 3 of this book which looks at the genetic and environmental causes of family problems, including poor nutrition.

As for the TFP, FIPs and similar schemes, we can rescue a few things. For a family of low social competency and mental capacity and with multiple problems, the concept of having one key worker to *analyse needs* and *organise support* from various agencies is surely sensible.

I was poor so you made me poorer. I was disabled so you called me a benefit cheat. I could not find work so you called me a scrounger. My child was hungry so you called me a bad parent. My mind was broken so you made me a criminal.

The anecdotal reports of many families welcoming such support cannot be dismissed. Several years ago looking at the FIP evaluations the author was struck by evidence that the projects had made an impact in one area: in easing school behaviour problems (see section 4.3).Tellingly, this did not involve parenting classes or threatening children, but involved the key worker acting as *an advocate* for the family, explaining, for example, the unrecognised mental health problems of the child. This brings us back to my focus: many schools did not have even one teacher with formal training in handling mental health problems and learning disability. That is why 2/3 of suspensions / exclusions involve such pupils…including our TF children.

Here is the key point: the *impact* of the key worker for the large majority of 'troubled families' who have serious health problems *will be minor* **if that worker, for all the flim flam about inter-agency working, cannot access NHS or other special resources.** This problem loomed large in *every* FIP programme evaluation since 1999. In the NE 2016 Synthesis Report we saw the identical comments. There was

'limited evidence for the efficacy of the interventions offered to families'

Surely this opinion is of central importance given that according to the DCLG '99% of the families were turned around'. In practice the

'therapeutic dimensions' of the programme (mental health, DA / DV and parenting) were 'not always clearly defined'

The report adds specifically

'there appeared to be little progress in addressing the health issues for families'

But remember 75% had a limiting, long standing illness or disability. 45% had an adult with a mental health problem. 52% had children with an SEN statement or other special needs. 60% of families were not in work because of disability.

There you have it, in a simple sequence: poor health, worklessness, poverty …and yes, for some mentally impaired youths, a short pathway into a criminal justice system notoriously unable to cope with mental health and disability issues. The prevalence of general learning disability in young offenders is **9X** that in the 'normal' population. (The death rate for mentally impaired prisoners is also **9X** 'normal' prisoners). One can only imagine the frustration of the well meaning key worker unable to get specialist medical help in such *almost universal* family circumstances.

How can this happen? Two reasons : firstly mental health / disability medical resources are extremely tight for the *general* population and in decline. See section 1.8.3. Secondly could it be there is a reluctance to 'waste' such resources on families identified by the last Prime Minister as simply criminal, morally degenerate and irresponsible? If resources are tight let's concentrate on the 'deserving'. For the 'undeserving' the best medicine is 'tough sanctions'. In the author's experience doctors are just as susceptible as the rest of us to state spin and misinformation. After all, it was German doctors in state institutions for the disabled, *aided by local authority officials*, who first agreed to euthanize the 'useless mouths'. Starvation and lethal injection eventually gave way to the mobile gas chambers. None of us are immune to relentless fake news and alternative facts, amounting to hate propaganda about disabled minorities…spun by nominally democratic governments.

Treating the 'whole family' also makes sense providing this is not translated into: all the families are the same and all the members are the same: namely criminal, feckless, irresponsible, drug fiends and alcoholics with pregnant under 18s. If such was the case one could work out a 'standard treatment' profile. The nearest we can approximate to a 'standard' profile is the dominance of the 75% with a limiting, long standing health condition or disability and the 80% on out of work benefits at some point…the two conditions being closely linked. We saw in section 1.5.3 that the various anecdotal reports on the families, selected to show how chaotic and dysfunctional they were, simply demonstrated the *dominance* of poor health, and usually, mental health and disability issues.

So if you do nothing else give the key worker role a health focus and formal powers to access real health support. This is not rocket science given the clear and overwhelming evidence in front of us. If this is not done the TFP and similar schemes can *never* deliver any significant benefits: like the many failed intervention schemes before it since 1997.

1.8.3   Not Helping The Troubled Families : A Brave New Britain

Despite the cant of politicians about wanting to help the 'poor' improve their 'life chances' the *reality* is very different and that reality impacts most on our kind of families : the sickest, the most mentally and physically disabled, the poorest, the least employable, the most socially vulnerable. The *reality* is continuously highlighted in articles and reports from charities and academic groups but these remain a minority sport and the public…and politicians…do not see the overall pattern. Let's finish with a few recent headlines.

'Early Intervention funding halved under coalition' (35)

An investigation by CYP Now, Nat. Children's Bureau & The Children's Society using the FoIA approached local authorities to assess the impact of coalition government funding cuts for early intervention by 55%. Spending is falling by 8.3% a year. Children centre funding is falling by 17.2% per year currently.

'Conservative election victory to signal deep spending cuts' (36)

The cuts amounted to £30 billion over two years. Of this £12 billion was in welfare savings. The benefit cap was reduced to £20K per family from £26K. Meanwhile the Conservative election manifesto made a commitment to 'eliminate child poverty'… by concentrating on the bad behaviour by our Troubled Families.

'Psychiatrists attack 'scandal' of child mental health spending' (37)

An investigation by the Royal College of Psychiatrists found that CCG spending on child mental health varied from £2.01 to £136 per child. Ten CCGs spend less than £10 per child and 25 CCGs less than £25 per child. At the same time there has been a 'big spike in anxiety, depression and other serious problems among under 18s *including suicide*.' NHS mental health services in 2016 were treating 234,000 children in England every month based on 60% of health trusts. Probable total ? ~400,000 per month.

'Benefits outstrip costs of investing in CAMHS analysis finds' (38)

The Centre for Mental Health carried out a cost-benefit analysis for several common children's mental health conditions 'Investing in Children's Mental Health'. They found that CBT produced big benefits for treating anxiety and depression : benefit / cost ratio 32 : 1. School based programmes to treat 'conduct disorders' in six to eight year olds cost £108 per child but benefits in improved behaviour was valued at £3,000 per child : benefit / cost ratio 28 :1. Aggression in adolescents cost £1,260 per child but benefits of £27,700 : benefit / cost ratio 22 : 1. Compare these ratios with the claimed TFP results.

'Malnutrition quadruples in last decade' (39)

16,000 cases of malnutrition were reported by hospitals in 2015. 900 cases were classed as severe : being in danger of death. The Liverpool University Faculty of Health head commented

'...what is really worrying is that for every person admitted to hospital there will be **5 times** that number getting care in outpatients and **50 times** that number getting GP care. These [hospital] figures are only the absolute tip of the iceberg.'

If Professor Capewell is correct, total malnutrition numbers are ~ **900,000**. The Trussell Trust meanwhile attributes benefit delays and sanctions as the major cause of food bank usage growth. Remember 40% of our TFP families had been sanctioned during the projects.

'Boost early years support to improve social mobility, commission says' (40)

The Social Mobility Commission painted a depressing picture of Britain in 2016 in the report 'State of the Nation: Social Mobility in GB'. Half a million poor children were not 'school ready' by the age of five. Children in deprived areas are twice as likely to have low quality childcare provision and are **27X** more likely to an Ofsted 'inadequate' school. The chair, Alan Milburn, noted that 'Whole sections of society and whole tracts of Britain feel left behind.' He points to a stark divide between London and areas like the north east and south west. Just 2% of young people in Yorkshire and Humberside will get an apprenticeship. Children on free school meals are half as likely to get an apprenticeship as wealthier peers.

'Government confirms life chances strategy has been dropped' (41)

Instead we will receive a 'social justice' green paper. Social justice means cutting benefits, etc. Cameron also took a hit when the cunning plan to *redefine* poverty by scrapping the '60% of median income' relative poverty measure was defeated. The original plan also included a voucher for 'parenting classes'. I mean Cameron *knew* that bad parenting caused our troubled families so re-programming the wider underclass rabble was the plan. It also transpired that the inter-departmental 'Child Poverty Unit' has been abolished.

'Families with disabled children 'missing out on childcare'' (42)

The Family & Childcare Trust found that 32% of all LAs are not promoting information on their childcare provision.

Yet the law requires that LAs to make clear the provision for SEND children in particular. Only 20% made their provision clear. Research by Contact a Family in 2015 found that 25% of parents of disabled 3 and 4 year olds were not accessing the 15 hours of free childcare entitlement. Guess who these people are. This is the Sure Start story again.

'UN accuses UK of 'systematic violations' of disabled people's rights' (43)

The UN Committee on the Rights of Persons with Disabilities was asked by various UK disability charities to consider the impact of austerity and benefit cuts on disabled people. They concluded

'… the threshold of grave or systematic violations of the rights of persons with disabilities has been met. Persons with disabilities have been regularly portrayed negatively as…making a living out of benefits, committing fraud as benefit claimants, being lazy and putting a burden on taxpayers…The committee also collected evidence about persons with disabilities whose mental health condition had severely deteriorated as a result of [ATOS work capability assessments]…in many cases the implementation of welfare measures [bedroom tax, sanctions…] has reinforced the dependency of persons with disabilities on informal [food banks] and formal family care…'

How did *Great* Britain respond? It dismissed the UN report with bovine excreta of the highest quality.

'The United Kingdom is proud of its record in supporting disabled people to lead more independent lives and participate more fully in society.'

This translates as: we will get them off state benefits come what may and harass them until they learn or die. You see it is not just our troubled families under attack, but now all the disabled and chronically sick 'useless mouths'. The Troubled Families propaganda merely provided a wedge to lever open the black pit in the 'Public Group Mind' in which lurks the worst of human nature. Let the reader confirm this from the evidence we have examined together. In case of any lingering doubt, DWP secretary, Damien Green added

'At the heart of this [UN] report lies an *outdated view* of disability which is *patronising and offensive*. We strongly refute its findings.'

As the sole carer of a learning disabled son and a stroke disabled wife and as the friend of several mentally impaired people, neglected, harassed and abused by rabid governments, how dare this ignorant man speak for me and mine…or for those driven to despair and suicide by the likes of him and his DWP predecessors (see Appendix S1 for the evidence). Nor does he speak for the thousands injured and the hundreds killed every year in state 'custody' and 'care'. I can say no more…

On our rabid politicians, let the Old Testament speak for me

'For your hands are defiled with blood and your fingers with iniquity; your lips have spoken lies and your tongue hath muttered perverseness.'

'The way of peace they know not; and there is no judgement in their goings: they have made them crooked paths: whosoever walketh therein shall know no peace.'

'Therefore is judgement far from us, neither does justice overtake us; we wait for light, but behold obscurity; for brightness, but we walk in darkness.'

Isaiah, Chapter 59

Appendix S1 : Benefit Sanctions : Death & the DWP

We saw that benefit, tenancy and child seizing sanctions were the primary tools used to control our Troubled Families. 40% of the families received sanctions and threats. But such tools are now also used in the wider context of welfare benefit claimants. The regular claim is that the several billions lost to 'fraud and error' each year is primarily due to false benefit claims by malingerers and cheats. This assertion led us to the dreadful Work Capability Assessment administered by the unspeakable ATOS. In fact around 2/3 of the 'loss' is down to administrative error. Blitzes by successive governments show that the cheating rate is a few percent. The claim is also that sanctions focus the mind and 'encourage' people back into work. Conditionality, make the scum struggle for their hand outs, is the big thing, including now disabled people and lone mothers. Putting aside the ethical issues is there any evidence that such a harsh regime pays off? Given the centrality of the DWP Jihad and programmes like the TFP there has been little attempt to establish the facts.

If the reader wants to explore the evidence I recommend the NAO review of 2016 (44) and, for complete independence, the review by the Joseph Rowntree Foundation (45).

In November 2016 the NAO published a detailed review of benefit sanctions (44). The report makes it clear that the DWP is not doing enough to find out how sanctions affect benefit claimants. They note that sanctions are common : 24% of job seekers had received at least one between 2010 and 2015. By the way sanctions are imposed for the slightest breach of the Byzantine rules, not because of suspected cheating (45). The NAO noted that the Coalition had increased the scope and severity of sanctions in 2012 with *no idea* of the effects on claimant behaviour. The NAO found that the DWP had no analysis at all of such effects although the data was available. The NAO undertook a preliminary analysis itself. They comment drily that it would be a good idea for the DWP to do more work on outcomes and costs and benefits.

Let's look at the NAO data. In 2015 3.5 million people claimed out of work benefits. 1.4 million of these were expected to look for or prepare for work. Those preparing for work are ESA chronically sick and disabled people in the 'work related group'. **800,000 referrals** for a sanction were made in 2015. 400,000 sanctions were imposed. A four week sanction involved a loss of £300. The maximum sanction period is 156 weeks. 26% of sanctions on JSA by private 'providers' were overturned in 2015.

In 2015 the DWP withheld £132 million from claimants in sanctions *but* had to pay out £35 million in 'hardship payments' under its own rules. So the net saving was £97 million per annum. The DWP estimated that it spends £30 – 50 million *applying* sanctions. However it also spends £200 million *monitoring* the sanction conditions set for claimants. So the total admin cost is £230 – 250 million versus the saving of £97 million.

So the benefit sanction system costs the tax payer £133 million to £153 million per annum. Does it save money?

The NAO also found that sanctioned claimants were equally likely to stop claiming benefits permanently as to get a job. The effect on the sick and disabled was worse: sanctions were more likely to have *discouraged* them from working....ever. (see also below, 45). The reader may feel that the gentle urging of the NAO that the DWP should check cost-benefit is a miracle of restraint. We saw it before in the PAC TFP Inquiry did we not? Of course the *overall impact* of the sanctions on the claimants and hence on 'wider public spending is unknown' according to the NAO.

However we might expect some negative impacts on mental health, malnutrition and survival crime and hence on NHS, LA and justice costs.

These numbers are impressive but there is more. The Work Programme, the flagship intervention to get the scroungers back into work, is administered for the DWP by 16 private providers. We noted the cost in section 1.3.6. It was **£629 million** per annum on average from 2012 to 2015. It's nice to know that somebody is benefiting from the government's mad, costly Jihad on benefit claimants. By the way, for our TFs the WP achieved just 11% with a member back into work.

Given all this the reader and tax payer might wonder how the hell the government justifies this nonsense. Well, by spin and misdirection of course. The DWP does cite some international studies purporting to show that sanctions work. The best place to review all the evidence is the excellent JRF report 'Welfare Sanctions and Conditionality in the UK' (45). They discuss the effects of 'very severe sanctions' in some US states which reduce welfare 'case loads' but there is little evidence of positive effects on *job entry*. i.e. the claimants just disappear from the system. The effect on earnings is also negative. In the UK it has been noted that large numbers of claimants exit the system to 'unknown destinations', not employment. Even some MPs have noticed! In 2014 the HoC Work & Pensions Committee recommended that 'benefit off-flow targets' be *immediately* replaced by 'off benefit and into work measures' for this reason.

The government rejected this on the grounds of 'cost', which is ironic. Of course all the government wants is a reduction in claims and benefit spending …who cares where the damn scroungers end up. There is some evidence that conditionality and sanctions are successful in this sense (45). People are driven off JSA and ESA or discouraged from applying in the first place. This can be seen in trends in the ratio claimant unemployed / survey based unemployed. In the early 1990s this was nearly 100%. It fell steadily through the nineties under New Labour and plateaued in 2010 at 60%. Huge numbers are not claiming JSA. All we might say is thank god for family support and food bank charities. So the issue comes down to a moral question: are we happy as citizens that the state 'saves money' by abandoning the poorest and most vulnerable, including our Troubled Families, to chance and fate?

The scroungers going to 'unknown destinations' includes those who die. Disability groups have carried on a running battle to force the DWP to release data on deaths…slowly winning.

In 2015 it emerged from FoIA requests that 80 people per month were dying shortly after being found 'fit for work' and rejected for ESA. 2,380 died between December 2011 and February 2014. Also 7,200 claimants died after being put in the ESA work related group...that is being fit enough to 'prepare' for work through, you guessed it, 'work related activities' (46). We have 9,580 deaths in total in two years. Some died due to their health condition (despite being fit for work) and some committed suicide. How many? DPAC and other groups eventually forced the release of 49 DWP secret, internal review reports since 2012 into 49 claimants who had died (47). There may have been other cases of deaths not released or studied. 40 of the cases followed a suicide. 33 of the reports made recommendations for *procedural* improvements. 10 of the claimants had definitely been sanctioned at least once. All the reports had been heavily redacted. So we can say 4,421 deaths per annum minimum with maybe one in five down to suicide: 884 suicides per annum. Total number of deaths down to sanctions, following suicide, despair, heart failure, strokes, starvation, etc: 2,000?, 3000?, who knows? Surely one death is too many in a civilised society?

Section 1 References

1. 'Conference will Celebrate the Success of The Family Intervention Programme' www. wirral.gov.uk/news/17-03-15
2. 'Wirral Intensive Family Intervention' www. catch-22.org.uk/programmes-services/wirral-intensive-family-intervention
3. 'The Troubled Families Programme: Financial Framework for the TFP payments by results scheme for local authorities' ; DfC&LG website; 28 March 2012.
4. 'Review of the Claimed Long Term Outcomes from Six FIPs', April 2008 ; This book Section 4.4; sub-section 3, How successful were the projects?
5. 'Review of The Dundee Family Project', June 2007; this book Section 4.2.
6. 'A Kind of Trouble: the 'recontextualisation' and 'operationalisation' of the TFP' ,Stephen Crossley; https //akindof trouble.wordpress.com
7. 'Investing in Children's Mental Health', Centre for Mental Health; 2015.
8. 'The Fiscal Case for Work with TFs'; DfC&LG website, February 2013.
9. 'Financial Framework for the Expanded TFP'; DfC&LG website, November 2014.

10. www. hmd.org.uk/genocides/disabled-people
11. www. en.wikipedia.org/ wiki/Aktion_T4
12. 'National Evaluation of the TFP : Interim Report Family Monitoring Data'; ECORYS Consortium, July 2014; DCLG website.
13. Written PAC TFP Inquiry Submission: Dr. M Barnes , City University of London and Mr. A Ross, Quant Consultancy; October 2016.
14. 'Think Family'; Cabinet Office, January 2008.
15. 'The Impact of Sure Start on 5 year olds and their families'; DFE RB067, November 2010.
16. 'Falling Through the Net'; Contact A Family, February 2013.
17. 'Psychiatric Morbidity Among Prisoners 1997 : Summary Report' National Archives (pdf).
18. 'Implementing Anti-social Behaviour Orders: Messages for Practitioners' ; Cabinet Office, 2002.
19. 'The Intensive Family Intervention Programme October 2012 to March 2015'; Wirral Council, March 2015.
20. 'Policy Based on Unethical Research'; Nick Bailey, University of Glasgow, www. poverty.ac.uk/news-and-views/articles/policy-built-unethical-research
21. 'Troubled Families Report Suppressed'; BBC Newsnight, August 8th 2016.
22. 'Troubled Families is a Fraudulent Scam'; Centre for Crime & Justice Studies, 29th February 2016.
23. 'A troubling attitude to statistics'; Jonathan Portes, NIESR, www. niesr.ac.ukblog/troubling-attitude-statistics# , 15.03.15
24. 'Handle With Care'; Centre for Policy Studies, 10.09.2006

25. 'Louise Casey: Social workers 'collude' with problem families'; BBC News, Brian Wheeler, www. bbc.co.uk/news/uk-politics-23158680 ; 03.07.2013
26. 'Policy Based on Unethical Research'; Nick Bailey, Poverty & Social Exclusion, 16.02.2016. www. poverty.ac.uk/news-and-views/articles/policy-built-unethical-research
27. 'The ASBO Gestapo: state sponsored disability abuse & human rights decay'; Professor David P Gregg, Green Man Books, October 2014. ISBN 978 1502517982.
28. 'Frontline worker: Troubled Families is a fraudulent scam'; Centre for Crime & Justice Studies, 29.02.16.
29. 'Louise Casey report into CSE represents a missed opportunity for children'; Community Care, www. communitycare.co.uk /2015/03/20/louise-casey-report-cse-represents missed-opportunity

30. 'Neighbours From Hell : The Politics of Behaviour'; Frank Field MP, Politico's Publishing, 2003.

31. 'Politicians From Hell : An Essay on the Politics of Poverty'; Professor David P Gregg, Green Man Books, 2015.

32. 'The Perfect Social Policy?'; Stephen Crossley, Centre for Crime & Justice Studies', 11.11.2015, www. crimeandjustice.org.uk/ publications/troubled-families-programme-perfect-social-policy

33. 'National Evaluation of Sure Start local programmes'; DFE RB073, July 2011.

34. 'Early Impacts of Sure Start local programmes on children and families'; NESS/2005/FR/013

35. Children & Young People Now, 06.05.2015.

36. Children & Young People Now, 08.05.2015

37. The Guardian (society), 17.11.2016

38. Children & Young People Now, 03.02.2015

39. Benefits & Work, 25.10.2016

40. Children & Young People Now, 16.11.2016

41. Children & Young People Now, 20.12.2016

42. Children & Young People Now, 26.01.2017

43. Benefits & Work, 08.11.2016

44. 'Benefit Sanctions'; NAO, HC 628, 30.11.16

45. 'Welfare Sanctions & Conditionality in the UK'; Joseph Rowntree Foundation, September 2014.

46. 'Death has become part of Britain's benefits system'; The Guardian, 27.08.2015

47. 'Suicides of benefits claimants reveal DWP flaws, says inquiry'; The Guardian, 13.05.2016

SECTION 2

AN OVERVIEW OF FAMILY INTERVENTION PROJECTS 1997 TO 2012

2.1 INTRODUCTION

The Troubled Families Programme has a long history of antecedents going back to the election of Tony Blair and New Labour in 1997. Blair soon announced that his government would be 'attacking crime and the causes of crime', an aim soon extended to anti-social behaviour in the underclass. Blair wanted to out do the Conservatives in a hard nosed approach to crime. In fact crime had been falling steadily for some years by 1997 and continued to do so irrespective of actions by future Labour and Coalition governments. The pattern on anti-social behaviour was somewhat different as we will see below. On several measures from the British Crime Survey, ASB was low and steady under the Conservatives before 1997. Within a few years of New Labour arrival ASB rose steeply and then plateaued. Blair had successfully talked up perception and fear of ASB in the population and then found he could not reverse it however draconian the ASBOs and other interventions became. One of these involved identifying ASB with poor parenting in the underclass. The lone mother became public enemy number one…along with her 'menace' children. So was born the ASB Family Intervention Project, later the Intensive Family Support Project and now the Troubled Family Project. Throughout the aim has remained consistent: **to grip the families; to grip the local support services**…by the throat until they change! Somebody, anybody but central government, had to be blamed! Failure has followed for nearly two decades because all governments have accepted the social model that poverty and bad behaviour in families is caused by feckless and irresponsible parents lacking in moral fibre and character. Thatcher articulated the model which all later governments, left and right, have followed.

'In western countries we are left with the problems which aren't poverty. All right there may be poverty because they [the poor] don't know how to budget, don't know how to spend their earnings, but now you are left with the really hard **fundamental character – personality defects'**

No mention here of long standing mental illnesses, learning disabilities and low IQs, just the feckless, work shy, morally degenerate, underclass residuum who cost the state money.

Not only that but to the Thatcherites (and later New Labour) that undeserving poor constituted an existential, societal and racial threat!

'They [the underclass children] are born to mothers who were first pregnant in adolescence in social classes 4 and 5. Some are of low intelligence, most of low educational attainment. **The balance of our population, our human stock, is threatened**'

Sir Keith Joseph
Intellectual Godfather of Thatcherism ; October 1974

SECTION 2.2   'FAMILY INTERVENTION PROJECTS'

: A Classic Case of Policy Based Evidence

(Published By The Centre for Crime & Justice Studies, 2011)

'There is no point pussyfooting…if we are not prepared to predict and intervene …pre-birth even… these kids a few years down the line are going to be a menace to society…'

Prime Minister Tony Blair; September 2006
(On the unborn children of lone mothers)

When powerful politicians 'know' they are right, a priori, the only hope for social justice lies in addressing the factual evidence. When the powerful deny and distort such evidence justice dies. Anti-social Behaviour Family Intervention Projects are a case in point.

Family Intervention Projects are now a key element in the government's ASB Jihad following the rapid decline and discrediting of the ASBO itself. The FIP is said to apply 'assertive and non-negotiable interventions' and provide 'intensive support' for 'chaotic families', so eliminating ASB in communities and stabilising family status, reducing homelessness and improving the 'outcomes' for children. These 'interventions' are supplied by councils or by agencies hired by them. Families may be re-programmed in their own homes, in temporary dispersed tenancies or in controlled core residential units, the ASBO Sin Bins of the media. The apparent balance of sanctions and 'tough love' support has a wide appeal to politicians and the uninformed electorate. Unfortunately in practice the FIPs fail in multiple ways: by targeting the wrong people for the wrong reasons; by targeting false 'causes of ASB' while failing to tackle the real underlying causes in those targeted ; by failing to deliver support in key areas like mental health ; by failing to deliver sustained changes in family behaviour or reduced ASB in the community. At root the FIP remains 'enforcement' led and 'sanctions' orientated where someone must be blamed and punished for bad behaviour. This ethos justifies forcing very vulnerable families with mental disorders into projects under threat of eviction, loss of benefits and removal of children into care.

This paper will re-examine the evidence for delivery from the FIPs by deconstructing the evaluation reports covering ~60 projects from the first in 1999. These are the Dundee Family Project (1); The 'Six Prototype Projects' evaluated by Sheffield Hallam University Centre For Social Inclusion (3, 4); the '53 FIP Phase: Early Outcomes' report by the National Centre For Social Research (7).

The Dundee Family Project began in 1996 and was evaluated for the period 1999 / 2000 by Glasgow University who published their report in 2001 (1). The DFP became the prototype, flagship model for all later efforts. Government reports and spin claimed over several years that it had achieved an '84% success rate with the most difficult families' Such ambiguous, misleading claims set the pattern for the next ten years. Caveat emptor! Let us look more closely at the claims on the basis of my detailed reanalysis of the results (2).

Firstly in what sense are the DFP families the 'worst'? The rationale for the FIPs is the reprogramming of families who have 'disrupted' their neighbourhoods causing 'untold misery to many'. It is surprising then that of the 56 families receiving 'interventions' only 8 had 'conflicts with neighbours'. We also learn that 'a small number' of these were recognised as victims in these conflicts. If 'small' is 3 then 5 out of 56 or 9% of the project families were 'guilty' of causing conflicts. But the primary reasons for FIP referral are given as 'conflict with neighbours, poor upkeep of [council] property and rent arrears'. We must conclude then that up to 91% of the families were referred for rent arrears, poor house upkeep and other minor misdemeanors …hardly the image of ASB fed to the public, surely?

The project demographics show us that most families were very poor, lone mother led and in poor health. 50% were on anti-depressants; 75% had an alcohol or drug abuse / addiction problem. We will see again and again over the years that most families were referred for mental health problems and social inadequacy rather than offending as the public understand it. In most cases these health problems are not addressed in the projects.

Are the project families perhaps 'the worst' in the wider sense of their ASB peers? Well altogether 126 were referred and 56 selected. We learn that the selection process was 'valued' by staff for its 'capacity to indicate a family's motivation to change'. Repeatedly 'family cooperation' is emphasised as a selection criterion. The less cooperative, the most resistant, families were eliminated from the start. By the way by failing to 'engage' these families risked eviction and loss of their children. Those who cooperated had these sanctions hanging over them …some motivation.

Secondly can the 84% success rate be justified? Well evidence for behaviour change was opinion based from 'semi-structured, qualitative interviews, self-completion questionnaires, case records and a small number of observations'. Note that behaviour outcomes were actually only assessed for 36% of families. Only in a few cases were outcomes assessed by independent observers. Detailed interviews covered only 10 out of 70 closed cases, or 14%. Even so there was a 'very high interview failure rate' and the sample 'underrepresented those who found it hard to accept the project'. No formal methods for assessing behaviour were applied and the study had no control group. Limited sampling, incomplete data sets, subjective assessments and badly biased samples are the norm in FIP evaluations as we will see.

There is worse. The 84% success figure applies only to the small number of families in the 'core residential unit' (or Sin Bin). If we include all three intervention types the overall 'success' rate is only 59%. However housing officers say 86% based on improved housing issues like rent. The views of social services staff based on family behaviour, risk factors and ongoing problems are markedly different at 39%. This also reflects the evaluators concerns who say

'long term mental health and relationship issues require attention after project work is ended yet social services may not have the resources to attend to this and specialist [medical] services are rarely available'

Their recommendations for better data collection and longer term evaluations to test sustainability were naturally ignored. Instead the government cloned the DFP in six new prototype projects and appointed a new evaluation team from the Centre For Social Inclusion at Sheffield Hallam University who became involved for some years (3,4). As in the DFP remarkable claims were made in government press releases about FIP success (9).

'Intensive Family Support Can Turn Around ASB in 8 Out Of 10 Families'

'In 85% of families complaints about ASB had either ceased or reduced …by the time they left the projects'

'92% of families were also found to be a reduced risk to their local community'

Let us deconstruct these claims (5). Firstly look at sampling. The 85% claim is based on only 15% (39 / 256) of families in the six projects. Secondly the claim only applies to the families who 'fully or partly engaged' with the projects excluding those who 'disengaged' or left. In fact only 42% of families fully engaged. Clearly the evaluation sample is biased. It is also difficult to reconcile this fact with the subjective opinion based view that 92% of families were 'found to be a reduced risk to their community'. By careful reading, including footnotes, we find that at exit only 22% had no ASB complaints (versus 4% at least, on entry) and 33% had reduced complaints. Note that 78% of families (even in the positively biased sample) still exhibited ASB. Nor do we have any idea about the frequency or severity of ASB complaints. However there are clues about the more serious end of the spectrum. At entry 68% of families had no contact with the police. At exit this rose to 76%, a modest 8% drop in police contact. How serious was their ASB if 68% had no police complaints against them to begin with?

To be fair the Sheffield evaluators were well aware of the above problems.

'It is impossible however to determine the extent to which project outcomes identified …are a direct result of the project interventions'

'It was not always noted whether family behaviour had impacted in any significant way on the community when initially referred and therefore it is impossible to chart changes that had occurred as a result of the project interventions'

'It was beyond the scope of the evaluation to carry out an independent assessment of the impact of these changes [in behaviour] on the wider communities where the families live'

Nevertheless the government claimed 85% or even 92% success rates and somehow concluded that FIPs deliver 'excellent value for money'. If ~90% of families were normalised, and stayed normalised, in terms of behaviour, so eliminating long term support costs, the latter claim would be true. However there is no objective evidence for this scale of behaviour change nor for its sustainability.

Concerned about just this issue Sheffield persuaded the government to sponsor a study of 'Longer Term Outcomes' (4). Although the tracking period was less than one year and the sample reduced to 21 families who agreed to cooperate (8.2% of all families) the outcome was clear enough as we will see(6). Also note that again the tracking sample was biased : for the bulk family population 42% were fully engaged with the projects. For the tracking sample this was much higher at 63%. We are dealing with the most cooperative and receptive families in this assessment.

The claim is that with a more 'nuanced analysis' (one taking into account changes or non-changes in ongoing health problems, etc) the success rate is now 43%. However looking more carefully reduced ASB can only be claimed in 31.5% of the tracking families (6). Recall that at project exit it was claimed that 85% of families showed reduced ASB (3). Accepting these figures implies that in less than one year unacceptable ASB has returned in 53% of the families. Claimed behaviour change is not sustained…even for a year. Why is this? Well the DFP suggested that much of the alleged ASB involved social inadequacy and mental health issues. What are the 'six projects' families like?

- 80% of families had mental / physical health problems and learning disabilities.
- 59% of the adults had clinical depression and anxiety problems.
- 54% of families had one or more children with a mental or physical disability.
- 72% were lone mother families
- 85% of adults were unemployed
- 59% of families were in debt
- 60% were found to be 'victims of ASB' and described as 'easily scapegoated' in disputes by project managers

These are chronic problems not life style choices. Across the FIPs over ten years we are dealing not with 'families from hell' but 'families in hell' with little hope of escape. Yet the level of medical support given in the projects is totally inadequate and parenting classes do not cure mental disorders. Having carefully examined the nature of the families and their 'crimes' the Sheffield team parted company with the government to write scathing reports on ASB strategy (10,11) Here are one or two extracts of their expert conclusions

'The subjects of ASB interventions often have mental health problems, learning disabilities and neurological disorders. This raises crucial questions about the extent to which the use of punitive control mechanisms

202

…can be justified…Disabled people with learning difficulties and mental health conditions may be particularly powerless to control behaviour that could cause alarm and distress…there are grounds for serious concerns about the way ASB interventions are being used against [such] people …'

Did the government listen and acknowledge this abusive mis-targeting and failure? Of course not. Instead they appointed new evaluators from the National Centre For Social Research to assess the next phase of 53 FIPs started in 2006 /2007. The NCSR team followed the FIP tradition by honestly reporting the limitations of data and information along with clear caveats about results in the body of their report (7). However by the time we read executive summaries and government press releases these have again disappeared and the declared results are carefully selected to paint a moderately positive picture (12,13). Ironically the detailed reporting gives the best insight into the limitations of FIPs of all the evaluations and is therefore invaluable to researchers. No doubt they will be 'sacked' for this! So what are the claims this time? Based on the first 90 families (of ~1080) to complete intervention we learn that (12,13)

- 61% of families with four or more types of ASB at project start up reduced their levels of ASB to 7% when they left.

- The proportion of families facing one or more 'enforcement actions' fell from 45% to 23%.

- The proportion with 'no risk factors' increased from 1% to 20%.

- The proportion of 5-15 year olds with 'educational problems' declined from 37% to 21%.

The minister for children and families declared

'These early results can't be ignored. The reduced levels of ASB …are substantial'

But are the results reliable? Well the data samples as usual are very small : they cover 8.3% of families in the 53 projects. In fact only 18 families across nine projects were interviewed, that is 1.7%. (8) The evaluators also tell us up front that

'These results cannot be used to assess quantitative impact as the IS did not contain a control group'

'The purposive nature of the sample design as well as the small sample size however means that study cannot provide any statistical data relating to the prevalence of these approaches , views and experiences'

That seems clear enough but there is more. The exit criterion which defines the end of intervention is that

'ASB had stopped or reduced to an acceptable level'

  So the 90 families are simply the first to meet this 'success' criterion (although remarkably 35% were still exhibiting one or more 'types' of ASB). We do not know from this tautological result when, if ever, the remaining 91.7% of families will meet the criterion. These 90 families were simply the easiest to re-programme. This is provable. In the bulk population 80% of families had some initial enforcement action against them but for the 90 families this was only 51%. The 90 sample is clearly not representative of the bulk population (8).

  It is also essential to realise that the measure of ASB used is qualitative, that is, the number of **types of ASB.** To talk of families 'reducing their levels of ASB' is grossly misleading. There is no quantitative information about the severity or frequency of ASB in the families. The evaluators note that

'Typically the information collected in FIPs consisted of a description of the problems a family caused **which could not be quantified...**no reliable results are available on the issue...because in the majority of cases information on complaints was not recorded numerically'

However the data base provides some clues on ASB severity.

- Although 62% of families were referred for rowdy behaviour only 1% had a fixed penalty notice for disorder.

- Although 54% supposedly had committed noise offences only 1% had a penalty notice for noise and less than 1% had a noise abatement order.

- Although 59% were involved in environmental damage (litter, etc) only 1% had a penalty notice for environmental crime.

  It is interesting that at referral only ~2.6% of individuals had an ASBO and ~8.3% of children had an ABC.

204

These facts about ASB incidence are obscured by data reporting at the family level although individuals commit offences. While 98% of families had 'reports of ASB' only 44% of individuals had such reports. Or equivalently while 2% of families had no ASB, 56% of individuals, the majority, had no ASB. While 42% of families were reported for 'harassment' only 9% of individuals were involved. The FIP 'blame the family model' badly distorts the apparent level of 'criminality' in the families. Rates are 'sexed up' by 3-5 X.

Having looked at all these critical caveats does the claim for a reduction from 61% of families having four or more types of ASB down to 7% reflect the overall picture? Well at the level of individuals, who actually commit offences, 56% had no ASB at referral while 86% had no ASB at evaluation. Therefore ASB has ceased (at least for several months) in 30% of individuals but we must remember that this is for the most responsive families in the 'first out' 90 family sample.

What about the claim for reduced 'enforcement actions' from 45% to 23% of families? Well taking court related legal actions we note that

'there appeared to be little change in the level of court orders and juvenile specific orders [by project end]'

Indeed juvenile orders fell from 13% to 11% and court orders from 8% to 7%. Notice the level of orders among individuals is low anyway. The vast majority of adults and children are not on orders. What about housing enforcement issues? At referral 40% had received a warning visit from officers versus 7% at evaluation but this may simply reflect a change in jurisdiction to the projects in some cases. Indeed 86% of families were in secured or assured tenancies at referral versus 82% at evaluation, a slight decline in housing security. We also note on housing issues that 47% received 'support to improve property' and 38% received 'financial management support'. As in the DFP, family housing defined 'ASB' appears to relate to property upkeep and rent arrears. In fact the earlier Sheffield evaluators made this comment on the social 'normality' of the families (6).

'Contrary to popular belief, the evidence suggests that rather than constituting a distinct minority distinguishable from the 'law abiding majority' **families tended to conform to the norms and values of the communities in which they lived'**

What distinguishes them across all the evaluations is a high level of mental and physical disorders and extreme poverty.

The presentation of the NCSR results on family 'risk factors' (mental health, poverty, disability...) is also telling (7). What the claimed result above actually means is that 99% of families had such risk factors at FIP entry and 80% still had risk factors at exit. The evaluators say in their conclusions section

'Sustainability is hard to achieve, particularly in the light of the multiple problems – including mental and physical disabilities- that many families continued to manage on a daily basis'

This is not surprising given that only 11% received professional psychiatric treatment or counseling. Remarkably given that 79% of children at referral had 'discipline issues' and that 69% of families were lone parent led, only 35% received the government hyped, cure all of 'parenting classes'. Of these only 18% received classes from outside professional agencies. So much for 'intensive support'.

The final headline claim of school improvement is also telling. The fall in 'educational problems' from 37% to 21% of 5-15 year olds must be welcomed. But please note in relation to the severity of these 'problems' that only 6% of children in the 90 family sample were excluded. We do know that a remarkable 47% of the children had ADHD or autistic spectrum disorders. We also know nationally that 2 / 3 of the children excluded from mainstream schools in 2005 / 6 had a learning disability and 1 / 2 the 78,600 children suspended had special needs (Bow Group survey). The majority of school problems in project families relate to mentally disordered children.

So what did the project staff actually do for these children? Did they rely on parenting classes to encourage parents to discipline the children? Did they punish the children? No. We are told that 57% of families had staff 'supporting children into education' and 67% had FIP arranged additional 'support' from schools. It is made clear that staff acted as 'positive advocates for children and parents' explaining their medical and social problems to the schools. Perhaps they also stopped disability related bullying? Remember in the DFP that 70% of the children had suffered bullying at school. The children (with chronic, underlying mental disorders) did not change ...the schools did. Nor is this surprising. A University of Bath study in 2007 concluded

'...most teachers are unequipped to deal with special needs'

As in other FIP phases the high frequency and persistence of untreated mental disorders does not support the assumption that the claimed improvements in family behaviour and status are sustainable. These families were again assessed less than one year after project exit. The evaluators say

'It is less clear whether these outcomes will be sustained in the longer term…more work is needed…across all 53 projects these longer term outcomes need to be assessed quantitatively'

On underlying health problems they also say specifically

'The evidence from family interviews suggests that families had not received much help with health issues…there was little change …many [mental] health problems typically require a long period to be resolved…[there were problems also] due to difficulties FIPs had in "levering in" health services…'

Enforcement rather than support still dominates the FIP model with ~80% of referrals coming from enforcement led council agencies and only 3% from health professionals. Only 8% of referrals come from the police despite the alleged 'high criminality' of the families.

So we return to our starting point. After a decade the recommendations of three teams of evaluators to develop an adequate FIP data and evidence base are still ignored. The government has had ten years to carry out the repeatedly recommended, comprehensive longitudinal studies of the 'successful' families leaving the projects to establish 'sustainability' of the claimed reductions in ASB, improvements in family status and community benefits. It has not done these things. Why? Because even with the limitations of successive evaluations they demonstrate the failure and abusive nature of FIPs, whatever the original good intentions, and objective long term studies would only confirm this. On the FIP concept, and delivery over a decade, the evidence tells us

This is not just social engineering : This is voodoo social engineering.

References

1. 'Evaluation of The Dundee Family Project'; Glasgow University www. Scotland.gov.uk/library3/housing/edfp

   2. 'The Dundee Family Project : A Commentary On The Government Evaluation Report'; D P Gregg January 2007.

   3. 'ASB Intensive Family Support Projects-An Evaluation of Six

207

Pioneering Projects' Centre for Social Inclusion website, Sheffield Hallam University. (see also 'ASB IFS Projects', Housing Research Summary No. 230, 2006; Department For Communities & Local Government)

4. 'The Longer Term Outcomes For Families Who Had Worked With Intensive Family Support Projects' ; Department For Communities & Local Government (see also DfCLG Housing Research Summary No 240, 2008) www. communities.gov.uk/publications/housing/familysupportprojects

5. 'Interim Review of the Government Evaluation report On Six ASB FIPs'; D P Gregg, March 2007.

6. 'Review of Claimed 'Longer Term Outcomes' From Six ASB Family Intervention Projects'; D P Gregg, 2008.

7. 'Family Intervention Projects : An Evaluation of Their Design, Setup & Early Outcomes' ; National Centre For Social research, 2008. www. dcsf.gov.uk/research/data/uploadfiles/ACF44.pdf

8   'A Review of the report 'Family Intervention Projects: An Evaluation of Their Design, Setup & Early Outcomes'; D P Gregg, October 2008.

9   'Intensive Family Support can turn around ASB in 8 / 10 cases'; Home Office press release on October 30 2006; see also ASB practitioners Area , HO website. www. respect.gov.uk/members/news/articel.aspx?id=8792

10 'Disabled Peoples' Experiences of ASB and Harassment In Social Housing : A Critical review'; CEIR, Sheffield Hallam University, for the Disability Rights Commission, August 2007. See the DRC website or www. shu.ac/research/ceir/DRC

11. 'Antisocial Behaviour & Disability In The UK' ; CEIR, Sheffield Hallam University : People, Places & Policy Online 2007; 2 /1 , pp 37-47

12. 'Success for family intervention projects'; Dept. For Children, Schools & Families press release, 10th July 2008.

13. 'Tackling families' anti-social behaviour'; National Centre for Social Research, Research Findings section, 2008.

SECTION 2.3   FAMILY INTERVENTION PROJECTS

: More Coalition Policy Based Evidence

(Published in abridged form by the Centre for Crime and
  Justice Studies 2013)

Professor D P Gregg (retired); January 2013

'Government support will focus more on quality outcomes …it is
in other words about producing more evidence-based projects'

Tim Loughton, Children's Minister
'Funding The Future' conference
London April 2011

In 2011 the Centre for Crime & Justice Studies published this writer's
critical review of FIP evaluations and government success claims from
1999 to 2009. (Family Intervention Projects: A classic case of policy based
evidence). Apparently the only criticism received was that the review did
not include the most recent 2010 / 2011 FIP results, presumably on the
grounds that FIP practices and success rates had transformed in a year after
ten years of failure. It therefore seems appropriate to provide a brief
commentary on some of the key FIP claims made during 2010, 2011 and
2012 as reported most recently in 'Working With Troubled Families';
Dept. for Communities & Local Government ; December 2012.

Let us begin with the DCSF research report of March 2010, DCSF-RR
215. The analysis was carried out for the government by the National
Centre for Social Research, NCSR, as was the last full evaluation report
this writer analysed. For brevity I will focus on the claims made for
reduction in ASB since both New Labour and Coalition governments have
used this arena to justify intrusive state intervention in 'chaotic' families.
But please recall that in previous FIP evaluations we learned that 80% of
these families had significant mental and physical health problems and
learning disabilities. In case I am accused of relying on 'old data' again
note that DFE-RR044 in late 2010, tells us that

'33% of families had one or more children under 16 with
  special educational needs'

In addition the written evidence to the Health select committee in October 2010 from the National Family Intervention Strategy Board, the FIP 'trade association', tells us that 40% of adults from 'families with multiple problems' face mental health problems : some 2.5 x more than English adults found with mental health issues at clinical review. The NFISB also quotes claimed FIP results on mental health with a reduction from 31% of families with problems to 26% at exit, a fall in just 5% of families. This modest result is not surprising since they say 'one of the biggest problems from FIPs is accessing health services…'.This writer in previous evaluations found that only 11-14% of families received professional mental health treatment or counselling.

DCSF-RR215 provides a detailed breakdown of the fate of families referred to the FIPs. The headline claim from this study, widely made by government agents, is that 64% of those reaching 'planned exit' had ceased any ASB. The drop was from 89% of families exhibiting alleged ASB at entry to 32% at exit, an 'actual' drop of 57%. Even this claim, according to the normal rules of research evidence, is invalid as we will see.

The ubiquitous Louise Casey, former Respect Tsar for Brown, now the Coalition Tsar for Troubled Families, told the Home Affairs select committee in 2010 that '66% of families' had ceased ASB. She also added

'You have to crack down …[some of the worst families] are deliberately choosing not to cope [with their children]'

Remember that Ms Casey is describing families where 33% have one or more children with special educational needs and 60-70% of the adults, mainly lone mothers, suffer from serious depression / anxiety disorders. Let us examine the 66% or 59% or 47% success claims in detail.

Summary results are provided for 2734 families offered an FIP placement. Of these 1013 had reached a planned exit. Some were still in the system. However the 66% success claim does not take into account 742 families who dropped out of the process. Surely these must be counted in assessing project performance? In fact at FIP entry we had 1013 x 0.89 = 902 later finishers and 742 x 0.89 = 660 later drop outs or, in total, 1562 families displaying ASB. After leaving the FIPs we had 1013 x 0.32 = 324 finishers and 660 drop outs or in total, 984 displaying ASB. The proportion still displaying ASB at exit was therefore 984 / (1013 + 742) = 0.561.The fall in ASB families was therefore (1562 - 984) / (1013 +742) = 0.329. So if we take the declared data at face value, the real fall in ASB families was 32.9 % not the headline 66% claimed.

However we can argue that this is not the end of the structural distortions in the reported results. All the earlier evaluations from 1999 to 2009 stressed that 'willingness to cooperate' was a key family selection criterion. For example the first full NCSR report 'FIPs : An Evaluation of Their Design, Setup and Early Outcomes' tells us in section 4.1.2 that FIP family selectors

'looked for evidence [that] family members at referral were motivated to engage with an FIP'

In fact we learn that 3% of families offered a project refused and a further 8% refused to accept a work plan. We learn that many problematical families did not even reach the formal referral stage e.g because ethnic communities choose to deal with their own problems; because many communities were too afraid to officially report dangerous families ; because some families were considered too far gone by communities and authorities for intervention. Page 123 also tells us

'there is a lack of evidence to actually verify whether FIPs were reaching the worst families…'

Given these observations it is interesting to note that a further 923 families of the 3657 families referred were 'not considered suitable for inclusion'.

Given the above was it because these families were considered too difficult and potentially uncooperative, if not dangerous, or not 'troubled' enough? It is interesting to calculate a conservative estimate of the 'success' of the overall FIP process including the rejected. Some 3657 families entered the system; 923 were rejected ; 742 joined but dropped out ; 1013 reached a planned exit ; 979 at the time of reporting were still in. We will assume those still in achieved the same success rate as those already at exit, that is, 979 x 0.32 = 313 would still display ASB. On the government ASB figures, at referral, we can say 3657 x 0.89 = 3255 displayed ASB. At planned exit 1013 x 0.32 = 324 still displayed ASB. The estimated families with ASB when all have left the system is 923 + 742 + 324 + 313 = 2302. This is (2302 / 3657) x 100 = 62.9%. The fall in ASB families overall is therefore 89 – 62.9 = 26.1%. This is a very long way from the headline claims of a 66% success rate.

It is also worth noting when considering the above success claims that Education Dept. statistical 'monitoring and evaluation summary', OSR 14/2011 of September 14th 2011, tells us that 554 families had been subject to FIP service two or three times.

We may ask if general FIP reporting has improved under the Coalition government. It has not. OSR14 / 2011, for FIP families exiting up to 31st of March 2011, tells us of a

'58% reduction in anti-social behaviour (from 81% to 34%) '

That is 81- 34 = 47% of families have reduced ASB compared to 89- 32 = 57% up to March 2010. In December 2012 an update, 'Working With Troubled Families', was published. The headline claims were for a reduction in ASB of 59%. That is from 77% to 31% an 'actual' fall of 46% of families.

Apparently FIPs are becoming less effective over time or the data is being more sensibly construed. It is difficult to know since detailed evaluation reports on FIPs with a proper discussion of data and assumptions as in earlier studies, no longer appear to be issued before public performance claims are made. The reader may think that any reduction in ASB is a good result but it is critical to also consider some of the dubious procedural and definitional facts behind ASB success claims, such as those made above, which were described in detail in my CCJS review paper. The FIP evaluation approach does not conform to the standards expected in 'scientific' research and indeed strong caveats by the evaluators themselves are repeatedly reported... but hidden in appendices. The caveats appear again in the latest 'Working with Troubled Families' report in its Appendix A. These caveats are never mentioned in the headline claims made by ministers.

- Firstly the measure of ASB used in these FIP evaluations is purely qualitative and largely subjective. There is no indication of the severity or frequency of ASB incidents, only a note of the 'types' of ASB attributed to a family. The first full NCSR report concedes on page 40 that

  'Typically the information collected by FIPs consists of a description of the nature of the problems a family caused which could not be quantified ...no reliable results are available on the issue because in the majority of cases information on complaints was not collected numerically'.

  We can have no idea of the actual impact on the community of the claimed reductions in ASB. The qualitative ASB measure is like saying that a man with four denominations of coin in his pocket is wealthier than a man with only one denomination of coin in his pocket, without knowing the actual wealth of each, which is nonsense. If only we could pay our taxes on that basis. The only 'quantitative' data presented is for police contact. 68% of families had no police contacts at FIP entry versus 76% with no contact at project exit. The (short term) improvement, under FIP 'intensive' supervision and the threat of 'sanctions' remember, is just 8%. Notice that for 68% of families at entry their alleged ASB, if any, was not serious enough to warrant any police attention.

- Secondly the subjective criterion for completing FIP intervention is that

  'ASB has stopped or reduced to an acceptable level'

  We have something of a tautology here. However in the first full NCSR report we discovered that 35% of the 'successful' families were still involved in one or more types of ASB. More recently from OSR 14 / 2011 noted above, 34% of 'successful' families reaching 'planned exit' were still displaying ASB. There is a remarkable degree of arbitrariness here in the definition of 'success' with much scope for wishful thinking. There is no external scrutiny.

- Thirdly all the reported results refer to family changes during supervision in the projects. There is limited data to show what happened after support ended. There has been no long term, large scale monitoring of families. The longest post project monitoring exercise lasted ~14 months. That showed a rapid decay in behaviour.

- Fourthly many of the claims are based on a very limited sampling of families and these samples are often biased, as accepted by the evaluators themselves.

* Fifthly it is important to recall that individuals commit offences not families. By reporting ASB and crime at family level, offending levels are hyped up because the typical FIP family has ~1.3 adults and ~3 children. In the first full NCSR report we find that only 2% of families have no reports of ASB but also that 56% of individuals had no ASB. (note: reported family ASB levels appear to have changed little from the first NCSR report to the later DFE- RR044 and the OSR 14 /2011 statistical release).

Taking for example, one of the ASB 'types' we find that 42% of families had reports of 'intimidation' but only 9% of individuals had such a report. While 62% of families had reports of 'rowdy behaviour' only 1% had received a fixed penalty notice which tells us something about the severity of this antisocial behaviour.

On an individual (actual perpetrator) basis the fall in ASB is even less impressive than my family analysis above suggests.

- Lastly the gold standard for medico-social research is the randomised , controlled trial as recommended in the Cabinet Office paper 'Test, Learn, Adapt : Developing Policy with Randomised Controlled Trials' (2012) which tells us 'RCTs are the best way of determining whether a policy or intervention is working.'

In fact if huge sums of public money are to be spent, such as the £450 million for troubled family interventions, it should be the only way. The ministers commissioning the several FIP evaluations since 1999 failed to accept the repeated advice of the evaluators to set up proper monitoring schemes. As a result all of the alleged changes in family behaviour and health cannot be attributed to the projects. In fact in Appendix A of 'Working With Troubled Families'; December 2012, we are told

'evaluations have not, or have not been able to, establish suitable control or comparison groups…most studies are limited in what can be concluded from them about the degree to which improvements for the families are attributable to the intervention…'

There is no indication in the recent statistical releases that things have improved. In fact OSR 14 /2011 of September 2011 shows that the qualitative approach to judging success has been extended to a wider range of measures. For example figures are now given for overall project success. That is, the proportion of families who leave the projects for a 'successful reason'. This is said to be 85% (for exiting families up to March 2011). However this number is based on a most peculiar type of button counting. In the tables recording 'reasons for leaving a family intervention' we learn that there are 10 reasons classed as 'successful'. Any **one** reason defines a family as a 'success'. However these families are referred in the first place because of 'multiple, complex, risk factors'. The (subjective) improvement in any one may not significantly reduce overall risk. This is actually stressed in bold type in the report:

'without an impact assessment we cannot establish whether the outcomes achieved by families can be directly attributed to the family intervention services...'

'In addition families may still be at risk when they complete a family intervention service even though the level of risk may have reduced'

This raises legitimate questions about the definition of success applied here and the exaggerated 'success rate' reported to an unsophisticated public. This is not the end of the distortions. There are also 6 reasons classed as inconclusive: defining 'neither a success or a failure'. However these include

- High risk cases: unsafe for staff to continue to visit the family.
- Family break up.
- Children taken into care.
- Family referred for another family intervention.
- Family referred to another support service.

In addition the sixth reason, 'family moved away' likely includes many cases where families, including the 'successful' families, were forced to move by vigilante neighbours, some 59% based on the earlier evaluation reports. It is difficult for this writer to see these reasons as 'inconclusive' and as anything but reflecting a failure of the FIP Intervention yet these families are not counted as failures. We also find that if a project worker defined both successful and inconclusive reasons this was also counted as a success. Clearly this introduces a bias we cannot correct since numbers in this category are not given. Finally there are only two reasons for defining a family as unsuccessful: the family refused intervention; the family failed to engage with the project. In fact just to make certain we read that

'after January 2009 these codes were removed for families leaving at the exit stage, meaning there were **no** unsuccessful reasons for leaving an ASB family intervention at the exit stage'

As we noted earlier, 34% of such 'successful' families reaching a 'planned exit' still exhibited ASB and still exhibited multiple, serious risk factors for which they had been referred to FIPs in the first place. (In terms of all families leaving, 62.9% still exhibited ASB). In an alternative calculation the evaluators include the families with both 'successful and unsuccessful' reasons. On this basis the success rate falls to 70% from 85%.

The unsuccessful family rate is not the implied 3.9% but at least 30%. Looking at this definitional system, stacking the deck to exaggerate 'success' and minimise 'failure' is still the name of the game. This is surely unacceptable.

Now it seems we have pre-emptive public claims for FIP efficacy even before the 'statistical' analysis, such as it is, is completed and the results made available for independent scrutiny. At the National Children and Adult Services conference in London in October 2011, the head of DFE's families at risk division talked of 'trends' emerging from the data

'Some data suggests those areas that have had family intervention operating for more than a year or two are showing measurable reductions in numbers [of children] in care'

This of course was reported uncritically in the press as, for example, 'Intervention Projects Help Cut Care Figures'. So much for objective 'evidence based policy' and responsible reporting to the media.

As mentioned earlier the most recent offering from the Department of Communities and Local Government is 'Working With Troubled Families' by Louise Casey. This contains only headline claims for reduction in ASB, risk factors, involvement in crime and school behaviour but no details. The numbers are very similar to the more fully reported results of 2010 and 2011. We have for example 77% of families at project entry with ASB and 31% at project exit. However in the last full NCSR report we learned that while 98% of families exhibited ASB at entry only 44% of individuals did so.

Reporting at the family level conveniently 'sexes up' the apparent rate of ASB and crime in the families. Assuming a similar scaling for the latest data suggests that the frequency of actual individual ASB at project entry is ~ 34.5%. This suggests that 65.5% of individuals were not engaged in ASB at all. Similarly the fall in individuals supposedly exhibiting ASB, by project exit, is ~20.6% not 59% or 66%.

The same 'sexing up' applies to the crime figures. The claim is for a 45% fall in crime. However the appendices tell us that only 36% of families were involved in crime at project entry. You would never guess this from the 'high levels of criminality' claimed by ministers in the media. But again crime is about individual offences. If we assume the same family-individual scaling as for ASB occurrence the individual crime rate at entry would be ~16.1%. Unfortunately only summary data is provided so we cannot know the full truth.

Similarly the claimed fall in 'truancy, exclusion, bad behaviour at school' is 52% on a family basis. The entry and exit rates are 58% and 28%. But remember the typical family has ~3 children so the individual rate could be as low as ~19% at entry. The other trick here is to lump together three different measures of 'bad' behaviour of very different severity. No details are provided but we know from the last full NCSR report that for the first 90 families in the exit sample, the entry frequency of school exclusion in families, the most 'serious' offence, was only 6%. At every turn results are presented in such a way as to increase the apparent culpability of the families, in order to justify to the public their forcible 'reprogramming', and to exaggerate the FIP success rate. These claimed improvement results are based on project exit data so we also need to recall that previous evaluations by the Sheffield Hallam team showed a rapid falloff in good behaviour within fourteen months of project exit and the end of 'assertive' family supervision and 'intensive' support.

The reporting distortions extend to the 'risk factors' responsible for many families being targeted by FIPs. In 'Working with Troubled Families' moderate claims are made for reductions in risk factors. However the headline claims fail to tell the whole story. To understand this we need to look carefully at the appendices again.

	Headlines	Actual Entry %	Actual Exit %	% fall
Reduction in families with Mental health problems.	24%	39	30	9
Reduction in families with Physical health problems	29%	10	7	3
Reduction in drug addiction	39%	32	20	12
Reduction in alcohol Abuse	47%	28	15	13
Reduction in no. of Adults not in work, education or training	14%	67	58	9

The headline reporting of drug and alcohol abuse reduction gives the impression of a high incidence of these problems in families. Actual entry frequencies are around 30% on a family basis but could be much lower on an individual basis with ~1.3 adults per family and ~3 children. We find 'high' substance abuse along with crime often flagged as justification for 'assertive' intervention in these 'shameless' families. The high entry incidence of mental health problems and economic inactivity in the families is striking as are the very modest reductions in these risk factors during the FIPs.

We are also told repeatedly that many families are put into FIPs because they have 'multiple risk factors', typically five of the seven measures of deprivation defined by the last government. As usual we are given no information on the distribution of risk factors across families which would enable detailed analysis. We can only get a rough feel for the situation. If a group of families had all the above five risk factors for example the average reduction per risk factor would be ~25%. Roughly 75% of the families would still be exhibiting all their entry risk factors. This crude estimate matches the reported result from the last full NCSR evaluation that 80% of exiting families still exhibited multiple risk factors. These results warn us that many families, 'successful' or not, referred 'blind' to an FIP again could easily be accepted for inclusion on the risk factor criterion. This puts the headline risk reduction claims in perspective.

Overall the writer contends that there are still serious, ongoing, problems with the definitional basis, data quality, sampling and data analysis in FIP evaluations. Applying the normal rules for scientific research the results would be considered invalid. There are also still very serious problems with how false public claims are made by government agents for the success of FIPs and about the supposed criminality of these vulnerable families. Remarkably this is happening at a time when ministers like Tim Loughton are lecturing charities and local authorities about the need for bidding for 'intervention' funding only for those techniques which are 'evidence based'. Compare this new government value for money initiative, and the earlier critical analyses we have shared, with Loughton's statement on September 14, 2011, about the latest official FIP statistical release.

'The statistics show an overwhelmingly positive picture of how intensive family intervention can successfully turn around the lives of families that have many complex problems...'

As we noted earlier the 'chaotic families' programme is now in the hands of Louise Casey (Companion of the Order of the Bath). Ms Casey's attitude to the use of 'evidence' in policy making was made clear as early as June 2005 when she told a dinner for Home Office officials and ACPO senior policemen

'Topic for the evening "Research: Help or Hindrance?" Hindrance thanks very much'

'Doing things sober is no way to get things done…I suppose you can't binge drink anymore…I don't know who bloody made that up. Its nonsense…There is an obsession with evidence based policy. If No. 10 says bloody evidence based policy to me one more time I'll deck them one…'

The Guardian, Daily Telegraph, BBC News, etc, etc.

These views, from the Coalition Troubled Families Tsar, are somewhat difficult to reconcile with the government's claim to be committed to sober, 'evidence based' intervention initiatives.

The Coalition government is obviously determined to repeat and extend the mistakes of their New Labour predecessors: where Brown targeted 50,000 'chaotic' families Cameron will target 120,000 at greater cost and, based on over a decade of evidence, with little useful effect. In re-launching FIPs in December 2011, as a response to the summer riots, David Cameron criticised conventional, coal face, local intervention efforts as

'a string of well-meaning, disconnected officials…no-one sees the whole problem, no-one grips the whole problem'

BBC News Dec. 15th 2011.

This is doubly ironic given the repeated FIP model failure to 'grip' anything and the recent report from the Childrens Commissioner, 'Nobody Made The Connection: the prevalence of neurological deficits in young offenders'. This report brings together all the medical evidence on the relative prevalence of common mental disorders in young offenders in comparison with the 'normal' population. Some of the results are shocking.

The prevalence of general learning disabilities (IQ <70) in young offenders is **9.2 X** that in the general population.

The prevalence of autistic spectrum disorders is **16.6 X** greater.

The prevalence of communication disorders (Tourettes, etc) is **12.5 X** greater.

The prevalence of dyslexia is **5 X** greater.

The prevalence of foetal alcohol syndrome is **4.3 X** greater.

The prevalence of ADHD is **2.5 X** greater.

In fact the Cabinet Office as early as 2002 knew that 60% of ASBO defendants had diagnosed mental disorders but this was ignored, and is still ignored, in deciding appropriate intervention. We can also add that repeated Mencap and Mind surveys suggest that people with mental disorders are **8 X** more likely to suffer physical or verbal abuse in their communities than 'normal' people. These are people easy to scapegoat if they kick back on abuse, being unable to defend themselves to the authorities if accused in local disputes. This point was made repeatedly by FIP managers themselves.

Sadly the mentally disordered, based on IPCC data, are also **9 X** more likely to die in police custody than 'normal' people. Talking of such mentally disordered 'troubled families' destined for the new round of Cameron's FIPs, Louise Casey told the press in late 2012

'we should be better at talking about things like shame and guilt'

Her boss Communities Minister, Eric Pickles added helpfully

'we have sometimes run away from categorising, stigmatising, laying blame. [We need] a less understanding approach.'

So ignoring all the medical evidence, the stage is set again for re-launching 'assertive, non-negotiable' intervention and tough 'sanctions' summarised in the New labour FIP mantra which underpinned their 'Together' and 'Respect' initiatives (run by Casey):

'grip the families : grip the local agencies'

The problem is that the decade long evidence base, from three evaluation teams, shows the FIPs failed to do this in key areas such as accessing NHS services for the many with mental health and disability problems or supporting re-employment in the many unemployed families. Referring back to the first full NCSR report, the later DFE-RR044 report in late 2010 reminds us

'The evidence from family interviews suggests that families had not received much help with health issues. This was partly due to problems with accessing the relevant services.'

This problem clearly remains intrinsic to the FIP model after a decade of projects and promises of 'intensive support'. Cameron further claimed that his council based, family 'Troubleshooters', would be 'paid by results' and only when

'they [the families] have stopped, and I mean completely stopped, anti-social behaviour'.

Given our earlier analyses Cameron is doomed to disappointment if he demands objective evidence of sustained ASB elimination. On the other hand all this local evidence on progress will be processed by Louise Casey. One can only hope Mr. Cameron will not find himself 'bloody decked' by Casey if he really does insist on objective ASB measures and proof of FIP delivery.

Meanwhile we have the reports of Graham Allen MP who has identified coal face intervention techniques where there is a strong, scientifically sound evidence base for efficacy and good cost-benefit (such as Multi Systemic Therapy ; Functional Family Therapy ; Family Nurse Partnerships and, I would add, school based Nurture Groups). These techniques start from the basis that the people we are dealing with are often cognitively impaired and socially inadequate: not intentional criminals in most cases and not shameful, guilty, parents 'deliberately choosing not to cope with their children' as Casey would have it.

There is also the excellent report 'Mental Health Promotion and Mental Illness Prevention: the economic case ' from the Dept. of Health , LSE PSSRU, the Centre For Mental Health and the Inst. of Psychiatry , Kings College, London, which shows remarkable medium term pay backs for various early diagnosis and medical interventions for the kinds of mentally impaired people mainly targeted by the FIPs for 'non-negotiable, assertive, persistent' intervention and 'sanctions'.

The MHP&MIP report is based on evidence from randomised controlled trials or the equivalent. In 2013 the national Audit Office reviewed early intervention initiatives and pointed out yet again the poor evidence on 'impact' and 'cost benefit' in many cases. They called again for 'more consistent and robust gathering of evidence for what works'.

On the other hand projects with a strong evidence base suggested returns of 4 to 1 (see above). They noted as an example the 2011 report on oversight of special education for 16 – 25 year olds which found the cost of support for a moderately learning disabled youngster through adult life ran to £ 2 to £3 million.

They estimated this could be reduced by £1 million with the right early support. NAO noted that despite the spin early intervention spending in health, education and youth crime has not increased over the years as a fraction of the departmental budgets. Meanwhile the failed FIPs cost hundreds of millions. The evidence base shows that the Coalition government should abandon the bloated, bureaucratic FIP programme and focus scarce funding on objectively proven, coal face, medical and professional support techniques for prevention and early intervention.

Mr. Cameron should realise that the populist 'families from hell' spin may no longer be working as it did, given current hard times. The 4Children survey of 2,000 people, part of their 'Give Me Strength' campaign in spring 2011, found that 70% did not agree with targeting family spending on the 'most chaotic families' but also supported less expensive support for families in crisis. 90% believed most families would benefit from 'practical help'. Only 3% wanted children from troubled families taken into care immediately which is a relief since the outcomes for children taken into state care have long been dreadful as recent cases have reminded the public. 4Children is strongly advocating the implementation of practical prevention and early intervention techniques such as those identified by Graham Allen.

On the other hand the Coalition government can be confident, thanks to a decade of deliberate denigration, that the public will not complain when planned changes in the benefits system disproportionately impact poor, lone parent families. The report,' The Impact of Austerity Measures on Households With Children' from the Institute of Fiscal Studies, for the Family and Parenting Institute in January 2012, predicted a fall of 4.2% in income for the average family with children in coming years. However, unemployed lone parents face an income reduction of 12% by 2014 -15. Some 500,000 additional children will fall into absolute poverty as a result. These include our 'chaotic families' of course, and these changes will not improve their already deprived and stressful lives.

Meanwhile Action For Children, who have dominated the 'FIP Industry' with 38 projects at one point, complained loudly in October 2011 that five of it's FIPs had closed in that year and that two more were threatened with closure. Given the history one cannot be sorry.

They have since continued lobbying with the rest of the industry.

Far too many vulnerable, mentally disordered families have been stigmatised; far too much money has been wasted for over a decade on grandiose social engineering schemes; far too much statistical spin has been falsely used to deliberately misdirect public opinion.
One cannot but agree with Graham Allen MP. Enough is enough.

'Billions of pounds are paid out year after year; indeed decade after decade, often without the faintest acquaintance with an evidence base'

Early Intervention: The Next Steps

SECTION 3

COMMENTARIES ON ASB FAMILY INTERVENTION PROJECTS & THE CAUSES OF ASB

3.1 INTRODUCTION

Sections 1, 2 and 4 present a formal analysis of the design and operation of the state family intervention initiatives and a quantitative dissection of the 'success' claims over two decades. In section 3.2 we look at the political propaganda around the various intervention programmes and the views of various experts about the nature of the families and alternative, medical and education based interventions. We also look at wider evidence for our contention that successive governments have shown no respect for science based and objective evidence in social and justice policy areas. Despite repeated exposures this pernicious approach continues unabated. If the facts and government spin disagree, the facts must be suppressed or ridiculed. The public do not understand that they are being repeatedly hoaxed about issues critical to their wellbeing... never mind the obscene and unjustified waste of taxpayer money.

We also show how the apparent 'high' criminality and anti-social behaviour of the learning disabled and mentally ill follows simply from the remarkably high level of abuse suffered by them in the community and their inability to deal with crises, or communicate their case to the authorities. We review the remarkable evidence collated by the Children's Commissioner for the many fold prevalence of learning disability and communications disorders such as autism, in young offenders in comparison to 'normal' youngsters.

We examine the views of justice experts and the HoC Human Rights Committee on how the Justice System fails those with mental disorders throughout the process and how Lord Bradley responded to these problems with his recommendations for reform. These are proceeding but slowly.

Section 3.3 examines the causes of the cognitive limitations we find in our troubled families. This has some relevance to how the state could effectively tackle most so-called 'anti-social behaviour'. We look at the evidence on IQ impairment related to interaction of genetics and environmental factors such as childhood and adult nutrition, vitamin deficiency, low level poisoning by heavy metals and the emerging evidence for multi-generational scale epigenetic effects.

Understanding of the links between behavioural problems and neurological faults is improving. The observation that applying a post cranial (external) magnetic field to the RTPJ region of the brain can 'turn off' or at least dampen the 'moral sense' in normal adults has important implications. The RTPJ is not normally fully developed until the late teens or early twenties.

Damage in that area into adulthood has obvious implications for some members of our families. It certainly removes the justification of the state to label people as 'morally' degenerate by choice. Fortunately understanding of neuro-plasticity is also improving and there is evidence that cognitive therapy and education can provide significant compensation in areas like suppressed IQ and conduct disorders. If the troubled families of the underclass have any future in Britain it must lie in these kinds of intervention …not in stoning to cast out devils.

SECTION 3.2

EXTRACT FROM 'THE ASBO GESTAPO' © D P GREGG

GREEN MAN BOOKS 2014   ISBN 978 1502517982

For example the Criminal Justice Act 2003 decimates the principle of the presumption of innocence. Section 101 allows evidence of the accused's 'bad character' to be presented to the jury. This is actuarial justice. The ASBO targeting and the forcing of whole families into 'ASBO Sin Bins' on the basis of statistical risk factors, that is of statistically derived, implied 'bad character' evidence, takes the logic one dangerous step further. This whole approach represents a fundamental shift in the basis of British justice. If people are to be routinely imprisoned or re-programmed 'just in case' or on the opinion of ministers, we have reached a very dark place indeed.

When Ms Blears moved to the Dept. for Communities and Local Government we will see that she took her belief that her interpretation of criminal 'intention' was sacrosanct with her, seriously damaging relations with the Muslim Council of Britain and finding herself facing possible legal action for defamation. Senior Muslim clerics are harder targets than mentally disordered youngsters and ill, poverty ridden families in sink estates.

Family Intervention Projects: the 'ASBO Sin Bins'

Although the National Audit Office report, 'Tackling Antisocial Behaviour', showed that ASBOs were failing, the government extended their punitive approach to even more intrusive actions. The Family Intervention Projects forced 'antisocial' problem families into so called 'ASBO Sin Bins' under threat of homelessness, removal of housing benefit and removal of children. To quote the Respect Taskforce, Respect Action Plan 2006

'Sanctions are key. The threat of sanctions or use of sanctions provide both a way of curbing bad behaviour and also a lever for persuading people to ...co-operate fully...'

'To ensure that failure to comply has consequences for families, contracts should identify sanctions that will apply if families do not adhere to the terms'

We will see that these sanctions are applied to people with serious mental disorders who may have little hope of complying. The Respect Taskforce Action Plan, 2006 and other related documentation tells us

'**We know** that intensive tailored action with ...clear sanctions can be effective in improving the behaviour of the most problematical families ...providing a more effective response to persistent ASB'

'**Based on evidence we know** this small number of families need an intensive, persistent and if necessary **coercive approach**'

'**The proven success** of FIPs is based on systematically linking **enforcement** and support to provide families with motivation... to change'

So we will now look at this evidence. An '84% success rate with the most difficult families' is often claimed for this intervention. However the author has analysed the government evaluation report on the Dundee Families Project which was the flagship model for later, cloned projects by now totaling over 60.

There is NO objective evidence for the delivery of substantive, long term community benefits (such as reduced ASB or crime) from these projects. Several published claims are false and many serious caveats by the evaluation authors were suppressed. Looking at the six later prototypes, a year after leaving the projects acceptable behaviour and home stability had fallen to 43% of families (or 32% by proper analysis) from the claimed

226

85% at exit. The rapid decay is clear. How many FIP families will be 'ASB' free and stable after a few years? It is also claimed that families' lives and tenancies are stabilized. However in the Long Term Outcomes evaluation of 53 recent FIPs (actually less than one year after project exit) evaluation we discover that 58% of the 'successful' families were forced to move home 'involuntarily' after FIP exit. The evaluators comment

'Ongoing concerns about personal safety dominated families' accounts with many reporting that since exiting the project they had been victims of crime, subject to ASB from neighbours and in a few cases were living in fear'

This is what happens when the state takes a vigilante approach to community problems and encourages simplistic scapegoating.

Come on, you say, the government would not set out to make false claims about social policy would they?

This problem of false claims about the 'success' of health related social engineering initiatives was ubiquitous with new labour who piled initiative on initiative, costing billions, without assessment of effectiveness. When programmes are independently evaluated more often than not they are failures. In July 2009 the British Medical Journal published research on the Young People's Development Programme which targeted young people aged 13-15 in danger of pregnancy, yes our future lone mothers, drug abuse and school exclusion. It covered 27 areas of England from 2004 to 2007 and cost £2,500 for each child. 2,371 kids took part so the sample size was adequate. After the 'reprogramming' of the girls by the YPDP a total of 16% became pregnant compared with only 6% in a matched control group on a conventional youth programme. Both groups were similarly sexually active. Yes attending a new labour anti-sex, re-education programme can make you pregnant!

In 2008 the HOC Health Select Committee reviewed the evidence for the children's Sure Start programme and concluded

'Sure Start programmes were being colonized by the middle classes who enjoyed the cheap, high quality child care they offer and extending provision universally would further dilute their focus on those who need them most'

The latter include of course our FIP families. The first Sure Start evaluation in 2006 showed that the programme actually had a negative effect on the poorest children.

Naturally the government was not pleased. A further commissioned study in 2008 disputed the negative effect, or at least muddied the water, but confirmed that any gains were modest. Only 5 of the 14 measures showed any gains. Sir Michael Rutter an authority on effectiveness studies and an advisor to the programme was also not happy. He told the Sunday Telegraph (16.09.06)

'Why we may ask did the government rule out any form of randomized controlled trials design, given its superior strength for determining efficacy? **It may be presumed that the reason was political... [such trials] carry the danger of showing that a key policy was a mistake'**

Indeed. But the lack of rigour as displayed in the FIP evaluations, then brings the whole exercise into disrepute which of course does not stop the government making false claims.

In March 2009 the House of Commons Select Committee on Health published a scathing report on such projects including the £33 billion Sure Start programme aimed at our poor, lone parent families. They concluded

'Ministers have spent large sums of money on social experiments ...but we do not know whether these experiments have worked...More public money must not be wasted on ineffective and possibly damaging interventions'

One adviser told the committee that proper evaluation showed that 'documents that passed for research often amounted to little more than propaganda'. That is exactly this author's finding on ASBOs and ASBO Sin Bins except that in these cases honest, serious caveats about the research evidence included by the evaluation authors were removed in evaluation summaries and government announcements.

This is intellectual fraud and a hoax on the public.

Well, you say, that is just your opinion.

No it is not. The government has form in this area. A report in July 2009 by the HOC Innovation, Universities, Science and Skills Committee criticized ministers for taking a cavalier attitude to scientific evidence. The report called on chief scientists within government departments to 'name and shame' ministers who flout scientific advice when formalizing policies. Of course advice need not be taken but data should not be distorted for political purposes. Later we will look at the criticisms of the Chief Government Statistician on misuse of knife crime statistics.

For now note that in August 2009 a letter was obtained under the FoIA from Professor John Beddington, the government chief scientific adviser, to the Home Secretary which warned of the risk of alienating their scientific advisers. He suggested that leading academics would be discouraged from working for government if they are reprimanded in public for expressing their honest professional views. Of course the government did not listen despite its claim of following 'evidence based policy'. In October 2009 Professor David Nutt, chairman of the Advisory Council on the Misuse of Drugs, was sacked by the Home Secretary for reiterating his research based conclusions on the relative 'harm' produced by a wide range of drugs which placed alcohol above cannabis, LSD and ecstasy in harm and just below methadone. He argued logically that action should be taken on alcohol. He also placed tobacco above cannabis and ecstasy in terms of damage done. He repeated that the risks of taking ecstasy, statistically, were no worse than horse riding, currently a legal activity. He told the BBC after his sacking

'In my view policy should be based on evidence...it's a bit odd to make policy that goes in the face of evidence...The danger is they are misleading us...Gordon Brown makes completely irrational statements about cannabis being 'lethal'...I'm not prepared to mislead the public about the harmfulness of drugs like cannabis and ecstasy...I think most scientists will see this as a further example of the Luddite attitude of this government, ...towards science'

Others agreed with him and Dr. Les King and Ms. Marion Walker, representing the pharmacists also resigned with the remaining council members asking the Home Secretary for urgent reassurances of their right to free speech on scientific evidence. Following that meeting John Marsden of the Institute of Psychiatry, Simon Campbell a former president of the Royal Society of Chemistry and Ian Regan a pharmaceutical consultant also resigned.Further support came from Professor Beddington, the government Chief Scientific Advisor, who said

'I think the scientific evidence [on cannabis versus alcohol harm] is absolutely clear cut. I agree with it'.

Similarly Lord Drayson, the Science and Innovation Minister in a leaked e-mail to No 10 declared himself 'pretty appalled' by the sacking and added 'as science champion in the government I can't just stand aside on this one'. Alan Johnson, Home Secretary, said in his sacking letter

'It is important that the government's messages on drugs are clear and as an adviser you do nothing to undermine the public understanding of them…I cannot have public confusion between scientific advice and policy'

So Johnson's position is clear: if policy and the scientifically verified truth are out of step it is the truth that must go. By the 2010 election eight experts had left the ACMD in protest at the government's approach to evidence. Johnson's actions caused such alarm that senior scientists including the President of the Royal Society and 26 others, many government advisers, published a statement of principles which the government must adhere to in future. It said for example

'Disagreement with government policy and the public articulation and discussion of relevant evidence and issues by members of advisory committees cannot be grounds for criticism or dismissal'

Remember it was Johnson who wrote to councils threatening dismissals unless they redoubled their efforts in the ASBO Jihad …whatever the evidence said about its failure and mis-targeting. Remember it was Johnson who defended the £47 million bonuses going to 50,000 MOD staff in 2009, as the UK forces body count reached 230, by saying that these civil servants also go 'into the front line' to develop anti-IED procedures and so on. But surely Afghanistan must be overflowing if 50,000 MOD staff are out there? Well official figures showed that actually only 104 were there at the time and General Sir Mike Jackson, former army head, described Mr. Johnson's claim, with admirable restraint, as 'somewhat disingenuous'. Johnson's grasp of factual reality seems somewhat tenuous does it not? Could we trust anything these new labour ministers said?

Now perhaps you see Mr. England why the author believes that the new labour government claims to create 'evidence based policy' were totally false and most certainly so in the ASB Family Intervention Projects programme and the ASBO Jihad.

Look, you say, this is all a bit technical, we still have to punish these families if they are bothering the neighbours or perpetrating crimes.

In the Dundee project only 6% of the 70 families targeted had been involved in neighbour 'conflicts' although widely portrayed in government spin as 'neighbours from hell' .Most were 'guilty' of poor (council) house maintenance, poor hygiene, rent arrears and internal family problems. 75% had significant physical and mental health problems; 50% of the mothers were on anti-depressants; many were very poor, unemployed, lone parent families. Some had been homeless on more than one occasion. The majority felt strongly they had been unfairly targeted.

Yes …these are the same evil villains targeted by the ASBO jihad. (But in the next 53 project phase only 2.6% of individuals had ASBOs. Only 8.3% of the children had Acceptable Behaviour Contracts)

The six 'prototype' FIPs had similar characteristics to the DFP. Many families were targeted as before for having 'risk factors' related to lone parenting, poverty and health. Lone mothers in families with 'no positive role models' ie no attached men, are particular targets of hatred. They are readily portrayed as 'scarlet, sexually promiscuous women', social deviants and benefit scroungers to boot, but above all, they are easy targets on which to pin the troubles of 'Broken Britain'. We will see later from direct statements by Gordon Brown that this targeting by 'risk factors', for offences which have not yet happened and statistically may never happen, was deliberate new labour policy. 80% of the families had serious mental / physical health and disability problems. 59% of the adults suffered from depression. 47% of the children with problems had ADHD / autistic spectrum problems. Despite these extremely high levels of mental disorder and the claims that FIPs provide 'intensive support', only 11% of families received professional counseling or psychotherapy. The claim that FIPs are 'support' led is false as far as medical needs are concerned. In practice they are still 'sanctions' led. The picture is one Dickens would recognize immediately. Meanwhile repeated surveys showed the absence of proper support for the young women who will become our 'chaotic' lone mothers.

In 2012 Family Action commissioned a survey of 2,200 pregnant women and new mothers. A third of the lowest income women had no family or friends who could offer support. A third of the women had no support from local councils, NHS, etc, despite peri-natal depression .They estimated that 300,000 babies would suffer because of this depression and 'poor bonding'. Remember 70% of our FIP mothers had serious depressive illnesses. Family Action repeated again the call for proper, medical, early intervention for such mothers to prevent the children becoming problems later. Does this sound familiar Mr. England? It is clear that FIP bullying and 'parenting classes' have not cured deep rooted mental health and learning disability problems nor ASB. Why then did new labour and now the Coalition government, insist on this failed approach? Because it is popular. The Home Office admitted this in a press release on 21.11.06 which actually adduced a Mori poll as supporting evidence for the FIPs. They report that

- 53% of people polled say poor parenting is one of the key causes of ASB.

- 80% agree that parents should be held responsible for the bad behaviour of their children.

- 55% say better parenting would do most to reduce crime.

So now we know: important social policy is determined by a popular vote and focus groups, not scientific or medical evidence. No wonder the findings of ten years of FIP evaluations were either ignored or ruthlessly distorted …they would not be popular with the public and worse, expose a major waste of our money. Consider Blair in 2007 trying to post-justify the ASBO Ghettos zapping vulnerable families.

'Visit the Dundee Family Project for an idea of how it can be done .It is very tough. It is intrusive. Forget general sociology. Concentrate on the facts…'

Well one fact is only 6% of the families had been involved in neighbour disputes and another is that 30-40% were targeted for rent arrears, poor council house upkeep and poor hygiene. However there is much evidence for physical disabilities amongst these families.

In the second batch of 53 FIPs 41% of the adults (mainly women) had muscular / arthritis / respiratory conditions. 69% were clinically depressed. This is why their houses were not maintained. Put simply: they were targeted for 'tough' and 'intrusive' sanctions because they were ill and inadequate. Notice Blair concentrates on the Dundee study and ignores the later Sheffield and NCSR work which made FIP failure very clear. If we 'concentrate on the facts', for the first ~60 projects to 2011, this 'tough', 'intrusive', policy simply does not work, but hey, remember new labour were the experts on 'policy based evidence'.

In assessing the FIPs the second issue is whether the projects have a wider effect on their communities in reducing either ASB by acting as a deterrent, or by reducing the 'causes' of ASB. We saw earlier that claimed FIP family 'improvement' rapidly decays after project exit. We also saw that the BCS data show no reduction in public concerns about 'neighbour issues' between 2001 and 2007. What about causes? Recall that many FIP families were targeted for several poverty and health 'risk factors' associated with ASB. Have risk factors improved in the UK as a result of numerous government poverty, ASB and education initiatives? Well 'Think Family' (DfCSF) tells us that the percentage of families experiencing '5 or more' serious disadvantages including our FIP risk factors between 2001 and 2005 had varied over the range 1.9 - 2.2% with no visible improvement trend.

Now 2% represents 140,000 deprived families but so far the FIPs had 'reprogrammed' ~1,500 and the planned expansion would eventually cover ~20,000 (at a cost of at least £218 million). So at best this 'major' FIP initiative would reach 1/7 of the 'high risk' families. Later the Coalition would tackle this. Families would be monitored by 24 hr CCTV in their homes to ensure children go to bed on time, eat proper meals and go to school. Mr. Ed Balls noted

'This is pretty tough and non-negotiable...'

By the way the 20,000 families would be drawn from a short list of 120,000 prepared by local authorities. This would be based not on offences committed but on risk factors suggesting which families have children who **might one day offend**. Yes this is actuarial justice on a large scale targeting, as before, poor lone mothers and mentally impaired children and adults. But now there was not even a pretence that intervention is justified by current anti-social behaviour.

In a No. 10 press briefing (14.07.08) Gordon Brown and his spokesmen confirmed that the families were selected 'as being **at risk** of becoming high rate offending'. They added that 'obviously it was quite likely that a significant proportion of those families would be subject to parental orders, ASBOs or similar'. In fact the evaluation of 53, second phase FIPs, remember, showed that only 2.6% of individuals had an ASBO and only 8.3% of children had an acceptable behaviour contract. When No 10 was asked, given these families are so bad, why not just condemn and punish them, they backtracked and replied that actually they were just 'at risk of offending'. Brown also added that 'we need to ensure that parents were made responsible for the actions of their children' making it clear that like Blair, he believes bullying and parenting classes can 'cure' the 80% of FIP families with mental / physical illnesses and learning disabilities. These exchanges suggest that Brown was fully complicit in the abusive 'ASBO Ghetto' programme. (By 2012 as the economy failed and following the Summer Riots of 2011, Cameron announced that 120,000 chaotic families would be 'reprogrammed'. These are again our poor FIP families with sick lone mothers and sick children, and 5 or more 'risk factors'. They were presented as trouble makers as usual but most were not offenders, merely inadequate and vulnerable).

Having brought the evidence that medical support to the 80% of FIP families with mental / physical / learning disability problems was totally inadequate to the children's minister ,Baroness Morgan, in 2008 the author was assured that the problem was solved in current FIPs and that each would have a dedicated 'medical professional'.

However this turned out to be a liaison role and the issue of inadequate local NHS funding was not addressed. She also claimed that the latest FIP results confirmed the positive effect of the claimed changes but data from the DfCSF website clearly showed no improvement in the proportion of people showing mental or physical health improvements (possibly) attributable to the FIPs. Baroness Morgan seemed to have general problems with figures.

In September 2009 the media reported that she had wrongly claimed £140,000 in expense by designating a holiday cottage in Wales, a five hour journey from the Lords, as her main residence while living in the family home in Muswell Hill. In the last section we will see that Baroness Morgan is by no means the only minister with expenses 'problems'. New labour ministers in general seemed to have a problem with numeracy and reality.

Despite all the government noise about improving medical support in the FIPs the author notes that in June 2008 the government confirmed that public funding for training family therapy and related professionals would be cut despite objections from, among others, the HoC Select Committee on Skills. Professor Stratton and Dorothy Ramsay, chairman of the Association for Family Therapy and Systemic Practice said in response

'On the one hand the government declares its support for families and the need to 'think family' and then it pulls funding from the very training necessary to turn this into reality...[It] threatens the well-being of vulnerable children, adults, families and communities...The stance is paradoxical...it beggars belief'

Indeed it does, but remember we were dealing with labour Newspeak and the Ministry of Doublethink. Clearly FIP families will continue not to get the professional help they need ...no wonder these projects are failing.
By the way Mr. England many 'normal' people suffer from acute depression or anxiety disorders serious enough to need treatment at some point, yet figures from the Royal College of GPs in 2010 showed that only 15% receive professional behaviour therapy while most are simply zapped with powerful, potentially addictive, drugs. While the problems are much greater in FIP families with 60-70% of adults suffering chronic depression and anxiety only ~11% receive therapy.

Given there is no evidence for even local deterrent effects of the 'ASBO Sin Bins' were we supposed to take the FIP expansion plans seriously when root causes would not be addressed? Was this initiative a cynical political gesture or was the government incapable of doing a few simple sums? Or could they simply be confused?

Or could it be that some civil servants, with Downing Street connivance, muddy the waters? Well this is what Louise Casey, Respect Office Tsar and then Brown 'community law & order' adviser, said in 2006 about how she advises government departments on ASB interventions like the FIPs

'If it is the Home Office I say 'enforcement', if it is the Dept. of Health I say 'support' and to the Dept. of Communities I say 'empowering' ...you have to play this game across Whitehall'

How can one adequately respond to this slime? It seems you also need a way with slogans, looking at the Respect Initiative documents.

'Respect - broader, deeper, further'
'Everyone is part of everyone else'
'The whole is greater than the sum of its parts'

Respect – costlier, shallower, triter ...remember we were paying for this gibberish. No wonder the FIPs are confused and schizophrenic in practice and mentally disordered families suffer. Ms Casey, remember, is an unelected civil servant who as we saw earlier also advises ministers to come into work 'pissed', will 'deck' anyone who suggests that policy should be based on evidence and who doesn't want to be quoted by the 'friggin Guardian'.

Remarkably in 2011 Cameron made her his 'Families Tsar'. Astonishingly we also find in the government FIP evaluation reports by Sheffield Hallam University that 60% of the FIP families targeted were identified as **victims of ASB**. The report 'ASB Intensive Family Support Projects '(DfCLG website) also tells us recent research demonstrates this is often the case. They say the results

'Highlight the need for agencies investigating complaints to develop well-defined investigatory policies and processes to ensure that all those involved in ASB cases are dealt with fairly'

Managers of two of the recent major FIPs also said this:

"The families were particularly vulnerable to being bullied and could be identified as those who are easily stigmatized, scapegoated and victimized by others in the community"

"The complainants whose voices are heard are sometimes simply those who have the resources and ability to shout the loudest".

This conclusion strongly supports the author's earlier comments about biased targeting in the ASBO process. The FIPs and ASBOs often punish mental impairment and social inadequacy not ASB. Most neighbour dispute ASB occurs in poverty ridden areas. To stop it, and save council and police time, the ASBO strategy is simple: define the party least able to defend themself as the villain and make the other party the victim. Issue an ASBO to the 'villain'. Hope that this sends a message to the local underclass. It does not and 70% of ASBOs are breached. The ASBO and ASBO Ghetto are also useful to control mentally ill council tenants guilty of rent arrears and poor council house upkeep as we saw. If we look at the second phase batch of 53 FIPs from 2006 / 2007 the dominance of a 'sanctions led' mentality and disinterest in an evidence based approach is perfectly clear. 80% of family referrals come from enforcement agencies: 62% come from council housing and ASB teams alone; only 8% come from police despite the supposed 'criminality' of the families; only 3% come from health professionals.

In 2007 a University College London study of housing and mental health found that 26% of formal housing rights cases involved tenants who had mental illness and a further 12% involved tenants with a physical illness or disability. By contrast only 11% of tenants with housing rights issues reported no illness. Many others reported stress related illnesses often attributed to problems with the housing authorities themselves. The standard response of many housing authorities is to apply sanctions, including eviction, not urgent medical treatment, often making mental illnesses worse. Remember that **69%** of the FIP family adults have clinical depression. Remember that ~80% of the homeless people selling the Big Issue have mental health problems. Remember also that 'official' homelessness, i.e people registered with local authorities, had doubled under new labour from ~40,000 in 1997 to ~80,000 at the end of 2008.
However the charity Crisis estimates from other government figures that including rough sleepers, people in hostels, squatters, those discharged from institutions, under notice of eviction and illegal overcrowding in 'concealed households', raises the real homeless figure to ~800,000.
So much for social inclusion in our Brave New Britain.

Hold on, you say, these mentally disordered people are clearly annoying people, disordered or not, and should be punished to deter them. What's unfair about that?

Well that summarizes government policy very well. However it is unfair if punishment is proved to be ineffective compared with proper medical treatments.

236

It is unfair if such people are often targeted for a disability, not ASB, and are unable to defend themselves in disputes because of poor verbal and reasoning skills. It is also a fraud on the public since ASBOs are supposed to be issued only where an order will 'protect' people from future ASB acts. Experience shows that in cases involving mental disorders ASBO conditions are massively breached.

So, you say, the ASBO process is unfairly biased. I still don't know how you can prove that.

We can get a feel for the scale of the problem of ASBO process bias with published data discussed earlier and in the next section. Firstly we can estimate the proportion of ASBOs going to mentally disordered people from various sources.

60% of ASBO targets had 'medical mitigating factors' in court. (Home Office)
38% of ASBOs went to mentally disordered youngsters. (BIBIC)
80% of the FIP families had serious mental /physical /learning disability health problems. (Government FIP evaluations)We will take a conservative estimate of 50% going to disordered people overall.

Secondly we need an estimate of the UK mentally disordered population including the learning disabled, the drug and alcohol addicted and the mentally ill.
We have that :There are 1 million children with alcoholic parents
(Think Family , DFCSF)
There are 350,000 children with drug addicted parents
("   "   "   )
There are 2.8 million with chronic alcohol dependency
(Royal College of Psychiatrists)
There are 1.3 million with chronic drug dependency
(Roy. Coll. Of Psych.)
There are 240,000 with functional psychosis
("   "   "   )
400,000 drug addicts receive incapacity benefits
(gov. DWP)

26% of people have disabling depression / anxiety disorders at some time in their lives. (Mental health Foundation) There are 1.2 million classed as moderate and mild learning disabled (Mencap). Some additional assumptions are needed. Considering the family data the numbers could refer to one or two parents and a typical poor, high risk family has ~3 children.

We know the poorest ere often lone mother led. Assume 1.5 parents. We should then estimate numbers of adults in the poorest families with alcohol addiction as 1 x 1.5 / 3 = 0.5 million and drug addicted 0.35 x 1.5 / 3 = 0.175 million.

Similarly the number of adults with acute depression / anxiety depends on the duration of the episode. Peak depression is in the 25-44 age groups but children also get depressed. 42% of people on incapacity benefit have depressive illnesses. Consider the 15-75 range overall. If we assume a total of one year acute illness we get 60m x 0.26 / (75-15) = 260,000. If we assume 3 years we get 60m x 0.26 x 3 / (75-15) = 780,000. We can now estimate upper and lower bounds on the 'mentally disordered' population.

	Lower bound	Upper bound
Moderate/ mild Learning disabled	1.2 m	1.2 m
Functionally psychotic	0.24	0.24
Depression / anxiety	0.26	0.78
Drug addiction	0.675	2.8
Alcohol addiction		1.3
Totals	2.375 m	6.32 m

The lower bound does not include other minor mental disorders. The upper bound may overestimate the severity of the social impact of alcohol / drug dependency. E.g. the DWP data shows only 400,000 drug addicts on incapacity benefits. DWP data for 2006 noted ~1.1 million people on incapacity benefit with 'mental illness'. We therefore take a rough estimate as the mean, 4.35 million.

By 2007 ~12,000 ASBOs had been issued although rates were then falling rapidly. We will work with total ASBOs as 14,000. So we have

Populations	4.35m mentally disordered	55.56 m 'normal'
ASBO numbers	7000	7000
Ratio ASBO / population	1 / 621	1 / 7950

Which implies the mentally disordered population is a remarkable 12.8 x more antisocial than 'normal' people. Do we really believe this? If not what else might be going on?

Well in the next section we will look in detail at the shocking level of abuse suffered by the disordered. For example Mencap and Mind surveys show that 82 – 88% of such people had received physical and verbal abuse from their neighbours. 25% were forced to move home. Now clearly the 4.35 million disordered people, without ASBOs, did not 'ask for' this disability abuse other than being different, weird, strange and unlikely to kick back. Incapable drunks or addicts did not incite people to urinate on them or to set fire to them on the street. Visibly learning disabled people did not incite others to chase them along the road and insult them. In the next section we will see the remarkable levels of general paranoia out there: people just waiting for a safe target on which to exorcise their demons. 27% of people think somebody is trying to irritate them. 10% think somebody has it in for them. (Institute of Psychiatry) The next question is how do 'normal' people fare in the abuse, intimidation stakes? Well recall the British Crime Survey of ASB which showed that 11% of people thought being intimidated, pestered, insulted was a fairly big or very big problem. 6% thought neighbour disputes were a big problem. Let's be generous and take the higher figure. So the ratio of frequency of abuse comparing mentally disordered and 'normal' people is 86 / 11 = 7.82 x. If you are mentally disordered, antisocial or not, you are nearly 8x more likely to suffer abuse and intimidation in your neighbourhood. This rather stacks the deck does it not? Suppose we adjust the ASBO / per head of population ratio calculated earlier for frequency of abuse. We have 12.8 / 7.82 = 1.64 x. Suddenly the ASBO rate per head for disordered versus 'normal' people does not look so different. Lets look at the mentally disordered who do get ASBOs.

Some may be guilty of Irritating but **involuntary** behaviours related to conditions like ADHD, autistic spectrum disorders, Touretes syndrome, bipolar disorders, schizophrenia, etc, etc. Such sufferers may be unaware of or unable to understand their impact on others. Inappropriate behaviour is common and easily redefined as antisocial. We will see later that some nameless behaviour disorders relate to chronic chemical imbalances and even to simple malnutrition and poor diet. Secondly some people targeted for being 'strange' may be physically normal and capable of kicking back at abusers. They may suffer from poor reasoning powers, an inability to plan ahead and an inability to foresee the consequences of their actions. However like the others, they also fall foul of a key problem: their inability to tell their side of the story to state agencies in disputes and in court. Verbal skills, quick thinking, lying, reasoning, appearance, attitude control are all impaired. As we noted from several sources including the FIP managers, the DPPs and HOC select committees, the mentally impaired often fail to get a fair hearing. How can we take this into account?

Suppose we simply assume performance in the above circumstances is proportional to IQ. We take the 1.2 m moderate / mild learning disabled to have a mean IQ of 60. What about the other 3.15 m disordered, the drunk, drugged and mentally ill? Clearly common sense experience suggests cognitive, communication, disinhibition and attitude impairments in such people. What is their 'effective' IQ? Let us make a range of assumptions.

Learning disabled	other disordered	mean IQ	dis. IQ / normal IQ
Nos. 1.2 m	3.15 m		
IQ 60	80	74.5	1 / 1.38
60	70	67.2	1 / 1.54
60	60	60	1 / 1.72

The table assumes a 20 – 40% deficit in effective IQ for the other disordered in comparison to mean population IQ of 100. This is reasonable considering also the higher frequency of addictions for, example, in the poorest families where starting IQ is already low. With these reasonable assumptions we quickly approach the remaining unexplained 1.64 ratio of ASBO frequency for the disordered versus the 'normal' populations. A mean effective IQ of 64 for the disordered population gives a corrected factor of 1.64 / 1.63 = 1.01x. The population difference has disappeared.

Let's be clear: whether the disordered were genuinely antisocial or not poor defence skills put them at a significant disadvantage in disputes with neighbours or council agents. It is also not unreasonable that the general 7.82 x factor for exposure to abuse suffered by the mentally disordered offers far more opportunity for inappropriate responses by such people whether you choose to call that antisocial behaviour or not. Overall the evidence clearly supports a system powerfully biased against the mentally disordered. Two years after new labour was kicked out the above analysis was vindicated as the Children's Commissioner for England published (in October 2012)

'Nobody Made the Connection: the prevalence of neuro-disability in young people who offend'

A team of eminent forensic psychiatrists reviewed all the published evidence on the prevalence of disabilities in the general population and in the youth offending population. The results surprised even this author in their clarity. Here they are in summary.

Disorder	prevalence general population	offending population	ratio
Learning Disabilities	3%	27.5%	9.2 X
Autistic Spectrum	0.9%	15%	16.6X
Dyslexia	10%	50%	5X
ADHD	5.3%	12%	2.3X
Communication Disorders	6%	75%	12.5X
Traumatic Brain injury	2.78%	6.86%	2.5X
Foetal Alcohol Syndrome	2.5%	11.3%	4.4X

These differences are massive by any standard. Note the huge differential in communication disorders and autism. Added to the information which has been noted repeatedly since 2000, they make an overwhelming case for our contentions. The truth is many knowledgeable people did 'make the connection' and were ignored by populist politicians out for votes.

The Children's Commissioner draws familiar conclusions and makes obvious recommendations. Firstly governments must intervene early to identify mental disorders and provide genuine medical support.
As we have seen in the ASBO Jihad even when disorders were recognized little was done. Secondly the commissioner demands that young people with such disorders must be recognized in the youth justice system and **diverted** out of the criminal justice system and into a medical support system. She concluded :

'Our findings call into question whether a criminal justice system that commits young people with neurodisability to custody is a fair and just system if those young people ...do not understand the consequences of their actions, nor have the cognitive capacity to instruct solicitors...'

Remember expensive imprisonment, ASBOs and the rest, do not solve the medical and societal problems, genuine or not, that these children and youths represent. Medical treatments may do (see below). While considering 'Nobody Made the Connection' and neuro-disability we might also ask from whence came the war on the 'lone mother' which justified the FIPs? The author has a suggestion. Antisocial personality disorder is a recognized cluster of disorders at one extreme merging into psychopathy or sociopathy. Consulting the voluminous literature we find that such disorders are 'explained' by the popular Bio-psycho-social-model (BPS) which posits both genetic and environmental factors (see for example 'Working with Personality Disordered Offenders'; Ministry of Justice). The key environmental factor is 'parental capacity', in other words the capability of the 'lone mother'. The ASB youngster is genetically inferior and his mother makes it worse.

Ah, you say, if these disorders are officially recognized why aren't the families from hell given suitable medical treatment?

Indeed Mr. England. As I explained that would be costly. However there is another reason. The BPS model has been used in other contexts to play down the role of genuine mental and physical illnesses and to blame patient behaviour on 'lack of moral fibre' and to an overindulgent society in assigning them a 'sick role'. This interpretation has been very popular in the insurance industry to deny sickness payouts. Sickness is due to 'psychosomatic' factors, malingering and character weakness. In respect to the FIP mothers does this sound familiar Mr. England?

Yes it does, but it's a jump to say new labour used this BPS model to justify their ASB family approach.

Later we will look at the new labour and Coalition blitzkriegs on the chronically sick and congenitally disabled on Incapacity Benefit. This was underpinned by the so-called work capability assessment developed under new labour, honed to a new level of viciousness under the Coalition and implemented by the ATOS company. The theoretical basis of the WCA is the BPS model adapted from the American insurance industry via the UNUM funded 'research' group at Cardiff University. Later we will look at the regular exchange of senior people between these organizations.
We will see that the WCA has been widely condemned for finding terminally ill and seriously disabled people 'fit for work' and by the High Court for discriminating illegally against people with mental disorders.
New labour knew all about the BPS model and I suggest used its 'pseudo-science' to covertly justify to themselves the ASBO Jihad and the populist Families from Hell narrative. Parenting classes can cure mental disorders on the cheap...or not. Despite the clear evidence of the inappropriate targeting and failure of sanctions led ASB policy, some government

advisers like the ubiquitous Louise Casey, recommended even more rabid sanctions. As she said in 2006 to what she calls the 'friggin' Guardian:

'We have lost the ability to be judgmental because we worry about being seen as nasty to poor people'

Or to put it more bluntly even new labour ministers, unlike Ms Casey, worried about being found out. Well they have been as we have seen and will see later. There is no appeal from FIP targeting.In fact the Sheffield academic team who prepared the FIP evaluation reports, so shamefully distorted by the government, wrote a report for the Disability Rights Commission demonstrating the scale and seriousness of this unfair, punitive targeting. They were scathing about the labour government's 'simplistic approach' which allows politicians to 'side step the more complex issues of social exclusion' and which 'serves to justify a focus on punishment'. The issue of whether mentally impaired people can help their behaviour is buried. They say

'...the subjects of ASB interventions often have mental health problems, learning difficulties and neurological disorders. This raises the crucial question about the extent to which the use of potentially punitive control mechanisms...can be justified. ASBOs in particular have DRASTIC IMPACTS on disabled people by not only failing to address root causes of disruptive behaviour , but the effects of employing a regulatory mechanism that can have exclusionary effects and even result in a custodial sentence, may serve to exacerbate their problems'

For many years mounting evidence that many health conditions often seen in ASBO recipients relate to executive dysfunctions of various kinds, in turn related to brain damage or development abnormalities and to faulty chemical control systems for dopamine, serotonin or cortisol, related either to very poor nutrition or to known genetic faults, has been ignored. Cambridge University work in 2008 confirmed that low serotonin in particular leads to aggressive, impetuous behaviour and can result from something as simple as missing meals. Serotonin levels also fall with insufficient blood glucose levels. Low IQ families on low incomes are particularly susceptible to a poor diet. We will look at this again later.

Well, you say, this is just liberals making excuses for criminals and yobs.

Is it? In 2009 Lord Bradley took evidence from many sources for his report on people with learning disabilities and mental illness in the criminal justice system which we will look at later. One eminent witness, based on direct experience, told him

'The failure to identify and provide support at an early stage is the reason some [mentally disordered] people offend in the first place'

The liberal in question was Her Majesty's Inspector of Prisons. The evidence for the failure of FIPs to deliver, the targeting of mentally disordered families and the heavy criticism of the FIP model by the Sheffield University evaluation team was brought to the attention of the Dept For Children, Families & Schools several times via my M.P. The responses were to say the least, unsatisfactory. Finally the unequivocal Sheffield evidence appeared to push the Dept. into a corner. The result? Well Beverly Hughes, minister of state, disowned the Sheffield evaluations in April 2009!

'The Sheffield Hallam evaluation ...does not provide a sufficiently robust basis on which to infer performance for FIPs as a whole'

But wait a minute... the Sheffield Hallam evaluations were the most detailed, sustained evaluations available. Government claims for FIP success for several years were based entirely on these evaluations and still are on several web sites. The reports were still cited by the Coalition Communities Dept. Families Tsar in 2013. The labour government had simply moved on now the evaluation limitations were pointed out to them. Let's look now in more detail at more recent FIP results.

The detailed 'Early Outcomes' evaluations by the NCSR, discussed earlier, for 53 current FIPs were now favoured by Beverly Hughes, based on data from only 9 projects and interviews with 18 families, that is 1.7% of all families. The 'quantitative' results covered only 8.3% for the first 90 families completing. The sampling is very limited. How can such data allow us to 'infer the performance for FIPs as a whole' as Ms. Hughes put it? This is a mystery. Not only that but the criterion for completing intervention was

'ASB has stopped or reduced to an acceptable level'

In other words the families don't get out until they are judged 'successful'. But this is a tautology...those who complete must be successful by definition! We are told that at exit only 7% of families had 'four or more types' of ASB versus 61% at entry. This sounds good until we consider the above criterion. These results only tell us about the first 90 families and nothing about the remaining 91.7% of families still in the

FIPs. Are the first 90 simply the easiest to re-programme? Remarkably there is clear evidence they are. In the bulk population 80% of families had some initial enforcement action against them but only 51% of the first 90 families. Remarkably we also find that **35% of the successful families are still involved in one or more types of ASB.** Is this success? Remarkably there is no quantitative data on the actual frequency and severity of the ASB either before or after the FIPs.Remarkably although we are told of the high levels of criminality and ASB in the families only ~ 8% of children had an Acceptable Behaviour Contract and only ~2.6% of individuals had an ASBO. What qualitative data there is on 'types of ASB' is very misleading. For example while 62% of families were supposedly involved in 'rowdy behaviour' only 1% had a fixed penalty notice for disorder. Although 54% supposedly had committed noise offences only 1% had a penalty notice for noise. By presenting data at the family level the degree of criminality / ASB is also 'sexed up' e.g While 98% of families had 'reports of ASB' this involved only 44% of individuals… the majority were not involved in ASB at all. The authors openly admit to serious limitations of the study. In fact the authors acknowledged several major caveats

'The IS findings should be treated with caution as the [8.3% of] families included in this analysis were the first to complete the service and might not be very representative of all the families FIPs work with'

Indeed not since successful 'completion' was defined by a large reduction in ASB…the criterion is a tautology.

'No reliable [quantitative] results are available on the issue [of ASB severity or frequency] because in the majority of cases information on complaints was not collected numerically'

'These results cannot be used to assess the quantitative impact of FIPs as the IS did not include a control group'

Indeed the claimed results are arguably scientifically invalid and even worse

'It is less clear whether these positive outcomes will be sustained in the longer term…More work needs to be done to assess the degree to which outcomes are sustained in the longer term'.

Indeed since families were evaluated only 5 to 10 months after leaving the projects. Nor was there significant change in underlying health and social problems.

'FIP families by their very nature tend to have deeply-entrenched and complex problems which can take time to reveal themselves, **let alone start to be resolved...**there was little change ...many health problems require a long period to be resolved ...the evidence from family interviews suggests that families had not received much help with health issues'

Remember that most families (99%) were referred to the FIPs because of 'risk factors' yet we learn that at exit 80% of families still had risk factors. Logically if these families were now referred to an FIP they would be accepted for re-programming again! Sheffield noted similar caveats but looked at 6 FIPs and more families over a longer evaluation period. Why dismiss the Sheffield results now? Because the authors had distanced themselves from the FIP model and government policy.

The recent 53 FIP evaluation suffers from severe data / analysis problems but has the virtue of making these even clearer than previous studies along with the preferential targeting of the most mentally disordered and socially inadequate people and the lack of medical support they receive. The author has brought these facts to the attention of several government agencies. Curiously he notes on the DfCSF Publications website (November 2009) that the full NCSR Early Outcomes evaluation report (DCSF – RBW047)

'...is currently out of stock and cannot be ordered'

Perhaps the author's analysis proved too embarrassing or too convincing? He wondered how long the NCSR contract will survive given their honest presentation of the FIP database and evaluation limitations...but see below for the government's cunning solution.

One final point of interest. Remember that the Sheffield team became convinced that the families were distinguished from their communities by greater mental disorders and social inadequacy. They say remarkably that

'Contrary to popular belief the evidence suggests that rather than constituting a distinct minority families tended to conform to the norms and values of the communities in which they lived'

How can this be said about the 'families from hell' and their yob children? Remember in the ASB process in resolving ASB neighbour conflicts the council agent selects the easiest target to be the villain and the more able, eloquent disputant to be the victim. The disputants are very similar in outlook and behaviour and the main point of difference is suitability to be targeted: that is being incapable of self defence because of a mental disorder or low IQ and 'fitting the profile' of risk factors: that is being a depressed lone mother in rent arrears with mentally disordered children and a dirty house.

Finally in March 2010 a new report on the 53 projects appeared on the DCSF website: DCSF-RR215, providing summary results for 1013 families who had by then completed reprogramming. The headline claim was that 64% of those reaching a 'planned exit' had ceased any ASB (or a drop from 89% to 32%). As usual the figure is grossly misleading. It does not account for 742 families who dropped out before completion. So we actually have 1013 x 0.89 = 902 + 742 = 1644 families with ASB at entry and 1013 x 0.32 = 324 + 742 = 1066 at exit. The exit proportion is therefore 1066 / (1013+742) = 60.7 % and the fall in ASB families is (1644 − 1066) / (1013 + 742) = 0.329 or 32.9% not 64%.

However this is not the end of the distortions. Earlier reports stressed that willingness to engage was a primary criterion for selecting families and some families were rejected as being to violent or disruptive to allow in the FIPs. It is interesting then that 923 of the families referred were deemed to be 'unsuitable' and rejected. On this basis we can legitimately add these 'refuseniks' into the overall project process numbers. The total offered the FIPs was 2734. Applying the above success rate to all the eventual number still with ASB would be 1531. The total number of families referred was 2734+923 = 3657. So, on the basis of problem family referrals the true success rate would be (821+1531) / 3657 = 0.246 or 24.6%, a long way from 64%.

Of course all this did not stop the ubiquitous Louise Casey telling the Home Affairs Select Committee in 2010 of FIP success ... that 66% of families who experienced the FIPs were no longer involved in ASB. On the families she said

'You have got to crack down on the very small number of absolutely problematic families that cause the most havoc in communities. That varies from the lowest level of disorder that we call ASB to the nastiest crimes... I think they are few in number but the problems they cause in communities are phenomenal...[some of the worst families] are deliberately choosing not to cope [with their children]'

Remember the majority of those parents 'deliberately choosing not to cope' have serious health conditions and children with a range of mental disorders. By 2009 the FIP expansion plan would cover 50,000 'chaotic' families ...hardly a few. By 2011 Cameron's plan would allegedly cover 120,000 'problem families'. Let us be clear. Most of these families are targeted for deprivation and statistical risk factors, including having one or more mentally disordered children and being poor and socially inadequate. Whole families are consigned to sanctions based 'ASBO Sin Bins' as a result for 'assertive, non-negotiable' interventions. This treatment is identical to the 'guilt by association' policy operated by North Korea. If one family member is targeted by the state, for any reason, the whole family is subject to the 'exterminate three generations' process which sends them all to the gulags…forever.

It is interesting that North Korea operates a huge network of informants. As we will see new labour encouraged similar 'citizen' networks, including training children to report on neighbours. The government mantra was 'See it: Report it'. As we will see, under new labour, the UK also shared with North Korea the highest classification of state surveillance intensity. It is interesting also that the 'follow up' studies on families some 9 to 14 months after exit, claimed no deterioration in ASB status. However the small print tells us these results are based on ~80 families who reached planned exit, a mere 4.5% of those processed in the FIP schemes and 2.9 % of those originally referred. Not only is the sample ridiculously small for drawing general conclusions but it represents those families still cooperating with the authorities… it is fatally biased by definition as the previous NCSR report acknowledged.

Of course there is still no quantitative data on ASB frequency or severity only numbers of 'types of ASB' reported. Basing judgments about ASB and ASB changes on such qualitative data is like saying that a man with 4 denominations of coins in his pocket is wealthier than a man with one denomination of coin in his pocket irrespective of how much money he actually has. If only we could pay our taxes on such a basis! It is also interesting that unlike all previous 'scientific' reports on the FIPs this report gives only numerical summary results. There is no analysis or discussion and no caveats about data quality or the conclusions that can legitimately be reached. One can only assume that the politicians did not want independent analysts challenging their results again. That is their choice but now the government had lost the ability to make any claims about the 'scientific' validity of evidence supporting the success of FIPs. As in the case of the Drug Advisory Board fiasco, the misuse of knife crime statistics, criticized by their own chief statistician, and the made up evidence to support illegally keeping DNA records, all credibility has been lost. This did not stop Allan Johnson, Home Secretary from making more unsupported claims in the HoC on 18.01.10

'FIPs have proved phenomenally successful…an independent study of the first 700 families to take part in FIPs show dramatic reduction not only in ASB but in …mental health problems'

Compare that with what we have seen. Hidden from public sight the National Family Intervention Strategy Board, in effect the FIP 'trade association' reported to the parliamentary Health Select Committee in October 2010 providing useful data. It seems 40% of adults from 'families with multiple problems' face mental health problems: some 2.5 X more than English adults found with such issues at clinical review. The NFISB also quotes FIP results on mental health with a reduction from 31% of families with problems to 26% at project exit, a fall of just 5% of families. This modest result, far from the public claims, is not surprising since they said

'One of the biggest problems from FIPs is accessing health services '

Recall that the author found that only 10 to 14% of families had access to mental health treatment in the projects despite for example 69% of adults having serious depressive or anxiety problems. Recall that new labour repeatedly claimed they had solved the 'access' problem but clearly it remained fourteen years after FIPs began in Dundee.

The change of government did not change the cavalier approach to FIP evidence. OSR 14 / 2011 in September 2011 shows how the qualitative approach has been desperately extended to try to paint a picture of FIP success. Figures are now given for 'overall project success'. That is the proportion of families leaving an FIP for 'a successful reason'. This was said to be 85%. However this is based on a most peculiar kind of button counting. In the tables recording 'reasons for leaving a family intervention' we learn that there are 10 reasons classed as successful. **Any one reason defines a family as a success.** However these families are referred in the first place because they exhibit serious 'multiple risk factors', typically several, according to the government. The subjective improvement in **any one** may not therefore significantly reduce overall risk. This is actually stressed in bold type in the body of the report.

'Without an impact assessment we cannot establish whether the outcomes achieved by families can be directly attributed to the family intervention services... **In addition families may still be at risk when they complete a family intervention service even though the level of risk may have reduced'**

So there is no proof a project is responsible for any family changes. So risk of future problems remains high even for 'successful' families. This definition of success is dubious in the extreme and will certainly mislead an unsophisticated public since the above major caveats are not declared when Coalition government ministers promote the FIPs. This amounts to fraud but it is not the end of the distortions. There are also 6 reasons classed as 'inconclusive': defining neither a success nor a failure. However these reasons include

- High risk cases : unsafe for staff to continue to visit the family.
- Family breakup
- Children taken into care
- Family referred for another FIP
- Family referred to another support service.

In addition the sixth reason 'family moved away' likely includes the many cases where families were forced to move by vigilante neighbours, some 59% based on the earlier evaluations. It is difficult for the author to see the other 5 reasons above as 'inconclusive'. Surely they all signal failure? If staff is afraid to visit a family is this not a failure of the FIP to improve family behaviour? Avoiding family breakdown and the taking of children into care is given as a major financial aim of the FIPs. Sending a family to another FIP or other services, for another try, is surely not a success? But these reasons are not recorded as failures. We also learn that if a project worker recorded both inconclusive and successful reasons this case was reported as a success. Finally only two reasons are given for defining a family as a failure: the family refused intervention; the family failed to engage during the project. In fact just to make things clear we are told

'After January 2009 these codes were removed for families leaving at the exit stage, meaning there were **no** unsuccessful reasons for leaving an ASB FIP at the exit stage'

34% of families reaching 'planned exit' still exhibited ASB and still exhibited multiple-risk factors for which they had been referred in the first place. In terms of all families leaving 62.9 % still exhibited ASB. The unsuccessful family rate is not the implied 3.9% but at least 30%. The definitions used exaggerate success and minimize failure in an unacceptable and dishonest way. At the same time ministers like Tim Laughton were lecturing charities and local authorities about the need for bidding for 'intervention' funding based only on those techniques which were 'evidence based'. Yet Loughton said on September 14th 2011 on the latest FIP statistical release

'The statistics show an overwhelmingly positive picture of how intensive family intervention can successfully turn around the lives of families that have many complex problems'

Compare this statement with our analysis above: it is blatant, unsupportable rubbish. Policy based evidence was still alive and well in the Coalition. When Louise Casey became Troubled Families Tsar for the Coalition the false claims for FIP success soared to new heights. In Summer 2012 Casey herself undertook personal 'research' by going forth to interview 16 families from hell selected from the projects out of several thousand families identified so far. The families appeared grateful and successfully reprogrammed in the anecdotal report. This was heralded in the press as a major event. Strangely the press was not directed to a caveat in the report which said

'The information [the interviews] gave us is not representative of the 120,000 families that are deemed to be troubled'

A number of real researchers also pointed out that these families were living under the threat of sanctions and their 'ethical approval' to be used in such 'research' had not been obtained, breaching ministerial guidelines. Casey's research such as it was, was equivalent to evidence obtained under torture. Complaints to the Dept. for Communities and Local Government elicited the remarkable response that

**'The report falls more properly within the description dipstick /
informal information gathering'**

Meaning that Ms Casey could ignore the government's ethical guidance on social research. So it seems we have finally moved from 'evidence based policy' to 'policy by dipstick'. But as Casey said in her infamous HO / ACPO dinner speech

'If No. 10 says bloody evidence based policy to me once more I'll deck them one'

To expunge this embarrassment one assumes, Casey was sent away to produce a 'real research' report which appeared in December 2012 with a great fanfare in the press. The idea was to brazen it out and rally the local council storm troopers. The usual headline claims were made about reductions in crime and ASB in FIP families based largely on an update of the 2010/2011 NCSR results we examined earlier. However careful reading of the extensive references showed that the only full FIP evaluations cited were those we looked at earlier from Sheffield Hallam University and the NCSR. This time the main claim is that involvement in ASB fell by 59%, a long way from the early FIPs claiming 85% ...but there is more. The appendix tells us 77% of families exhibited ASB on project entry and 31% at exit, a fall of 46% of families.

But notice that at entry 23% of families had NO ASB. Compare these numbers with the 98% of families exhibiting ASB at entry in the last major NCSR evaluation. We were told in that report that only 44% of individuals had ASB at entry. Reporting at the family level 'sexed up' the ASB frequency. If we estimate the number of individuals with ASB at entry for the latest data using the same proportion we get ~35% and at FIP exit ~14%, a fall of 21% of individuals. However the main point in these recent results is that only ~35% of individuals, probably youngsters in a multi-child family, allegedly exhibited ASB at FIP entry. Yet Coalition government ministers and Ms Casey continue to claim the families are all targeted for making their neighbourhoods a misery. In fact we have known for years that most are targeted for 'risk factors', mainly for being lone parent led, poor and in debt and mentally disordered. This is making the generous assumption that the data is valid. However hidden in the appendices are the usual strongly worded caveats about this 'research'.

- The evaluations had no control groups so that any claimed improvements could NOT be objectively attributed to the projects.
- The outcome evaluations were 'in most cases' based on 'subjective assessments' by FIP project workers who have something of an interest in declaring their projects a success. There was no independent, objective scrutiny of outcomes.
- The evaluation evidence is 'qualitative in nature' based on 'interviews and case studies with small numbers of families'.

Previously we saw that these samples were biased by definition. And finally the researchers say 'this means that the evidence, of course, should not be taken as representative of all [120,000] troubled families'.

Note that the claimed results **are not classed as official government statistics** which says it all. There is no indication of independent validation by the Office for National Statistics which has sometimes been claimed for previous reports. The Coalition has continued the new labour government misrepresentation of the families and project success measures. But then as Ms Casey said at the infamous HO / ACPO dinner

'Topic for this evening: Research Help or Hindrance? Hindrance thanks very much'

Look, you say, these FIPs have been going on for over a decade, surely if they did not work they would have been stopped.

Why Mr. England?

What matters for governments is to appear to be doing something, anything, to garner popularity in a difficult area. The public are easy to mislead. However, every now and again the truth slips out. In January 2013 the Families Tsar, Louise Casey, spoke at a cross party meeting at Westminster on Sure Start and child protection. Along with anecdotal horror stories about chaotic families she spoke off the cuff about previous family intervention schemes.

'Will any of these things touch those families? The answer is they haven't yet.'

Casey has had many years to reprogramme tens of thousands of 'families from hell' and now admitted that she has failed. Finally you had it from the nags own mouth.

Let's get back to new labour and see what Gordon Brown did towards the end of his reign. Despite all the clear evidence of the failure of ASB FIPs Brown still believed, or claimed to believe in them. He even endorsed the discredited Dundee project which he claimed to have visited. In September 2009 when new labour was in third place in the polls behind the Lib Dems, a desperate Gordon turned again to ASB to distract attention and appeal crudely to the electorate. He told us again that 'the decent hard working majority feel the odds are stacked against them in favour of a minority ...' and as a result this minority of irresponsible families would be targeted. Another

'50,000 chaotic families would be subject to FIPs with ...clear rules and clear penalties'.

He repeated again that if youngsters breached ASBOs the parents would be punished...and put on an order themselves. Gordon must have been desperate if all he could do was recycle discredited ASB interventions. But fear not! He had another cunning plan. Using his unerring 'moral compass' Gordon zeroed in on the unmarried lone mother again. He told us

'From now on all 16 and 17 year old parents living on state support will be placed in supervised, shared homes where they will learn their responsibilities and how to raise their children properly'

As the election approached in March 2010 Brown announced in Reading

'We are expanding FIPs to cover **all** problem families in the country'

and he justified this by quoting the second phase, 53 project results

---

253

evaluated by the National Centre For Social Research we discussed earlier.

'Of the first 700 families to go through the system 2 / 3 are no longer involved at all in ASB'.

Well we saw earlier that the actual short term 'success' rate is arguably 24 % and certainly no more than 33 %. Mr. Brown who condemned the 'misuse of crime statistics' by the Conservatives failed to mention these pertinent facts. The new labour tradition of distorting and spinning the truth continued. Later we will see Brown caught out and humiliated for giving false data to the Chilcot Inquiry on army spending and equipment supply in Afghanistan.

In the labour party manifesto of 2010 the position was reinforced again

'For the 50,000 most dysfunctional families who cause misery to their neighbours, we will provide Family Intervention Projects- proven to tackle ASB – a no-nonsense regime of one-to-one support with tough sanctions for non-compliance'

Remember most of these families were targeted for rent arrears or dirty gardens or 'having risk factors' like being 'lone mother led' with mentally disordered children and Brown himself said that they were only 'in danger of offending' when pressed. What can their neighbours be like if such problems cause them 'misery'? After all the evidence we have seen how could labour say FIPs are 'proven to tackle ASB'? These statements are simply blatant lies. The manifesto was remarkable on law and order in many respects. It proudly claimed

'We have brought in a right to petition local authorities to end 24 hour licensing where problems arise'

Are we supposed to have forgotten that labour brought in the 24 hour license in the first place and that late night drunken disorder had increased as a result? How about illegally keeping the DNA of one million innocent people which we will examine in detail later? The manifesto says

'We are proud of our record on civil liberties and have taken the DNA profiles of children off the database…'

Yes… because all the UK Children's Commissioners, the EU and the United Nations expressed outrage at the keeping of children's DNA, innocent or not. How could even new labour hacks dare to write such slime? Incredibly in a 'political profile' interview on ITV before the 2010 election Brown declared that he would like to be seen, above all, as the 'children's champion'. Given all we have already seen and what is to come this beggars belief.

Finally on disadvantaged, vulnerable young women, the new labour position was clear...the lone mother 'enemy of the people' and her 'menace' children will be forced into ineffective reprogramming in the projects or, if under 18, locked up for their own good in 'slag hostels'.
As Tony Blair said 'there is no point pussyfooting' and Gordon had finally taken that view to the limit. Notice 'all' poor, underclass 16 and 17 year olds are to be included no questions asked. All are presumed guilty...surely the ultimate example of 'actuarial justice'. With such rhetoric from the top was it surprising that in some northern cities organized rings of Asian sexual predators targeted such vulnerable young girls in state 'care'? In Rochdale in 2012, 9 Asian men were found guilty of serially abusing and prostituting up to 50 vulnerable under age girls. Many of the girls were under state 'supervision'. Look, the governments of Britain have no regard for these white 'slags' so why should we?

There you go again, you say, exaggerating a minor problem.

Minor, Mr. England? In May 2013 an Oxford paedophile ring involving 5 Pakistani and 2 North African men was found guilty of 59 offences including rape, trafficking and organizing prostitution involving dozens of girls aged 11 to 15 years old. The judge described the treatment of these vulnerable girls as amounting to torture in many cases. The media characterized the girls as having 'chaotic' backgrounds and 'dysfunctional' families. Sounds familiar, does it not? The majority were in 'state care'.
Other 'gangs' were identified in Derby and Telford. In August 2014 Professor Alexis Jay published her extensive report into organized child sex abuse in Rotherham. It turned out that at least 1,400 children some as young as eleven, had been sexually abused, beaten and trafficked over a period of sixteen years by organized British Pakistani gangs. The professor noted

'The utter brutality is what shocked me most...it is really hard to describe it...[yet] South Yorkshire Police regarded many child victims with contempt...it continues to this day'

Most of the children were under state supervision. Many children had complained to social workers and the police but were ignored. The children were dismissed as 'undesirables', not worthy of protection by the police.

Youth workers who gave warnings to the local council were reprimanded and downgraded. Council staff told the professor that they were scared of pressing the Pakistani connection because the labour council would call them racists. Some staff reported that managers had directed them to bury the Asian connection. Senior police witnesses told the inquiry that 'influential' Pakistani councilors acted as 'barriers' on grooming issues. The Deputy Council leader over the period 2011-2014 was Jahangir Akhtar. However three reports on the abuse problem had been written from 2002 to 2006 and the findings suppressed or ignored. New cases were still emerging up to 2013.This is where new labour 'multiculturalism', political correctness and the denigration of underclass children from dysfunctional families had taken us. Surely this poison is pure evil?

That is conjecture, you say

When the report came out Dennis McShane the former Rotherham MP, admitted that he had not said anything because 'as a liberal leftie' he had not wanted to 'rock the multicultural boat' (Daily Telegraph 30.08.14). Other labour MPs spoke out. Ann Cryer reported that when in 2002 she exposed a sex-abuse scandal in Keighly involving Pakistani men, she was criticized as a racist. She noted 'at the time I was dealing with this, political correctness [about minorities] was playing a big part' Simon Danczuk the Rochdale MP who helped expose the Cyril Smith scandal also slated the warped thinking of council services management.

'Sit before children's services managers and you're likely to hear endless waffle about guidelines, policies, procedures, strategy and thresholds. But they won't mention the kids. Cold, remote theory rules…you end up with situations like Rotherham …where political correctness and cultural sensitivity are more important than child rape…This is dogma for breakfast, lunch and dinner'

Well said sir. If you want more chapter and verse Mr. England have a look at 'Easy Meat' published by the Law and Freedom Foundation in 2014 which recounts many similar scandals of industrial scale sexual abuse of children in 'state care', ignored by police and councils. I repeat: British governments and their agents have no regard for these troubled 'underclass' white girls from anti-social families so why should sexual predators from our ethnic minorities think and act differently? Their own culture, quite rightly, closely protects their own young girls.

By late 2012, two years into the Coalition government, the FIP claims were still unraveling. From the beginning it was said that the FIPs 'gripped' the 'worst' families.

This author showed again and again from the official FIP evaluation reports that this was not true …the easiest families were chosen. In 2014 the Heads of Young Peoples Services Convention met in Sheffield and claimed, like the author, that local authorities were 'cherry picking' easier to help families to make sure they received incentives under the Coalition 'payment by results' system and of course because FIP selection criteria strongly depended on identifying 'co-operative' families as a matter of principle from the beginning. So inevitably out of the woodwork came the ubiquitous Louise Casey, Troubled Families Tsar, threatening hell and damnation.

'If they don't target the difficult families and reduce their [state] dependency, then in two or three years time they will still be highly dependent and costing them [the local councils] money. I am very happy to hear from **quiet** whistleblowers'.

Notice the word **quiet.** Louise does not want the public learning the truth about the FIPs and woe betide any professional who speaks out too loudly. So what can we do? If we believe in simple genetic determinism the scope is limited. Increasingly unions which could precipitate such problems will be identified by screening. It is perfectly ethical to give the partners clear genetic counseling on the risks. If risky unions go ahead it will be increasingly possible to screen very early embryos for faults which provides another decision point for the parents. What the author fears of course is that the state will apply compulsion… as Blair said 'pre-birth even' to these possibly 'menace' children. This is the cheap and easy way out for the state. However recent evidence suggests that in many circumstances environment plays an important role and genuine remedial action in areas like education can significantly improve outcomes for such children. We will explore this in the next section. By 2009 more independent evidence emerged of the labour government's failure to tackle 'the causes of crime' and ASB.

A world expert on crime, Professor Irwin Waller, reviewed the effectiveness of government policy in a major report for the Policy Exchange think tank. He blamed the government's obsession with **'central control'** and punishment for **'widespread failure'** of the crime reduction strategy since 2002 and failure to address the causes of crime which we have seen relate closely to mental disorder and poverty. The report concludes that

'After a decade of unprecedented spending on policing, courts and prisons England and Wales have a crime rate **twice** the European average'

Prevention has not been adequately addressed here as it has successfully been in Europe. That is why crime here cost us an estimated £78 billion a year. Happy?

State Targeting of the Mentally Disordered.

So this is the position. The majority of youngsters caught up in the ASBO meat grinder have involuntary behaviours related to dietary stress, a mental condition or a learning disability related to genetically moderated brain development abnormalities. Usually they are in the poorest families. The evidence is clear: serious medical conditions are being punished, not treated; mentally impaired youngsters and their families are being branded as 'wicked' enemies of the state.

No, no, no, you say, the courts wouldn't let these things happen ...there must surely be safeguards?

Well the courts must follow the law however distasteful they may find it. I repeat, going back to ASBOs, the ASBO process is set up to almost guarantee success and it does, **98 %** of the time. But, yes, there are safeguards in principle ...but none in practice. First of all even ASB defendants have the right to mount a defence in court. However in all elements of the criminal justice system it is well known and accepted that the mentally ill and the learning disabled do not make 'credible' witnesses and are very vulnerable to prosecution attacks if the defendant (or to defence attacks if the plaintiff). In many cases for that reason, and under heavy pressure to save court time, no defence is presented. You don't believe me? Well listen to Sir David Calvert-Smith Q.C., the last Director of Public Prosecutions in a Voice disability conference in 2003:

'The vulnerable [disabled] have been ignored, abused and exploited and trying to redress the balance has been seen as too difficult'
The problem is clearly well known but remained unaddressed a decade on. The outgoing DPP, Sir Ken Macdonald said this in October 2008

'Disability hate is widespread...there is a vast amount not being picked up...This is a scar on the conscience of criminal justice. All institutions involved in CJ, including my own, share responsibility'

In March 2008 the Parliamentary Joint Select Committee on Human Rights published a major report on learning disability

'A Life Like Any Other? Human Rights of Adults with Learning Disabilities'

The report provides evidence for massive discrimination in the public sector. On the treatment of the learning disabled as victims of crime and as alleged perpetrators of crime the committee concludes

'We are concerned that the problems highlighted by this evidence could have potentially very serious implications for the rights of people with learning disabilities to a fair hearing, as protected by the common law and by Article 6 ECHR. Some of this evidence also suggests that there are serious failings in the criminal justice system which give rise to the discriminatory treatment of people with learning disabilities'

Once convicted because of these failings the discrimination continues

'We are deeply concerned that this evidence indicates that, because of failure to provide for their needs, people with learning disabilities may serve longer custodial sentences than others'

Not only this, but the mentally impaired are in great danger in custody. According to IPCC data 96 people died in custody or shortly after release in the year 2007/2008. Past IPCC data shows that ~50% of these were mentally impaired. The IPCC now also collects data on 'near miss' incidents where people were saved. In 2008 there were 1,053 near misses and at least 83% of these involved some mental disability, mental illness or addiction. The death rate is **9X** that for normal prisoners. This is even worse than the **4X** death rate for black people.

Look, you say, all this is terrible but there must be safeguards for things like ASBOs with so many children and youngsters being involved.

That is so on paper. In this case we have the comprehensive Home Office "Guidance on ASBOs and ABCs" and the similar Youth Justice Board Guidance. This rulebook required ASB teams to investigate the mental health background of all defendants. For a wide range of 'vulnerable people' it calls for a multi-agency approach to assessment before any intervention is decided including application for an ASBO. It calls for 'expert medical input' to the design of any intervention and a prior assessment of medical and social support needs. This information appears under the Home Office ASB practitioner advice segment 'How do I tackle ASB when an individual has a disability or mental health condition?' That is clear enough and we have it repeatedly from Hazel Blears herself in House of Commons statements and in letters to my M.P. Here is Blears written answer about safeguards which appears in Hansard (12th September 2005; column 2514w)

259

"It is for local authorities to determine what medical history should be considered when applying for an ASBO…If there is evidence that a perpetrator of ASB is suffering from a medical condition, mental health condition, disability or is vulnerable in any other way then a practitioner with specialist knowledge should be involved in the assessment process to determine the cause of the behaviour and whether an ASBO is the most appropriate tool…The assessment should account for known medical conditions or disabilities as well as uncovering undiagnosed problems"

In fact the original ASBO concept included the issuing of Individual Support Orders along with enforcement actions. In practice only ~10% of ASBOs had such ISOs attached despite the high levels of mental disorders. Even 10 years after the ASBO started this problem was not fixed (Challenge & Support Project Guidance: Youth Taskforce 18.02.08)

'However too often enforcement measures are used in isolation without consideration of appropriate support…Police, ASB teams and Registered Social landlords do not readily have access to the agencies that can undertake an assessment of a young person in order to determine the appropriate support that should be delivered. Also these agencies are not able or best placed to facilitate delivery of that support…'

So much for government claims of a 'multi-agency' approach. The picture is the same for medical support in the ASB Family Intervention Projects. Local authorities also have a statutory duty to assess any person who may be in need of community support at the start of preparing an application for an ASBO under the NHS and Community Care Act 1990. They have a similar duty to children aged 10-17 under the Children's Act 1989. However these safeguards are often ignored …hence the 38% of ASBOs issued to mentally impaired young people and the 60% of people with diagnosed medical mitigating factors who end up in court. They also have a duty under the Disability Discrimination Act 2005 to assess and take into account the mental disorders of tenants in social housing against whom they are taking action e.g. for eviction. However only half of councils are aware of this obligation and of those so aware, many ignored it. There is unequivocal proof of this. In 2005 the British Institute for Brain Injured Children surveyed All ASBO and Youth Offending Teams in the UK. The YOTs recorded a 38% incidence of ASBOs going to young, mentally impaired people. The extensive range of conditions listed showed that expert medical diagnoses had been obtained. The ASBO team officers recorded only a 5% incidence of mental health problems, notably a small number of ADHD cases and a few special needs cases.

No other medical problems were recorded. This is a remarkable result. For the same population the YOTs recognized a **7.4 X** greater incidence of serious mental conditions than the ASBO teams. The ASBO teams nationally were clearly and deliberately ignoring medical conditions which should engage the Home Office safeguards for 'vulnerable' people. Even worse the DDA 2005 contains a statutory requirement for ASB targets in social housing to receive psychiatric assessment **before** enforcement action is decided. This was clearly not happening, with council ASB teams making their own medical judgments. This is a scandal.

But why, you ask, would councils act like this?

Well the author had assumed that councils had been inspired to join in the ASBO Jihad because they believed it would be popular with voters and because of various government financial inducements. However my correspondence with a leading academic authority on ASB interventions, who advises governments, suggested another reason which shocked even me. He believes councils avoid medical assessments as a deliberate policy.

'I think that you make crucial points about medical factors. Indeed, there is a wider point about local authorities being reluctant to officially acknowledge and define medical conditions because of the cost implications of this re [special] school places , support etc. Hence ASB mechanisms are utilized to manage some cases where this is clearly inappropriate'

A similar picture emerges from educational research. Remember that 47% of our family children with problems have an ADHD / autistic spectrum disorder and that 2 / 3 of children excluded from mainstream schools are mentally impaired. Remember that new labour policy is 'inclusion' in the mainstream. However Professor Carl Parsons of Canterbury University, a recognized expert on inclusion, notes

'It means access to what other children get, even if it's in a watered down form…It could be argued that not all the money that was saved from closing special schools followed children into the mainstream…I'm not sure that most schools have got a grip on varying their provision …to be able to accommodate the educational needs of this wider range of children.'

Inclusion, even if teachers and carers are untrained in special needs, is cheaper. My academic colleagues are not alone in these views. SANE has said that the mental health services are simply 'passing the buck' back to the criminal justice system. The CEO of SANE has also argued that ASBOs are often seen as the cheaper option by local authorities. Remember 38% of young ASBO recipients have **diagnosed** mental health conditions and 80% of the FIP families have mental and physical disorders with 47% of the children having a problem being ADHD / hyperactive /autistic spectrum. If this contention is accurate we should be ashamed that councils acting in our name are doing this. As we will see below neglect of the mentally disordered by the state is endemic and shameful, but deliberate criminalization of such people to save money is unspeakably wicked.

ASBO teams, councils and magistrates courts are routinely ignoring other legal guidance. The Sentencing Guidelines Council says

'Some factors may indicate that an offender's culpability is unusually low …factors indicating significantly lower culpability [include]…mental illness or disability…'
Similarly the Justice's Clerks Society states that

'The court should be cautious when considering applications that relate to offenders with defined medical / mental problems that give rise to ASB'

Hold on, you say, how can Home Office and legal safeguards and the DDA be ignored by the ASBO teams they helped to set up and train? Well the Home Office assured me and my M.P. that they have no powers to intervene and indeed, no responsibility, if local authorities flout the safeguards …although they have expressed 'concern'. You get the picture? The apparent vulnerability safeguards will reassure the do-gooders and any curious MPs but in practice… let the councils get on with it…it's not our problem. That's why we didn't make the safeguards statutory …get it?

No, you say, that can't be a deliberate policy.

Consider: the new labour government notoriously flooded the statute books with thousands of new laws. Do we believe they would have accidentally missed the need for statutory safeguards in this area? And remember the Home Office had all the 'offender' statistics we have explored …they knew perfectly well who the ASBO net would gratuitously catch: the mentally impaired and socially inadequate. The fact is that successive new labour Home Secretaries while supporting the safeguards in Parliament when questioned, undermined them in the media to appear tough, so setting the tone for local council officers on the street …do what you like, mentally disordered or not. Hazel Blears said this in Community Care magazine in November 2005:

'Just because someone has a disability or is vulnerable in some way does not mean **their real ASB** is any less frightening to those around them'

This can only be read in one way: it does not matter if this 'real' behaviour is caused by a mental condition. It does not matter if the behaviour is involuntary and there is no intention to cause alarm. It does not matter if 'those around them' are ignorant, intolerant, prejudiced and merely irritated. The correct course is imposition of sanctions not treatment. That is the ASBO model.

The interesting question is why errant councils have not been pursued under the new DDA 2005. The author has no good answer to this despite having brought the situation to the attention of the Equality & Human Rights Commission....a body in some disarray as we will see.

Well, you say, surely they could go to the Local Government Ombudsman. It must be his job to monitor council misbehaviour.

Indeed it is. However it turns out the local government ombudsman cannot inquire into complaints against a council if the matter concerns preparation for a legal case brought by that council. If a court issues an ASBO that seems to preclude ombudsman involvement full stop. This is beyond his or her statutory brief. However it is interesting to go onto an LGO web site and look at the record of decisions against local councils. A remarkable number concern complaints by disabled or ill people, or their families, about neglect or mistreatment. So there you have it: nobody apparently had the responsibility or the power to monitor or police these so-called safeguards in the ASBO process.The mentally impaired are totally exposed in this inherently biased, draconian, legal meat grinder and local authorities have financial incentives to use ASBOs rather than costly medical treatment and special schools.

Of course a defendant could mount a legal appeal after the allowed interval but not on the grounds that their local authority, deliberately or through incompetence, failed to follow Home Office Guidance ...even though if that guidance had been followed the vulnerable defendant most likely would never have seen an ASBO court. Remember: the guidance is not statutory. Also we have seen that **98 %** of ASBO applications are approved because of the biased nature of the process. An appeal is essentially a rerun of the original case. What do you think the chances of success are? It is to be hoped that at some point the DDA 2005 will be brought into play but remember our near destitute, lone parents in social housing will find it difficult to organize legal help or even recognize their rights. So much for legal appeals in the UK.

Given the scathing statements of the Council of Europe Human Rights Commissioner about ASBOs the European Court is a possibility (see below). But how many of the poor, marginalised, and mentally impaired people unfairly caught by the ASBO process could summon the resources or wits to go to Europe? Besides several relevant articles such as the right to a fair trial and the right to privacy and right of free association are conditional rights and subject to local over-rides. Besides the labour government had been criticised by the European Court dozens of times for human rights violations with little effect on its behaviour (see below).

After ten years of criticism of the ASBO Jihad and the criminal justice system abuse of mentally disordered people the government commissioned Lord Bradley to look into the matter. His report was published in April 2009 and widely welcomed by mental health organizations. He concluded that health and social care for such people was essential at every stage from before arrest, through the courts and into prison. He also concluded that

'The majority of offenders with low level [mental] disorders are not dangerous and could be better treated outside the criminal justice system. Appropriate checks on mental health **before** ASBOs and penalty notices are issued to avoid **'accelerating vulnerable people into the criminal justice system rather than appropriate [medical] services'** But as we have seen such safeguards both statutory and guidance based exist already and were widely ignored by councils.

1. All police custody suites to have access to diversionary services for vulnerable people. Perhaps that will reduce the horrific death rate in custody of such people. Remember they are 9X more likely to die than you.

2. Immediate implementation of trained support for vulnerable defendants in court just as vulnerable witnesses are now supported.

3. Community sentence alternatives for vulnerable people which the evidence shows can be very effective if backed up with support..

4. Prison health screening of new inmates should include learning disability. The Prison Reform Trust found that 26 prison boards, more than half who replied to a survey, had no services for the learning disabled. One third did not even respond. This despite an estimate that (at least) 23% of under 18 prisoners have IQs less than 70.

5. Organised rehabilitation for mentally disordered prisoners leaving prison including health support.

Bradley's conclusions about the neglect of the mentally disordered correspond closely to the evidence we have explored together. How long will it be before the government accepts the evidence and acts? Remember 75% of the 86,000 UK prisoners are classed as 'intellectually impaired' and it costs £50,000 per annum to keep such people locked up. Reform could save money as well as reducing abuse.

Unfortunately, with labour, we were dealing with an evidence proof government. Having invented the failed ASBO and the failed 'ASBO Sin Bins', new labour, desperate for a new gimmick, introduced the 'Drinking Banning Order' or 'Booze ASBO' in September 2009.These BASBOs will ban 'offenders' from bars, off-licenses and certain areas for up to two years. You will recall that despite the media frenzy and the puffed up labour rhetoric only 0.11% of people have reported unacceptable public drunken behaviour to the police. You will recall that 44% of ASBO recipients had proven alcohol or drug addiction problems. You will recall that ASBO breach rates are ~70%. Shall we take bets on the % of BASBO recipients who will breach? Liberty made the key points.

'How many times can you spin a new 'crackdown' without tackling the causes of offending behaviour? It will be jelly bean ASBOs for sugared-up kids next. Surely its time to call last orders on endless new legislation'

Even the chairman of the Magistrates Association said

'We are not satisfied that these [BASBOs] will work as effectively as perhaps some ASBOs have. Clearly the issue is about tackling why these people have an alcohol dependency'

So …less effective than ASBOs eh? Shall we say a 90% breach rate by people who are clearly sick and need urgent help which the evidence shows they will not get in jail, or in the community… as we will now see.

In 2010 the Independent Commission on Youth Crime & Antisocial Behaviour published their review of the new labour approach we have examined with familiar conclusions.

I suppose, you say, this was more 'do-gooders', wringing their hands.

Well Mr. England it did include a number of academics who actually knew about the issues but also Lord Macdonald CBE, the former Director of Public Prosecutions, Ian McPherson QPM, Assistant Commissioner of the Metropolitan Police and Andrew Webb director for Children and Young People for Stockport Metropolitan Borough Council and police lead on youth offending for the Association of Directors of Children's Services. Stockport of course is right next to the ASBO capital of Britain, Manchester. I suggest that these gentlemen have seen the effects of ASB and youth crime policy, close up and personal, from the sharp end. Here are the key conclusions of the Commission.

'Across England and Wales… large sums of public money are wasted.
- Investment in **proven** preventative interventions and constructive sanctions has been too low.
- Not enough children who could be turned away from a life of crime at an early age are receiving timely help and support.
- Those who become involved in more persistent offending are too often treated in ways that do little to help them lead law abiding lives – and may serve to make offending worse.

The Commissions concern over poor results is matched by dismay over the quality of past political debates about youth crime:

- 'For many years politicians appear to have been caught in a war of words on the basis that public opinion would favour whichever party sounded 'tougher'.
- **The facts were a notable casualty,** to the point were three out of four people still believe that crime is going up despite sound evidence that it has been falling for the past 16 years.
- The consequences of this punitive arms race have been expensive for tax payers but have not improved public confidence.'

I submit Mr. England that this is completely in line with the points I have made to you earlier. Finally in July 2010 the new Coalition government responded to the overwhelming evidence on ASBO failure. Home Secretary Theresa May announced it was 'time to move beyond the ASBO' and a 'criminalizing and coercive approach' to punishments which are 'rehabilitative and restorative'. This was widely interpreted as the end of the ASBO. She condemned new labour's 'top-down, bureaucratic , gimmick laden approach' which 'too often criminalized young people unnecessarily, acting as a conveyer belt to serious crime and prison'. She promised an approach based on communities working with the police on earlier intervention to stop bad behaviour. Local people should be encouraged to intervene. If this meant an end to the arrest of people who do try to stop children behaving badly on the street or people who defend their properties from damage and the encouragement of individual pro-social behaviour it must be welcomed. However the ongoing danger of vigilantism must be recognized. It is unfortunate that the mis-targeting of ASBOs, and the other 'ludicrous' interventions, at the mentally disordered was not acknowledged and this signaled the likelihood of ongoing injustice. Indeed May soon announced the 'Anti-social Behaviour Injunction' and the 'Criminal Behaviour Order' to replace the ASBO, and yes, reading the definitions we see, in essence, the ASBO re-branded, but more rabid.

SECTION 3.3 HOW TO TACKLE ASB & DYSFUNCTION
(The ASBO Gestapo; 2014)

OK, you say, it looks a though government's current approach to ASB is ineffective but they have to do something. What can they do?

Well in the next section we will see a few hints of government thinking and I will argue that even more rabid action against the underclass, the young and other undesirables is in the air. If you mean positive interventions then we have already reviewed some: improving the access of mentally disordered and disabled people to medical treatment and genuine support. Two specific areas look promising based on properly conducted scientific trials with children and young offenders…something never achieved in ASB FIP evaluations.

Nurture Groups are a purely voluntary, school based intervention of intensive emotional and teaching support for children with behavioural problems which could lead to SEN statements or exclusions. Several studies show significant improvements in cognitive and emotional development, social engagement and behaviours indicative of secure attachment. Typically 87% of the NG children were able to return to the mainstream and most sustained their improvement after several years. Of the control group without NG placement 35% were placed in special schools and 45% still needed extra support in mainstream. This is significant when we recall that 2 / 3 of exclusions relate to mentally impaired pupils and 42 % of our FIP children have ADHD and 54% were SEN. On a longer time scale remember that 75% of adult prisoners are classed as intellectually impaired and 80% of young prisoners have two or more mental health problems. Recall also that one of the few positive interventions in the Family Intervention Projects involved FIP staff acting as 'positive advocates' for children and families in schools and in this way reducing 'educational problems' from 37% of families to 21% …a modest but important result.

Remember also the government's pledge to 'Think Family' and the supposed 'intensive' psychological support for families in the FIPs? The government apparently was backing family therapy but only 11% in recent projects received professional input. However we noted earlier that in June 2008 they pulled the funding for training FT practitioners. Do they now doubt family therapy effectiveness or is it a matter of cost again? Well the Cabinet Office report, 'Realising Britain's Potential' from 2008, quotes a major US study in support of therapy efficacy including reduction in crime rate achieved by

Nursery education   14%   Psychotherapy for juvenile offenders 19%

Functional family therapy   16%   Adolescent diversion projects 19%

Juvenile education programmes 18%   Nurse family partnerships   17%

There is also evidence that simple nurse-visit programmes can effectively address maltreatment which has been associated with child ASB. Remarkably the CO report also mentions Family Intervention Projects as though the US evidence had been taken on board and the above types of intervention widely implemented in the UK. They have not after ten years of FIPs and fiascos like Sure Start.

One ray of light emerged in 2011. Graham Allen the labour MP, was commissioned by the Coalition to review coal face, evidence based, intervention techniques. He found strong evidence for the efficacy and good cost-benefit for techniques such as Multi Systemic Therapy, Functional family Therapy ; Family Nurse Partnerships and so on. These techniques start from the basis that the people we are dealing with are sick, cognitively impaired and socially inadequate : not intentional criminals and not morally degenerate and not 'choosing not to cope with their disordered children'.

In the same year we had the excellent 'Mental Health Promotion and Mental Illness Prevention' from the Dept. of Health, LSE SPRU and the Centre For Mental Health and Inst. Of Psychiatry, Kings College London, which shows remarkable medium term pay-backs for various early diagnosis and medical interventions for the kind of mentally disordered people mainly targeted by the FIPs and ASBO teams for 'assertive, non-negotiable , persistent' interventions and 'sanctions'. The Coalition should abandon the bloated, bureaucratic superficial, FIPs and focus on evidence based, coal–face, medically sound techniques. As Graham Allen said

'Billions of pounds are paid out year after year; indeed decade after decade …often without the faintest acquaintance with an evidence base'

Well, you say, OK, work in the schools and with doctors but once these kids are in prison it's too late …let them rot.

Well yes, re-offending rates are high (74% within two years for 18-20 year olds compared to ~65% for all adults) but just suppose something cost effective could be done. In 2009 the Healthcare Commission published damning evidence of the failure to diagnose and treat mental health problems in young offenders. A third was sentenced without any medical information being supplied to the court. In a third of cases a survey found that the information supplied was 'unbalanced unverified or inaccurate'. Despite this widespread lack of medical evidence for 66% of offenders a remarkable 25% of young people on crime-prevention schemes, community orders or custodial sentences were found to have some form of disability. 50% of these had a learning disability, 20% a physical disability and the remainder a mental health problem. The care deficiencies were often due simply to NHS PCTs providing inadequate funding to the Youth Offending Teams. This is not about being 'kind' to offenders…the joint author was HMI of Prisons. The CE of the Healthcare Commission said

' If we a truly serious about breaking the cycle of crime and preventing young offenders from becoming adult offenders, we must make sure that health needs are addressed. It is clear that in too many cases, the NHS is letting these young people down'

Remember it costs ~£50,000 a year to keep an adult in prison and remarkably there is evidence that simple, cheap health actions could save this money. Earlier we discussed the role of biochemical imbalances of possibly genetic origin, in aberrant behaviours. Long term tracking studies have for example pointed to genes controlling key neuro-chemicals, such as the MAOA (monoamine oxidase A) gene, having a role in some types of ASB but caution is necessary. We have seen that ASB is not a coherent 'thing' but a wide range of disparate behaviours. Similarly the 'causes' of ASB are disparate. People targeted because of ADHD, OCD, autistic spectrum disorders are not the same as learning disabled, low IQ people targeted for kicking back against abuse and getting in trouble. People with early onset ASB are not the same as people with adolescent onset ASB. The late onset type may simply 'grow out of it'.

Evidence of genetic factors will continue to emerge. In September 2010 the Lancet published a major study at Cardiff which looked at the DNA of 366 ADHD children and 1,000 'normal' children.

Children with ADHD were twice as likely as the controls to have small sections of DNA in the areas studied missing or duplicated on chromosome 16. 7% of the controls had such faults against 14% of the ADHD children. Of course this was not a comprehensive study of the whole genome and many disorders are controlled by multiple gene faults. Also the faults found were of forms already known from studies of autism and schizophrenia. The results caused an outcry from the psychologists who favour 'nurture' as the cause of ADHD and so on. Bad parenting must be the cause…the government says so.

Nevertheless twin and adoption population studies of children show genetic and environmental effects contribute to the variance of ASB observed but in complex ways. Children with a vulnerable genotype will react badly to certain environmental factors including maltreatment and 'bad' parenting (so called GxE). If a parent shares a vulnerable 'risk' gene the 'rearing environment' may be poor. This is called passive rGE. However an affected child may also evoke negative parenting responses even if the parent is 'normal' (evocative rGE). . This is an area where professional parenting programmes and multi systemic therapy might help to control difficult behaviours. Subtyping of children to guide intervention is important. One approach is to add to a description of the ASB a location on a 'callous/ unemotional' scale. Children with high CU traits are said to be motivated by self-interest and respond well to rewards but fail to respond to punishment. Others may respond better to punishment. The range of sub-types out there perhaps explains the failure of 'one size fits all' interventions like the ASBO and the FIP. The good news is that genetic vulnerabilites may be countered. Growing knowledge should support better cognitive behaviour therapy targeting and perhaps (benign) pharmacogenic interventions.

However there is more to the story. A large body of evidence links poor nutrition to aggressive or impulsive behaviours and reduced IQ. For example in 2002 Dr. Gesch of Oxford made a study of 231 young offenders in a British prison. One group was given nutritional supplements to approximate a normal diet for four months. The other control group was given placebos. The trial was also randomized double blind. The behaviour of the placebo group did not change. The enhanced nutrition group showed a 37% reduction in violent violations and a 26% reduction in total violations compared with the pre-trial period. Other trials exist in the UK and the USA demonstrate similar results. To put the case beyond doubt Dr. Gesch has secured a $2.3 million grant from the Wellcome Trust and a detailed three year study involving blood chemistry analysis and cognitive tests covering 1,000 prisoners is under way in three British prisons.

Heavy Metals and Crime

It should also be noted that forty years of research shows that the same pattern of significant excess of metals such as aluminium, lead, mercury and cadmium and defects in zinc, chromium and selenium occour in both hyperactive children and violent young criminals. Cadmium for example occours in cola drinks and cigarette smoke. Aluminium is a persistent neurotoxin yielding loss of intellectual function, memory, the ability to concentrate, and in old age, dementia. It is common in junk foods and coloured sweets but it can be blocked by a good diet and iron, calcium and magnesium supplements. Lead interferes with glutamate neurotransmission pathways and disrupts retention of newly learned information. IQ is affected. It is also linked to schizophrenia. It is also linked to impulsivity and aggression. Zinc deficiency can cause memory problems and cognitive and motor function impairment in children. Selenium deficiency can cause hypothyroidism yielding fatigue, mental slowness and cretinism. The role of chromium is not understood but chronic deficiency leads to loss of weight, glucose intolerance, mental confusion and nerve damage. Even calcium deficiency can cause hyper-excitability and impulsivity.

Hold on, you say, just because these metals can cause behaviour problems doesn't mean that there is a difference between poorer and wealthier groups that explains crime and so on.

That's true Mr. England. There are though many cross section studies of lead poisoning that suggest the higher is local lead pollution, the higher is local poverty and crime but this is not proof of causation. Some would say it is poverty that 'causes' crime.

Well there you are, you say.

Fortunately in recent years research has progressed beyond cross section models. What we need are longitudinal studies that link variations in lead levels in the environment to variations in crime over many years. We now have that. 'The Urban Rise and Fall of Air Lead and the Latent Surge and Retreat of Societal Violence' Professor H Mielke and Sammy Zahran; Environment International ; Vol 45 ; August 2012, pages 48-55, provides the smoking gun. Mielke tracks the rise and fall of atmospheric lead emissions from leaded petrol from 1950 to 2010 in six major US cities. He compares this with data on aggregated assault rates over time. The use of leaded petrol rose rapidly from 1950 and peaked in the early 1970s and then fell off to zero by the early 1980s as evidence built up of the neurological damage aerial lead caused. By 1986, far too late the US Clean Act was extended and all lead was removed from petrol.

Within a few years lead levels in the blood of US citizens fell by 80%. Remarkably the pattern of the rise and fall in violent crime follows an identical pattern in the six US cities but with a lag of 22 years. Just to be sure Mielke then looked at the correlation of year on year difference in the two variables and adjusts for other factors. The link persists. 90% of the variation in aggravated assault is accounted for by lead variation. Mielke concludes that exposure of children to lead in the early years leads to neurological damage which manifests in adult criminal behaviour.

The same pattern of growth and decay in leaded petrol usage occurred in the UK and Europe but somewhat later. Curiously crime has been falling steadily in the UK, despite New Labour scare mongering, since 1995 and is still falling, contrary to expectations, through the major recession which began in 2008. This continuing fall is difficult to explain by other means. (Some have suggested the fall in the proportion of young men in some populations). It is these kinds of impacts in nutrition and environmental poisoning, which contribute to the large proportion of IQ variation in the poorest families attributable to 'shared environmental' factors in the Turkhelmer study we examined earlier.

Childhood Nutrition

Other research on poor youngsters points to a high frequency of nutrient deficiencies in Thiamin, Riboflavin, folic acid and omega 3 fish oils. The latter deficiency for example is linked clinically to impaired attention, impulsivity, poor memory, impaired cognition and depression, symptoms which should be familiar from our examination of FIP children.

Other major studies clearly demonstrate the links between poor childhood nutrition, low IQ and later aggressive and anti-social behaviour. A study by the University of Southern California Social Science Research Centre tracked 1,000 children for 14 years including indicators of malnutrition, IQ, family income, health, occupations, education levels, etc. Behaviour in school was assessed at 8, 11 and 17 years. The children were Caucasian, Indian and Chinese. (Jianghong Liu, American Journal of Psychiatry; November 2004). Malnourished children showed a 41% increase
in aggression at age 8 compared with a control group receiving normal nutrition and a 51% increase in violent and antisocial behaviour at 17. The report comments

'Poor nutrition characterized by zinc, iron, vitamin B and protein deficiencies , leads to low IQ which later leads to ASB. These are all nutrients linked to brain development'

ASB increased with number of indicators of malnutrition. Remarkably even in the USA 7% of toddlers suffer from iron deficiency and 9 to 16% amongst adolescents. The authors say

'There is more to ASB than nutrition but we argue that it is an important missing link. Biology is not destiny. We can change the biological disposition to ASB and aggression'

Hang on, you say, these are foreign studies...what about UK and European evidence?

Fair comment. In February 2008 the Cabinet Office Strategy Unit published 'Realising Britain's Potential' which pulled together a mass of data on recent demographic, social and crime trends. It looked at the fate of children from high social class and low social class families over time. Poor children with high initial attainment test scores at 22 months declined in score down to the level of poor children with low initial scores by 122 months. Children from the highest social class with low initial scores improved to match those in their class with the highest initial scores. These results were found for children born in 1970 and in 2000. It is clear that environment pulls down the ablest poor children and raises up the least able children in richer families. ..exactly the effect discussed above. The Cabinet Office report concludes

'Providing all children with the best start in life will be crucial to tackling gaps between people from different backgrounds'

Going back to child nutrition a study of the Jamie Oliver 'Feed Me Better Campaign' published in 2010 by Oxford and University of Essex researchers showed significant differences in academic achievement between a London school included and others excluded from the scheme. In Greenwich the end of primary school test scores for English rose by 4.5% and in science by 6% compared with other non-scheme schools in similar areas. Staff at the school claimed to notice clear changes in behaviour including higher attention levels after the improved lunches. Attendance rates also increased by 15% which they attribute to reduced authorized absences due to illness. The researchers could not rule out a placebo effect since there was no 'in school' control group. However given the Gesch results the new results are very suggestive. So you see Mr. England government is well aware of the realities but still we allow social mobility to decline and lock up the poor, mentally impaired instead of providing real, early remedial support. Even later on, given the above evidence, there is hope for effective interventions. For example the cost of providing nutritional supplements for every UK prisoner would be

273

~£3.5 million a year compared with the total prison budget of ~£4.5 billion in 2006 according to the HO. Considering all the evidence Dr. Gesch now says :

'Having a bad diet is a better predictor of violent behaviour than past violent behaviour. In fact predicting future criminal behaviour from a criminal past has statistically little better than a random chance of being correct.'

Please remember this when we consider the new labour approach to 'actuarial justice' below and recall the 'risk factor' approach to targeting our FIP families. He goes on :

'[Diet] also affects perception and insight to the extent that a nutritionally deprived person may not have the mental faculties to differentiate appropriate from inappropriate behaviour. Over 1,000 juvenile delinquents showed a 44% drop in anti-social behaviour when put on a low sugar diet'

'Tackling crime must involve getting tough on the causes of ASB i.e. getting tough on nutrition'

Why is this so significant? Well remember that our lone parent, mentally impaired ASB families are amongst the poorest in Britain. Do they have nutritionally adequate diets? Well 'Think Family' on the DfCSF web site tells us these 'chronically ill, disabled or infirm' families, in 'poor quality' housing, have very low (below 60% of median) incomes and that

'the families cannot afford a number of food and clothing items ...the [government claimed] reduction in child poverty may not be reaching such families'

We noted earlier the recent Cambridge work on low serotonin levels, poor diet and aggressive and impulsive behaviours. Is it not remarkable that the new labour government continually preached about the effects of obesity and poor nutrition on physical health but blatantly ignored the proven effect of poor nutrition on the human brain ...also a 'physical' organ and a very vulnerable one. But they KNOW that antisocial behaviour is caused by 'bad parenting' and 'wickedness', and that is where the votes are, so why look at alternative evidence of causation?

Neurological Development.

This point needs emphasizing.

The physical brain is the source of ALL behaviours, capabilities and 'moral' judgments. In recent years research has shown that simple interventions can cause marked changes in all of these. Transcranial Magnetic Stimulation can temporarily modify parts of brain function. By feeding magnetic pulses into the ventral occipito-temporal cortex the speed of reading in 'normal' volunteers can be slowed (Dr. J Devlin; UCL; Journal of Cognitive Neuroscience, March 2010). By applying a magnetic field to the right temporo-parietal junction, a small area behind the right ear which is involved in our perception of others' thoughts and beliefs, subjects can be induced to make morally dubious decisions including those that could lead to harm. (Dr. Liane Young, MIT; March 2010, Proceedings of the National Acadamy of Sciences, USA). Dr. Young noted

'You think of morality as being a really high level behaviour. To be able to apply a magnetic field to a specific brain region and change people's moral judgment is really astonishing. '

Professor Colin Blakemore, the leading neuro-scientist commented

'It [the brain] is responsible for everything that we do, every belief, intention and action. We can move our muscles but to do this we need impulses from the brain. In the same way, moral and ethical choices are just functions of the brain, just as picking up a cup of tea is'.

That is not to say that experience and education cannot modify inherent brain function for the better. There is evidence for 'neuroplasticity' even in damaged brains which is good news providing appropriate therapy is accessible.

Dr. S J Blakemore of UCL noted

'The [MIT] study suggests that this region – the RTPJ - is necessary for moral reasoning. What is interesting is that **it is very late developing – into adolescence and beyond right into the 20s'**

How developed is the RTPJ in the adult learning disabled and those with ADHD and, in the extreme, the sociopath? If the moral sense, if knowing right from wrong, is so sensitive to physical and chemical interventions, or internal physical or chemical faults on what basis can we justify demonizing and criminalizing people who have such faults or who are particularly susceptible to external disturbances? If this region of the brain develops late even in normal children, what justification is there for making the age of criminal responsibility as low as 10?

How can we allow children of 10 to end up in the Old Bailey on rape and murder charges? How can we apply punitive ASBOs to young children for non-criminal behaviour? Could this RTPJ region also be sensitive to poor long term nutrition and to metal poisoning and other childhood stresses?

People with malfunctioning or undeveloped RTPJ regions and other mental disorders require treatment. If treatment is not possible and there is a real risk to public safety then they must be removed to a place of long term confinement. What is morally indefensible is to fail to supply medical treatment to such people while publicly demonizing them as 'evil menaces' and scapegoating them for community abuse. In February 2009 a major report for the Joseph Rowntree Foundation found that 2010 targets for child poverty reduction set by Blair a decade ago would be missed by 600,000 families. The author said :

'During the recession the families who remain out of work will need extra money if they are to avoid severe poverty which will do irreparable harm to children'

Just to reinforce the point the DfCSF released data for January 2009 on the number of children receiving free school meals : 1,095,430. This reflects families on 'poverty' incomes but underestimates it by a factor of two according to the Child Poverty Action Group. 16% of our primary school children qualify. Remarkably in our affluent capital, home of parliamentary democracy, the proportion is 34.5% and growing as the recession hits the poorest families hard. Remember poor nutrition impacts brain function, effective intelligence and behaviour. Forget morality : think malnutrition if you want to tackle ASB.

Oh come on, you say, a poor diet is not that bad surely.

Well governments continuously encourage us to 'eat healthy' with dire warnings about physical diseases while ignoring the mental health implications. Consider the recognized eating disorders which give an idea of the broader consequences. A report by John Henderson of the Dept. of Health for Pro Bono Economics in 2012 found from sampling that ~310,000 young people between 10 and 24 had a significant eating disorder in England alone. These disorders disrupted their ability to work, to take on normal responsibilities and to conduct a social life. The charity estimated that 1.6 million people of all ages in Britain have such a debilitating disorder. They note that 40% of the people they help have not even been to see a GP. The result is loss of education, poor career prospects and premature death (including an enhanced suicide rate).

Here we have a group of diseases with massive physical and mental consequences which are readily apparent. Unfortunately the chronic behavioural effects of poor nutrition in vulnerable families go unnoticed by governments except as reasons to stigmatize, blame and criminalize them.

Even more striking is the emerging evidence of the effects of poor diet during pregnancy. In September 2013 the results of the five year Europe wide Nutrimenthe Project was published. This had tracked 17,000 mothers and 18,000 Children looking at development and behaviour. It found unequivocal evidence of the effects of omega 3 DHAs, long chin ployunsaturate fatty acids, minerals such as iron and zinc, B vitamins and iodine levels during pregnancy, on later child behaviour and test performance in literacy, spelling and grammar. The study also noted the effects of parental education, wealth, age and the genetic make-up of the mother and child. The latter factors can interact with nutrient take up in the womb and in breast feeding. The Nutrimenthe site also records recent studies from around the world demonstrating the critical role of early nutrition. Sadly this turns out to be merely the beginning of the story.

Epigenetics

We will see that a recurring theme in the Coalition rhetoric is the 'multi-generational' nature of the 'lack of achievment' and 'ongoing problems' in the Families From Hell. We noted Louise Casey's admission that 'nothing' so far had 'touched' these families' problems despite repeated, often vicious, state interventions. There is a reason for this and it does not bode well for a quick fix. In recent decades it has become accepted that in some circumstances environmental factors and stress during pregnancy in particular can not only create physical and mental deficits in children, but that those deficits can be passed on, via actual genetic changes, to future generations: so called epigenetic changes. Sometimes the normal DNA error correction processes can be bypassed and the genome altered with dire, long term, consequences.

In 2013 Cambridge researchers found that epigenetic factors in sperm and ova, such as methyl groups, were not completely eliminated in the normal DNA error correction processes. About 1% of induced changes got though. In 2011 Salk Institute workers concluded that methyl groups, to take one example, can influence the activity of thousands of genes. Such influences may be benign or not. Potentially this means that epigenetic effects can have hundreds of thousands of times more influence than spontaneous mutations, the traditionally assumed mechanism of genomic change.

Not only this but such epigenetic changes were not random, like mutations, but concentrated at 'hotspots'. The Salk group showed that epigenetic mutations could be passed on for thirty generations (see The Edge of Uncertainty, chpt 4; Michael Brookes, 2014 for more examples).

And I suppose all this is based on animal studies, you say.

Actually recent human studies are also highly suggestive Mr. England. The Swedes have always been careful record keepers in areas like agriculture, health and mortality statistics. The Karolinska Institute recently compared periods of famine and plenty in northern Sweden in the nineteenth and early twentieth centuries. Three generations and their health were tracked. Some very remarkable results emerged. Incredibly after allowing for socio-economic factors a boy near puberty who overate in a good crop year could reduce the life expectancy of a grandson by 32 years. Other studies seem to confirm surprisingly large epigenetic multi-generational effects. In the 'Dutch Hunger Winter' the Arnhem region was deliberately starved by the Nazis as a collective punishment. The results echoed down at least two generations in health areas like breast cancer, coronary heart disease, schizophrenia and both obesity or low birth and adult weight depending on the stage of pregnancy when starvation occurred. Various US studies showed that a birth weight deficit persisted in African American babies in comparison with both white American and black African babies, irrespective of current socioeconomic status and for a long time period. Data for the period 1897-1935 showed a 7% deficit. In 1988 the deficit was 8.6%, statistically unchanged. The suspicion is that this persistent deficit is the imprint of epigenetic changes during the deprivations of the slavery years. If so God forgive us. Low birth weight is associated with hypertension, cardiovascular disease and diabetes…and a shorter life expectancy…all present in excess in the African American population.

The message of emerging studies is stark. The shadow of deprivation, of poor nutrition, of 'environmental pollution' and stress during pregnancy falls not just on that foetus, but on two and perhaps many more future generations. The cost of state neglect of one underclass generation echoes down the decades. If you, the state, want to save big money on Troubled Families stop child deprivation now, support her children and continue the medicine for a hundred years for her impaired descendents. Your alternative is to reset the genetic clockwork the Nazi way. One thing is clear: to condemn the Troubled Families of the underclass for the effects of state and societal neglect, suffered perhaps generations ago, is an obscenity.

David Cameron, Eric Pickles, Iain Duncan Smith and your successors, please note. And how much multi-generational damage have your 'welfare reforms' added to an already sad legacy?

Meanwhile we had yet another new superficial health initiative: Change4Life which invites the above families to join the 'lifestyle revolution' with the tagline 'Eat well, Move More, Live Longer'. The evidence based truth for these families, considering all we have seen, is that they will 'Eat poorer, Be Criminalized More, Die Sooner'. Recall the scathing report on dozens of such government social engineering schemes by the HOC Select Committee on Health in 2009 which described them as 'ineffective and possibly damaging' and branding positive 'research' claims as 'propaganda'.

Well, you say, things are difficult for everybody at the moment but the hard working majority just soldier on.

Indeed Mr. England but I suspect that you do not realize how badly your family has been hit. The Joseph Rowntree Foundation did a review in mid 2012 which was shocking in its conclusions. They calculated that the average working family would need an additional £9,000 per annum over what they earned in 2008 before the banking scandals, to maintain the same standard of living. After 4 years of frozen wages, increased taxes, increased child care and public transport cots and high inflation have you kept up Mr. England? It is extremely unlikely that you have. Your cost of living alone has risen by 16% over inflation in that period. This is nothing new.
In August 2009 the Times exposed another cunning Brown plan to zap poor benefit claimants. Under current arrangements claimants of housing allowance can keep up to £780 per annum if they use their initiative and find accommodation below the allowed maximum cost. This affects some 300,000 people. Brown, despite an outcry from his own backbenchers, intends to stop this, effectively reducing claimants income by up to 20%...claimants who include the very poorest families. Now imagine the impact on the poorest families. Note that by April 2009 Save The Children who normally operate in the poorest parts of the Third World began giving money to British families in dire need. Their research showed that among the parents in poverty **48%** have already reduced the amount they spend on food. STC say :

'Now families in poverty face the problem that not only is their income woefully inadequate, but prices for essentials are dramatically increasing... We are seeing an element of malnutrition...

we're seeing stunting [of children's growth] here too [in the UK]...these children are more likely to experience stress, more likely to suffer ill health and less likely to do well at school'

Stunted, malnourished, ill children in the UK? Surely not, according to the government. In fact on March 1st 2010 in his Reading pre-election speech Brown told us

'Let us go back to the facts : a society in which not just crime and ASB is down but also child poverty , illiteracy and ill health have all fallen , cannot be called a broken society'.

Recall that the BCS, he now admires, shows clearly that crime has been falling steadily since 1995, two years before Blair came in, and has shown NO variation in response to the many new labour initiatives. Fear of ASB increased under new labour thanks to their propaganda and they failed to then control it. Compare the above with what we have seen about ill-targetted 'crime initiatives', poverty, services for the old and mentally disordered, life expectancy differences and falling social mobility. As to literacy the government's own data show 1 in 4 children cannot read or write properly when they finish primary school.

The 'success' of Brown's education policy became clear in 2012 with the OECD review of developed countries spending and delivery, 'Education at a Glance'. As we proceed bare in mind OFNS figures record that education spending increased from £35.3 billion in 2000 to £63.9 billion in 2009. The OECD tell us that this spending explosion generated

'no improvement in student learning outcomes'

And our class sizes were larger than in most developed countries at 26 pupils compared with an average of 21. We also had more NEETS with 15.8% compared with the developed average of 14.8% in the EU. At the same time Britain fell from 17th place to 25th for reading in 15 year olds, 24th to 28th in maths and 14th to 16th in science based on the same tests in 70 countries. Compare this with Brown's glowing report above.

What about health? The Mid Staffordshire Hospital Trust scandal broke in 2012 and demonstrated the madness that resulted from New Labour's obsession with chasing NHS management targets at the cost of focusing on the care of patients. Some 1,200 unnecessary deaths occurred there in one hospital. Gagging orders prevented us knowing how many other hospitals suffered similar failings but we can guess.

What about child health? A survey in the Lancet by the London School of H&TM in March 2013 pointed to 2,000 preventable child deaths every year in Britain. It turns out that the UK has long had the worst record among 14 European countries for unnecessary child deaths under age 14.

By the way new labour spent over one billion pounds over the three years to 2008 on positive media spin about government policies such as Change4Life. The 2010 budget for the Central Office of Information (or Ministry Of Truth) was £391 million.

Welcome to the legacy of Blair and Brown's Brave New Britain. It will take years to dismantle it even assuming the political will to do so in future governments. Don't hold your breath.

IQ, Poverty & Education

The Gini coefficient which measures population income inequality rose from 0.26 in 1979 to 0.39 in 2011, an increase of 50%. Many groups, even the Tories, had recognized the growth in inequality and the decay of opportunity under new labour. In October 2009 a Conservative report presented shocking data on educational inequalities.

In 2008 47% of pupils receiving free school meals, some 33,909, failed to get a GCSE higher than grade D. Children in the most deprived areas are 20 times more likely to be in a 'failing' school than children in the richest counties. Deprived children are effectively barred from 'core' subjects like English, maths, and physics. In 2006/7 there were ~6,000 successful Oxbridge applicants. Only 45 of these were children who had received free school meals. The Office for Fair Access says that currently, intelligent children from the 20% richest families are 7 X more likely to get to university than similar children from the poorest 40% of families. In the 1996 the ratio was 6 X. Remarkably Michael Gove, the then (Conservative!) shadow children's secretary, said

'Education should be the engine of social mobility. But most schools in the poorest areas are classed as 'failing' and children eligible for free school meals are nearly 200 times more likely to leave school without a single GCSE than they are to get three As at A level'

Look, you say, these kids are just thick …what do you expect?

Yes there is a gross correlation between poverty and lower mean IQ but to assume a priori that this justifies giving up on the education of the poor is monstrous. Amongst other points the evidence shows that environmental

281

factors like poor nutrition can have a marked effect on intellectual ability and behaviour. Remember 75% of prisoners are classed as 'intellectually impaired' and the majority of our ASBO yobs and families are mentally impaired. Most poor children can benefit from education including, diversion from crime, and a reasonable proportion will flourish.

That, you say, is typical liberal, wishful thinking.

It must be admitted that the whole issue of 'nature versus nurture' is contentious but even limited studies show that more than simple genetic effects are in play. In one the correlation coefficient between measured IQ and 'socioeconomic class' was -0.72 : the lower the 'class' the lower the IQ. (Crawford et al; British Journal of Clinical Psychology, (2001), vol. 40, pp87-105) Roughly 50% of IQ variation is associated with 'class'. However 'years of education' also correlates with IQ, with a coefficient of +0.65 : the more education the higher the IQ. Education accounts for roughly 42% of IQ variation. Of course correlation is not proof of causation, the direction of any causation is unclear and we could argue that class and extent of education are linked and so on. Nevertheless putting both factors in to a simple regression equation leads to a good predictor of measured IQ. The data sample also excluded people with obvious neurological or psychiatric disorders and therefore some of the most impaired in all social classes.

Such studies are suggestive but no more. However if we look at recent evidence some clarity emerges and, although difficult, it is worth summarizing because it has huge policy implications.

In 2003 a major paper disentangling the genetic and socio-economic influences on IQ with emphasis on low income families, was published. (Professor Turkhelmer; Psychological Science; Vol. 14, No 6, November 2003). The work was based on a very large database of identical and fraternal twins. The data was so extensive that in effect, the influence of identical genes (in identical twins) versus non-identical genes (in fraternal twins) and socioeconomic variables (income, parental education, occupation, etc) on children's IQ variation could be calculated for each socioeconomic group. It was found that IQ variation attributable to genes was small for the most disadvantaged families but as high as 90% for moderate income families. Conversely the variation in IQ attributable to a 'shared family environment' was 60% for the poorest socioeconomic families falling rapidly to near zero for the moderately well off families. 40% variation was attributable to 'non-shared environmental factors' in the poorest group. In simple terms the richer families in general have such a good environment that genetic differences show up in IQ variation.

(There is a level playing field for all who are rich enough). Within the poorest families group genetic differences are swamped by the effects of poor environmental factors. These include poor nutrition (which we will explore later), heavy metal poisoning (eg lead), limited stimuli, stress and low quality schooling. These results are clear and statistically significant. The bottom line is that improving the 'environment' of the poorest families including improved education and health care, can improve their effective IQs and economic outcomes. Providing a more level playing field in the most basic factors will increase their potential for social mobility.

Remarkably there is also direct evidence of environment impact on IQ which does not require a degree in statistics to understand. Suppose we took some poor children on the edge of 'mental retardation' and put them at random in a control group were no additional help was given or into a group receiving intensive educational support from 6 months to five years old. If these kids are a lost cause and their fate is fixed by genes (their 'bad seed') we would predict no difference in IQ between the two groups. In fact in the famous Milwaukee Project this was done. At 5 years the control group had a mean IQ of 83 and in the intensive support group, 110. At adolescence the formerly supported group IQ was still 10 points ahead of the control group. By the way all these kids were black. The intensive educational support up to 5 more or less eliminated the 10-15 point difference in mean IQ said to exist between blacks and whites. So much for racial inferiority.

In other studies groups of poor siblings who had been split with one being adopted into upper middle class families and the others staying put in poverty, have been analysed. The IQ of the moved children rose over time by 12 to 18 IQ points depending on the study.

Remember genetic mixing will continually generate 'able' people whatever the 'mean' starting population condition in a particular socio-economic group. If you doubt this examine the personal histories of Michael Faraday and Thomas Henry Huxley, those giants of Victorian science, and many others. On a personal note the author was born into one of the poorest districts of Liverpool in the 1940's but, thanks to public libraries, a decent technical high school and post war Old Labour governments, he went to university on state grants and eventually did quite well like many of his poor, local contemporaries. Although age is taking its toll his inductive IQ was once 162... not too bad for a poverty stricken, 'thick scouse kid' perhaps? It is shocking that sixty years later there are many poor children denied the advantages I had ...and this after thirteen years of recent 'labour' governments supposedly committed to social inclusion and mobility.

Well that's unfortunate, you say, but opportunity for most of us is still there.

But is it? For a moment consider the children of the decent hard working majority …your children. In 2009 the Milburn report on social mobility looked at the bias in access to top jobs. He found that 50% of top professional jobs go to kids from private schools: that is just 7% of kids. He pointed out that 75% of judges, 50% of doctors and 45% of senior civil servants were also still from private schools. The 15% of poorest children (those on free school meals) obtained only one third the qualifications of the other 85%. Some of these differences no doubt relate to innate intelligence and talent but according to Milburn success still depends far too much on 'who you know' not 'what you know' in Brown's Britain. The deck is stacked whether you are of normal or sub-normal intelligence, working class or lower middle class despite new labour spending an additional 28 billion per annum on education every year since 1997.

SECTION 4 :

FORMAL REVIEWS OF THE GOVERNMENT EVALUATION REPORTS OF FAMILY INTERVENTION PROJECTS 1997 – 2008

4.1 INTRODUCTION

In this final section we will examine the official FIP evaluation reports commissioned by successive new labour governments from British academic groups from Glasgow University and Sheffield Hallam University. The evaluations are remarkably consistent in three respects.

Firstly the families targeted are remarkably similar over the years: poor, inadequate, chronically sick, learning disabled, mentally disordered. Only a minority is anti-social and much of that is low level, but all have high and long term, state 'support costs'…thanks to unemployment and disabled children.

Secondly the academic analysts, within the sometimes doubtful framework set by government, appear to report accurately what they find while also emphasizing strong caveats about data quality and gaps. They repeatedly point out weaknesses in the ability to draw strong inferences from much of the outcome information. They all, from the first project onwards, emphasize the need to confirm claimed results from long term monitoring…which never happened. All their caveats were ignored.

Thirdly they all point to the long term medical problems of the families and the difficulties of the projects to mobilize professional help from the NHS and so on…despite repeated government claims that the FIPs successfully 'grip' all the support agencies and force co-operation. The picture across all project phases up to and including the Troubled Families Programme, is one of repeated denigration and false rhetoric against the families and stark lessons about state intervention **not** learned. Seeing the whole history laid out it is hard to believe that the abusive, costly farce is still continuing to the detriment of very vulnerable UK families.

SECTION 4.2   THE DUNDEE FAMILY PROJECT

A COMMENTARY ON THE GOVERNMENT
EVALUATION REPORT

(www. Scotland.gov.uk/library3/housing/edfp)

Professor D P Gregg (retired) ; January 2007

1. INTRODUCTION

The Dundee Families Project has been widely heralded in the media and local government circles as the highly successful 'flagship model' for state intervention in 'antisocial' problem families. It has been cloned several times. The public is repeatedly told that the project 'had an 84% success rate with the most difficult families'. Usually the criteria of success used in the project are not discussed. Sometimes claims are made for delivery of significant reductions in antisocial behaviour, crime and the frequency of children taken into care which do not feature in the evaluation report. Recent critical evaluations of antisocial behaviour interventions by the National Audit Office suggest little has changed.

A careful reading of the strangely structured ,Dundee, evaluation report paints a far less positive and much more tentative, being kind, picture of delivered outcomes than that presented in the widely disseminated, headline results : a picture which strongly calls into question the cost effectiveness of these expensive state interventions. Decisions on the use of public funds should be based on the full facts not on selective 'sexing up' of raw data. This commentary attempts to address that problem from the viewpoint of an experienced research scientist and management consultant

.
2. CHARACTERISTICS OF THE PROJECT FAMILIES

We are told that the families involved were 'poor' and that very few had 'working members'. Many were lone parent families with child care and control problems. There was 'a high incidence of physical and mental health problems'. 50% of the mothers were on anti-depressant drugs. Drug and alcohol abuse featured in about 75% of the cases and addiction in 33% of the cases. [note : We are not told the IQs of family members nor the frequency of learning disability but we know that 35% of ASBOs are issued to mentally impaired people and that according to the Home Office one of the highest 'risk factor' groups for antisocial behaviour is the physically /mentally disabled and ill cluster . Only the lone parents and the homeless are said to be more dangerous!].

Clearly these are socially inadequate, disadvantaged people with serious health issues. (However we will see later that health services involvement in the project was marginal). So just how antisocial are they?

3. CHARACTERISTICS OF THE ANTISOCIAL BEHAVIOUR (ASB) EXHIBITED

56 families received 'outreach, dispersed tenancy or core residential block ' interventions. 70 cases overall were eventually closed. We are told that 'neighbour disputes, poor upkeep of property and rent arrears' were the most 'prominent' antisocial behaviours exhibited by project families. However in section 4.7 we learn that 'conflict with neighbours' was involved in only 8 cases : i.e 11.4% of closed cases. In section 4.31 on 'housing, family and other needs' we learn that 'neighbour issues' are involved in only 5 cases : i.e 7% of closed cases. However in section 8.10 we also learn that 'a small number of families were recognised by other agencies to be the victims rather than the protagonists in neighbour difficulties'. So some of the 5 or 8 project cases involving neighbour conflict may actually involve the victims of antisocial behaviour ! How many , 2,3,4 ? We are not told. [note : the DRC tell us that 25% of disabled people have been forced to move home by serial neighbour abuse ; in a 3 month period 33% had been physically abused]. It is interesting also that 70% of the project children interviewed said they were bullied at school. Presumably these victim families are considered acceptable collateral damage in the war on ASB.

The public have been told that ASB is about 'neighbours from hell'. In fact a maximum of 7% to 11.4% of project cases concerned this issue. (or if the small number of project families who were actually victims in conflicts is 2, the frequency could be as low as 4.3%. If it's 3 the minimum frequency is 2.8%). Issues of poor property maintenance / damage, cleanliness /hygiene and rent arrears feature much more prominently. We might ask just what is meant by antisocial behaviour in this project ? We are also told in addition that only 2 out of 3 referrals actually cited antisocial behaviour, however defined, as a factor. This diffuse, loose approach to the definition of antisocial behaviour may explain why 'some project staff believed the term was employed in an over-inclusive and often stigmatising manner'.

We will see that there is much evidence in the report that wider and very frequent social inadequacy and mental and physical heath issues are being conflated with a small number of instances of (apparently) real antisocial behaviour (as promoted in the media by government).

In this respect the Dundee Project is no worse than the other government ASB interventions : remember 35% of ASBOs go to mentally impaired people despite clear Home Office 'safeguards' for vulnerable people.

4. THE FAMILY SELECTION PROCESS

Over the project life 126 families were referred to it. 70 cases were eventually closed. 56 families received ' outreach, dispersed or core block' interventions. We are told repeatedly the project 'places emphasis' on 'family cooperation'. Families 'must agree to accept the service, though often they may have few other options'. In plain English the other options (or sanctions) included eviction from council property and removal of children into care (9 out of 20 families had previously been evicted more than once).

We are told in section 8.20 that project staff 'valued' the admission process for its 'capacity to indicate a family's motivation to change'. In other words the 56 families selected for intervention were carefully chosen to maximise success. This is confirmed in section 8.9 where we are told that 'other agencies need to deal with the most resistant families'. So when we are repeatedly assured of an '84% success rate with the most difficult families' we can see this is being rather economical with the truth.

Given that the families were carefully selected for their 'cooperation' and motivation to change' it is remarkable that the success rate across all interventions was only 59% (particularly when based on the soft, largely subjective and peripheral, criteria discussed below).

5. THE PROJECT SUCCESS CRITERIA

The key point to make is that the project and evaluation applied nothing like the randomised , controlled trials recommended by NICE for socio-clinical intervention projects. There was no independent assessment of outcomes against the formal measures normally used to evaluate e.g. behaviour changes. There were no control groups in the project. This government have used conformity to NICE trial standards to promote and underwrite the apparent success of other social intervention strategies (e.g. the 'super-nanny' scheme). It is therefore surprising that the Dundee Family Project and its clones are still put forward as state intervention flagship models. Let's look at the actual criteria of success used. We are told that the project 'has been very successful in terms of its image, collaborative agency relationships and production of change in families'. We will examine these in turn.

5.1 PROJECT IMAGE

A key measure of success is said to be that the initial 'negative image' of the project was replaced by 'local acceptance' and by 'prominent and positive national publicity ' (section 8.12). It seems local residents 'witnessed hardly any problems from the core block'. However given the core block protocol involved 24 hour monitoring and control of the families , including exclusion of visitors, this is hardly surprising. Also recall that the families were under threat of sanctions such as homelessness. Also as we saw earlier 'some' of the few families involved in neighbour conflicts were in fact victims not perpetrators.

The 'positive national publicity' is frankly irrelevant except to the political sponsors of the project. It delivered nothing, as we will see below, to the taxpayers who paid dearly for it. The author also wonders how 'positive' the publicity would have been if the real facts of the project had been fully and clearly presented to a wide audience.

5.2 INTERAGENCY COOPERATION

'Grip The Agencies' is a key mantra in the Respect Agenda. In the Dundee Project we are told in section 8.13 the project 'has set **close and good** working relationships with **most** of the **key agencies** working with ASB'. Such cooperation is certainly to be welcomed. However a closer reading of the report shows this statement to be again economical with the truth to a degree most people would find unacceptable.

We do learn that 'senior staff' and 'stakeholders' have been 'very supportive' of programme cooperation at the 'strategic level'. To anyone familiar with bureaucracies this is not surprising : sponsors of high profile , political projects are compelled to exude cooperation and good will in public and such projects are never allowed to fail. However in section 8.37 we read that 'at the front-line level difficulties were apparent' and most project staff expressed 'dissatisfaction with social services input'. Although initially family referrals from social services were much higher than from housing by 2000 social service referrals had ' dropped markedly'. The report comments dryly that ' recent [social services] reluctance merits closer examination'. In fact a closer reading of the report shows very large differences in views about project conduct and success between social services and housing departments. Social services gave a much lower rating of success. As we will see housing appeared to focus on containment and control while social services tried to support the families and address underlying causes.

The author suggests that the 'control' agenda came to dominate the project and social services disengaged. This has important implications for long term community outcomes from such projects as we will see. [note : the control and sanction model now seems to dominate government thinking on ASB. Nothing seems to have been learned since the Dundee Families Project].

We are also told that while project staff strove to build good relations with housing, social services and the police, health service links were given 'less priority' despite the 'high incidence of physical and mental health difficulties' in the families. This reinforces the author's view that addressing causes of behaviour was in practice not a project priority. The report concludes, frighteningly, that project staff 'did not always recognise' the 'prominent role' of health professionals in 'child protection' issues. Staff acknowledged this in considering future project training needs and the report urged the involvement of a psychiatric nurse in future projects. The project did at least 'establish relations' with 2 local agencies concerned with addiction problems although 'communications difficulties' had occoured. (33% of families had addiction problems).

Given that improving child behaviour was said to be an important project aim it is also remarkable to learn that 'education services were not represented at project meetings and contact was not frequent'. We are not told why this was.

In summary education was not actively involved; health service links and inputs were marginal ; social services effectively disengaged from the project in it's later phases. This leaves housing and the police (the containment and control arms) actively participating. It can be argued that **most** agencies and **key** agencies were not involved in **close and good** working relations in the project despite the headline claim. Was inter-agency cooperation successful? What do you think?

5.3 FAMILY BEHAVIOURAL OUTCOMES

From the point of view of the community what matters is that behaviours that are considered to be 'antisocial' are eliminated and eliminated cost effectively. As we noted earlier only 5 or 8 project cases (7% to 11% of total cases, but possibly significantly less if some families were indeed victims) involved 'conflicts with neighbours'. [note: while central and local government focuses attention on such cases they are in fact in 14th place in public concerns about ASB. They are seen as a 'fairly big or big problem' by only 6% of people and a 'big' problem by 2%.

Source : 'Experiences and Perceptions of ASB In The UK' , Home Office report 2004]. For the Dundee families issues such as poor upkeep or maintenance of (council) property, cleanliness / hygiene , rent arrears and internal family conflicts and problems were much more prominent in case profiles than neighbour conflicts. This should be born in mind when judging claimed levels of success in changing family behaviours.

An equally important issue is the source of evidence for behavioural changes. Section 8.3 tells us that this came from 'semi-structured , qualitative interviews, self-completion questionnaires, analysis of case records and a small number of observations'. Those interviewed included senior stakeholders, project staff and families. We are told that 'only in some cases' were case outcomes checked 'externally' i.e. by independent observers. The evaluation research was done 'on a part time basis' only. [note: behaviour changes were not assessed using any of the several formal measures recognised by NICE. Control groups were not included in the project design].

Apparently 'virtually everyone interviewed' praised the work of the project. It would be rather surprising if senior stakeholders and project staff did not. A great deal is therefore made of the 'generally positive' attitude of the families to the project. It is easy to understand that the focussed and intensive attention and support given by social services, perhaps for the first time, was appreciated. However 'improved access to housing' was given top billing as the reason for positive views of the project in the adult interviews. In other words they were glad not to be made homeless. Similarly the children focussed on their improved 'housing situations'. We might conclude that being faced with homelessness and family break up might encourage even people of low intelligence and poor social skills to be positive about the project when asked. A loaded gun to the head tends to focus hearts and minds. But this is not the end of the story.

When we look more closely a different picture again emerges. There were 70 closed cases. However the initial evaluation interviews covered only 20 families. 'Follow up interviews', presumably more detailed, covered only 10 families or 14% of the project total. This is a very low sampling level on which to base strong conclusions. There was also clear, systematic sampling bias. We are told in section 8.5 that there was a 'very high interview failure rate' and that consequently 'the families interviewed may have under represented those who found it hard to accept the project'. The author suggests 'may have' can reliably be replaced by 'certainly '. This bias and the very low level of family sampling invalidates the presented conclusions about overall family attitudes to the project. This must be born in mind when considering the claimed levels of 'success' in behaviour change and the likelihood that solid , long term community benefits were delivered.

The **formal** results reported on behaviour changes attributed to the project are opinion tables (4.24) presented on a crude scale: little change; better; much better. Note there are no categories for worse or much worse. An a priori assumption of success is built into the scale. This is bad practice to say the least. Irrespective of whether deterioration occurred or not it tells us something of the approach to evaluation issues in the project. Even accepting this 'dodgy' scale there are massive differences between housing and social services opinions which are enlightening. Housing staff say that 24 of 28 , that is 86% showed Improved behaviour. Social services staff say that only 9 of 23 families, that is 39%, showed improvement. Recall that there were 70 closed cases and 56 families received core block, dispersed or outreach interventions. On a closed case basis it appears that only 36% of family behaviour outcomes were actually assessed. This is a very low sampling frequency on which to make strong, public claims about project success in behaviour change.

Why is there such a large level of disagreement about behavioural outcomes (assuming, at least, the same sample of families is being considered) between housing and social services staff? Different criteria are being applied. Housing 'needs' were identified in the project as rent arrears, home maintenance and cleanliness while family 'needs' involve health issues, drug and alcohol abuse, parenting and child issues. We are indeed told in 8.22 that 'some time after' the project, closed cases were 'generally doing well' in 'housing management' but some 'still poorly' on 'family issues'. So the high level of success reported, 86%, is about housing management issues not antisocial behaviour as usually presented to the public. On the other hand the social service views show us that the chronic, underlying causes of family dysfunction have not been successfully addressed in 61% of cases , even in the short term and under intensive 'treatment'. If the causes of 'antisocial behaviour' have not been addressed what can we expect for the long term delivery of substantive community outcomes? This is explored below.

'Success' evidence is also recorded by type of intervention. The project's 'own evaluations' suggest that 56% of outreach, 82% of dispersed and 83% of core block cases were successful. The overall picture, taking into account actual case numbers, is of a 59% 'success' rate. However 'because case numbers were small' we are told that the evidence on the 'comparative success of the 3 main service types' was 'inconclusive'. This is rather important considering the very high cost of the core block service as discussed below.

A second critical issue is the sustainability of positive behaviour changes in the long term , after the project ended, and how these translate into substantive community benefits. The raw core block results look impressive as presented to the public. However we learn that 'some' of the core families 'found it hard to re-adjust' when they left the block. Consider what this implies. 5 out of 6 core cases noted are claimed as successful. If we take 'some' to mean 2 then on leaving the block 3 out of 6 cases were unsuccessful or at risk. If 'some' means 3 then 4 out of 6 cases , 67% ,were in doubt.

Is there other evidence of family deterioration after the project ? There is. We saw earlier that, in the majority of closed cases sampled, underlying family needs and causes had not been met. We are also told in section 8.35 that 'long term mental health and relationship issues…require attention after project work is ended yet social work may not have the resources to attend to this and specialist services are rarely available'. In section 8.36 , in wonderfully hyperbolic language, we are told that the 'handling' of 'family disengagement' from the project was not 'optimal'. Not surprisingly given the stigma of 'antisocial behaviour' there was 'difficulty in securing tenancies for families to move on'. Some families deteriorated and received inadequate monitoring and support. Poor 'hygiene' in several homes led to 'renewed neighbour rejection'. This comment appears to confirm that the few (5 or 8 out of 70) cases of 'neighbour nuisance' in the project were not about aggressive ASB but about negative responses to social inadequacy. Perhaps these were the same project families said to be 'victims' in the few neighbour conflicts? Finally, just to reinforce the core block difficulties ,section 8.26 tells us 'project staff held mixed views about the core block with **most** wanting it's functions re-examined'.

The changes in family behaviour analysed above relate to internal project measures in the short term. The key issue is whether these changes are sustained long term and whether they translate into substantive community benefits. What is the evidence for this? Sustainability was discussed above. On community benefits we learn that senior 'stakeholders 'nearly all agreed' that the project 'gave long terms benefits to families 'who engaged well, in 3 ways'. These are said to be: avoiding high cost options (e.g children in care}; reducing behaviours (e.g. crime); promoting quality of life. Let us deconstruct all this. These are simply opinions and not based on long term field evidence since no long term evaluation had taken place. These are simply a list of possible benefits **if** the internal behaviour changes recorded in the project translated into other, desirable, sustained behaviours in the community. No evidence is presented for such outcomes in the report although such outcomes have been spun in the media as fact.

It might be argued that the high profile publicity given to the project and the tough approach taken would have a deterrent effect on other ASB problem families. [note : the government's emphasis on publicity in ASB matters suggests this is an aim]. However section 8.45 refutes the hypothesis of any wider community effects. So we find that education services saw little effect on school related problems. The project was also said to have had little effect on 'problems faced by services such as housing and police in Dundee'. The numbers of evictions had 'dropped markedly' since the project was established but the evaluation team attribute this largely to 'changes in housing department policy' although some senior stakeholders held the (unsubstantiated) opinion that the project had contributed.

The author submits that if we take into account what the evaluation report **actually says** the conclusion is far removed from the headline '84% success rate' spun to the media, public and to local councilors to justify further projects.

Given the above analysis of claimed behaviour changes and benefits the question of project cost-effectiveness is moot. In section 8.42 the authors admit 'the expense per family is high' yet give an **opinion** that the project 'does offer good value for money'. Section 8.43 argues that the cost of the project is balanced by the annual costs to housing and social care expended if the project did not occur. Fine, but we are looking for evidence of higher cost-benefit from the project in comparison with normal interventions by these agencies. The cost per family is 'high' but the evidence for sustained, improved community benefits is not there as we have seen. How then can the project offer 'good value for money'? The author's fall back on the argument that **if** 'children being taken into care is avoided' then 'long-term gains will accrue'. Fine but there is no evidence in the report this happened. Yet we are then told that 'approximate calculation suggested the project had saved more money …than was required for its operations'. We have shifted from potential but totally unproven avoidance of long-term costs to certainty in the bottom line! This kind of sloppy (or sly?) analysis is common enough in the evaluation of government ASB intervention projects as we will see. To be fair, elsewhere again, it is 'emphasised that a complex and long-term study would be required to demonstrate this [good value for money] conclusively. That would itself be very expensive '. For this project the author has shown that neither long term, substantive, community benefits, nor cost-effectiveness have been demonstrated. Yet on the basis of misleading, headline claims of success other UK local authorities had been persuaded to clone the Dundee Project at great cost to local tax payers.

6. CONCLUSIONS

This is a remarkable project 'evaluation' report. Headline statements on 'positive' aspects of the project in some places are later strongly diluted or contradicted in other places. It is difficult to gain a coherent picture of the evidence. A reader with limited attention span or motivation to build the overall picture will be easily mislead by the headlines. The author has attempted to bring the scattered evidence, or lack of it, into a more focussed form. In doing so a very different picture emerges compared to the headline '84% success rate with the most difficult families' widely claimed by the promoters. Here are some points to note :

1. The family selection process eliminated families 'not highly motivated to change'. 56 families received interventions out of 126 referrals. We can conclude that the 'most difficult [ASB] families' in Dundee did not in fact take part in the project.

2. Only 5 to 8 of the 70 closed cases involved 'conflicts' or 'issues' with neighbours. Some of these few families were identified as victims not promoters of ASB. The most prominent 'ASB' problems were said to be inadequate property maintenance/ damage, cleanliness/hygiene, rent arrears and internal family conflicts and issues.

3. Most of the families had serious physical and mental health and substance abuse problems. Few were working. Lone parenting was high. These were clearly socially inadequate people, not the archetypal ASB yobs presented to the public.

4. Inter-agency cooperation was claimed as a key success factor. Yet, despite the 'high incidence of physical and mental health problems' , health services involvement was marginal. The education service was clearly not involved. In later years the social services department (heavily criticised by project staff and so disillusioned) largely disengaged.

5. Changes in family behaviour were assessed by crude opinion surveys from staff, senior stakeholders and families. None of the formal measures of behaviour change accepted by NICE were used. There was no control group for the project. There was no independent, comprehensive, evaluation of cases. There was no evaluation of actual, long term delivered benefits to the community such as reduced crime and ASB or fewer children taken into care. Surveys of education, housing and police authorities saw no spin off effects on 'problem'

levels across Dundee at the end of the project.

6. Family attitude to the project from final interviews was said to be positive. However only 10 families out of 70 were interviewed in any detail. We are told of a 'high interview failure rate'. The authors admit the results therefore 'under represent' the views of those not happy with the project. This result is clearly not reliable. Family attitude clearly affects the likelihood that improved behaviours will be delivered back into the community. The family interview failure rate does not bode well for this.

7. Overall 59% of cases sampled were claimed as successful but housing And social services had very different views. The latter gave only a 39% success rate apparently because underlying family needs and health issues (the causes of ASB) had not been addressed successfully. The 86% housing reported success related to issues like house up keep, cleanliness and rent arrears. Note that these success results are based on less than 36% of the families in the project , a low sampling level on which to draw key conclusions.

8. Several pieces of evidence point to deterioration in family status at the end of the project and particularly for core block families. Support for them clearly evaporated.

9. 'The small number of cases' means that evidence for the relative effectiveness (success) of core block , dispersed and outreach interventions is said to be 'inconclusive' even on the soft 'success' criteria used. Most staff wanted the functions of the core block in particular to be 're-examined'. Given the high cost of core residential block intervention it's cost -effectiveness is doubtful.

10. The overall cost-effectiveness of the project is not demonstrated in the evaluation. Claims of 'good value for money' are based on opinion and gross assumptions that claim family behaviour changes will persist and long term community benefits such as lower crime and ASB and lower levels of children in care will happen.There is no evidence in the evaluation to support this. It is said that comprehensive cost-benefit analysis would be 'too expensive'.

11. Overall the isolated claim of '84% success rate with the most difficult families', repeatedly used to promote the approach of the Dundee project and its clones, is grossly misleading in comparison with actual project delivery as described in the government evaluation report. No objective, field evidence is presented for medium or long term delivery

of substantive community benefits or for cost-effectiveness.

Any effective approach to bringing the poorest and most socially inadequate families back into the main stream of society must be welcomed and supported. If that approach is 'cost-effective', so much the better. If that approach also removes the sources of friction and disdain for the socially inadequate, disabled and ill in the 'normal' ,majority community so much the better. However there is an obligation on the state to be certain that such intrusive intervention is both effective and fair. If it is ineffective and punishes inadequate families for their inadequacies and health problems that form of intervention should be totally unacceptable in a civilised society. The waste of public money is a secondary consideration.

The Dundee project approach exemplifies a wider problem. The recent National Audit Office report "Tackling Anti-social Behaviour" of December 2006 reviews the government's various approaches to ASB interventions. For example it records that 55% of ASBOs are breached; 33% are breached 5 or more times. The report makes some other remarkable statements. In judging the success of various interventions to date they say:

"We are not therefore able to draw conclusions as to whether other forms of intervention or **no intervention** would have achieved the same or a better outcome".

Based on the many perceived weaknesses of current intervention approaches the NAO makes several telling recommendations : the recording of local case information should be improved to support claims of effectiveness ; targeted (social, medical) support should be provided to individuals ; ASB agencies and ASB coordinators must be trained to deal with young people and people with complex (health, disability) needs ; ASB coordinators must take advice from support agency professionals ; formal evaluation schemes should be developed so cost-effectiveness can be proved. These failings should be familiar. They closely match those identified by the author. Clearly little has been learned since the Dundee project was designed.

The NAO report concludes that there is international evidence that other interventions such as education, counseling and training are more cost effective methods of addressing ASB. It concludes that research is needed to understand the 'causes' of ASB and for development of new, preventative, interventions based on that understanding. The author completely supports this last point: there should be no place in this important field for crude, voodoo social engineering promoted on the basis of sexed up evidence, sound bites and dodgy dossiers.

The primary 'benefits' of the various ASB interventions on individuals and yob families so far appear to be political : they allow central and local government to claim that 'tough ,immediate' action is being taken. This is a benefit only in terms of (perhaps) public 'perception' and (perhaps) votes. In fact public perception of yob families puts them in 14th place as a source of ASB concern as we noted. As the public become aware of the lack of real community delivery from these interventions and their high costs we must hope there will be a well deserved political reckoning.

SECTION 4.3   INTERIM REVIEW OF THE GOVERNMENT EVALUATION REPORTS ON SIX ASB FAMILY INTERVENTION PROJECTS

(Professor D P Gregg [retired] March 2007)

1 INTRODUCTION

 Six Family Intervention Projects (FIPs) , five managed by National Children's Homes (NCH) have occoured since the 'pioneering' Dundee Families Project (DFP) which was also managed by NCH. Two included core residential units (so called 'ASBO Towers') in addition to outreach and supervised ,dispersed tenancy 'services'. These projects are being evaluated by Sheffield Hallam University's Centre For Social Inclusion (SHU) using family case file data and interviews with project staff, referral agencies and a small sample of families. The comments in this note are based on "ASB Intensive Family Support Projects : Housing Research Summary 230" (HRS230) and the equivalent full report (AIFSP) issued by the Dept. For Communities and Local Government and the interim 'technical' report currently available on the SHU web site.This note reviews the results claimed in the reports and makes broader comments on the limitations and contradictions of FIP design and operations. Further comments will follow as additional FIP evaluation information becomes available.The 'intensive support' offered to extremely vulnerable families in these projects, for the first time in most cases, must be welcomed but there is no quantitative, independent evidence of long term, positive impacts on the families or their communities. The positive claims of 'remarkable' success as widely reported are not supported by careful analysis of the detailed evidence. There is no objective basis for the claims of 'excellent' value for money. Even more disturbing the supposed 'intensive family support' is still rather limited in critical areas like family mental health which is acknowledged as a root cause of their supposed ASB. In 60% of cases these mentally impaired, very poor, socially inadequate families were found to be victims of ASB. The large scale, national roll out of FIPs will divert funding and attention from the key aim of understanding the root causes of ASB and the development of the truly effective, preventative interventions called for by the National Audit Office.

2. REVIEW OF THE CLAIMED PROJECT RESULTS

2.1 Caveat Emptor.

Before discussion of the detailed results it is important to realise that these are based on the subjective opinion of project workers, made often on the basis of ambiguous criteria and often on samples of only 15 to 20% of the families in the projects. The project information bases and evaluations are a long way from the standards approved by NICE for assessing other ASB intervention schemes (e.g. randomised trials with controls, recognised clinical measures for judging aberrant behaviours and independent assessors) . Similarly the 'positive' qualitative , anecdotal evidence from family interviews is based on only 13.3% of families in the projects. Despite this we are told (in the full AIFSP report, page 117) that 'for the vast majority of families the projects had helped them achieve remarkable changes'. We will find below that this claim is unsustainable for many indisputable reasons. Meanwhile on page 132 (AIFSP) in the summary, and contrary to the above headline, it is admitted that

' it is impossible however, to determine the extent to which the positive outcomes identified and recorded by staff as part of the data gathering exercise are a direct result of the project's interventions rather than other factors'.

HRS230 also tells us, in discussing project impacts, that :

'it was beyond the scope of the evaluation to carry out an independent assessment of the impact of these changes [in family behaviour] on the wider communities in which the families lived'.

Caveat emptor.

2.2 Family Engagement in the FIPs.

We are told in the HSU interim report 'a general indicator that can be used to measure the IMPACT of interventions is the extent to which

...families engaged in the process'. Remarkably we then learn that only 42% of families 'fully engaged' with the project in the 2003-2004 period (a sample of 109 families). Full engagement was 48% in the 54 closed cases at the end of 2005.This is later defined as : actively cooperating with the assessment process and the aims of their support plans. This means 58% (of 109 families by 2005) did not fully engage with the projects. (or 52% in the closed case sample). In fact 26% completely disengaged and these cases were closed. It is difficult to reconcile these figures with the HRS230 headline claim that project workers gave the opinion that for 92% of the families 'risk to the community ' had been reduced or eliminated and with the widely repeated claim for these projects of an 84% success rate.

2.3 Project Impact Measures from Case Files.

  Six years after the DFP, case evidence recording has clearly not improved. The organisers and practitioners do not seem to have actioned the lessons and recommendations of the DFP evaluation which is a cause for concern. We are told in the HSU interim report that ' **in a significant number of case files detailed outcomes were unknown**' ; nor was it clear to the evaluators that the results 'are representative of the total sample of service users' ; nor that ' improvements noted were sustained over time'. Given the strength of the published claims for FIP success these statements are remarkable. We will examine the claimed impacts with the above in mind.

2.3.1 Reduction In ASB Complaints.

  Elimination of ASB complaints against the families was 'a key aim' of these projects. The headline claim is that there were positive outcomes on ASB in 'a total of 85% of closed cases'. This is often presented as an 85% reduction in ASB achieved by the projects. Both these claims are very misleading in several respects. Firstly the results are based on only 16% of the families in the projects. This small sample may or may not be representative of the full population. Secondly the sample and the 85% claim only include families who 'fully or partly engaged 'with the projects and excludes those who disengaged or left the projects. That sample is clearly biased. Thirdly some families already had zero complaints at referral. This is not taken into account. Fourthly the subjective project worker assessments are not compatible with other data provided in the report. We will examine these points in turn and try to estimate the true situation on ASB complaint reduction. The results presented in G8.1 (full AIFSP report) are for only 41 families who 'fully or partly engaged' i.e. cooperated in the assessments and followed their service plans and aims.

This is only 76% of the 54 closed cases available. Nine families disengaged from the project. In 3 of these cases ASB complaints increased. 4 families also left due to 'changed circumstances' including children leaving home.(note : 24% of families had 15-17 year old children at referral ; children leave the projects at 16). We will assume a conservative, neutral outcome for these 4. The full sample would then be :

No complaints at project exit	12	families
Stable and reduced	23	
Stayed the same	6+4	
Increased complaints	6+3	

Also on page 30 (AIFSP report) we learn that 5 of 157 families had no ASB complaints at referral. For our 54 family sample that would imply 2 families. So the number of 'no complaint' families possibly attributed to the projects would be $100x (12-2)/54 = 18.5\%$. We will return to this.

  On page 129 we are told that after case closure 'in 24 cases' complaints about behaviour 'were still prevalent and tenancies remained unstable'. This data can only be reconciled with G8.1 opinions in the following way. The 'increased +stayed the same' category above stands at 19 instead of 24. Therefore 5 of the stable /reduced families must be moved. This gives :

No complaints at project exit	12	22.2%
Stable/ reduced	23-5	33.3
Stayed the same	6+4+5	27.8
Increased	6+3	16.7

To be clear ASB complaints had ceased in only 22.2% of families sampled by project exit but only 18.5% of cases (at maximum) can be attributed to the projects. At project end 77.8% of families still had ASB complaints. At best we can say that an additional (in project worker opinion) 51.8% of families had reached the point were tenancies were not at risk. This is very different to the headline claims of an 85% reduction in ASB. There is also a problem with the definition of tenancy 'stabilisation' we will return to below. Notice that we are not told the scale of the reduction of ASB for the 33.3% of families where this is claimed. Was it 5, 10, or 50%? Clearly whatever the 'risk to tenancy' threshold assumed by the workers the actual scale of reduction is what is of interest to the community.

  The reduction of ASB, whatever it is, is attributed to factors such as increased parental control and the development of communications and conflict management skills. However some of the reduction may actually relate to the 'enforcement' aspects of intervention. 34% of families were targeted because of antisocial visitors to their homes. This often related to groups of youngster and associated noise, etc. 70% of families were targeted for youth nuisance. It is therefore interesting that page 121 tells us that 'complaints about [visitor] behaviour often stopped completely after a family had been re-housed'... presumably in dispersed or core residential cases at least. It also reports that 'ASB in some cases reduced as a result of a family member being removed or leaving voluntarily'. So in how many of the 18.5% of families in which ASB ceased and the 33.3% in which ASB reduced were these improvements actually related to imposed structural changes in the families rather than improved parenting skills and behaviour? Clearly this has relevance to the question of whether claimed improvements were sustained after project closure. (note: the average family had 3 children. Removing one still leaves a potential long term problem). This difficulty is recognised in the full AIFSP report. In section 10, "Gaps in The Evidence Base" it recommends research extensions to actually measure

'the sustainability of interventions in terms of family functioning and behaviour'.

Even the 18.5% and 33.3% improvement estimates we found may be optimistic as predictors. To reinforce the 'quantitative' analysis we are also told that

'the vast majority of service users interviewed confirmed that by the time they left the projects complaints of ASB had completely ceased or reduced significantly as a result of project intervention'.

Well they would, wouldn't they given that their project participation was under threat of sanctions such as eviction and family break up. Even families with low IQs are unlikely to say: 'no, we are still as bad as ever'. However the above statement hides a bigger distortion. The 'vast majority' claim applies to an interview sample of only 34 out of the 256 families in the projects: a sample of only 13.3%. Later we will see that this sample is likely to be biased (see section 4). Neither is there any independent evidence of whether the claimed qualitative improvements in behaviour were sustained in the community after the alleged 'intensive' project support and the immediate threat of family eviction and other sanctions ended. HRS230 tells us: "an independent assessment of the impact of these changes on the wider community was in fact "beyond the scope of the evaluation". But surely long term community impacts such as reduced crime and ASB are the primary deliverables used to justify these projects to local councils and the public? Indeed they are: caveat emptor.

2.3.2 Complaints to the Police.

   This data (G8.5 AIFSP) provides valuable evidence on those ASB complaints presumably serious enough to be brought to the attention of the police. It is also useful since it should be based on objective recorded data not project worker opinion and ambiguous criteria : either complaints reduced or they did not. At first sight the results look impressive. 90% of families showed either no or reduced complaints by project exit. It is surprising that more has not been made of this result. Or as we will see , perhaps not .Firstly the results apply to only 39 families who ' fully or partly engaged' out of 256 families in the projects : a sample of 15.2%. As usual the 39% of families with no complaints and the 51% with reduced complaints refer only to those who engaged. We are also told that 6 families disengaged i.e. 11.1% of the 54 closed cases (note: the disengagement level of the total population is significantly higher at 17%-26%. The closed case sample is apparently not representative). 3 families had increased complaints, 1 stayed the same and 2 reduced. The other 9 families are not mentioned. As before we try to reconstruct the full sample.

No police complaints at exit   15 families   27.8%
Reduced complaints   20+2   40.7%
Stayed the same   1+1+9   20.4
Increased   3+3   11.1

As usual the scale of complaint reduction in the 40.7% of 'reduced' cases is not given. Was it 5, 10, 50%…? Already our 90% of families with 'improvement' has fallen to 68.5%. However footnote 27 , page 124, tells us that in 'some cases ,households were not known to the police when their cases opened'. This is a rather significant point. If they were unknown to the police there were no complaints at that point. So how many were unknown? G6.2 perhaps gives us an indicator: 68% were not in 'ongoing contact' with the police. It is difficult to reconcile G8.5 and G6.2 evidence.

* at case opening 68% of families had no contact with the police.
* at case closing 68.5% had had no complaints (27.8%) or reduced
   complaints (40.7%) to the police.

   This is something of a puzzle unless the closed cases were not representative of the total population. However G6.2 at least gives us both before and after measures, for a bigger family sample, which are presumably consistent. At case opening 68% of families had no 'ongoing contact' with the police. At case closure this was 76%. This implies a modest 8% reduction in the number of families in police contact and presumably in associated complaints. This is a far cry from the 90%

improvement implied by G8.5.

2.3.3 Eviction and Tenancy Stabilisation.

A key objective of FIPs , it is said, is the stabilisation of tenancies and the avoidance of family eviction. The results presented for these measures are again based on project workers opinions not independent assessors but there is less room for ambiguity in the meaning of the stability measure : a simple yes or no.

Results are given for 41 families out of 256 : a sample of only 16%. We are told that at project exit 78% of families who fully or partly engaged had stable tenancies. No common criterion for this judgement is defined. 15% were considered unstable. Of the families who disengaged 8 were unstable and 1 partially stabilised. 4 families were 'changed circumstances'. As before we reconstruct the full sample (of 50 in this case).

Stable at exit	32	families	64%
Unstable at exit	18		36%

The key question is what was the stability pattern at project start up for these families? Chapter 5 (AIFSP) contains much useful information for a much larger sample of families (n =157). 33% had received a 'notice of seeking possession' (NOSP) or a 'notice to quit' (NTQ) prior to project referral. These families were clearly at immediate risk of eviction. The report says however that these notices 'may not necessarily' relate to ASB but may be due to reasons such as rent arrears. (page 184 tells us a recent survey showed the 'vast majority of evictions' in general are due to rent arrears. Footnote 20 , page 69 reports that 59% of project families were in debt at referral , 69% of these debts related to rent arrears. i.e. 41% of the families in total. We can assume that no amount of parenting master classes is going to remove the problem of poverty or the related eviction threats). Page 69 admits that at start up 'we [the evaluators] defined the threat to tenancy broadly'. In addition to the unambiguous NOSP/NTQ cohort they included families with a warning from the landlord and those having ABCs or ASBOs .

It is though conceded that these' may not be a direct threat to the home'. Threat definition is clearly critical to interpreting family status at referral and project exit. What criteria did workers apply in the exit survey? If they applied the 'broad' criterion we can say the following for the 157 sample : 113 were at threat at referral I.e. 100 x 113 / 157 = 72%. Therefore 28% were not at threat. Applying this to our sample at exit we could claim an improvement during the projects of 64 - 28 = 36% in stable tenancies. This is a long way from the headline claim that in 80% of cases tenancies were successfully stabilised.

If project workers applied the more precise criterion of membership of the NOSP/NTQ cohort the gains attributable to the projects were less. At exit 36% were still unstable versus 33% at start up (with 41% having rent arrears). If this is the case the projects achieved nothing substantive. This example demonstrates the effect the failure to define transparent, consistent criteria has on our ability to evaluate project impacts. (See also the section below on family breakdown).

2.3.4 Impact on The Wider Community.

Improving the community is a 'key aim' of the projects. Unfortunately page 117 (AIFSP report and the HRS230) tells us that

'it was beyond the scope of the evaluation to carry out an independent assessment of the impact of these changes on the wider communities in which the families lived'.

Yet again we must rely on project worker subjective opinions and forecasts gleaned from the case files and risk and risk criteria are not defined. We are told that at exit 51% of families who fully or partly engaged posed 'no risk ' to the community. 41% posed a 'reduced risk'. 8% posed an increased risk. These figures lead to the headline claim of a 92% success rate. As usual these results apply to a sample of only 15.2% of project families. We are told that 10 families disengaged leaving 5 as 'changed circumstances'. We conservatively reconstruct the full closed case sample as :

No risk at exit	20 families	37 %
reduced risk	16	29.6
stayed the same	5+5	18.5
Increased risk	3+5	14.9

We are not told by how much the risk 'reduced' for the 29.6% of families. Was it 5, 20, 50% ?
That would surely be of great interest to those in the community. As for other impact measures the key question is what was the level of risk when these families entered the projects? It is the difference between start and exit risk that might be attributable to the interventions. Page 124, footnote 26 does tell us this:
'It was not always noted whether family behaviour **had impacted in any significant way** on the community when they were initially referred and

---

305

therefore **it is impossible to chart changes** that had occurred directly **as a result of the project interventions** but the data clearly indicates that the situation had not deteriorated over the course of support'.

In other words the best result the data can support is **no change**. This is very different to the headline 92% community risk improvement claim. Are there any other indicators of community impact? Family contact with the police, implying more serious complaints , is arguably a reasonable proxy for community risk. G6.2 (AIFSP) told us that at referral 32% of families were in 'ongoing contact' with the police. At case closure this was 24%.

Also 70% of families had youth nuisance as one reason given for referral. Contacts with youth offender teams (YOTs) may therefore be of relevance. At referral 22% had contact with YOTs. At exit this had risen to 26%. Together these proxies support a 'no deterioration' claim for community risk but not the headline 92% improvement claim. The evaluators themselves are clearly concerned about the validity of community impact claims. In the "Gaps in The Evidence" section of AIFSP they say:

'there are limitations to the evaluation evidence base, particularly in relation to the assessments of the impact on the community'.

As a result they highlighted the need for further independent research on this issue.

2.3.5 Risk of Family Breakdown

Preventing family breakdown and the associated costs to the state is said to be a 'core objective' of the projects. This important objective can again only be judged on the basis of project worker opinion. Neither are the criteria used by the workers defined. The presented results are based on a sample of only 15% of the families in the projects. We are told that 48% of this sample had reduced risk at closure; 45% stayed the same ; 8% had increased risk of breakdown.
As usual these numbers apply only to those who fully or partly engaged in the projects. For the 9 families who disengaged , 6 stayed at the same risk and 3 had increased risk. We reconstruct the full closed case sample as :

Reduced risk   19 families   35.2%
Stayed the same   18+6+5 = 29   53.7
Increased risk   3+3   11.1
As usual we are not told the degree to which risk reduced for the 35.2% families or increased for the 11.1% of families . Was it 5, 20, 50%?

To quantify project cost effectiveness which depends strongly on family breakdown prevention we need to know. In 64.8% of families the risk of breakdown stayed the same or increased by exit. So how did the projects change things? Page 125 (AIFSP report) tells us that at referral ' **64%** of families were considered to be at high or medium risk of family breakdown , often due to multiple problems that **may not be easy to resolve in the short term** '. Frustratingly the decreased / increased risk data at exit are not related to the low, medium, high risk groups. This makes them fairly useless as evidence. We can however attempt a conservative reconstruction. At referral we know

Low risk	Medium risk	High risk
36%	32	32

At exit we appear to have a net decrease in risk in 35.2 - 11.1 = 24.1 % of families. Assume that this improvement was spread across all risk categories. Assume , generously, that the improvement in risk was large enough to move the families one risk category lower. At exit we would then have:

Low	Medium	High
36+8 = 44	32+8-8=32	32-8=24

So 56% of families would now be medium or high risk. Being generous we might say that families at medium or high risk of breakdown had fallen by 64 - 56 = 8% during the projects. However recall that this 'gain' applies only to a sample of 21% of the families in the projects. This small difference could simply be a sampling effect. In fact a difference of this scale would be seen in over 7 out of 10 samples of this size even if the medium / high category proportion remained at 64% at project end. It is also interesting to recall that applying a precise definition of threat in the case of tenancy stabilisation suggests only a small positive or zero change due to project interventions.

2.3.6 Impact On Children's Health and Well Being.

The children of the projects had remarkably high levels of medical / psychiatric needs. 54% had a learning disability or ADHD or a physical disability. 19% suffered from depression or other mental health problems. 17% had drug related problems. 53% had statements of SEN or attended special schools or had educational statements. 36% of families were classed as having 'children in need' or at medium or high risk of being taken into care at referral. Despite all this we are told that many families had previously received little support from other agencies (interim SHU report). With the supposed 'intensive support' given in the projects

307

one would hope for marked improvements in 'health and well being'. The scale of improvements is however unclear. We are told 'it was sometimes difficult to ascertain exactly what criteria projects workers had used when assessing the impact of interventions...' and that 'often the changes were small' and involved such things as 'a healthier diet, improved daily routine and regular check ups at the dentist'. Given the severity of children's problems this is disappointing.

The data on mental health at project exit relate to 38 families : a sample of 14.8% of project families or 70.3% of closed cases. An improvement is claimed in 40% of families. These are only the families who fully or partly engaged. We are not told what happened in the remaining 30% of closed cases. This is very unsatisfactory. Let us be generous and assume no change for these families in reconstructing the full sample. As usual criteria are not defined.

Improved mental health	15 families	27.7%
Stayed the same	21+16	68.6
Worsened	2	3.7

As usual the level of improvement for the 27.7% of families is not quantified. Was it 5, 20, 50%? The results are depressing but as page 64 (AIFSP) tells us

'This finding highlights the deep rooted and intractable nature of many of the mental health problems and suggests in some cases longer term mainstream interventions are required'.

Let us translate this into clear English: 'some' cases actually means 72.3% of cases; 'mainstream' means getting proper, professional, medical help for these children. But surely providing such help was one of the key aims of the projects? The reality is presented in G6.2 which lists family contacts with support agencies at case opening and closure.

Thirteen key agencies are listed. The list does not include the NHS. Contacts with a 'mental health worker' are noted. Recall that 80% of the families have significant mental health and disability problems. At referral only 9% were in contact with a mental health worker. At exit this figure was still only 17%. Put it another way : at start up 89% of the families with problems had NO mental health worker. At exit this had 'improved' to 79%. It is hard to reconcile these stark facts and the possible 'small changes' in health in 27.7% of sample families with the glowing headline claims of project success i.e. of 'significant improvements in children's health...'. Or even more misleadingly:

'given the high levels of concern over the health and well being of family members , particularly children and young people, these findings represent

encouraging indications that the projects were successful in putting families in contact with agencies that could address the causes of problem behaviours'.

Do you think the evidence supports such claims? It does not. If the 'deep rooted and intractable' mental health problems have not been addressed for most families how can it be predicted that problem behaviours in the community have been reduced or eliminated in 92% of families? It cannot.

Project impact on schooling is also reported in respect of 44 families. This is a sample of only 17.2% of families. At referral 'concerns' included non-attendance, truancy and 'some problems' in 29% of regular attendees. 4 families had no schooling problems. However 'concerns' also included 34% with special educational needs or statements (38% at exit).
At exit 16 families had improved on attendance (7 'markedly'), for 10 attendance remained 'problematic' and for 18 schooling problems stayed the same or worsened. So we have

Improved	16 families	36.4%
not improved	12	27.3
problematic/worsened	10+6	36.3

Any improvement must be welcomed but for 63.6% of families things did not improve or worsened. Can these results justifiably be reported in the headline claims as 'significant improvements' in 'educational attainment'? It would also be interesting to know the reason for increased attendance in the improved cases. We can see that the improved percentage is close to the percentage of children with special needs, namely 36%. Is this a coincidence or have conditions and support been improved mainly for the learning disabled children? Page 66 (AIFSP) tells us that it was not always clear 'whether these schooling concerns had been formally acknowledged prior to referral'. One of the 'key project interventions' was to ensure that 'where children had special needs ...appropriate support [was] provided'. Such children also suffer disproportionately from bullying at school. (as recorded in the Dundee Families Project report). Was this also , finally, addressed ?

2.4 The Subjective Evidence

Without objective quantitative evidence for project 'impacts' the evaluators had to rely on subjective and anecdotal evidence gleaned from case referral agencies , project staff and families. That is perfectly legitimate in principle. The devil however is in the detail. We are told in the interim SHU report (relating to 109 of the families) that 'the majority of referrers viewed the projects in 'a positive light' for 'a variety of reasons'. The reasons cited are interesting. Referrers welcomed 'the tailor made packages of support'; 'the intensity of support'; 'the independence of the projects' from local authority agencies. Notice that these views are related to project design and procedural issues, not results achieved. In further comments more negative aspects emerge. We learn that 'some referrers had reservations about making a judgment on how successful the projects had been with all types of families'. Perhaps these reservations related to the 58% of families who did not 'fully engage' in that sample of 109 families? (or to the 52% in the closed case sample of 54).We learn that

'reservations were also expressed about how successful any one project could be at addressing long-standing, deep- seated problems at the root of a family's behaviour'

Despite this we are assured 'most referral agencies' judged the projects as 'helping to reduce the risk of eviction in the long term'. No risk probability estimates are attempted which is unhelpful in evaluating cost-benefit. Overall this material adds little to our ability to quantify project impacts. Some project families were also interviewed. 'Overwhelmingly' the assessments were 'positive'. Adults in families felt better as a result of the support offered. Is this surprising if we consider the family history profiles.

* 72.2% were led by lone mothers clearly struggling with multiple children.
* 85% of adults were not in paid work.
* 59% were in debt.
* mental and physical health was poor in 80% of families: 59% of adults were clinically depressed; 21% had problems such as schizophrenia, obsessive-compulsive disorder, anxiety disorders and stress.
* 54% of families had a child with learning difficulties or ADHD or a physical disability. 19% had mental health problems.
* 79% of families had at least one child judged to be 'vulnerable'; 38% had a child at risk of being taken into care.

The reports conclude these are some of the poorest, most mentally impaired and disadvantaged families in the UK. **These are not 'families from hell' but 'families in hell'.** Yet HRS230 tells us that 'the multiple support needs' implied by the above profiles 'in many cases had not been addressed by other agencies'. Naturally the families interviewed were pleased, finally after years of neglect, to receive some focused attention to their problems. Who could fail to welcome this result? However the situation is actually far more equivocal.

Remarkably, if we look carefully at the report, we find the first stage of family interviews covered only 29 families of the 109 studied: that is 26.6%. We can assume by definition that this 26.6% were among the 42% who 'fully engaged' with the project. We don't know the attitudes of the 73% not interviewed except that around 6/7 of them were 'not fully engaged'. The second stage of interviewing in Autumn 2005 involved 24 families including 19 from the first set. This means that 34 families in all out of 256 were actually interviewed about their project experiences. i.e. only 13.3%.As in the DFP these sampling levels are very low. The DFP evaluation at least admitted that the sample was biased in favour of cooperative families unlikely to express negative comments. It must be remembered that families were under threat of eviction if they did not cooperate. The SHU report actually confirms this. They tell us the projects had a

'significant effect...particularly where the service users felt that the projects had prevented them from loosing their home'.

We also need to consider whether the improved state of mind of the 26.6% of families interviewed in the first stage or the 13.3% overall survived the removal of intensive support at the project end and indeed how these internal improvements translated into sustained improvements in behaviour in the community. All we have to judge this is opinion. As noted earlier the prediction that 92% of families offered a 'reduced risk' in the community is not supported by a close look at the so-called quantitative case file data. Police and YOT contact data suggest a small change at best during the projects. This interview sampling of only 13.3% of families, the selected anecdotal evidence and a 'fully engaged' figure of only 42%-48% of families, does little to change this conclusion.

3. COST EFFECTIVENESS

These projects are repeatedly described as very cost-effective. A large section of the evaluation report (AIFSP) deals with estimating the costs of projects and the costs of family eviction, family breakdown and children taken into care. The author has little chance of assessing the validity of these estimates. However other data in the public domain suggests the cost estimates for children taken into care are of the right order of magnitude. The average total cost per closed case is said to be around 32K for a project involving outreach, dispersed and core residential interventions.

The average project family had 2.9 children. The cost of family break up for such a family is given as 250K per annum. At first sight the projects look like good value. However it is necessary to be very careful. The claimed cost savings depend totally on the reduction of family break ups and the avoidance of children being taken into care which can be attributed to the project interventions. This point is acknowledged in several places in the final AIFSP report and in HRS230. For example in claiming 'excellent value for money' for the projects HRS230 goes on ' as they have the **potential** to reduce considerably the short term and long term costs of many agencies'. But 'potential' is not delivery. There was no independent assessment of whether claimed improvements were sustained beyond the end of project interventions. In section 11 of AIFSP , 'Gaps In Evidence' the authors draw attention to 'the limitations of the evaluation evidence base'. They go on to recommend further research to actually establish :

* the sustainability of interventions in family functioning and behaviour.

* the longer term impact of family project interventions on existing support and supervision services.

Only with such objective data can cost effectiveness be evaluated. The impact evidence we evaluated earlier is subjective, opinion based, exaggerated and ambiguous.

* We have seen that 'underlying, deep rooted' causes of 'family problem behaviour', namely serious mental health and disability issues are still undressed in 79% of the 80% of families with such problems (63% of families in total).

* Because of ambiguities in criteria definition the fraction of tenancies 'stabilised' due to interventions is anything from zero to 36%. However even these positive estimates are based on a sample of only 21% of families in the projects.

* G4.1 in AIFSP tells us that at referral 19% of families were at high risk of children being taken into care and 20% were at medium risk. On that basis ,assuming the projects did no harm, the maximum potential target for avoiding the costs of care is 19%.Unfortunately there is no data for the exit situation. Page 56 (AIFSP) also tells us that at referral only six families had a child already in care or in controlled residential accommodation i.e. only 3.8% of families. This is rather a long way from 19% or 39%.

* The high and medium risk of family break up group at referral was said

to be 64%. On generous assumptions it was 56% at exit implying a reduction possibly due to project interventions of 8%.However the exit estimate is based on only 15.6% of families in the projects. Because of limited sampling a difference of 8% from the referral level could occour by chance in 77 out of 100 such samples. The odds are the change is not real.

Looking at this set of results it is easy to see why the evaluators felt the need for objective, independent, field, assessment of project impacts. For the sake of obtaining a feel for the cost saving potential of projects let us be generous and assume the project interventions reduced family break up in 4% of families , the actual fraction with a child in care at referral. This assumes that the number in care would have doubled without such interventions.

Number of families in a typical project 256 / 6 = 43.
Total cost 32,000 X 43 = 1,376,000.
Saving if a family with 3 children is stabilized, £250,000 per annum.
So savings for 4% avoidance is 0.04 X 43 X 250,000 = £430,000 per annum.

We get breakeven if these families were stabilised for a period of 3.2 years. If one child in each family avoided care the breakeven period is 9.6 years. The cost leverage of this project design does imply potential. However the objective, quantified evidence on frequency of avoidance of care and sustainability of family behaviour changes in the medium and longer term is essentially zero. The headline claim in HRS230 that

'the cost analysis of the IFSPs indicates that this form of intervention offers excellent value for money'

is grossly misleading and not supportable on the basis of the published evidence.

4. FAMILY TARGETTING PROTOCOLS: Bias, Intolerance and Neglect.

The evaluation reports, if read carefully, and seen in the context of other research, provide a powerful insight into how our families find themselves in FIPs or as the targets of other state interventions such as ASBOs. This is at the heart of the issue and the author makes no apology for exploring it at some length. ASB interventions will not be effective until causation is fully understood and acknowledged honestly. The major change distinguishing the six FIPs under review from the original DFP is the sharpness of focusing in family targeting. The concentration is now much more on families allegedly displaying ASB recognisable in the popular media archetype promoted by the government as we will see. Whatever the motivation this helps us to see even more clearly the correlation between important factors in the ASB phenomenon which are very revealing.

1. High levels of alleged 'media headline' ASB.
2. High levels of mental/physical health problems and disabilities in the target families.
3. High levels of ASB perpetrated AGAINST the target families.
4. Decreasing levels of tolerance of 'difference', including mental impairment, and increasing paranoia in the community, related to government misinformation.
5. Decay of medical, educational and social support services for the mentally ill and learning disabled in the community and in specialist in house units over the last decade.

We will explore these factors and why the FIP targeting appears to be in practice biased and punitive in a counterproductive way, whatever the good intentions of those involved. In the DFP less than 10% of the families targeted had been involved in 'neighbour disputes'. In the six FIPs under review the frequency of 'neighbour conflict and disputes' was much higher at 54%. 'Youth nuisance' was also higher involving 70% of families. Nevertheless this still means that 46% of families targeted were NOT involved in neighbour conflicts and 30% were NOT engaged in youth nuisance. In 34% of cases ASB complaints were due to visitors to family homes, not the families themselves. (note: this does not prevent such families being evicted by many councils). We learn however that 36% of families had noise complaints, 33% for garden condition and 30% for rubbish. The DFP approach of defining poor council house upkeep as ASB is apparently still with us (50% of referrals, by far the biggest slice, were still from 'housing'). Overall HRS230 assures us that 'the majority of cases concerned 'low level but persistent nuisance behaviours'. The SHU technical report is even more enlightening. The family interviews explored to what extent the families believed complaints against them were 'justified and reflected reality'.

Most had a strong 'sense of unfairness that they had been singled out by the authorities'. Most families disputed all or some of the ASB complaints. Many claimed exaggeration. Many could not understand why they had been targeted. Some of the behaviour admitted was seen as part of normal family life in that community. Remember these are the families who 'fully engaged' with the projects yet their sense of injustice is strong despite cooperating. What might the 58% who did not fully engage have said about their targeting? We don't know because they weren't interviewed.

What is clear is that the current approach to targeting is counterproductive. Later we will see that it is also admitted to be unfair. It should be noted that some families cited the growth in intolerance in their community and the exercise of personal grudges for their targeting. We will come back to this.

The SHU evaluation also looked at the perceptions of the referral agencies. The ratings given for the scale of ASB behaviours were very diverse. The consensus view indicated largely 'low level complaints' as the cause of referral. It is very telling that 'the majority of referrers were reluctant to use the term anti-social' to describe family members. They felt that 'labeling families as anti-social was counterproductive to achieving change'. It is also telling that the families found the ASB label 'embarrassing', 'upsetting' or 'humiliating'. Clearly the families did not see the ASB label as a badge of honour. Most referrers also made it clear that 'the families were not always entirely responsible for their ASB due to underlying causes'. No doubt these included the pervasive, un-addressed, mental health and learning disability issues for which no support had been given.While accepting their behaviours as 'problematic' the 'cause of problem behaviour was clearly associated with individual pathology or circumstances beyond the families control'. Quite remarkably given the repeated government demonisation of these families the parents were 'often described in positive terms as being caring' by referral agencies. These views perhaps explain why the families felt such a strong sense of injustice at being targeted and stigmatised …for that is still the way participation in these projects is promoted by senior members of the government for the benefit of the media.

Let us review some of the 'individual pathologies' underlying the alleged ASB. HRS230 you recall tells us that over 80% of the adults targeted had significant mental/physical health problems including clinical depression, schizophrenia, obsessive-compulsive disorder, anxiety disorders and stress. 27% had alcohol or drug dependency problems. The HSU report says 25% (28% in AIFSP) of families had one or more children with special educational needs. 19% had ADHD. Curiously the IQ of family members is not recorded. This is relevant: the Home Office tells us that 55% of persistent young offenders had statements of special educational needs or attended special schools ; 75% of prisoners are 'intellectually impaired' ; 35% of ASBOs go to mentally impaired youngsters.

The correlation between mental ill-health and disability and alleged ASB is strongly highlighted by comparing the status of families assigned to the core residential and outreach groups. Look at the relative frequency levels of families with particular health problems.

Problem	core/outreach relative frequency
Mental health	1.8 X
Learning difficulties	1.5 X
Physical disabilities	1.4 X
Depression	1.2 X
Alcohol dependency	1.4 X
Health related dependency	1.5 X
Average ratio	1.47 X

The core families are clearly even more vulnerable than the already very vulnerable general family population. The report notes however that the number of agencies involved at referral was the same for core and outreach families.

Strangely only for drug dependency is the relative problem level significantly lower for core families at 0.64 X. We can also look at the relative frequency of occurrence of ASB problems for core and outreach families.

ASB Problem	core/outreach relative frequency
Neighbour disputes	1.08 X
Youth nuisance	0.62 X
Harassment	0.64 X
Other crime	0.86 X
Drug nuisance	0.41 X
Vandalism/rubbish	0.69 X
Property damage	0.66 X
ASB visitors	0.75 X
Garden	0.67 X
Average ratio	0.71 X

For 8 out of 10 categories of ASB the frequency of core families having problems is markedly lower than for outreach families. In only one category is the core family problem behaviour markedly higher: the ratio is 2 X for 'violence' (i.e. 55% versus 27% of families). This is a curious result given the low ratios for problems like harassment (0.64 X) and property damage (0.66 x) for the core families, the very similar levels of family 'violence' frequency for core (64%) and outreach (68%) families and the similar frequencies (64% versus 59%) for neighbour disputes. The 2 X ratio for 'violence' is hard to reconcile with the average ASB problem ratio of 0.71 X. One might conclude that the core families, while generally significantly less anti-social, lack self-control when situations of conflict arise and they are pressed too hard. The high frequency ratios for mental illness (1.8 X), learning disability (1.5 X) and alcohol dependency (1.4 X) relative to outreach suggest this is so. These results raise the issue of who initiates conflicts. Is it our core families or others? Page 38 (AIFSP) tells us that 59% of project families have been the victims in neighbour disputes and 20% have been subject to violence. We are told that 'some of the families were particularly vulnerable to being bullied …easily stigmatised, scape-goated and victimised by others in the community'. The author suggests these are some of our core families. Core residential blocks, 'ASBO Towers' or 'sin bins' are the highly visible flagship symbols of FIPs in the community. Somebody has to go in them and that has to be the 'very worst' families; not necessarily the most antisocial, just the strangest and most vulnerable and those most easily goaded into the violent reactions that justify the 'very worst' label. We will return to this later.

If we add in the 72% of lone mother families, 82% of adults not in full time work and the 59% of families in debt we have a clear picture of mentally impaired ,very poor, socially inadequate people unable to cope with the expectations of our complex, modern society. Surely, as the comments of the referrers hint, the state response to this should not be criminalisation or the threat of eviction but effective, long term medical and psychiatric support. (We will see that such support has decayed dramatically in the last decade).

What we have in these projects is the modern equivalent of communal stoning to cast out devils. The attitude difference to mental versus physical impairment is stark. Would we employ such coercive sanctions and criminalisation against the chronically ill and physically disabled: pick up thy bed and walk or we'll stop your benefits ? Would we label them as anti-social for absorbing state resources? Perhaps in the near future, under New Labour, we will. This brings us back to the claim by many families of growing intolerance of mental health problems and social inadequacy in the community. The most remarkable statistic in HRS230 is that:

"60% of families were reported by project staff and / or referral agencies to be victims of ASB"

(note: in the DFP 70% of the children had been bullied at school).HRS230 points to 'emerging research' which highlights 'the difficulties' in distinguishing ASB victims from perpetrators. Is there any independent evidence to suggest why FIP families are as likely or more likely to be victims rather than instigators? There is.

In 2005 a Disability Rights Commission survey found that 50% of disabled people interviewed had suffered 'physical or verbal abuse' in the last three months ; 33% had suffered physical abuse ; 25% had been forced to move home by serial neighbour abuse ; 60% had given up complaining to the police who took no action. (note: it is widely accepted in the criminal justice system that disabled and mentally ill people do not make credible witnesses .The relevance of this to FIP selection and ASBO targeting is obvious) . A recent Mental Health Foundation survey found that 47% of people with mental health problems had suffered discrimination at work. The government Social Exclusion Unit says that 83% of people with mental health problems felt 'stigmatised' in the community ; 55% named prejudice as a key barrier to employment. The Disability Discrimination Act 2005 points to the high frequency of disability discrimination in the provision of public sector services. There is much more that could be said. HRS230 implicitly acknowledges the above issues and highlights the **need** for ASB agencies:

"to develop investigatory policies and processes to ensure all those involved in ASB cases are dealt with fairly"

Lets be clear: the current processes are intrinsically biased against mentally impaired, socially inadequate people. This is true for all the ASB interventions. In the ASBO process the complainant is encouraged to concentrate on his subjective feelings about events. There is no need for 'investigators' to prove 'intention' to cause annoyance, etc by the alleged perpetrator. There is a built in assumption that the complainant is the victim. As we have seen the mentally impaired accused is not considered 'credible' a priori and is less likely to have complained about disputes. 97% of ASBO applications are granted and 37% go to mentally impaired people. The HRS230 statement suggests that at last this 'inequality of arms' in ASB interventions is being recognised... in the DCLG at least.

Let us return to the issue of intolerance in the community. Is it increasing and if so, why? There is ample evidence that people (the decent, hard working majority) are more fearful now and therefore less tolerant of 'difference'. Lets consider a few examples :

* A large survey for the Institute of Psychiatrists in 2006 found that 27% believed that people deliberately set out to irritate them ; 10% think somebody 'has it in for them'; 5% believe there is a conspiracy against them ! The researchers expressed 'astonishment' at the level of paranoia they now found.

* British Social Attitudes 2006 found that only 52% of people would be

more concerned that an innocent person be convicted than that a guilt person walked free. Twenty years ago that figure was 70%.

* A YouGov poll to mark Holocaust Memorial Day 2007 found that 41% of people believed that prejudice and intolerance were now so strong that another Holocaust could happen in Britain today (note: in the Nazi Holocaust the first victims murdered were around 220,000 disabled children and adults of the Greater Reich).

What is driving these attitudinal trends? Many think it is government propaganda on the 'war on terror' and what Blair calls 'the war on low level terrorism at home' i.e. antisocial behaviour. 'Neighbours from Hell' and 'Hoodies' have been built into apocalyptic nightmare threats totally at odds with the government's own social statistics.

The British Crime Survey report 'Experiences and Perceptions of ASB in the UK' has 'hoodies' or rather 'teenagers hanging around' in only 6th place among public ASB concerns. Although 28% expressed concern about this 'problem' less than **3%** had personally experienced a distressing incident. Similarly 'neighbour disputes' ranked 14th and were seen 'as a very big problem' by only **2%** of people. The FIPs are targeting a 2% problem, ranked 14th in people's ASB concerns. Why? Because of the government jihad on ASB. Because the families targeted, unlike mobile' hard to catch' ASB perpetrators ,are strange, easily scape-goated, sitting ducks in council property, who lack the mental abilities to defend themselves and the harassment and punishment of this 'pond life' makes good press. The most mentally impaired, if abused or attacked in the community or unfairly targeted by the authorities, are likely to respond badly and even violently so confirming their guilt. These families are those who HRS230 tells us have serious mental health and disability problems which 'had not been adequately addressed by other agencies'.

Let's look at this state neglect which seems to be at the root of most of the 'families from hell' targeted by FIPs and ASBOs. This government has systematically reduced the medical, educational and social service support for the mentally impaired and disabled. There is massive evidence for these contentions. The author will merely quote a few concerned authorities :

* "43% of beds in children's psychiatric units have been lost since 2003"
                                        Royal College of Psychiatrists.

* " The Special Needs education system is not fit for purpose"
                          House of Commons Education Select Committee.

* " 84% of Local Implementation Teams supporting schizophrenics in the Community are rated as weak or fair".

Healthcare Commission.

* " People with a learning disability are more likely to experience major illness and die sooner. They face difficulties accessing services and they are less likely to receive adequate treatment"

Disability Rights Commission.

* " Only one in thirteen families with disabilities get help from social services. Disabled children are 13 times more likely to be excluded from school".   MENCAP.

* " The cost of bringing up a disabled child is 3 times higher than for a healthy one. 55% of disabled children live in or at the margins of poverty".   Cabinet Office Review.

* "300,000 children in poor housing suffer from long term illness or disability"   SHELTER.

* " Carers for the chronically sick and disabled face a bleak picture : 33% are forced to live on benefits ; 31% are in debt ; 63% felt socially isolated ; 45% said their own health had deteriorated significantly "

Carers UK Survey.

* " A successful system of care would transform this country , empty a third of our prisons and halve the number of prostitutes and homeless"

Centre For Policy Studies.

* **" Services for disabled children and their families are a national disgrace "**

The Children's Commissioner For England.

Do you recognise these people? The people described above are our FIP and impaired ASBO families. Charles Dickens would have know them.

"This boy is ignorance ; this girl is want. Beware them both, and all of their degree, but most of all beware this boy for on his brow I see that written which is Doom" said the Spirit.

"Have they no refuge or resource? " cried Scrooge.

"Are there no prisons? Are there no workhouses?" said the Spirit.

A Christmas Carol; 1843.

Would Dickens believe that a century and a half after his time we have learned so little? The social failure of the FIP families is easy to understand in the light of the facts: it is our failure in the duty of care we owe to the most vulnerable. The government created the problem of 'social exclusion' through gross neglect. It encouraged a fearful, intolerant society for it's own political ends which seem to centre on increased state control of our lives. Now the two themes come together. It victimises the socially excluded, demonising them as part of the war on 'low level terrorism' to justify coercive interventions in their lives (and increasingly ours) through criminalisation or attempts at crude, ineffective social engineering. We should be ashamed that we let
it happen.

5. FAMILY INTERVENTION PROJECT PHILOSOPHY

From the beginning the FIP model has been schizophrenic in it's aims and approach moulded by powerful political considerations. Page 157 (AIFSP) in addressing 'organisational issues', says ' all projects [are] working in a highly pressurised and political context'. They add 'projects can be captured to serve the interests of specific groups and agendas - such as social landlords, residents, or influential political and policy groups'. In this context note that 50% of families were referred by council housing departments, by far the biggest referral group. Many referrals seemed to relate to house up keep issues and rent arrears (41% had rent arrears).

The FIP model is said to balance enforcement and support elements. Some observers view the model as an improvement on the punitive and ineffective ASBO since it introduces this element of support for alleged ASB families and claims to address underlying 'causes'. One can see that many well meaning people have been seduced by the opportunity to introduce support resources, if only for a limited time, into what was a purely punitive approach. (In practice in key areas like mental health that support still appears to be very limited relative to the high identified level of need). However the potential effectiveness of support is undermined, as we have seen, by the still coercive core philosophy of the FIP. Even the agencies and staff involved in these projects are conflicted. In the original DFP the difference in perception of the nature of the exercise between the housing arm and the social services arm was stark : that of enforcement versus support. More tellingly there were major differences in the ratings of project success with social services giving much lower scores. Feelings were so strong that social services largely disengaged from the project in later years. (see : Evaluation of the Dundee Families Project on the Scottish Executive Online site). It is now six years later. Have the serious and divisive problems discussed above been resolved?

Demonstrably they have not. The SHU report tells us there was:

"a clear view...that the 'problem' was definitely not perceived in the same way by all agencies...a **fundamental difference of opinion** between the way enforcement led and welfare led agencies viewed families' circumstances was highlighted. **Conflict** appeared to be particularly acute in relations between housing practitioners and social workers ".

Clearly nothing has changed in six years. These serious conflicts are not even mentioned in HRS230, the executive summary document which councillors and other decision makers are most likely to read. Indeed HRS230 talks misleadingly of the 'shared guiding principles' and the 'multi-disciplinary' approach as a 'key strength' of the projects. Of course one of the key political aims of FIPs is to 'Grip the Agencies', as the Respect Office calls it, and force effective cooperation. It would not do to admit that the projects failed to do that. We have seen for example that the opinions of key stakeholders in nine agencies were sought (page 183, AIFSP). However education departments and the NHS were not included. Of the nine agencies six were concerned with enforcement and only three with support. This is not the impression given by the headline claims. But then we have already seen that grossly distorted headline claims have been made about the 'impacts' of the projects on the welfare of their communities, the other key political aim. The FIPs have not succeeded, in part ,because philosophical conflict is built into their design.

The conflation of 'enforcement' and 'support' functions in projects still dominated by an enforcement viewpoint will not succeed. We also explored this in section 3 where the referral agencies while keen to obtain intensive support for their families expressed disapproval for the inappropriate ASB labeling. We noted that even the families who cooperated fully, under threat of eviction or other sanctions, expressed a great sense of injustice at their targeting and stigmatising. We noted that 52% (in closed cases) did not 'fully engage' with the projects perhaps for that reason. The project statistics themselves paint a picture of very poor, mentally impaired ,disabled ,socially inadequate people who's serious needs demand direct, ongoing medical and psychiatric interventions, truly independent of enforcement agencies, not demonisation and quasi or actual criminalisation.

6. CONCLUSIONS

The emperor is stark naked. There is a massive reality gap between the headline claims promoted by government agencies for the great success of FIPs and the data and comments presented in the SHU technical report , the full AIFSP report and the original DFP evaluation report. Here is a brief review of how this happened. We are told that 'extent of engagement' by families is an 'indicator' and 'measure' of project 'impact'. Remarkably then 58% of families did not 'fully engage' with the projects and 26% completely disengaged in the first stage. 52% did not engage in the closed cases sample. This makes a nonsense, for example, of the HRS230 claim that in '92% of cases the risk to local communities had reduced or ceased '. Case files provide other 'impact' data but this is also misleadingly reported. The qualitative 'impacts' claimed in the headlines turn out to be based on samples of only 15% to 21% of total cases. The potential for biased sampling is clear. We learn in fact that 'in a significant number of cases files did not record detailed outcomes'. We also learned that for all impact measures the headline results reported relate only to families who 'fully or partly engaged' with the projects. Those results are biased by definition. In many cases the quantitative scale of improvements is not defined. For many impact measures statistics at project exit are not related back to the equivalent statistics at project start up. It is often impossible to determine what if any changes have occurred and how, if at all, these relate to project interventions. There are no control groups against which to judge changes. It must also be understood that the results are based on project workers opinions not independent measurements. The results are not based on controlled randomised trials. Criteria for judging improvements in families are often not defined. Standard measurement schemes for evaluating, for example, children's behavioural problems are not deployed. In many cases the blatant weaknesses in the 'quantitative' opinion results are supplemented by anecdotal data from interviews with families. This is hardly reliable data given the coercive context of family recruitment to the projects and the ongoing threat of eviction. More to the point only 13.3% of families in the projects were interviewed.This is a remarkable catalogue of caveats for a technical evaluation report making such strong claims of success. The reader must bear these critical points in mind in what follows. Caveat emptor. Here are the specific claims.

It is claimed that in 85% of families ASB complaints had either ceased or reduced so that tenancies were no longer at risk at project exit. This claim was examined in detail in section 2.3.1. Considering all closed cases, in 18.5% of families we could argue that project interventions had led to ASB complaints ceasing. However this result may be due to enforced structural changes in families rather than improved behaviour. In 33.3% of cases project worker opinion was that ASB had reduced sufficiently to stabilise tenancies. To be clear, this means that ASB complaints were still occouring in 77.8% of families. Please note that these results apply to a sample of only 21% of the families in the projects. There is no evidence either that any changes in behaviour survived the end of the projects. The AIFSP report admits this and recommends more research to 'establish the sustainability of interventions in family function and behaviour'

Large reductions in ASB complaints to the police were also claimed. This issue was examined in section 2.3.2. However worker opinion data is in conflict with police contact data. The contact data is at least consistent. At referral 68% of families had no ongoing contact with the police. At exit this was 76%. We could argue that project interventions led to 8% of families ending police contact and presumably complaints from the community. This is a long way from a headline claim of reduction/secession ASB in 85% of families.

It is claimed that in 80% of families tenancies had been successfully stabilised and the risk of homelessness reduced by project exit. This claim was analysed in section 2.3.3. These results apply to a sample of only 15% of families. Taking all the available closed case opinion data into account 64% of families had stable tenancies at exit. The key issue is what was the stability level at project referral ? Unfortunately there is significant ambiguity in how stability was defined. The change in stability may be anything from zero to 36% of families.

The related issue of family breakdown is also analysed. At exit it is claimed that risk of breakdown had reduced in 48% of families. In section 2.3.4 this is re-examined. We note that at referral 64% of families had a high or medium risk of breakdown. Using the exit opinion data in a conservative way the fraction at high / medium risk can be estimated as 56% at exit. This suggests 8% of families may have stabilised during the projects. However these estimates are based on a sample of only 21% of families. Because of the limited sampling an 8% change could be found by chance in 77 out of100 such samples. The odds are there was no change.

The most crucial FIP claim is for a major reduction of the 'risk to local communities' in 92% of families based on project worker opinion at project exit. This is a forecast not a delivered result. It is based as usual on a small sample of 21% of project families. The issue is analysed in section 2.3.4 but the detail is irrelevant in this case. The data Is acknowledged to be useless. I quote AIFSP and HRS230 :

' there are limitations to the evaluation evidence base particularly in relation to the assessment of the impact on the community'

This is because

'it is impossible to chart changes that occurred directly as a result of the
Project interventions but the data clearly indicates that the situation had
not deteriorated'

A claim of no deterioration is surely a very long way from the headline
claim of significant reduction of community risk in relation to 92% of the
families. Caveat emptor.

The 'carrot' promised in these projects to justify coercive intervention is
intensive support to address family problems. The issue of children's
health and well being is central to this because of the high level of multiple
needs and the youth nuisance problem in 70% of families: 54% of families
had children with learning or physical disabilities or ADHD ; 19% had
other mental health problems; 17% had drug problems ; 53% had SEN or
educational statements or attended special schools. The reports claim a
child mental health improvement in 40% of families. This claim is
examined in section 2.3.5. If all closed cases are considered the
improvement is actually in only 27.7% of families. The low improvement
figure is explained by the 'deep rooted and intractable nature' of the health
problems. But surely the projects were supposed to attack these problems,
the root causes of ASB, intensively? Just what medical / psychiatric help
did the families get? At referral 89% of families with mental health
problems (80% of the total) had NO mental health worker. At exit 79% of
such families had NO mental health worker. An additional 8% of families
got mental health worker support as a result of the projects. No information
is provided about contact with NHS specialists. However page 64 (AIFSP)
says the low level of health improvement achieved in the projects 'suggests
in some cases longer term mainstream interventions are required'. Here
'some' means 72.3% of the families. 'Mainstream' means direct NHS
mental health specialist support. The project families received a lot of
'stick' but very little 'carrot'.

The projects are repeatedly described as offering 'excellent value for
money'. However looking closer we read that the projects merely 'have the
potential to reduce considerably the short and longer term costs of many
agencies'. This is the 'carrot' promised to councils considering signing up
for projects. Delivering the potential means achieving substantial changes
in family behaviour and stability during the projects and maintaining these
after exit from the project for several years. Section 3 of this report and
conclusion points 1,2,3 have dealt with these impact issues. There is
evidence for a modest reduction in families in police contact of 8% during
the projects. 8% of family tenancies may have become stable during

the projects but because the family sample was small this change could have occurred by chance in 77 out of 100 such samples. In fact the evaluation summary, page 123 (AIFSP report) tells us in addition:

'it is **impossible** to determine the extent to which the positive outcomes identified…are a direct result of the project's interventions rather than other factors'.

There is no objective, independent evidence on which the 'excellent value for money' claim can be based. This is acknowledged in the 'Gaps in the evidence base' section (AIFSP) where the authors recommend further research to quantify

'the longer term impact of family project interventions on existing support and supervision costs'.

Overall the headline claims for project success and long term, positive, cost effective impacts in the community are not substantiated by the evaluations when these are examined carefully. The project worker positive opinions on project 'impact' are also backed up by interviews with the families. However these were carried out with only 13.3% of the families in the projects. This is a very small and possibly biased sample.

Nevertheless the subjective opinion data collected from referral agencies and families is very enlightening. Referral agencies mostly took a positive view but mainly for procedural reasons .There were many reservations about outcomes including the extent to which these projects could successfully address 'long-term and deep-rooted family problems'. The families interviewed were 'overwhelmingly positive' primarily about the 'intensive support' they received and the fact often stressed that their cooperation reduced the threat of eviction hanging over them during the projects. It is clear that the families were both mentally impaired and socially inadequate. Over 80% had serious mental/ physical health issues and/or learning disabilities. 72% were led by lone mothers clearly struggling with multi-child families to raise. 82% were not in work. 59% were in debt.

Despite this catalogue of deprivation HRS230 tells us that 'in many cases [these multiple support needs] had not been adequately addressed by other agencies'. The intensive help promised (but arguably not delivered : see point 4 above) by the projects must be welcomed BUT was only necessary because these families had been long neglected by the state. Indeed there is massive evidence that medical, educational and social support for such families has been in sharp decline for the last decade.

Remarkably these positive attitude results are based on interviews with only 13.3% of project families…the ones who fully cooperated. We do not know how the other 86.7% responded to the offered 'support'. We do know that only 48% of families were fully engaged and 24% completely disengaged from or left the projects. So 2/3 of those not interviewed were not fully engaged. Were these people positive about the projects and support received? We do know that 'the level of antagonism felt by families towards statutory agencies , particularly social services cannot be overstated' (AIFSP report). Most families, even those fully engaged, felt they had been unfairly targeted and stigmatised. It may be difficult to accept support when threatened, particularly if targeted 'unfairly'. Neither is there any evidence that the 'feel good' factor in the 13.3% of families interviewed survived the end of the projects or translated into long term behaviour improvements in the community.

The targeting of families for the FIPs remains problematical. Referring agencies remain uncomfortable with the term ASB and believe it's use is 'stigmatising' and 'counterproductive'. In fact 46% of the families were not involved in 'neighbour disputes' and 30% did not engage in 'youth nuisance'. 30 to 36% were targeted for noise, garden condition and rubbish complaints. The majority of cases are described as 'low level' nuisance. The HSU report tells us the parents 'were often described in positive terms as caring ' by referring agencies' who often saw mental impairment and 'factors beyond the families' control' as root causes of 'problematical behaviour'.

The overall picture from the evidence is not of 'families from hell' but of 'families in hell'.

The most remarkable statistic in HRS230 when considering family selection protocols is that referrers and project staff identified that:

"60% of the families were the victims of anti-social behaviour"

HRS230 cites 'emerging research' evidence that this is not unusual and that it is difficult to distinguish victims from perpetrators. This supports our very vulnerable families' views about unfair targeting. We are told in AIFSP that

'some of the families were particularly vulnerable to being bullied …easily stigmatised, scape-goated and victimised by others in the community'.

The author has shown in section 4 that these are the families with the highest incidence of mental health and disability problems. Unfair targeting is clearly a problem. HRS230 agrees stating:

"the need for ASB agencies to develop well-defined investigatory polices and processes to ensure that all those involved in ASB cases are dealt with fairly".

Many families claimed they had been unfairly targeted because of intolerance of their impaired status and because of grudges. They lack the intellectual resources to deal well with prejudice and abuse in the community or the authorities 'investigating' disputes. The author has provided evidence in support of increasing intolerance of 'difference' in UK society and a remarkable growth in paranoia. In part the author contends this paranoia originates in overblown government propaganda about ASB which is not supported by their own statistics. Intolerance of the mentally ill and the mentally and physically disabled is also astonishingly pervasive today and well documented.

Six years after the DFP the FIP model remains schizophrenic in concept and operation, driven by political considerations and subject to high jacking by particular pressure groups. The HSU report tells us of 'fundamental differences of opinion' and 'conflict' between the 'enforcement led' and 'welfare led' agencies. The evidence from the projects tell us the referral agencies see it as 'counterproductive' to stigmatise these mentally impaired and socially inadequate families. Yet they refer to these projects in order to access 'intensive' help for their clients which they should have had long before. If they had received adequate medical, educational and psychiatric support the 'low level nuisance' variant of ASB attributed to these families may not have developed in the first place. If 'enforcement', threats and stigmatisation in the community did not drive these projects perhaps the 52% of families (in closed cases ; 58% in the larger first stage sample) who did 'not fully engage' and the 17% (in closed cases ; 26% in the first stage sample) who 'completely disengaged' would have cooperated and benefited.

HRS230 concludes that the FIP evaluations have made a 'significant contribution towards understanding the underlying causes of ASB '. It is hard to know if this is meant to be tongue in cheek. The evaluations have certainly highlighted that the FIPs target some of the most mentally impaired ,poor and socially inadequate families in the UK. Families whose multiple needs have been long neglected. They highlight that the majority are themselves victims of ASB and point to clear unfairness in the targeting process which works against the mentally impaired. All the evidence is there in AISFP and HSU but not presented in a way that leads the reader to a balanced view of causes and outcomes.

Such a presentation would no doubt have negative political consequences.

It is to be hoped that behind closed doors in the DCLG , if not the Respect Office, the true implications of these projects are being fully spelled out as the author has briefly attempted to do. It is noticeable that Family Intervention Projects are now being called 'Intensive Family Support Projects'. It is to be hoped this signals acknowledgment of the real FIP lessons rather than yet more verbal spin aimed at diverting independent observers and decision makers concerned about the coercive and intrusive nature of these projects.

It is difficult to criticise an intervention project model that appears, if only for a limited time, to offer desperately needed help to very vulnerable families, even if under coercion. However as the author has showed in areas like mental health and disability treatment that support is very limited in comparison with the scale and frequency of the family problems and has failed in the majority of cases.

The national roll out of these FIPs will cost the tax payer a great deal of money and as discussed there is no independent ,quantitative evidence of long term benefits to the community or the families, nor of cost-effectiveness, other than wishful thinking. There are political benefits of course: Look at us, we are taking tough action against the 'families from hell'! Apart from misleading the public these projects will absorb funding which should be dedicated to serious research aimed at understanding the root, not the superficial, causes of ASB and developing truly effective , preventative interventions. (see below).The funding needed to provide proper, ongoing medical, educational and psychiatric support to the mentally ill, disabled and socially challenged is of course orders of magnitude greater than this and is unlikely ever to be forthcoming to our national shame.

7. COMMENTS ON ASB CAUSATION

There is NO royal road the resolution of the ASB problem. The long term solution to the ASB variant related to our FIP families, and the more serious forms, will require following back the chain of causation to loci where truly effective preventative interventions can be applied… without the need for criminalisation or coercion. Despite the claims of HRS230 we are not yet at that point. Research evidence, well known to the government, points to a genetic component to ASB and some types of criminality. Some of the longitudinal studies have tracked in detail the development of large populations of children over three decades. Other recent research is based on large scale twin studies. The results are said to support a complex interaction of genetic and environmental factors in the origin of ASB. If the roots of ASB, like many chronic physical illnesses, are proved to be genetic will the state continue to criminalise and impose coercive, punitive, interventions on the bearers of such genes ? Will they still be blamed for genetic defects beyond their control? Some 'experts' are already advocating the use of genetic markers to target children, or the foetus, for 'early intervention' by the state. Since these possible genetic /ASB / criminality correlations are probabilistic this amounts to implementing pre-emptive 'actuarial justice'. Not all children with the 'bad' genetic markers would go on to develop ASB or criminality. Genetic determinism has a dark history and great caution must be applied to the emerging evidence. The spectre of state sponsored abortion after screening for 'bad seed' is not so far fetched. Sterilisation of the 'parents from hell' is another option some repressive governments would not flinch to return to. It would be very cost-effective of course. If this dark vision seems improbable today recall that recently cleft palate and club foot were added to the official list as reasons for allowing an abortion in this country.

On a more upbeat note gene therapy can now be successfully applied to some genetically determined physical illnesses and disabilities. In the medium term perhaps something can be done to repair mental impairment, addiction and those 'with' antisocial personality disorders…the controlling factor is funding and political will power. However just suppose the prisons could be emptied ? We have 80,000 prisoners. Remember 75% of prisoners are intellectually impaired and 80% of children in custody have two or more mental health problems. It costs 50K per annum to keep an adult in prison and 70K for a child. That would fund rather a lot of medical research.

SECTION 4.4   REVIEW OF THE CLAIMED 'LONGER TERM OUTCOMES' FROM SIX 'ASB FAMILY INTERVENTION PROJECTS'

"A new approach, a fantastic opportunity "

Respect Initiative: Family Intervention
Project Showcase

1. INTRODUCTION

Since 1999 the government has funded seven prototype Family Intervention Projects also known as 'ASB Intensive Family Support Projects' and more commonly as the 'ASBO Sin Bin' projects.

These projects enforce outreach, supervised tenancy and core residential unit interventions on the targeted families. Sanctions for non-cooperation include eviction and loss of all benefits. The projects which last three years also supposedly offer intensive support to families to change their unacceptable behaviours and address the underlying causes. The author has already analysed previous project evaluation reports including

"ASB IFS Projects: Housing Research Summary 230"
Dept for Communities & Local Government (HRS230)

The equivalent full report also sponsored by the DfCLG from Sheffield Hallam University Centre for Social Inclusion (AIFSP)

The interim 'technical' report written for DfCLG by the Sheffield Hallam University team (SHU)

The Dundee Families Project; Scottish Government report with Glasgow University.

   Review of the previous evaluation reports cast serious doubt on the claimed achievements of these projects. There was no independent, objective, quantified evidence for the claimed, purely opinion based, benefits either to the families or their communities.
The authors of these 'government' evaluation reports acknowledged this and recommended a detailed follow up of a sample of families after project exit to measure 'longer term outcomes' i.e. to provide evidence for sustained benefits to families, communities and value for money. That final evaluation is now reported in:

"The Longer-term Outcomes Associated With Families Who Had Worked With Intensive Family Support Projects "

HRS240; DfCLG summary and full report,
www. communities.gov.uk/publications/housing/familysupportprojects

   The current paper reviews that final evaluation. The authors of Longer Term Outcomes (LTO) are to be congratulated. While keeping faith with their financial sponsors and putting the best possible, positive interpretation on the evidence they actually expose the severe limitations of the projects in practice and their effective failure as 'social engineering' tools to combat ASB. Analysis will demonstrate that the headline claims of success in 71 % or 43% of families are actually disproved by considering the full tracking sample data set. Remarkably this study of 'longer term outcomes' is based on families' experiences within 12 months of project exit. Very little of the supposed stabilisation of tenancies, presumed to result from reduced ASB, can be attributed objectively to the projects. In fact 57.1% of families moved home during the evaluation period, often 'involuntarily'. Levels of family breakdown remain high as do concerns about children's welfare and challenging behaviour and 'deep rooted' problems, often related to long term mental health issues and learning disability, remain unaddressed for many families. This litany of failure casts doubt on the sustainability of even the now more modest claims of improved family behaviour and welfare in this latest report.

Remarkably the study gives direct evidence for rapid behaviour decay. The previous major evaluations (HRS230; AIFSP) claimed that in 85% of families at case closure ASB was ended or greatly reduced. A year later detailed analysis of LTO data shows ASB largely ceased in 31% of families in the tracking sample. This implies that around 54% of families have suffered behaviour decay in one year if we accept the study data. At that rate all families would 're-offend' within a few years. One cannot speak of delivering 'long term' sustained ASB relief to the family communities on that basis. It follows, along with ongoing family support and intervention costs, that project cost effectiveness, by any reasonable measure, is zero.

The LTO study is nevertheless invaluable in highlighting the high level of inappropriate targeting and referral of families with serious mental health and learning disability problems (80% of families) to the projects by enforcement (housing & ASB team) officers contrary to the DDA 2005 and the Home Office ASB Guidance safeguards for vulnerable people. Shamefully a large proportion of these families were found to be victims of ASB and disability abuse. Mind has found that nearly 90% of mentally impaired people in social housing have been so victimised.

These negative results are important given government intentions to replicate the IFSP model in a further 73 intervention projects at a cost of around £ 345 million pounds over three years. Unless drastic changes are made this money will be wasted. We are all being hoaxed… again.

2. IS THE TRACKING SAMPLE REPRESENTATIVE OF THE TOTAL
   PROJECT POPULATION?

Before we can judge the validity of the claimed benefits of the projects it is essential to be confident that the small tracking sample of families underlying this study is representative, in several ways, of the general population of families experiencing the six projects.

2.1 Tracking Sample Size And Data Quality.

We are told that 38 families involved in projects over the period 2004-2006 gave 'informed consent' for their progress to be tracked. However 10 families declined to be involved or were not being monitored and for a further 7 families there was no 'direct contact' with the evaluation team. So family input to the final tracking study was from 21 families or (21/256) x 100 = 8.2% of all families in the projects : a rather limited sample on which to draw major conclusions on performance or indeed to justify some hundreds of millions of further investment in a national roll out of these projects. However other 'evidence' was collected from 'agency officers' involved with the families (see LTO , table 1.1) . 17 local government housing officers were interviewed along with 7 officers representing all other agencies such as social services, youth offending teams, police, ASB enforcement officers, medical services and education. Government policy on IFSPs and the previous evaluations have stressed the critical importance of a 'multi-agency approach' (or as the Respect Office memorably put it 'Grip the Agencies') yet only 7 people are now representing the views of the 'other' agencies. So in only 7 cases do we have any input on 'long term outcomes' from these agencies, that is, for only 25% of the tracked families and 7 / 256 or 2.7% of the project families. Is this credible or incredible? One of the factors making the data collection 'very resource intensive' we are told, is that 57.1% of the families, despite claims for home stability, had moved 'during' the evaluation period. Recall that 10 families fell off the radar completely. These facts do not suggest that exited families were in any sense being closely monitored. Was the level of ASB and other problems therefore under reported in this study?

2.2 The Level of Family Engagement.

In the previous technical evaluation report, HSU we are told that:

"a general indicator that can be used to measure the impact of interventions is the extent to which families engaged in the [project plan & evaluation] process".

The current LTO report, P33, tells us :

"project workers reported referrals based on adults willingness to engage with the project".

These comments tell us two things. Firstly the family populations in the projects were selected a priori on the basis of likely cooperation ...the most difficult families were eliminated from the projects at the first hurdle and at later hurdles. Secondly the original tracking sample of 38 (out of 256) who gave 'informed consent' for tracking were even more cooperative than the general population and therefore more likely to have a positive response to 'interventions'. Is there direct evidence for this sampling bias? There is. In the two earlier evaluations up to 2006, using much larger sample sizes, families were classified into three 'engagement ' groups :

Fully engaged with project   42 – 48 %

Partially engaged   32 – 35 %

Disengaged during project   26 --17 %

For the tracking sample 17 families were fully engaged, 8 families partially engaged and 2 families disengaged. (LTO, table 2.1) For one family this critical data was not recorded! So we have

Fully engaged   63%   Partly engaged   29.6%   Disengaged   7.4%

We see that disengagement in the tracking sample is only one third that in the general population while full engagement is 40% higher. The tracking sample is NOT representative of the general project population and therefore the claimed 'long term' success rates must inevitably be biased upwards.

2.3 Longer Term Outcomes?

The whole rationale of this third IFSP evaluation report is to test the 'longer term' sustainability of the changes in family behaviour and other benefits claimed in the earlier reports (HRS230, HSU,AIFSP). The project period studied is 2004 -2006. We are told in table 2.1 that families worked with projects from 3 to 36 months with an average engagement of 19.5 months. If we generously assume all families began in early 2004 and we know the final interviews occurred in May – September 2006 then evaluations took place some 10 – 14 months after project exit. No mention of this is made in the headline summary. However on P14 we are told

"the majority of families had exited **within** the previous 12 months"

Confirming our rough estimate above. Even more remarkably we are told on P18 that 6 families had exited 'only recently'. What is recently? One month? Two months? It is difficult for this author to translate 'within 12 months' into 'longer term outcomes'. Also if we remove the recent 6 the sample is now only 22 families or 8.6 % of project families. Of course if these families were included in the 'reduced ASB success' group we have a major source of bias ...there was little time in these families for ASB to have re-occurred by final interview.

If we accept the data at face value it does provide useful information on the decay of behaviour after project exit. The earlier reports claimed a significant reduction in ASB in 85% of families with a similar percentage of 'tenancies stabilised' at case closure. LTO tells us that in 71% of families. ASB complaints had 'largely ceased' and tenancies were stabilised by final interview. The authors say a 'more nuanced analysis' suggested a success rate of 43%. Let's take these numbers as meaningful for now. They imply that 'within 12 months' family behaviour has deteriorated in

$$85 - 71 = 14\% \text{ of families} \qquad \text{or} \qquad 85 - 43 = 42\% \text{ of families.}$$

The latter figure implies that in a year over 40% of families have fallen by the wayside!
If that rate continued within a year or so the anti-social behaviour of all families will have returned. As we will see the LTO report provides much detailed evidence in support of this simple extrapolation.

3. HOW SUCCESSFUL WERE THE PROJECTS?

Let us accept for the moment that the tracking sample data is worth analysing despite the many problems and while remembering that the evaluation period is less than one year. It is time to examine the claims for successful family outcomes based on the full study data set.
3.1 ASB & Home Stability

3.1.1 The Basic Data Reported

Reducing ASB in the community is a key objective of the projects linked to the second key objective of stabilising the tenancies of problem families. Delivery of these objectives yield the claimed major political and economic benefits of the projects. P108 in the conclusions section tells us that for 71% of families

'complaints about ASB had largely ceased and, as a result, the family home was secure'.

However we are then told

'a more nuanced analysis …showed that (12 / 28) 43% of families had achieved resoundingly successful outcomes'.

  We will now explore the claims that 'ASB had largely ceased', that the 'family home was secure 'and that this is 'as a result' of reduced ASB and indeed the project interventions. We will find that detailed tracking sample data contradict these claims. We will find that the 'more nuanced analysis' shows that the underlying 'deep rooted, multiple problems' of these families have not been successfully addressed which implies that ASB and family troubles will continue even in the 'resoundingly' successful families. The projects, despite the claims, have not addressed the 'causes' of family ASB although they have starkly exposed them and for that we should be grateful. Let us summarise and then comment on additional critical data scattered through the report :

1. The degree to which ASB complaints have reduced for the families is not quantified. Was it 5%, 10% or 50%? Where is the objective evidence?

2. We learn that 6 families had to be re-referred to projects after exit because of renewed ASB. Remarkably 3 of these families are in the 'resoundingly' successful group (P35). A footnote on P43 also tells us that 2 families in the 'partially successful' group had been 'recently re-referred' to projects.

3. For the 'partially successful' group we are told that for 2 families no ASB at all was evident at referral to the projects. The team described this as 'inappropriate referral'. Clearly no ASB at final tracking interview should not be a surprise.

4. For the resoundingly successful group P26 says that for 3 of the families a single issue 'usually concerning children's behaviour or a 'clash of lifestyles' had led to project referral. For these we are told 'sustaining change was comparatively easy to achieve'. Were these borderline 'inappropriate' referrals?

5. For 4 families the only source of evidence about reduced ASB and improved family circumstances is their own statements.

6. Table 2.3 tells us that (16 / 28) or 57.1% of all families had moved home 'during the course of the evaluation'. In fact 58.3% of the 'resoundingly' successful group moved home within a year of exiting the projects. This somewhat muddies the water over claims for improved home stabilisation.

3.1.2 Inappropriate Referral & Re-referrals.

Two families in the partially successful group were inappropriately referred and 3 in the resoundingly successful group must be considered borderline. In assessing reduced ASB these families should be removed or reassigned. Removing them leaves only 23 families in the tracking sample (9% of all project families). Alternatively if we remove the 2 definites and demote the 3 doubtful to partially successful we get :

(12-3) / 26 =34.6% resoundingly successful versus 43% claimed.

and (8-2+3) / 26 = 34.6% partially successful and failed 30.8%.

Put simply: the tracking sample data is fragile. Here is another example.For 4 families (sr) there is no independent evidence of significantly reduced ASB. Given the long familiarity of these families with FIP coercive philosophy, and particularly the sanctions of eviction and loss of benefits for failure to cooperate and change behaviour, do we think they would emphasise ongoing problems? Which group would they be reported under : resounding success, partial success or failure? Certainly not the latter. Strictly they should be removed from the sample. If there was no overlap with the 3.1.2 families this reduces sample size to 19 families (7.4% of all project families).

Let's look now at re-referral. Table 2.2 tells us that

'for 20 families no significant further complaints of ASB were reported by the final interview '.

However we then learn that 6 families had been re-referred to projects for ongoing ASB. We might expect that all 6 were members of the failed group of 8 families but a footnote on P43 says 2 families (rr) in the 'partially ' successful group had been 'recently re-referred' and P43 tells us that 3 families(rr) in the 'resoundingly' successful group had also been re-referred. In the case study described for one of these families re-referral followed written warnings. We are told that 'these setbacks' demonstrate that

'stability is hard to achieve particularly in the light of multiple [family] Problems (especially mental health conditions) '

Indeed. In fact the earlier evaluations (HRS230, AIFSP) found that 80% of the families had such 'deep rooted' problems. We will return to this later. We must conclude that these re-referrals are not one off flukes. 5 'successful' families have re-offended. What should be done with them? The headline claim is that that in 71% families ASB had 'largely ceased'.

This is unsustainable on the evidence presented; in fact ASB continued in 8+3+2 = 13 families or 46.3% of the tracking sample. This implies that in 15 families ASB did significantly reduce. However as we discussed earlier 2 families were definitely 'inappropriately referred' (ir) ,3 were borderline (bir) and 4 self-reported (sr) success with no independent evidential support. Taking ALL the data into account we can now reconstruct an alternative interpretation of the study results.

Resounding Success	12 – 3 (rr) – 3 (bir) -2 (sr) =	4	21%
Partial Success	8 – 2 (rr) – 2 (ir) – 2 (sr) =	2	10.5%
Failed	8 + 3 (rr) + 2 (rr) =	13	68.5%
Total		19	

   This reconstruction records significantly reduced ASB in 31.5% of families, a long way from the headline 71%. However we noted that the evaluators consider degree of 'engagement' of families as a 'measure' or predictor of success in improving behaviour, etc. In the tracking sample we found that 92.6% were fully or partly engaged. For earlier, larger samples of project families this figure was around 78%. The tracking sample had a significantly higher engagement. So what behaviour improvement would we expect applying tracking sample data to the bulk project population? Assuming simple proportionality we get 31.5 x (78 / 92.6) = 26.5% families with significantly reduced ASB. It is important to emphasise another factor in relation to claims of behaviour change. The report repeatedly stresses the importance of 're-referral' in keeping the families stable. For example P36 says

'The tracking study illustrates the critical role that re-referrals can play and indicates the need for IFSPs to adopt a **long term** view of outcomes and effectiveness…'

But P32 also tells us that

'Some families continued to be supported by a range of organisations such as CAMHS [children and adolescent mental health service] ,YOTs [youth offending teams] and social services after the projects had withdrawn their support'.

The level of re-referral, even in 'successful' families, and this other ongoing support speaks for the fragility of claims of sustained behaviour change after project exit. If ongoing support is 'critical' then the projects have NOT eliminated the associated costs : the basis for government claims that the projects offer 'excellent value for money'. Recall that most families had exited projects 'within 12 months' (and 6 within a few months) of the final evaluation interviews. Recall also that at case closure, for a much larger sample of families, it was claimed (AIFSP, HRS230) that in 85% of families ASB had ceased or been greatly reduced. Our analysis of all the tracking sample data suggests an actual success rate of 31.5% of families in this respect. If we accept the project exit success rate this means that 'within' a year ASB has re-occurred in $85 - 31.5 = 53.5\%$ of families.

If these rates of decay continued then all families would be re-offending within a year or two. Is this conclusion too harsh? Let us turn to the other side of the reduced ASB argument now and see. In all the evaluations claims of reduced ASB and increased stability of the home or security of tenancies go together: indeed each is used to support the claims for the other.

For example if a tenancy is judged to be secure by an agency officer then ASB 'must have' reduced significantly due to the project. This circular reasoning is dangerous and misleading.

In the current LTO report we are told that for '75% of tracked families their current home was secure' at final interview (c.f. 71% with no ASB) and compared with 86% with home at 'risk' at referral (Table 2.2) Let us look closer at this impressive claim. Table 2.2 also tells us that a remarkable 57.1% of families 'had moved home during the course of the evaluation'. We learn that the reasons families moved 'could not be explained simply by reference to housing histories'. Indeed. We might expect that this home instability was focused on the 'failed' families group. However, the rate of movement for the 'resounding success' group was 58.3%. This data clearly shows that while 75% of homes were secure at last interview 57% of families had recently moved home! We cannot infer that the 75% stability figure resulted from project interventions. The maximum stabilisation we could with certainty claim is $75 - 57 = 18\%$ of families. Is this reasonable? It is if we explore the implications of moving home. It means families leaving their problems behind them. We know that 60% of families in the wider project population had been victims of ASB (HRS230, AIFSP) and according to project managers are 'easily scapegoated' in neighbour disputes. If so moving solves the problem of abusive neighbours. If we assume the other 40% are indeed families from hell removing them from their original neighbourhoods also solves the original problem. Since families moved within a year of project exit there had been little time for ASB problems to restart in the new neighbourhoods. As the LTO report tells us the moves, many 'involuntary', 'represented a chance to start afresh'.

Indeed, but then the 75% stability figure is meaningless: the 75% home stability 'resulting from the projects' inference is not supportable on a proper reading of the evidence. What is the true position?

At referral we know that $100 - 86 = 14\%$ of homes were not at risk. If 75% were stable at final interview the improvement is in a maximum of $75 - 14 = 61\%$ of families. If however only 18% of stable homes at final interview could be attributed to project interventions then the maximum possible IFSP contribution is stability for $18 - 14 = 4\%$ of families. This is a rather modest result compared with the many headline claims from this and earlier evaluations. Of course the branding of families with the Mark of Cain to the point where 'staying put' becomes intolerable (or as we will see, dangerous) or forcing family moves could be counted as a successful project 'intervention'.
The problems at least moved somewhere else. However simple eviction would have achieved the same result, would it not, without the added project costs.

3.1.3 Conclusions on ASB and Home Stability.

We have found taking into account **all** the reported tracking sample data that (for a period of a year after case closure) 31.5% of families displayed significantly reduced ASB compared with referral and that for $18 - 14 = 4\%$ of families home stability improvement occurred for reasons other than 'mechanically' moving home.
Whether these changes can be attributed to project interventions is moot. In fact P24 in LTO tells us

'It was difficult to ascertain with any certainty the exact role that the projects played in bringing about particular outcomes for individuals and families. Indeed many other factors where present in families' lives…'

Recall that the LTO report tells us specifically that some families continued to receive support from several agencies including social services, YOTs and CAMHS teams after project exit. The last evaluation report (P123, AIFSP), based on a much larger family sample, was even blunter about the position at case closure :

340

'It is impossible however, to determine the extent to which the positive outcomes identified ...are a direct result of the projects' interventions rather than other factors'

This section has looked at the core frontline objectives of ASB reduction and home stability improvement, outcomes of importance to the 'enforcement' and 'political' agencies involved. However the projects had wider 'welfare' objectives and success or failure in these other areas, important in themselves, has a strong impact on the issue of sustainability of the core frontline objectives. The results below raise further concerns.

3.2 Wider Project Objectives : A Portrait of Failure .

The LTO evaluation report presents results as a continuum from failure to resounding success by subjectively rating families against 4 core IFSP objectives. These are:

- Prevention of repeat cycles of homelessness resulting from ASB and family breakdown.
- Addressing unmet support needs.

*   Promotion of social inclusion: health, education and wellbeing.

- Increased community stability.

The report also presents 'a more nuanced analysis' of family outcomes taking into account the 4 objectives and on this basis defines 43% of families as 'resoundingly successful' .
The 'continuum' description of outcomes based on qualitative opinion data leads to highly subjective results. However taken with 'family circumstances' this 'more nuanced analysis' shows that in many cases the projects have not succeeded in tackling ' deep rooted' family problems and that this casts doubt on the medium and long term sustainability of claimed beneficial changes.

Family Breakdown & Child Welfare

We saw earlier evidence for this in the significant short term re-referral rates even in 'successful' family groups. Now we add to this the evidence for ongoing problems given in Table 2.3. We learn that in 13 / 28, or 46% of families

'There are ongoing concerns about children's wellbeing associated with children's challenging behaviour'.

341

From the earlier evaluations (HRS230) we know that 72% of families had lone parents and an average of 3 children and where the majority of ASB was child and youth related. On this basis as children get older we might expect that in families with 'ongoing concerns', 46%, ASB problems are likely to re-occur even if currently suppressed in some families. Recall it was less than a year since most family case closures.

Table 2.3 also provides another startling statistic: 10 families by final interview had suffered family breakdown with children taken into care or in custody. That is 35.7 % of sample families suffered breakdown. But one of the key objectives of the IFSPs is to prevent family breakdown and the associated costs. Has this been achieved? Well at project referral the previous evaluation reports (AIFSP, HSU) tell us that 32% of families were at 'high risk' of breakdown and 38% had a child at risk of being taken into care. On this basis the expected level of family breakdown has occurred within a year of project exit which means the projects failed to provide the promised stabilisation. As we saw earlier tenancy instability has also continued with 57.1% of families moving home, often involuntarily the course of the evaluation'.

The report also mentions 'welcomed' changes in family structure, namely new babies in 4 families. However average project family size is already ~3 children and 72% are lone mother led while 59% are suffering from severe depression. Recall 80% in total have some mental disorder. Will a new baby increase or decrease the families ability to cope, particularly when the authorities are committed to the Blair social model that these babies ' a few years down the line ,will be a menace to society' ?

Unmet Family Needs

Addressing 'unmet support needs' of the families is another key objective. Little is said about the achievement of this target in the LTO report except that some families continued to receive help from social services, YOTs and CAMHS teams after 'project support was withdrawn'. This must be welcomed but what did the projects provide? We know from previous evaluations (HRS230, AIFSP) that 80% of project families had serious mental health and learning disability problems at referral. Disappointingly the LTO report fails to mention this but does point out that 'depression related illnesses' affected many families. In fact in the overall family population reported in the earlier evaluations 59% of adults suffered from serious depression. 54% of children had ADHD or another physical or mental disability. 53% had SEN statements and / or attended special schools. Given this appalling litany of problems we might expect that the families had received massive medical support before project referral.

342

In fact the earlier evaluations (HSU, AIFSP) tell us that only 9% were even in contact with a mental health worker. As LTO (P43) tells us the tracking families' experiences

'highlight the high thresholds that characterise access to existing mainstream services and the subsequent lack of support by other welfare agencies'.

Indeed. So what did the projects themselves provide? Well the earlier reports (HS, AIFSP) tell us that at case closure 17% of families had a mental health worker. This is an improvement over 9% but it means that 79% of the families with serious mental health needs still did not have access to specialist, mainstream, support. Can this by any definition be reported as a success? How could this have happened despite good intentions?
Why is it that mental health issues dominate the project family circumstances but are not in practice addressed? LTO provides an explanation.

'Where social tenants suffer from a mental health problem, under the DDA 2005 a psychiatric assessment **must** be carried out **prior** to enforcement action being taken. The tracking study provided anecdotal evidence that such practice could be **undertaken in a cursory way.**'

No account is taken of mental illness and disability in defining ASB by the enforcement led agencies who typically refer families.
These families are simply 'bad' and once on the projects we will bully them into better behaviour …forget all this medical mumbo jumbo.

The 'enforcement agencies' systematically and deliberately ignore issues of mental incapacity in the ASB Crusade. We have unimpeachable evidence for this. In 2005 the British Institute for Brain Injured Children used the FOI Act to survey all Youth Offending Teams and ASBO teams in the UK with respect to ASBOs issued and mental impairment. The YOTs reported that 37% of ASBOs had gone to mentally impaired young people and recognised a wide range of mental health issues including schizophrenia, OCD, clinical depression, autism, Aspergers Syndrome, suicide risk, self harm, psychosis, personality disorders, ADHD and generalised learning disabilities and SEN statements.

By contrast for the same population the ASBO enforcement officers reported only a 5% incidence of mental impairment. This difference in reporting is huge and statistically highly significant. The ASB teams clearly discount mental health issues despite the fact that the DDA forbids this as do the Home Office safeguards for 'vulnerable people' in the official Guidance on ASBO and ABC procedures. This is a national disgrace. We will see later that Home Office use of 'statistical risk factors' to target minority groups is probably responsible for this abomination.

Increased Community Stability

One of the primary reasons for this third LTO report is to quantify the 'longer term' impacts of the projects on the community. This has two aspects :

1. A sustained reduction of ASB in the communities where the families live.

2. Cost savings to local authorities from the elimination of the need for ongoing agency intervention and support to the families.

Structurally the LTO study could not hope to demonstrate these results and in practice it has failed to do so. We have seen that

1. The tracking sample was pitifully small covering only 10.9% of project families at best.

2. The views of all agencies other than housing came from the opinions of 7 people.

3. The 'longer term' evaluation period was actually less than 12 months.

We also found the claim that in 71% of families ASB had largely ceased, was untrue. The best that could be claimed taking all data into account is 31.5%. 5 of the successful families had been re-referred to the projects because of renewed ASB and some were still receiving support from other agencies such as YOTs and CAMHS. However since the previous evaluations claimed 85% of families at case closure this implies that in one year ASB had returned significantly in 85 -31.5 = 53.5% of families. If this 'decay' continued all families would be exhibiting renewed ASB in a year or two.

The associated result that 75% of homes were stable at final interview did not take into account that 57.1% of sample families (or 58.3% of 'successful' families) had moved home during the evaluation . These families had 'a fresh start' and escaped their problem contexts. There had been less than a year by final interview for ASB problems to restart in their new locations. We showed earlier that the maximum home stabilisation that could be attributed to the projects occoured in only 4% of families.

We also noted that for 46% of families concerns about children's wellbeing and behaviour continued and 35.7% of families had suffered family breakdown by final interview. But at referral 38% had a child at risk of being taken into care and 32% of families were at high risk of breakdown. On the basis of these figures the projects achieved nothing on these issues.

On the basis of these analyses it is difficult to see how a sustained reduction in ASB can be claimed now or will be delivered to the family communities (new or old) in future. So what evidence does the LTO report team present for sustained community benefits? Opinions.
In the projects some 95.7% of families received 'outreach interventions'. LTO P109 tells us that such interventions are 'more difficult to define and measure' however the study

'provides **some** evidence that there **can be** a number of benefits to local communities …'

We also learn that

'Furthermore a number of stakeholders reported that IFSP interventions were effective in bringing relief to many communities …'

It is true that there **can be** benefits to communities if the projects had delivered but considering **all** rather than just **some** of the evidence strongly indicates they have not delivered. Recall that in the tracking study opinion was dominated by 17 housing officers. All other agencies were represented by just 7 people. As to stakeholders opinions recall that these projects are high profile, politically motivated interventions designed to show the government is vigorously addressing ASB. Stakeholders cannot afford to be negative about outcomes. The LTO summary provides a clue to present thinking

'IFSP interventions were **believed** to be a more effective and sustainable solution to ASB as compared to **other forms of enforcement action**'

Belief is a wonderful thing but has no place in justifying intrusive and costly social policy. The much vaunted 'evidence based policy' mantra of this government is clearly dead. Or perhaps the above can be translated as

'ASBOs have failed on many criteria and we can't deny the evidence anymore so lets promote IFSPs ...they are all we have now. We can claim they offer support and the evidence for their failure, based on the 7 prototypes, is not yet widely known'

We will see later that this appears to be exactly the government's position. Note also that IFSPs are described as 'enforcement actions' which is accurate since as we have seen the key 'support' elements in projects are clearly secondary and inadequate.

Finally we should note that the LTO evaluators, despite working hard to demonstrate positive results, say this (P109) about the '**limitations of this approach**'

'**It is too early to make claims with any certainty about the longer-term sustainability of the changes that IFSPs had helped engender. This is partly because some families [the majority] had only recently exited the IFSPs , but it also reflects the fact that families working with IFSPs often had deep-rooted problems , suffered from multiple deprivations and were therefore likely to continue to be vulnerable to external influences**'

This seems a perfectly clear bottom line which one hopes will be presented unspun to the media, interested local authorities and Parliament.

3.3 Project Cost-Effectiveness

Given the evidence for the rapid decay of behaviour and family wellbeing in the tracking sample families and the clear admission that these families will require ongoing, multi-agency support for their 'deep rooted' problems it is pointless to try to analyse the cost effectiveness of the projects. The LTO evaluators wisely do not try but say simply

'Although local stakeholders could not place a precise financial value on the impact of IFSP interventions or the value to the wider community the projects were **perceived** to offer excellent value for money'.

'[the IFSP way of working] **is seen as being** highly cost-effective in the shorter term and **the longer term**'

In section 11 of AIFSP , 'Gaps In Evidence' , the evaluation team called for further research to actually establish 'sustainability' of claimed changes in family behaviour and functioning and the 'longer term impact' on existing support and supervision costs. The LTO study was defined to provide this critical evidence. The above sentences are the conclusions offered by the LTO study. This author contends that whatever the 'perceptions' of stakeholders the LTO study actually demonstrates that claimed behaviour changes decay rapidly after project exit even with some continued support, as we have seen. The headline claim in the last evaluation report HRS230 was that

'the cost analysis of the IFSPs indicates that this form of intervention offers excellent value for money'

'Analysis' has now been replaced by 'perception' and 'belief' and the full LTO study data base shows the claim for sustained family change and therefore excellent value for money is dead.

4. EVALUATION TEAM COMMENTS ON THE FAMILIES

The LTO evaluators stress repeatedly the extreme level of deprivation and poor mental health of the project families, their mistreatment and scapegoating in the community (AIFSP) and the poor support they previously received from the authorities. The sympathy for the plight of the families in the LTO team and indeed in many project practitioners is clear. Indeed one senses a degree of admiration for how many of these families bravely struggled to 'improve' despite profound and 'deep rooted problems'. One senses a strong desire to demonstrate that a welfare / support led intervention is superior to the sanction / criminalisation led alternatives in the ASB Crusade.

However this author contends, from the evidence, that the limitations in the current IFSPs are so profound that a complete rethink is essential. That will not occur if the severe problems in IFSP philosophy and practice are underplayed. Let us look at family circumstances. On LTO P63, 64 we are told the families predominantly lived in deprived urban estates described in the ACORN classification as

'experiencing the most difficult social and economic conditions in the whole country' and providing ' limited opportunities to improve their conditions'.

LTO points to many families living in 'extreme stress' in their communities under the debilitating impact of 'mental health conditions' . LTO mentions high levels of depression but gives no data. In the full AIFSP report however we learn that 59% of adults had severe depression. 80% of the families had serious mental health conditions and learning disabilities including schizophrenia , OCD, anxiety disorders, autism-

Aspergers, ADHD, statements of SEN ,etc. 54% of families had a child with a learning or physical disability. 72% of families were lone parent led and families averaged 3 children. Recall that at referral only 9% had contact with a mental health worker. Yet LTO, P67 makes it clear that the psychiatric assessments required by the DDA 2005 'prior to enforcement action' were carried out in a 'cursory way'. (Recall that while YOTs found that 37% of ASBO recipients had serious mental health problems the ASBO teams reported only a 5% incidence).

How could this happen? Well the full AIFSP report tells us that project managers characterised the majority of families as 'easily scapegoated' in neighbour disputes and less able to explain themselves to enforcement officers. In fact AIFSP discovered that 60% of the families were **victims** of ASB. (note: this may be an underestimate. Mind found that nearly 90% of mentally impaired people in council housing had been victimised). LTO provides an update of this remarkable situation.

'Ongoing concerns about personal safety dominated families' accounts with many reporting that since exiting the IFSP they had been victims of crime, subject to ASB from neighbours , and in a few cases were living in fear'

Did IFSP inclusion actually increase ASB against the families, giving their neighbours permission 'to have a go' , knowing that retaliation by the families would be punished , unquestioningly, by the enforcement teams ? Is this why 58.3% of even 'successful' families moved during the LTO evaluation period? Perhaps. Or perhaps the vulnerability of the families to intolerance, lack of understanding and abuse was there ab origine as the 60% victimisation figure suggests? But why would these families be singled out? Are they just innately anti-social? How did they differ from their neighbours? LTO provides an important insight.

'Contrary to popular belief , the evidence suggests that rather than constituting a distinct minority distinguishable from the 'law abiding majority' families tended to conform to the norms and values of the communities in which they lived'.

Surely this cannot be right? It can. The distinguishing feature of these families **is** simply their portfolio of serious mental health problems which either make them direct targets for abuse or lead to behaviours which are strange or worrying and might be described under the ubiquitous anti-social behaviour catchall... with a little encouragement for ASB teams looking for easy cases...or worse. We will see in the last section that there is compelling evidence for deliberate Home Office encouragement of the targeting of mentally impaired, lone parent families.

It is worth briefly considering some of the mass of evidence for community abuse and neglect of the mentally ill and learning disabled.

* A large scale MENCAP study (1999) found extremely high levels of 'bullying' with 88% of learning disabled respondents suffering abuse within the last year. 66% reported frequent (once per month) bullying.

* A study by the DRC (2004) found that 82% of respondents with mental health problems had been physically or verbally attacked. 35% had been physically attacked within the previous three months.

* In 2008 Mind found that nearly 90% of people with mental health problems in council housing had been victimised.

* The Joint Parliamentary Select Committee on Human Rights report 'A Life Like Any Other?' (2008) commenting on the failure of police and other authorities to tackle disability abuse and to treat the learning disabled fairly say

' We are concerned that …this evidence could have potentially very serious implications for the rights of people with learning disabilities **to a fair hearing**…evidence also suggests that there are **serious failings** in the criminal justice system which give rise to the **discriminatory treatment** of people with learning disabilities'

Specifically the previous evaluation summary (HRS230) expresses concerns that vulnerable, mentally impaired people have been unfairly treated in the targeted families .They say the evidence

'highlights the need for agencies investigating complaints to develop well-defined investigatory policies and processes to ensure that all those involved in ASB cases are dealt with fairly…'

This seems very clear. For a majority of the families mental health and learning disability problems lead to abuse in the community (perhaps stimulating retaliation) which is ignored by the authorities, or to mental health related behaviour which can be classed as ASB , and to unfair targeting in disputes by enforcement officers who ignore government safeguards for vulnerable people. The targeting may be deliberate policy. In the projects these mental health and learning disability problems are not successfully addressed; indeed AIFSP tells us that at project exit only 17% of families even had a mental health worker.

The admiration of the LTO team for the families is now quite understandable since despite their multiple disadvantages and mistreatment in the community and by state agencies the families tried to change and 'exercised a high level of personal agency and strength' within the limits of their 'emotional capacity'. The picture painted overall by LTO and the earlier evaluations is not of families from hell but of **families in hell desperate to escape.**

The limited success of the projects is also understandable now. You cannot bully someone with a serious mental health condition into 'good behaviour'. You cannot miraculously cure a learning disability with parenting classes. The projects can do nothing to address the high levels of intolerance and abuse in the wider community which mentally impaired people suffer, nor do they counteract bias and disability discrimination in the state enforcement agencies, but quite the opposite if we look at the analysis of media images by the LTO team.

The government has done little to counter the sensational and pejorative reporting of 'ASBO Sin Bin' , 'Tearaway Towers' , 'ASBO Ghetto' projects in the popular media and the characterisation of the families as dangerous, violent and feckless 'neighbours from hell'. Is it any wonder that families are reluctant to get involved given this a priori stigmatisation? Is it any wonder that at project exit 57% of families had to move home? How has this happened? We know that this government is a master of spin so surely they could set the right tone? Or have they chosen not to? Consider this typical press handout from Louise Casey, the ASBO / Respect Tsar

'These families can **cause untold misery** to those who live alongside them and **destroy entire neighbourhoods with their frightening and disruptive behaviour'**

11.04.07

Recently the official project language has changed again. Instead of 'Intensive Family Support Projects' we now have ' Family Intervention Projects'… after all families from hell must justify sanctions and state enforcement actions , not support. The government sponsors of the IFSPs have worked up the vigilante media with their tough political rhetoric and now have to pander to the monster of unfairness they have created. Voices pointing to the potential effectiveness of a true support led approach are lost as are the few civil liberties groups who understand and protest the outrageous targeting of vulnerable, mentally impaired people in the ASB Crusade.

5. CONCLUSIONS ON THE 'LONGER TERM OUTCOMES' STUDY

LTO is the third and last evaluation report on the AIFSPs by the Sheffield Hallam University team. These reports are an invaluable resource to anyone currently trying to unravel the IFSP saga. In future they will become a classic source of information for sociologists on just how the ASB Crusade became an exercise in disability discrimination for political reasons. The collected data paints a stark picture of the limitations of theses projects in underlying philosophy, field practice and results delivery. The headline claim is that 71% of families had greatly reduced ASB and that 75% of homes were stable at the end of the evaluation. However what the LTO team call 'a more nuanced analysis' taking into account ongoing ' deep rooted' and 'multiple problems' (which could lead to renewed ASB) classed 43% of families as successful. Already we should be alerted. In fact the data quantity and quality do not support the claimed results even before other factors are considered.
In summary

1.   Claims are based on opinions relating to a tracking sample of 28 families i.e. 10.9% of all project families.

2.   The coverage of evidence even within the 28 is very patchy e.g. The views of all agencies (social services, YOTs, police, health service, education, ASB enforcement officers…) except housing are confined to the opinions of 7 people.

3.   The level of family 'engagement' with the projects in the tracking sample is significantly higher than in the general population of families at case closure. But 'engagement' we are told is a predictor of family success. Therefore the tracking sample is biased.

4.   The majority of families had left the projects within 12 months of the final LTO interviews. 6 families had left only very recently'.

In summary the tracking sample data base is opinion based, extremely small, patchy in coverage, biased in favour of recording success and relates to a period of less than 12 months after case closure. The rationale for the LTO study was to provide solid, detailed evidence for the 'longer term' sustainability of reduced ASB in the community, increased home stability, and increased family wellbeing. All we have in fact are a small number of opinions recorded less than a year after families left the projects. This is not a 'longer term' assessment of 'outcomes' but it still has useful lessons to teach.

On the incidence of ASB for example the claimed reduction in 71% of families does not take into account

1. that 2 families had not in fact been referred for ASB. A further 3 families had been referred for a 'single problem' which was 'easily resolved'.

2. that 6 families had to be re-referred to projects for renewed ASB. 3 of these were in the 'resounding success' group and 2 in the 'partially successful' group. Only 1 was in the 'failed' group.

3. that 4 families self-reported 'success' without corroboration from any agency.

4. that some families continued to receive ongoing support after project support was withdrawn at exit.

If we take out the 'inappropriate referrals' and reassign the 're-referral families' the ASB reduction 'success' group is 31.5% of families , a long way from the headline 71%. The LTO team 'continuum of outcomes' approach rather obscures this fact. Please note that so far we have not even addressed the 'deep rooted' problems which led the 'more nuanced analysis'of the team to put success at 43%. The new ASB reduction estimate is uncertain. However it provides useful information. We noted that the previous evaluations by the team claimed significant reductions in ASB in 85% of families at case closure. A year later we have levels of 31.5%. This must mean that significant ASB has reoccurred in 53.5 % of families. Crude as this estimate is it implies that if such decay in behaviour continues **all** families will be re-offending in a year or so.

LTO provides no evidence of sustained behaviour change in the community other than the opinions of a few stakeholders. The only evidence for the cost-effectiveness of IFSPs is also opinion i.e. that for some 'stakeholders'

'the projects were **perceived** to offer excellent value for money'.

The claims of reduced ASB and home stability march in step in these evaluations; one supports the other. In LTO we are told that 75% of homes were stable at final evaluation. We are left to assume that this is an outcome of the projects. However this is misleading since at referral 14% of homes were already stable. Even more remarkably 57.1% of all families had moved during the evaluation. 58.3% of 'resoundingly successful' families had moved. We are told such moves provided a 'fresh start'.

They also allowed families to escape their problem locations. Living in their new locations for less than a year we can argue ASB complaints have simply not had time to mature and surface. So to what extent did the projects stabilise tenancies? We need to allow for those who moved. 75 – 57 = 18% could reasonably be attributed to the projects but 14 % were stable anyway at referral so the project contribution could be a mere 4%.

The wider objectives of the project recognised the need to prevent family breakdown and improve family health and wellbeing in the longer term since it is recognised that renewed problems here could lead to renewed family behaviour problems. What does the tracking sample results tell us? At final interview

1. 10 families (35.7%) had suffered family breakdown with children taken into care or into custody.

2. In 13 families (46%) there were ongoing concerns about children's welfare and challenging behaviour.

3. 57% had moved home, often 'involuntarily'.

Have the projects made an improvement? Well we know that at referral (AIFSP) 32% of families were at high risk of family breakdown and 38% had a child at risk of being taken into care. Well breakdown has happened at the expected rate. We must sadly conclude that there has been no improvement in these problems and the projects have achieved little or nothing.

An important IFSP objective is to meet the unmet needs of the families. LTO and the earlier evaluations make it abundantly clear these are dominated by 'deep rooted' mental health and learning disability problems which had not been addressed. 80% of the families had such problems. 59% of adults, mainly lone parents, had severe depression. 54% of the children had a learning or physical disability. At referral only 9% of families had a mental health worker (AIFSP) .What did the projects achieve? At case closure for the general family population, a mere 17% had a mental health worker although for the tracking group 'some' had contact with CAMHS teams. It is clear that ongoing mainstream medical support for the general population of families was not available. The LTO report states how difficult access is for these families.We have also shown from LTO and earlier evaluation evidence that many of the vulnerable families were widely abused in their communities. 60% of all families were identified as being victims of ASB. Recall that 80% are mentally impaired. This is in line with wider evidence from the DRC, Mencap and

Mind that the level of disability abuse in the community is generally very high (71% up to 90% in social housing). We also discussed evidence that ASB and other enforcement teams fail to take account of DDA 2005 and Home Office ASB vulnerability requirements to assess such people **before** enforcement action is taken and the **'serious concerns'** of the Parliamentary Joint Select Committee on Human Rights about state agency learning disability discrimination in the criminal justice area.

Given the level of community and state agency abuse the LTO team are right to admire the 'high level of personal agency and strength' exercised by some of the families. These people tried to change against all the odds and some succeeded ...temporarily. They deserve better from us than scapegoating, stigmatisation, criminalisation and half hearted support. No amount of bullying will cure mental illness. No amount of parenting classes will cure learning disability. They are not, in the main, families from hell but **families in hell desperate to escape.**

This author welcomes the LTO teams' finally frank bottom line

'It is too early to make claims with any certainty about the longer-term sustainability of the changes that IFSPs had helped to engender. This is partly because some [the majority of] families had only recently exited the IFSPs , but it also reflects the fact that families working with IFSPs often had deep-rooted problems , suffered from multiple deprivations and were therefore likely to continue to be vulnerable to external influences'

But as this analysis has demonstrated the reduction in ASB is far more modest, considering all LTO data, than claimed and significant decay of family behaviour is already apparent within a year of project exit. Little has been achieved in stabilising families or improving wellbeing, particularly in the mental health arena. They still face prejudice and abuse in the community and neglect and discrimination from state agencies: the 'external influences'. The future of all the project families remains deeply shadowed.

6. WIDER POLICY IMPLICATIONS

The LTO study following this analysis has demonstrated two results with wide implications for future policy decisions in the ASB Crusade :

1. That the IFSPs have not met their objectives of producing a high level of sustained change in 'ASB' in the families nor have the underlying 'deep rooted' causes been successfully addressed.

There is no objective evidence to support claims of 'excellent value for money'.

2. That a large majority , 80% of the families, because of significant mental health and disability problems, have been abused and scapegoated in the community and then deliberately targeted by enforcement agencies (housing and ASB teams) without prior psychiatric assessment and contrary to the DDA 2005 and Home Office safeguards.

Before we look at policy implications we should place the 'ASB family from hell' problem in the wider ASB context. The British Crime Survey report 'Experiences and Perceptions of ASB in the UK' lists 16 categories of ASB concern defined by the British public. 'Neighbour disputes' was ranked in 14th place, being seen as 'a very big problem' by 2% of respondents. Can this be correct? Why has so much effort (apparently) been aimed at a 2% problem which as we have seen mainly affects the poorest communities in Britain? Is the government really so altruistic about the 'underclass' that it concentrates the resources of its ASB Crusade in this area? Or is it that 'neighbour disputes' in the poorest areas involve sedentary, easy targets in social housing who can be bullied at will? It is easy to act tough when the target lacks the intellect and resources to fight back. Who cares about 'pond life' anyway? Make an example of some of them …it will focus the minds of the rest. Let's be clear : the IFSPs are addressing a limited ,2% problem for political reasons and because many other ASBs, of much greater concern to the public, are difficult to address.

Of the 'pond life' sub-class our 80% of mentally impaired project families are even more vulnerable and Result 2, above, should be a matter for great ethical concern. But beyond the ethical issue the evidence shows that a repeat of the 'enforcement led approach' to vulnerable families will lead to future project failure and further waste of public money. This contention is absolutely critical. The author has presented evidence already from the DRC, MENCAP and the PJSCHR on this issue. To reinforce this evidence he now presents a brief summary of other recent work on this problem. The author recommends consulting the DRC report

'Disabled people's experiences of anti-social behaviour and harassment in social housing : a critical review'

And

'Anti-social behaviour and disability in the UK'

These reports look at the results of many studies on this issue showing the extreme level of abuse and disability discrimination suffered by mentally ill and learning disabled people …particularly in deprived areas. In a formal, academic style the authors are nevertheless scathing about government ASB thinking, policy and motivation. On the vulnerability of these families to the state enforcement agencies the DRC report says their findings

'point to evidence that the subjects of ASB interventions often have mental health problems , learning difficulties and neurological disorders. This raises crucial questions about the extent to which the use of potentially punitive control mechanisms …can be justified …ASBOs in particular have drastic impacts on disabled people by not only failing to address 'root causes' of disruptive behaviour , but the effects of employing a regulatory mechanism that can have exclusionary effects and even result in a custodial sentence ,and may serve to exacerbate their problems'

On the IFSPs the second report says

'It appeared that agencies favoured a reliance on ASB interventions in which the problem was framed not as mental health impairment but as a 'parenting problem' with the focus on parents failing to 'take responsibility' or being 'unable to cope' '

'Failure to conform to normative [behaviour] standards justifies punitive action. Disabled people with learning difficulties and mental health conditions may be particularly powerless to control behaviour that could cause alarm and distress…Indeed the very process of being labelled 'anti-social' may serve to obscure the underlying health conditions that contribute to complaints'

And in conclusion

' …it is clear that there are grounds for serious concerns about the way in which ASB interventions are being used against people with mental health disorders and learning difficulties'

These results, from academics with intimate experience of the issues, are very much in line with this author's conclusions. For interested readers here are the website addresses where copies can be downloaded.

www. shu.ac.uk/research/ceir/downloads/

www. extra.shu.ac.uk/ppp-online/issue_1_300108/article_5.html

The reader will discover that both these reports were written by the same Sheffield Hallam University team who carried out the IFSP evaluations for the government which were reported in HRS230, AIFS, HSU, HRS240 and the full Long Term Outcomes report we have now analysed. A reader might think that with the IFSP evaluations completed the Sheffield authors finally feel free to express their uncensored views on the grossly inappropriate 'interventions' of the ASB Crusade, but this author could not possibly comment. They do not mention in their review compelling evidence that the targeting of mentally impaired families is not an unfortunate accident related to overzealous, ignorant ASB teams, but deliberate policy. The government Crime Reduction website provides information and guidance to these teams, to local authorities, and the police, on tackling ASB. www. crime-reduction.gov.uk/toolkits

Statistical risk factors are provided for various population groups. We are told that the highest risk group for ASB, are the 'lone parents' at 41%. The 'mentally ill / physical and mentally disabled' cluster has a risk factor of 32%. At 25% we find the homeless. These people should be very familiar to the reader… they are our IFSP families. The author has a letter from the Justice Minister (Hazel Blears) to his M.P. commending the resource efficiency of using these risk statistics to target particular minorities. What we have now is a self-fulfilling prophecy. In case any doubt remains about a priori targeting and stigmatising of vulnerable groups we have this from Tony Blair himself, the prime sponsor of ASB policy

' There is no point pussy-footing… if we are not prepared to predict and intervene more early… pre-birth even… these kids a few years down the line are going to be a menace to society…'

The Prime Minister ; September 2006
On The Unborn Children of Lone parents

Unfortunately this government does not admit to and does not learn from its mistakes. The 1999-2001 evaluation of the first IFSP at Dundee demonstrated all the problems found in the later 6 projects but it was claimed as an outstanding success. The hoax continues. Last year, given the 'proven success' of the 7 prototype IFSPs it was announced that 53 projects would be rolled out across the country. The 7 projects have historically cost around 1.4 million pounds each. However one recently started project is expecting costs of £ 800,000 per annum. The national roll out would cost **£ 74 million** on historical costs or **£127 million for 3 year projects** on the latest cost example.

357

However that is not the end of the story. Ed Balls, the new Secretary for Children, Schools & Families said in mid 2007 that

'It's a failure every time a young person gets an ASBO... I want to live in a society that puts ASBOs behind us'

Commentators suggested a retreat from the failed ASBO policy, well established by bodies like the National Audit Office, but this was denied. However Mr. Balls, under the Youth Task Force Action Plan, is launching a new initiative, the Intensive Intervention Projects for young people. Yes we are told that they are based on 'the successful Family Intervention Projects' developed by the Respect Taskforce. The 20 projects will concentrate on 'tough enforcement, non-negotiable support and early prevention' which sounds rather familiar. The target individuals will have to agree a contract and will receive 'an assertive and persistent key worker'. There will also be Parenting Early Intervention Pathfinder projects with obvious intentions: tackling 'bad parenting'...another familiar theme. In describing this programme no mention is made, despite the massive evidence from ASBO and IFSP experience, of mental health problems and learning disability as important underlying 'causes'...at least in the frequently targeted vulnerable minorities. Tackling 'causes' is down played...after all, families from hell only deserve punishment.

The cost of the initiative is apparently £ 218.5 million over the next three years. If we add in the 53 new IFSPs the total cost is around £ 345 million. Given the very poor and decaying medical support services for the mentally ill and learning disabled and their families in the UK and the findings of the IFSP evaluations on the critical role of 'ongoing support services' it is sad to see £ 345 million wasted on populist political stunts doomed to failure. Think what could be done with that money by mainstream mental health services working directly with these families.

Based on historical project size the intervention projects will reach around 3,000 families which sounds impressive. However recall that the British Crime Survey found that 2% of respondents thought neighbourhood disputes' with problem families was 'a very big problem'. On that basis some 300,000 families from hell are out there causing havoc and destruction. The new ASB initiative will reach just 1% of them. As with ASBOs and the prototype IFSPs we must conclude that the Youth Taskforce Action Plan is merely a symbolic gesture to reassure voters that the government is taking tough action. Will this gesture be any more successful than the ASBOs and prototype IFSPs ? It is hard to think so since the same failed 'intervention / sanctions' model is being applied yet again. Nor is there any evidence that this initiative will attack the 13 ASB problems above 'neighbour disputes' in the BCS, top 16, public ASB concerns. The hoax continues.

Professor D P Gregg (retired), April 2008

"The only thing necessary for the triumph of
evil is that good men to do nothing"

Edmund Burke

SECTION 4.5   A REVIEW OF THE REPORT

"Family Intervention Projects: An Evaluation Of Their Design, Setup & Early Outcomes"

Professor D P Gregg October 2008

'There is no point pussyfooting...if we are not prepared to predict and intervene early...pre-birth even...these kids a few years down the line are going to be a menace to society'

Prime Minister Tony Blair M.P
On The Unborn Children of Lone Mothers
September 2006.

1. INTRODUCTION

Family Intervention Projects popularly known as 'ASBO Sin Bin' projects are now a key element in the government crusade against 'antisocial behaviour' following the discrediting and decline of the ASBO as an intervention. Unlike the ASBO, which is seen as a purely punitive intervention, the FIP is said to 'challenge' the antisocial behaviour of families while preventing eviction and homelessness and improving 'outcomes' for their children in line with the Every Child Matters policy. The FIP is said to address the root causes of ASB. Families may receive 'assertive and persistent' interventions, including 'intensive support', in their own homes, in temporary dispersed tenancies or, in a small number of cases, a controlled core residential unit , the Sin Bin of the media. These interventions are organised by local authorities or by agencies hired by them. In principle the FIP appears to be a more balanced approach than other state interventions such as the ASBO. Unfortunately as we will see, in practice, the FIPs fail in multiple ways : by targeting the wrong people for the wrong reasons, by targeting false 'causes' of ASB, by failing to tackle the real underlying causes in the families targeted (mental impairment), by failing to deliver support in key areas like

359

mental health and by failing to deliver sustained improvements in behaviour in the community or in family stability. At root the FIP remains an 'enforcement' led intervention, dominated by local authority enforcement functions, where someone must be blamed and punished. This ethos justifies forcing very vulnerable families into projects under threat of eviction, loss of benefits and loss of children. If these contentions needs further support remember that policy is set from the top and consider the Tony Blair mission statement given above.

The current review analyses the data and conclusions in the recent report (FIPEO, 1) on 53 FIPs, written by the National Centre for Social Research and sponsored by the Respect Task Force and the Department for Communities and Local Government. The 53 projects were set up during 2006 / 7 but these included 19 existing projects co-opted into the scheme. The projects involve around 1080 families in total. However the results presented are based on only 90 families who completed intervention during the short evaluation period and included interviews with only 18 families and associated project staff. This remarkably low level of sampling is typical of FIP evaluations as is the biased nature of the sample and these factors make it hard to take the claimed results seriously as we will see.

Although the current FIP evaluation report (1) relates to projects set up in 2006/7 under the Respect Action Plan the FIP design is not new. The first FIP was the famous Dundee Family Project of 1999 evaluated by Glasgow University for the government (2) and later reviewed by this author (3). The Dundee project, despite many problems of design and operation noted by the evaluators, became the template for later FIPs. Remarkable headline claims for reduction in ASB were made for this first project which careful analysis of the actual data does not support (4,5,6,7). The evaluators also pointed to the inherent and unresolved schizophrenia between project staff involved from the 'enforcement' arm and staff from the 'support' arm which remains to this day. In practice an 'enforcement' ethos dominated. The evaluators also expressed concern about the poor data quality used to support success claims. This problem, as we will see, persists nine years later.

Following the 'success' of Dundee a further six FIP prototypes were set up and monitored up to 2007. The projects were analysed on behalf of the Home Office and the Dept For Communities and Local Government in a series of detailed reports by the Centre For Education Research and Social Inclusion at Sheffield Hallam University (4,5). This team found all the problems noted in the Dundee project but again the early reports superficially seemed to show large reductions in ASB. However careful analysis, particularly of the last report on 'Longer Term Outcomes'

(6,7) demonstrated rapid decay in behaviour within a year of families leaving the FIPs (5). The Sheffield team has also expressed concern in several reports about the targeting of mentally ill and disabled families (~80% of the families) and their lack of medical support. In fact having finished their government contract this team is now writing scathing criticisms of this inappropriate targeting including a report for the Disability Rights Commission (8,9). Remarkably regulatory ASB process safeguards for mentally impaired, vulnerable people, appear to be routinely ignored in family referral and selection. This may be unlawful and is certainly shameful. The current report, under review here, by the National Centre for Social Research, continues the FIP tradition of putting the best possible gloss on the outcome results while recording serious caveats about FIP operation in the bulk of their report. These caveats disappear by the time government agencies report the results to media and public in glowing terms (10). This review will look at those caveats in detail.

2. FAMILY DEMOGRAPHICS

"FIPs were working with very disadvantaged families"

FIPEO, page 2

We begin with a review of family health and demographics because these factors are central to the targeting of families by FIPs. They also shed light on the underlying causes of some alleged ASB which are misread and inappropriately attacked in the projects. To be clear, for the targeted families poverty and 'deprivation' do not cause ASB, nor does 'poor parenting'. As we will see for most of these families behaviour branded as ASB is 'caused' by significant mental impairments which generate serious executive dysfunctions which require treatment not sanctions. Community prejudice and disability abuse, encouraged by state and media propaganda, also play a role.

Tables 3.11 ,3.13 ,3.14, 3.15 in FIPEO (1) show just how 'disadvantaged' the families are. Here are some highlights of that data :

69 % are lone parent families (63% are lone mothers)
56 % have 3+ children   41 % have 1 - 2 children
> 62 % are out of work   (26% unknown)
> 61 % were receiving out of work benefits (32% unknown)
> 24 % were in significant debt (76 % unknown / not in debt)

The above also highlights the frequent incidence of missing data in the 'comprehensive' FIP Information System (IS), for example on debt. In the

7 prototype FIPs recorded debt was much higher at 59 % of families of which 70 % involved council house rent arrears …frequently the reason why these families were referred to the projects (2,4).

Table 3.11 presents 'risk factors' for ASB at referral which we will see strongly influenced that referral and family inclusion. We see that :

63 % of families had mental / physical health problems
69 % of the adults suffered from depression
25 % of families had one or more members with a disability
14 % of children had statements of special educational needs while
41 % had a low educational attainment and
25 % had a lack of basic numeracy / literacy and
23 % had difficulty with daily tasks

Note that as in earlier FIPs over 80% of families had members with mental / physical health or disability problems (2,4).Note again that the SEN status of 43 % of the families was unknown. In the 6 prototype projects 54 % of families had a child who was SEN or 'attended special schools / units' (4). Table 3.13 presents details of mental health problems. In summary:

42 % of the children were ADHD / hyperactive
29 % suffered from depression / stress
30 % lacked confidence
13 % were self-harming
10 % suffered from panic attacks
9 % had speech / dyslexia problems
5 % had Asperger's syndrome
18 % had other mental conditions

The reader may wish to compare this sad litany of mental illness and disability with the archetypal image of the 'yobs and families from hell' usually portrayed by government spokesmen and continuously repeated by the media.

Altogether **47 %** of the children had an ADHD / autistic spectrum disorder known to cause executive dysfunctions and hence inadvertent and involuntary behaviour problems. These are recognised medical conditions requiring professional medical treatment not legal sanctions. The FIPs promise 'intensive support' to these families and yet : only 19 % were 'involved' with a medical professional at referral ; only 3 % were referred by a health professional ; only 26 % had unqualified FIP staff support for mental health issues and only 11 % received professional counselling /

psychotherapy. Yet these medical 'risk factors' were used to force families into FIPs, under threat of eviction and loss of children under a false promise of 'intensive support'. That is the scandal at the heart of the ASB FIP crusade.

Neither is the physical health of the families good which also accounts for many problems they are involved in. Table 3.15 (1) gives this data for the adults :

36 % had a poor diet and 8% digestive system problems
30 % lack exercise
41 % had muscular / arthritis / respiratory problems
10 % had difficulty taking medicine
 9 % had difficulty seeing a GP
 9 % had epilepsy
 5 % had diabetes

   Could it be that 30 % of the parents lacked exercise because 55 % had a debilitating illness rather than because of sloth or poor motivation? Is this why they had difficulty maintaining their homes? (we note that this was a common reason for FIP referral in the 7 prototype projects , as discussed below (2,4)). Is this level of physical ill health the reason why 69 % of the adults suffered from depression and why lone mothers had problems controlling their (often mentally impaired) children?

   Overall the families present a sad picture of ill health and neglect. It is interesting that nowhere is the term 'learning disability' used and data on SEN is missing for 43% of the families. No comment is made on the extremely high incidence of mental disorders in the children associated with 'executive dysfunction' and behavioural problems although the alleged rationale of the FIPs is to address the 'causes of ASB' (9). The DDA 2005 requires that families in social housing must have a psychiatric assessment before authorities can impose ASB sanctions or interventions and similar procedures are described in the Youth Justice Board Guidance on ASB interventions and in Home Office ASB Guidance on vulnerable people. As we will see in describing the family referral process FIPEO makes no mention of this.

3. THE FAMILY REFERRAL PROCESS: Or Never Mind the (Data)
                                        Quality, Feel the Width
The FIP approach is said to

'focus on the most problematic families who persistently perpetrate ASB
 and who are at risk of loosing their homes'

'take a whole family approach which recognises the inter-connectedness between problems faced by different family members'.

We will examine how these principles work out in practice in targeting families. The second principle in practice means blaming ill, lone mothers for their inability to control their (usually mentally impaired) children. Families were referred by a wide range of agencies but the process is dominated by just a few agencies :
41 % local authority (LA) housing dept. / social housing associations
21 % LA ASB teams
14 % LA social services
9 % schools / local education authorities
8 % police
3 % health professionals

In total 80 % of referrals came from agencies with an 'enforcement' role versus 20 % with a 'care' centred role. This pattern does much to explain the dominance of the 'sanction led' FIP ethos in practice. Nevertheless the low level of police referral at 8 % is surprising given that we are told repeatedly of the high frequency of 'criminality' in the families. We will see that individual criminality is actually low.

In addition to ASB / criminality and eviction risk FIPEO also uses 'risk factors' to target families which included the health problems we explored, parenting problems (i.e being a lone parent) and school problems (being mentally impaired). Another factor mentioned as influencing family inclusion was that they were 'motivated to engage with the FIP'. This rather suggests the 'easy' families were selected. In fact we learn that 8 % of families approached either refused project inclusion or were considered **'too dangerous'** to include. It seems that in practice 'the most problematic families' were not addressed by the FIPs.

3.1 ASB AND CRIMINALITY

What about ASB , the core issue ? Remarkably FIPEO presents only qualitative data for the level of ASB reported for the referred families. This is because the referring agencies did not record data on 'number of complaints'. Therefore the scale and severity of ASB is unknown. Only the number of types of ASB is reported.

2 % of families had none; 11 % had 1 type; 12 % had 2 ; 14 % had 3 ; 60 % had 4+ This is a very peculiar distribution suggesting a very diverse population of 'offenders'.

Clearly the families are far from being equally 'bad'. Note also that although only 2 % of families had no ASB reported we later discover that **56 % of individuals had no ASB**. Repeatedly in FIPEO family level data gives a very misleading picture of family 'guilt' and the real incidence of ASB / criminality. This reporting style is a natural consequence of the a priori 'blame the family' ethos.

FIPEO reports ASB type according to the Home Office classification which is not helpful in identifying actual problems. We have

Type 1 ASB disregard for community / personal well being 87 % of
           Families includes noise 54 % / nuisance behaviour 70 %)

Type 2 ASB environmental damage 59 % (includes property damage
           48% / litter – rubbish 26 %)

Type 3 ASB misuse of public space 49 % (includes street alcohol
           drinking 22 % / drug / solvent abuse 35 %)

Type 4 ASB acts directed at people 42 % (includes intimidation /
           harassment 37 %)

The definitions of the individual 'offences' are not given. How severe was the behaviour involved in these various categories? We are not told. Intimidation can be anything from kids playing ball to 'teenagers hanging around' to threatening behaviour. We learn more from the more meaningful data on actual enforcement actions against the families. Table 3.6 in the report gives criminal involvement of the families. We learn that in 33 % of families a member had been arrested in the six months prior to referral. In 24 % of families a member had been convicted of a criminal offence in the previous 12 months which means that 76% of families had no criminal convictions. We have no data on the severity of offences. Was it dog fouling, littering, or murder? Remember even the breach of an ASBO or other order is a criminal offence. Drinking in the street can also lead to arrest and we saw that misuse of public space was apparently common. Further clues come from legal actions recorded in Table F8.

15 % of families had a child with a 'juvenile specific' court (supervision / referral) order.
11 % of families had a member with an ASBO and 2 % with a CRASBO
6 % had received fines
< 1 % had a drug intervention order
< 1 % had a crack house closure order

This does not look like a crime wave and paints a different picture to the qualitative ASB type data. 85% of families did not have a child with a juvenile order. 87% did not have an ASBO. However Table F8 also records pre-court actions:

25 % of families had a child with an Acceptable Behaviour Contract (ABC).
14 % had received a verbal warning
2 % had a parenting contract
1 % had a Fixed Penalty Notice (FPN) for disorder
1 % FPN for environmental crime
< 1 % FPN for noise
< 1 % had a noise abatement notice
< 1 % seizure of noisy equipment
< 1 % seizure of alcohol from youngsters

Note that although a key mantra of the FIP is that 'poor parenting' causes ASB and we will see that 79% of families had child discipline problems, only 2% of parents had a parenting contract. Note that **20 % of families had NO involvement in legal enforcement actions** and in **28%** of families the data on enforcement was not even recorded. It is instructive also to compare the qualitative ASB type data with the above

* 62 % of families at referral reported for rowdy behaviour and 42 % reported for harassment

   versus only 1 % fixed penalty notices for disorder.

* 54 % reported for noise offences and 27 % for being noisy neighbours

   versus only 1 % PN for noise ; < 1 % noise abatement notice ; < 1 % seizure of noisy equipment

* 59 % for environmental damage

   versus 1 % penalty notices for environmental crime ; < 1 % litter abatement notices.

* 49 % misuse of public space

   versus < 1 % seizure of alcohol orders ; < 1 % drug intervention orders; < 1 % crack house closure orders ; < 1 % seizure of vehicles.

We must conclude that the severity of ASB / criminality related to these families is actually rather low despite the misleading headline FIP claims such as

' families had high levels of ASB and criminal activities ' FIPEO, Key Findings ,P2.

There is another factor to consider which alters the picture presented in FIPEO dramatically: **offences are committed by individuals, not families, despite the central FIP blame and guilt by association model.** We need to take into account that the average family consists of ~ 1.3 adults and ~ 3 children , 4.3 people in all. What effect does this have on reported offence frequencies? It means that for ASB / criminality at the individual level as few as :

5 % of children have 'juvenile specific' court orders
8.3 % of children had an ABC
2.6 % of individuals had an ASBO
3.2 % of individuals had received verbal warnings

The ASB frequency data also changes significantly

ASB Type	Family level %	Individual level %
Disregard for community / personal wellbeing (noise)	87	39
environmental damage (litter)	59	17
misuse of public space (street drinking)	49	14
intimidation / harassment	42	9
No ASB reported	**2 %**	**56 %**

Reporting by family increases apparent 'offending' rates by 2.5 x to 5 x the real individual rate. We have already noticed that even at the family level enforcement action is very low and lower still when we now look at estimated individual levels. Reporting by Home Office ASB type at the family level is grossly misleading and exaggerates family criminality. It would be interesting to compare this data with the average for the local communities the families lived in. Are they really so different from their neighbours? They are different in the remarkably high levels of mental and

367

physical illness and disability among adults and children : recall that 47 % of children had ADHD / autistic spectrum disorders ; 69% of adults have depression ; 25% have a disability. But FIP referrers know that 'poor parenting' is a risk factor for ASB and therefore poor parenting must be responsible for bad behaviour, not children's mental impairment combined with adult illness. And of course statistically crime 'runs in families' justifying the targeting of whole families under the pretence of offering support. This false reasoning amounts to actuarial justice directed against poor, mentally impaired, lone mother families as we will see.

3.2 HOUSING PROBLEMS

The second major factor influencing referral to FIPs is said to be housing. 41 % of referrals came from LA housing departments or (social) housing associations and 76 % of families were in social housing with 14 % in private rentals and 2 % owner occupiers. Surprisingly although 43 % had received a housing officer visit / warning 69 % were in secure or assured tenancies and a further 7 % in starter or assured short hold tenancies. 24 % had a notice of seeking possession (NOSP) order. Only 7 % of all families were in temporary accommodation. Only 21 % in total were in near term danger of eviction.

Nor are we told the reasons for housing action. The reader is left to infer it must be related to ASB in the community. Previous FIP evaluations have provided much more information on eviction (2,4) .The flagship Dundee Families Project which provided the FIP model quoted housing surveys which showed that ' the vast majority of evictions were for rent arrears' (2). In the DFP itself 'major' referral factors were

'poor upkeep of [council] property and rent arrears'

In the later six prototype FIPs (4,5) we find that 41 % of families had been referred for rent arrears, 33 % for garden condition and 30 % for untidy houses and rubbish. 59% were in debt versus the claimed 24 % (plus 76 % unknown / not) in FIPEO families. 33 % had NOSP orders versus only 24 % in FIPEO. For the current projects are the 26 % of families targeted for litter / rubbish ASB under 'environmental damage' actually guilty of having dirty council houses? Referral as 'noisy neighbours' in the six projects was comparable at 33 % versus 27 % in FIPEO. So why is there no mention of poor council house upkeep and rent arrears for the current FIPEO families? Can they be so different? Well Table 4.3 tells us that FIP staff delivered 'support to improve property' to 41 % of families. But why if poor house upkeep is not mentioned as a referring factor? By contrast despite 63% of the families having mental / physical health problems and

25 % having disabled members only 18 % received medical support. Council house upkeep must surely have been really important to receive more attention than ill health ? Box 4.1 also tells us 38 % of families received help sorting out rent arrears and other debt. We must again infer that rent debt was very important to the FIPs , again more important than the high levels of ill health. But then 41% of referrals came from LA housing. We must conclude that using the Home Office ASB type classification conceals rather than exposes the true reasons families were referred to the current projects : as in the previous FIPs many were referred for being guilty of social inadequacy and mental ill-health , for being poor and for having rent arrears.

3.3   FAMILY RISK FACTORS : The Worst Families ?

We have seen that 56 % of individuals had no reports of ASB ; 42 % of families had no legal enforcement actions ; for those with enforcement actions the rate was 1.2 per family ; 87 % of families had no member with an ASBO and as few as 2.3 % of individuals had an ASBO ; 75 % of families had no children with an ABC and as few as 8.3% of children had one ; the levels of legal enforcement actions for specific offences within the Home Office ASB types was remarkably low compared with the claimed qualitative occurrences ; only 21 % of families were at short term risk of eviction. Given these facts why were many of the 'non-offending' FIPEO families targeted? In what sense were they the most problematical families and compared to whom?

Three primary reasons are given for referring families to FIPs : high levels of ASB and criminality ; high risk of eviction ; general risk factors related to family demographics. We have questioned the issues of ASB and housing. Can the 'risk factors' explain family targeting? Table 1 summarises all these factors for families accepted for the FIPs and families found 'not suitable'. The differences between families expose the thinking processes of the selectors.

TABLE 1   FAMILY CHARACTERISTICS AT REFERRAL

Factor	Accepted for the FIPs	'Not Suitable' for the FIPs
ASB / CRIMINALITY		
Average No of ASB types for families with 1-3 types	0.8	1

% of families with 1-3 types	37	56
% with 4+ types	60	28
% families with enforcement actions / unknown	80	68
children with ABC s	~ 8.3 %	~ 3.3 %
individuals with ASBOs	~ 2.6%	~2.1%
no conviction in last 12 months	76	82
enforcement status unknown	28 %	40 %
HOUSING		
Not in secure ,fully assured tenancies	24 %	50 %
status unknown	17 %	44 %
DEMOGRAPHICS / RISK FACTORS		
Workless families	62 %	39 %
Work status unknown	26 %	59 %
In debt	24 %	9%
Debt status unknown / no debt	76 %	91%
Lone parent	69 % (63 % mothers)	68 %
No positive role model	63 %	30%
No personal /social Boundaries	61 %	29 %
Child discipline issues	79 %	60 %
Overall health problems	63 %	46 %

Mental health problems	32 %	18 %
ADHD / hyperactivity	42 %	?
Disabled	25 %	13 %
SEN	14 %	?
SEN status unknown	43 %	?
Lack of literacy / numeracy	25 %	9 %
Difficulty in daily tasks	23 %	4 %
Individual children excluded from school	6 %	?

Inspection of Table 1 immediately highlights one reason for family inclusion in an FIP versus exclusion : for many important parameters less data is missing for the included families. They are simply better known as we will see. This makes selection in part a data lottery.

On ASB 'severity' the biggest differences between inclusion and exclusion is in the number of types of ASB reported. 60% of included families had 4+ types reported compared with 28% of excluded families. However we questioned earlier the value of counting types as a measure of ASB frequency or severity. Even so why were the 28 % of excluded families with 4+ ASB types not included in place of some of the 37% of included families with only 1-3 ASB types if ASB type is so important?

If we look at enforcement action frequency as a measure of severity there is little difference between families. 80% of included had actions / status unknown versus 68% of excluded; an estimated 2.6 % of included individuals had ASBOs versus 2.1 % of excluded ; 76 % of included had no member convicted versus 82 % of excluded ; 8.3% of children in included families had an ABC versus 3.3 % of excluded. On enforcement / legal action the big difference is that enforcement action status was unknown for 28 % of included families versus 40 % of excluded. Were the most ASB families selected? Who could say with this data quality.

We must conclude in part that families were included for ASB on the basis of a crude qualitative measure which did not reflect ASB severity or frequency or because data was simply better known for the included families. This is a sloppy, potentially unfair way of running a selection process …unless of course the die was already cast, a priori for the included families? We will see. Housing is said to be the second major factor in selection and in particular security of tenancy and risk of family homelessness. Lets be clear about this situation : where there was a threat of home loss it was primarily from the LA housing dept / (social) housing association itself. What is the direction of causation here? Families were 'encouraged' to join the FIPs under threat of eviction, loss of benefits and loss of children. We do not know to what extent a wish to include families in the projects (for various reasons, poor house upkeep, rent arrears, etc) precipitated a threat to their tenancies by the authorities.

We learn from FIPEO Table 3.9 that 76% of included families were in secure, fully assured or assured shorthold tenancies at referral versus only 50% of the families excluded. This means on the face of it many more of the excluded families may have been at risk but the tenancy status of 44 % of the excluded families was unknown while remarkably, the tenancy status of 17 % of the included families (that is 100 families) was also unknown at referral ! What is going on here? Risk of homelessness is claimed as a major FIP selection factor in government propaganda but on the basis of the inadequate quality of this data how can it be?

This leaves us with the general 'ASB risk factors'. Even if ASB is quantitatively low based on the above project data, with only 2.6 % of individuals with ASBOs and only 8.3% of children with ABCs, and even if 76% of family tenancies are secure, 'risk factors' can save the day for the FIP referral agencies and selectors. Remember the FIP model is that families, not individuals, are problematical, antisocial and criminal and that 'bad parenting' is largely to blame. On this basis an issue with one child can justify intrusive state intervention irrespective of the particular facts concerning a family. It is just a matter of going down the a priori checklist as we will see.

The biggest differences between included and excluded families (and presumably the bulk community population) lies in the demographics of poverty and health: the major risk factors for ASB. First a similarity : in both groups 68 – 69% of families are lone parent. This is not surprising since the Home Office crime fighters training website www. crime-reduction.gov.uk/toolkits tells us that lone parents are the most antisocial group in the UK (statistical risk factor 41%).It turns out that the included families are simply the poorest, most inadequate and most ill of this already deprived minority group. 61% of included families receive 'out of work benefits' versus 29% of the excluded. 24% included are in debt versus 9% excluded although remarkably the debt status of 76-91% families is unknown.

On child behaviour we note that 'lack of personal / social boundaries' is 61% for included versus 29% for excluded, almost identical to the 'no positive role model' with 63% versus 30%. These differences merely reflect the 62% of families led by lone mothers. Remember the HO knows lone mother = bad parenting.

Learning disability and mental health indicators show big differences between included and excluded: overall 63 versus 46% ; mental health 32 versus 18% ; disabled 25 versus 13% ; lack of basic literacy / numeracy 25 versus 9% ; difficulty with every day tasks 23 versus 4%. Remarkably the SEN status for 43% of included families is unknown and 100% unknown for the excluded families. 47% of the included children are ADHD / autistic but the level is again unknown for the excluded families. (In the 6 prototype FIPs 54% of families had children with SSENs or who attended special schools / units (4)).

3.4   FAILURE OF PROTECTION FOR VULNERABLE PEOPLE
       IN THE ASB PROCESS

Mental health / disability is clearly a key discriminator in family selection. Again this is inevitable since the HO Crime-reduction training website tells us that this health cluster has one of the highest risk factors for ASB : 32% versus 41% for lone mothers. Selectors can't go wrong (in justifying their actions) if they target the mentally impaired. Of course this may mean selecting families in secure tenancies, with very low levels of ASB and criminality as we have seen. It must also be remembered that several Mind / Mencap surveys have found that 80-90% of mentally impaired / disabled people in social housing have suffered physical or verbal abuse from neighbours. In the 6 prototype FIPs ~60% of families had suffered similarly. What is ASB in these circumstances? Strange, involuntary behaviours presented by mentally ill children and adults seen through the filter of community ignorance and bigotry perhaps? Or ill advised defensive action in response to disability abuse in the community? What is remarkable is that the government recognises that mentally ill / disabled and other vulnerable groups must receive special protection in ASB investigation and interventions design. **However in all the FIP descriptions and evaluations these safeguards are not mentioned as part of the ASB referral / inclusion process.** To be clear some safeguards are in non-statutory guidances but some are controlled by legislation with clear legal obligations. The team which evaluated 6 prototype FIPs for the government (4,5) said this about the situation

'where social tenants suffer from a mental health problem, under the DDA 2005, a psychiatric assessment must be carried our prior to enforcement action being taken'.

The Home Office and the Youth Justice Board ASB guidance contain similar requirements for all vulnerable ASB accused in any form of housing (11,12). The situation has been clarified in Parliament more than once. The Justice Minister, Hazel Blears said this in the HoC :

'if there is evidence that a particular perpetrator of ASB is suffering from a medical condition, mental health condition, disability or is vulnerable in any other way then a practitioner with specialist knowledge should be involved in the assessment process to determine the cause of the behaviour and whether an ASBO is the most appropriate tool...'

Written Answer : Hansard ; 12th September 2005 ; column 2514w

The HO guidance also makes it clear that local authorities

'have a duty under the NHS and Community Care Act 1990 to assess any person who may be in need of community services.

Similarly under the Children's Act 1989 it says

'when applying for an [ASB] order against a young person an assessment should be made of their circumstances and needs ...to ensure that the appropriate services are provided ...'

With ASBOs in the vast majority of cases, no medical assessment is taking place which is why at least 38% of ASBOs go to mentally impaired young people (13). In the case of FIPs things are worse.
High levels of mental illness / disability (80%+) are actively used to justify family inclusion via 'the risk factor' argument (even if their ASB is trivial, involuntary, or defensive) but the FIP evaluators in several reports mention no assessments to identify and take into account disorders at the referral / selection stage , nor assessments relevant to the DDA 2005 protections and other statutory requirements. To add insult to injury only 18% received medical support 'arranged' by the FIPs from the NHS (FIPEO, Box 4.2) while only 11% received psychotherapy / counselling. These vulnerable families are taking a threefold hit in a way which is not only hideously unfair but may also be unlawful.

4. FIP 'EARLY OUTCOMES & IMPACTS'

4.1 CAVEAT EMPTOR

'across all 53 FIPs these longer term outcomes need to be assessed quantitatively'
FIPEO report page 147

Government FIP sponsoring departments and the delivery agencies have made glowing claims of success for these projects. Unfortunately they have NOT reported the numerous caveats rightly stressed by the NCSR evaluators. The above quote sums up the situation : the current results pertain only to a small sample of families who left the FIPs around 5 – 10 months before assessment and are based largely on qualitative data. This is not new. FIP evaluations since 2000 have repeatedly warned of the poor quality of project data and the consequent weakness of evidence for success claims. These warnings have been ignored for eight years and the evaluations presented by government departments and their proxies as 'proof' of how wonderful the FIP is. At best this is wishful thinking (i.e. surely it's better than those nasty ASBOs?). At worst it is blatant intellectual fraud. Before we examine the FIP 'deliverables' it is essential to bring together these caveats which highlight the invalidity of the current early outcome claims. We should consider

1. Were the, 'most problematical' families targeted as claimed ?

2. Is family sampling and data quality adequate to support the outcome claims made ?

3. Are the claimed 'early' improvements in family behaviour and stability likely
to be sustained ?

4.1.1 The 'Most Problematic Families'?

' there is a lack of evidence to actually verify whether FIPs were reaching the worst families (i.e. we cannot compare the families referred / accepted by FIPs with the potential target groups of families in the local area) '

FIPEO report, page 123

In section 3 we noted the surprisingly low frequency of legal enforcement actions against families and individuals despite claims of 'high levels of ASB and criminality'. Recall that only 13% of included families had a member with an ASBO, or ~2.6% of individuals, at referral. 56% of individuals had no record of ASB and 79% of families were in secure tenancies. We noted that the included families were largely distinguishable from the excluded families in terms, not of actual ASB actions and criminality, but in 'risk factors', i.e. extreme poverty and higher levels of mental health / physical health / learning disability problems. It is true the included families were the most 'problematical' in health terms. On this basis the report is misleading in giving the impression that the included families are the worst in unjustified, bad behaviour. An argument could be made for the dominance of 'risk factors' in selection i.e. that the aim of FIPs is to anticipate and prevent future ASB. However in that case it is unnecessary to claim non-existent 'high levels' of ASB etc in the targeted families. However given the coercive, punitive, nature of FIPs and their stigmatising image in the media and community, encouraged by the government, perhaps the public would not stand for mistreatment of vulnerable people who had not offended significantly, but simply might do in future?

Secondly the dominance of mental health / disability 'risk factors' in selection might be acceptable if the promised 'intensive' family support was actually delivered. However as we saw in section 3 only 11% received counselling / psychotherapy through the FIPs. Remarkably FIP staff arranged external 'parenting classes', the flagship of FIP support, for only 18% of families although 79% had 'child discipline issues'.

The above suggests a lack of clear thinking in the handling of FIPs or a system dominated by the political need to paint the 'correct' picture to keep the uninformed public on side with the ASB Jihad. Either way the FIPs illustrate the danger of an actuarial justice approach in social engineering… particularly when the targets cannot defend themselves. The FIPEO report also supplies direct evidence that the included families were not the 'most problematical'. We noted earlier that 8% of the families approached were considered 'too dangerous' or refused to join an FIP. Section 4.1.2 tells us that FIP selectors

'looked for evidence [that] family members at referral **were motivated to engage with an FIP'**

given the above it is clear that the 'most problematical families' were eliminated at the start.

Section 7.2.1 gives interesting reasons why the worst families 'were missed' at selection including

- some ethnic minority communities dealt with ASB problems themselves rejecting outside interference. By definition their 'worst' families did not appear in FIPs.
- communities too scared to report the worst families.
- communities feeling a family was so far gone that nothing could be done.

These circumstances would clearly exclude the worst families from FIP recruitment. We also noted in section 3 that in many instances the availability of key data used in selection was unacceptably limited. The selected families in many cases were simply better defined in data terms. In these circumstances selection becomes a data lottery.

Overall the evidence shows that the families included in the FIPs were the 'most problematical' only in terms of ASB 'risk factors' : poverty and significant mental health problems. The most dangerous families in communities were excluded either by the communities or by FIP selectors. Cooperation of families at referral was a key selection factor. On this basis it is simply false to claim that the FIPs targeted the 'most problematical families'. The FIPs are harvesting the low lying, easy to target, fruit.

4.1.2 Biased Sampling & Poor Data Quality

The FIPEO report purports to represent the outcomes from 53 FIPs. 19 projects existed before 2006 and were 'rebadged' as FIPs and 34 were set up during 2006 and 2007. 885 families were referred to an FIP between Feb. and Oct. 2007 and 692 'agreed to work' with an FIP. Quantitative evidence in the FIP Information System (IS) refers to these families. However 'early outcome' **results were reported for only 90 families** who completed the intervention during the evaluation study. The total number of families in the 53 projects is not given. However we know that 34 projects hosted 692 families and on that basis the total is ~ 1080 families. This means that the **'early outcome' claims are based on a sample of only ~8.3% of families in the projects.** Only 9 FIP 'case studies' were carried out and these involve interviews with a total of **only 18 families.** This is a sample of **only 20% of families who completed intervention and 1.7% of all families in the project.** This is a remarkably low level of sampling to make strong claims about family rehabilitation across 53 projects. Indeed the evaluators themselves say on page 19, FIPEO

' The purposive nature of the sample design as well as the small sample size, however, means that the study cannot provide any statistical data relating to the prevalence of these approaches, views and experiences'.

We noted in section 3 the poor quality or absence of much of the 'quantitative' data including, critically, the severity of ASB among the families. On page 40 the evaluators concede

'Typically the information collected by FIPs consisted of a **description** of the nature of the problems a family caused which **could not be quantified** …**no reliable results are available on the issue** because in the majority of cases information on complaints was not collected numerically'

Reliable data on legal enforcement actions by contrast paints a very different picture than the 'descriptive' data with surprisingly low levels of ASB / crime as discussed in section 3. Much other data is missing on debt, tenancy status, SEN status and so on leading to selection bias simply due to missing data.

Neither are we given complete data relating directly to the 90 families who's 'outcomes' are described. Were the families who completed intervention during the 'study' representative of the full family population? Were they perhaps the least problematical families who finished first? We cannot say. However the evaluators provide useful clues. The duration of interventions were evenly split between under 26 weeks ; 27-52 weeks ; over 52 weeks directly suggesting a range of problem severity in the sample and section 2.4 tells us that the basic criterion determining time in project was simply continuing for 'as long as it takes'. Or as section 4.4 says

'Typically they stopped working with families when there was evidence that

* the families' ASB had stopped or reduced to an acceptable level

* the family had reached the point were they were capable of sustaining positive outcomes without continuing FIP support'

The FIPEO summary section confirms that 'staying involved for as long as necessary' is one of the factors 'critical to FIP success'. This evidence clearly implies that the 90 families completing intervention were not typical of the ~1080 families in the 53 FIPs **by definition.** Remember most projects only started in 2006 / 07. These 8.3% of total families are simply the first to conform to 'the long as it takes' policy. They are the ''least problematical' families **by definition.** The sample of 90 is meaningless and says nothing about the future level of 'success' across the other 91.7% of FIP families. By definition the 'most problematical families' will be the last to leave…perhaps some unknown fraction never will. The evaluators admit this in section 6, page 93, but not in the executive summary.

'The IS findings should be treated with caution as the families included in the analysis were the first to complete the service and might not be very representative of all the families FIPs work with'

Far from 'might not be very representative' we can guarantee the 90 families, due to the leaving criteria, are definitely NOT representative of the ~1080 families in the projects. The sample is badly biased. Remarkably careful search of the data reveals this. Compare F 3.3 and F 6.3. At referral 80% of the 692 families in the 34 projects had some enforcement action recorded but for the 90 family sample only 51% had enforcement actions at referral. Clearly the 90 sample assessed is far less 'antisocial'than the bulk family population. The evaluators also concede on page 93 that

'These results cannot be used to assess the quantitative impact of FIPs As the IS did not include a control group'

This is in addition to the problem of severe sample bias which renders the outcome results largely meaningless. This of course is lost in the public claims of government agencies for FIP success. This omission amounts to an intellectual fraud on the public.

4.1.3   Sustainability of Family Improvement.

The criterion determining the end of FIP 'intervention' for a given family is apparent success in reducing ASB and a subjective judgement by FIP staff that the reduction will be sustained. The report provides qualitative evidence for a **current** reduction in ASB but provides NO evidence for long term sustainability. From the point of view of communities this makes the glowing claims of FIP success irresponsibly premature…or dishonest.

It is important to realise that the evaluation monitoring period was from February to October 2007, the period in which 90 families completed intervention. 53 projects were set up in 2006 and 2007 with 34 starting from scratch. We are not told the 'time out of project before evaluation' distribution but clearly time out of project was short for all families. Take the most favourable limiting case : an early start in January 2006 with groups completing after 6, 12 and 18 months intervention and a late evaluation in October 2007. This gives an average time before evaluation of $(16 + 10 + 4) / 3 = 10$ months. For a start date in June 2006 we would have an average of ~5 months and so on. 5 or 10 months is surely no basis for judging the medium, let alone long term, sustainability of improvement claims? Because the individual levels of ASB are surprisingly low at FIP referral and the vast majority of tenancies were secure we noted that 'ASB risk factors' were used to beef up the case for targeting most families.

If the key underlying risk factors have been eliminated by the projects this could be adduced in support of longer term sustainability. However by the end of intervention 80% of the sample families still had active risk factors. As section 2.4 tells us

'FIP families by their very nature tend to have deeply-entrenched and complex problems which can take time to reveal themselves, **let alone start to be resolved**'

Indeed. Specifically we noted that 63% of families had significant mental / physical health problems and 25% had disabled members. 47% of the children had ADHD / autistic spectrum disorders. 14% were SEN children although shamefully the SEN status of 43% of families was unknown though we know that 25% lacked basic numeracy / literacy and 23% had difficulties with everyday tasks. Despite this litany of mental impairment only 11% of families received 'counseling 'psychotherapy' and only 18% in total had 'FIP arranged' support from the health services. Not surprisingly Table 6.6 shows little improvement in mental health by project end. 36% of families with problems at the end compared with 38% at project start. Similarly for physical health with 14% at the end versus 16% at the start. There is an improvement for drug / alcohol abuse but these problems are frequently symptoms of underlying mental health conditions such as depression and stress. Since these conditions have not been eliminated will the short term improvement in substance abuse be sustained?

In terms of socioeconomic risk factors workless families hardly changed with 79% workless at project start and 74% workless at the end. Families in secure / assured tenancies actually fell slightly from 86% at the start to 82% at the end.

Overall given the 'deeply entrenched and complex' family risk factors have not been eliminated the assumption that the claimed improvements in ASB and family stability will be sustained is not supported by the evidence. In fact the conclusion section tells us

'It is less clear whether these positive outcomes will be sustained in the longer term'

In the detailed discussion in section 6 we are also told

'more work needs to be done to assess the degree to which outcomes are sustained in the longer term'

This hardly represents the full picture of continuing 'deeply entrenched' problems and risk factors discussed above. Nevertheless FIPEO is clear enough and there is no excuse for government agencies to ignore this severe limitation in claiming FIP success. This is not a new problem since each of the previous technical evaluation reports since 2000 has strongly emphasised the lack of any evidence for sustainable outcomes (2,5) , which fact has evaporated from government media claims.

The FIPEO authors seek to support the case for sustainability by quoting the final report of the six prototype FIP evaluators (5), or rather they quote the 'official' summary version which says

'6 months on [after project end] there had been no significant complaints about ASB in the families they interviewed. Equally the threat of homelessness of these families had been reduced and the family home was secure at the point of interview'

However if we look at the detail of the final report (5) we learn that

* Only 35% of the small family sample tracked (i.e. ~20 from 256 families or 8.2%) showed NO ASB after 6 months while at project exit the figure was 85%. Therefore behaviour had deteriorated in ~50% of families in less than a year. At this rate all families would be reoffending within two years.

• While 75% of tenancies were stable at final interview we learn that 57% of the families were forced to move home during the evaluation period due mainly to fear of vigilante neighbours (60% had already been victims of disability abuse at referral).

• As in the current 53 projects ~80% of families had serious mental health and disability problems and these were not addressed. Only 17% had even a mental health 'worker'.

Far from 'proving' sustainability the evidence from the final report on the six prototype FIPs shows the opposite. Over nine years this pattern of uncritically reporting summary claims for FIP success has been repeated by FIP evaluators and government agents. Over nine years perfectly clear and damning caveats about the limitations of the FIP evidence have been 'lost' or suppressed, lessons have not been learned and acted on, and vulnerable families have continued to suffer to no good end for themselves or the community. Given the cost of these ineffective projects ignoring repeated evidence of failure is a hoax on the public.

4.2   SUMMARY OF THE CLAIMED OUTCOMES

It should be clear by now that the data and evidence upon which these claims are based is very poor to the point were they could be dismissed. However the claims are worth examining if only to highlight the bankruptcy of the FIP operation.

4.2.1   Reduction In ASB And Criminality.

Figure 6.1 shows that 65% of families had no reported ASB at the end of intervention compared with 8% at the start. This means of course that 35% of families were still engaged in ASB (but of fewer ASB types). However at the more realistic individual level 56% of individuals had no ASB at referral versus 86% at project end (Table 6.1). So ASB occurrence had ceased in only 30% of individuals. 9% of individuals still engaged in 1 type of ASB at project end compared with 9% at the start but there was a larger reduction in the 4 or more types category : 18% down to 1%. Note again that because FIPs did not record numbers or severity of complaints there is no way to judge any quantitative change in ASB from project start to end point. However it is important to remember that these results are effectively tautological in that intervention was only terminated when FIP staff took a judgement that

'ASB had stopped or reduced to an acceptable level'

It is not surprising in the least that the frequency of '4 or more ASB types' had dropped from 18% to 1% is it? What does 'an acceptable level' mean? If 12% of families are deemed a success while still displaying 1, 2, 3 types of ASB this suggests the ASB in quantitative and severity terms was low from the beginning. Should we be impressed that ASB had stopped for 30% of individuals during the 5 to 10 months after leaving the projects? Perhaps not if we consider the rate of decay found in the six prototype FIP evaluation discussed in section 4.1.3. How long before the 30% becomes zero %? Because of the tautological exit criteria these results tell us nothing about what will happen to the bulk population of families in the 53 projects. Remember the 90 families reported represent only ~8.3 % of this population and the evaluators admit that the 90 family sample is biased. Consider enforcement actions which are largely brought by local authority agencies.

We are told that ABCs etc had fallen from 21% of families at referral to 4% for the 90 families who met the exit criteria. Remember these families are not representative of the bulk family population. Also the 'reduction' may simply reflect the transfer of 'jurisdiction' to the FIPs from other agencies such as LA housing. Orders may simply be timing out with no new orders issued while families are being reprogrammed in the FIPs. It is interesting for example that visits from housing officers dropped from 40% of families to 7% during the projects. Does this reflect better behaviour or transfer of jurisdiction?

If we consider court related enforcements which are more likely to be brought by the police or YOTs and reflect more serious 'offences' the picture is different (Table 6.3). Juvenile specific orders at entry were in 13% of families at entry and 11% at exit. Court orders were 8 % at entry and 7% at exit. We are also told (page 99) that

'there appeared to be little change in the level of court orders (e.g. ASBOs , parenting orders, individual support orders) and juvenile specific orders (e.g. referral, supervision, curfew…) …this may partly reflect the longer duration of the penalties…'

The fall in enforcements under LA control likely did relate to change in jurisdiction to the projects rather than behaviour change. Note also that it is surprising that at the start 49% of families had NO enforcement actions against them versus 76% at exit so enforcements have ended for only 27% of families. Most improvement is in the 1 action families whose frequency fell from 27% to 10%. So the biggest shift was in the 'easiest' families. But 24% of families classed as successes still had 1 or more actions against them. 35% of successes still exhibited 1 or more classes of ASB. 7% were still involved in 'harassment and intimidation'. A reader might conclude that the criteria for judging 'an acceptable reduction in ASB' are surprisingly loose… unlessthe majority of the ASB was in reality, trivial.

4.2.2   Preventing Homelessness?

The report summary tells us

'The risk of families being evicted had also reduced considerably [by FIP exit]'

It is difficult to reconcile this definitive statement with the facts presented in the body of the report. Table 8.4 tells us that of the 90 successful families 86% were in secured or assured tenancies at referral compared with 82% at exit. The author finds it hard to see an improvement here.

———

At project start 12% of the later 'successful' families had a formal notice of seeking possession. By project exit this was 3%, an improvement for 9% of families. The problem of eviction was small at the start and got smaller. It is reported that at referral 40% of families had received a visit from a housing officer and that this had fallen to 7% by exit. As we asked above does this reflect an improvement in behaviour or jurisdiction transfer to the FIPs and temporary protection during 'reprogramming'? Table 4.3 tells us 47% of families received FIP staff support to 'help manage' the 'risk of eviction'. The reasons for housing interventions at referral are not made explicit. The implication is ASB was to blame. However we know from earlier FIP reports that ~40% of families were targeted for rent arrears and 30-35% for poor council house / garden upkeep and rubbish management.

Some hint that the current families were similarly targeted is that Table 4.3 FIPEO notes that 43% received 'support to improve property' while 38% received 'financial management support'. To confirm this Box 4.1 on finance and budgeting begins with 'sorting out rent arrears'. Emphasis on these 'housing related' support actions strongly suggests the major role of non-ASB factors in housing actions and FIP referral. It is worth noting that while 80% of the families had serious health / disability problems only 18% had NHS support organised by the FIPs. Poor council house upkeep and rent were obviously far more important, but then 41% of all referrals, by far the largest group, came from LA housing departments / associations.

4.2.3   Outcomes For Children.

The report summary says

'The outcomes for children and young people were also **reported** to have improved'

Note the evaluators change to the passive voice : caveat emptor. Improving the health and educational prospects of children in the families was seen as an important aim of the FIPs and has been used sell the FIP interventions as 'support led' on many occasions. Was it accomplished? In the 90 families ' truancy / exclusion/ bad behaviour at school' apparently fell from 52% to 24% of families. Is this useful result what it seems? At referral we are told (in Table 3.11) that 56% of families exhibited 'truancy / exclusion / bad behaviour at school'. This means of course that 44% of families did NOT have a child with these problems. Of course families are not excluded, children are. Considering individuals changes the picture significantly. 60% of 5 to 15 year olds did NOT have these problems and 92% of 5 to 15 year olds were NOT excluded from school.

In fact only 6% of the children in the 90 families were excluded which seems low. We are not told the general frequency of exclusions in the communities the families came from unfortunately. How atypical were the families? We do know that 47% of the children had ADHD / autistic disorders which affect behaviour adversely. 14% were SEN but SEN status was unknown for 43% of families. (In the six prototype FIPs 54% of the children were SEN or attended special schools / units).

A national study by the Bow group in 2008 found that

* Of 9000 children excluded from mainstream schools in 2005 / 06 6000 Had a learning disability.

* Half of the 78,600 children suspended from mainstream school had special needs.

* The NAS found that 60% of children with autistic spectrum disorders had been attacked at school similar to the 70% of project children in the six prototype FIPs.

A University of Bath schools study in 2007 concluded that

'most teachers are unequipped to deal with special needs'.

So are our family children innately 'bad' and 'antisocial' or ill and disabled and subject to teachers untrained to deal with their impairment and special needs? It's easier to brand them as antisocial and make them someone else's problem is it not, especially when the government makes it respectable to do so? The evidence on claimed behaviour improvement in the 90 families is suggestive. 57% of families had FIP staff 'supporting children into education' and 67% had FIP arranged support from schools/ education departments. Section 5.4.8 makes it clear that the FIP staff acted as positive advocates for the children and parents. Given the above national data on the inability of mainstream schools to deal with mental impairment such advocacy must be welcomed. The number of families with a child in the 'truancy / exclusion / bad behaviour' group fell from 52% to 24% in the 90 family sample but had children's behaviour really changed or had FIP staff 'advocacy' forced schools to acknowledge and adjust to the children's multiple medical and social problems and reduced the horrific level of bullying faced by mentally impaired children? We also have to ask whether 'advocacy' alone provides a permanent solution particularly when such support ends with the FIP. A key question then is to what extent the health and demographic status changed, permanently, for the better. The answer is disappointing but hardly surprising.

90 families	Project start	Project end
Mental health problems.	38%	36%
Physical health Problems.	16	14
ADHD / autism	47	47
Disabled	25	25
Workless	79	74
Full time work	7	5
Families receiving out of work benefits	79	82

To confirm the above FIPEO Section 5.4.7 tells us

'The evidence from family interviews suggests that families had not received much help with health issues'

while 6.3.2 tells us

'There was little change… many health problems typically require a long period to be resolved… also due to difficulties FIPs had in 'levering-in' health services …'

Table 7.1 is also worth considering. It shows that while it was easy for FIPs to arrange interactions with LA housing groups (88%) it was easy to arrange interactions with health services and social services much less frequently : 66% and 42%. This is not surprising given the dominance of LA enforcement groups such as housing in project set up. The same pattern was seen in previous FIP evaluations over the last eight years. The problem of getting badly needed professional medical support for these families has not been solved by the FIPs. This is a major failure which destroys the 'support led' credibility of these interventions. Indeed despite high levels of mental health / disability issues only 11% received 'counseling / psychotherapy' and 26% overall 'support with mental health issues' from medically unqualified FIP staff. The 'deep rooted' health and poverty problems of the families and their children have not changed. Given this are the modest improvements reported likely to be sustainable?

'Poor parenting' is blamed as the primary cause of children's alleged ASB and improvements are also claimed in this area. 67% of all families accepted for the projects were labelled for this crime. However for the 90 families who completed only 60% were 'poor parents'. Yet again the 90 sample is less problematical than the bulk project population.

What is poor parenting? It appears to be a crude projection of child behavioural problems straight onto the parent. So 79% of family children are said to have discipline issues (although only 13% had a juvenile specific order). For the bulk population while 67% are lone parent and 62% are lone mother, 63% were targeted for providing ' no positive role model' and 61% for 'lack of personal and social boundaries'. By contrast families 'not suitable' for intervention had only 30% with 'no positive role model'. Essentially having parenting problems is pre-defined by being a lone mother suffering from depression (69% of adults) struggling with an average of ~3 children at least one of whom probably has ADHD / autistic disorder (47%) or is SEN / disabled.

Surprisingly given the political prominence of 'poor parenting' in government propaganda only 17% of families received 'parenting classes' from unqualified FIP staff and 18% from other agencies or a total of 35% compared with the 79% of families with alleged child discipline problems.

For the 90 families poor parenting was said to affect 60% of families at referral dropping to 32% by project end. However 35% received parenting classes. Was attending a parenting class simply assumed to stop poor parenting? The criteria are subjective after all. We have also seen that positive advocacy at schools seems to have reduced school problems for 28% of the families without affecting underlying causal health issues. Positive advocacy may have done some good at school. So did parenting classes really change behaviour and achieve anything except a self fulfilling prophecy and a psychological warm glow? Just as in the case of mental health the coverage of support for this allegedly key cause of bad behaviour is remarkably low compared with the claimed scale of the problem. We have here another FIP credibility gap. There is more cause for concern. Section 4.3 says

'It was clear some FIP staff were providing advice and guidance about parenting without formal training **... concerns were voiced about the risks associated with unqualified staff delivering parenting interventions'**

What fraction of the 17% of the parenting classes / advice given by the FIPs used unqualified staff? We are not told. Underlying causes related to mental health of adults and children remain unaffected by parenting classes and most other FIP interventions and as section 6 tells us

'there was little change…many health problems typically require a long period to be resolved…There appears to be very little change in the level of court orders and juvenile specific orders'.

5 SUMMARY & CONCLUSIONS

It is tempting to simply dismiss the outcomes claimed in this report for a whole list of technical reasons. However that would deprive the lay and expert reader of an opportunity to appreciate the multiple failures in the ethos and operation of these projects and the dreadful plight of the families they target.

5.1 PROBLEMS WITH FAMILY TARGETING PROTOCOLS

Three key factors are said to dominate family referral and selection : high levels of ASB and criminality ; high risk of eviction; ASB statistical risk factors. We have seen that by using qualitative measures of ASB , not numbers and severity of complaints, the scale of 'family ASB' is exaggerated. This can be seen by noting the much lower frequencies of pre-court and court related enforcement actions. For example while 62% of families were reported for rowdy behaviour only 1% had fixed penalty notices for disorder ; while 54% were reported for noise nuisance less than 2% had received a penalty notice , noise abatement notice or had equipment seized.

FIP ethos is dominated by the idea that 'poor parenting' is the cause of ASB. This justifies branding whole families as antisocial and reporting 'offending' at the family level which grossly exaggerates criminality. For example while qualitative measures suggest only 2% of families had no ASB fully 56% of individuals had no ASB ; only ~5% of individual children had 'juvenile specific ' court orders and only ~8% had an ABC. Only ~3% of individuals had an ASBO. Everything appears to have conspired to 'sex up' the data on family offending. In fact there is little difference between those families accepted into the FIPs and those classed as unsuitable. The same is true of eviction risk with only 21% of families in near term risk of eviction. In fact 78% of included families were in secure / assured tenancies compared with only 50% of families found unsuitable. Nor are we given an analysis of the reasons for eviction risk. Was it ASB or something else? From earlier FIPs we know that 30-40% of families were referred for rent arrears or poor council house upkeep.

We also noted that about this proportion of FIPEO families received education / support from FIP staff on these very issues.

Serious ASB and high risk of eviction appear to apply to only a minority of the families and individuals targeted. Why then were they selected? Analysis shows that so-called risk factors play a major role. Comparing included families with those found unsuitable we found much higher frequencies of poverty, unsupported lone mothers (without access to positive role models) and mental health and disability. 63% of included families had significant mental / physical health problems versus 46% unsuitable ; 69% of adults (mainly lone mothers) suffered from depression; 47% of the children had ADHD / autistic spectrum disorders ; 25% of included were disabled versus 13% unsuitable. In previous FIPs 54% of the children had learning difficulties, had SSENs or attended special schools. We noted that this pattern of targeting is unsurprising since the Home Office crime reduction training web site identifies, lone mothers and the mentally / physically ill / learning disabled cluster as the highest risk groups in Britain for ASB. The FIP selection process is staying true to these a priori risk statistics. This is actuarial justice in action against vulnerable people unable to defend themselves.

The selection pattern reflects the high frequency of FIP referral from enforcement led LA agencies such as housing and ASB teams. 84% of referrals come from enforcement led agencies, just those for whom the crime reduction website was designed. Selection for social inadequacy and mental impairment might arguably be justified if the FIPs concentrated on providing access to mainstream medical treatment but this happened for very few families. Instead families received assertive 'advice' and parenting classes which the evaluators admit did not change underlying family problems.

We also saw that the claim that the FIPs targeted the 'most problematic' or 'worst' families was contradicted by the evidence. In fact the evaluation shows the worst (i.e. most dangerous) families were eliminated by the selection process or never reached referral.

The most remarkable feature of the FIPEO description of the family referral / selection process is that no mention is made to the safeguards for vulnerable people in the ASB process given in Home Office and Youth Justice Board ASB Guidances and in the Disability Discrimination Act 2005. This required LAs to make a psychiatric assessment of any person with mental health problems or disability before any ASB intervention is decided. This applies to children, their carers and to impaired adults.

The failure of FIP referral / selection to apply such safeguards may well be unlawful.

5.2 CLAIMED EARLY OUTCOMES

5.2.1 Evidence Reliability

'the IS findings should be treated with caution as the families included were the first to complete the service and might not be very representative of all the families FIPs work with'

'It should be stressed that these results cannot be used to assess QUANTITATIVE IMPACTS of FIPs as the IS did not include a control group'

FIPEO page 93

We noted that the public claims made for the recent 53 projects make no mention of the serious evidentiary limitations acknowledged by the NCSR evaluators which largely invalidate these claims. We saw that family sampling and data quality is very poor leading to biased results. Partial results are only available for 90 families, the first to complete FIP intervention. This is only ~8.3% of all families. Only 9 FIPs out of 53 were looked at in any detail and only 18 families and associated staff were interviewed. That is only ~1.7% of all families in the projects. These are very small samples upon which to claim success for the 53 FIPs. However there is a worse problem acknowledged by the evaluators above : sample bias. We noted a wide range in apparent severity of ASB across the family population at referral. Our 90 families are simply the first to reach the exit criteria of 'significant reduction in ASB' and a subjective judgement that this would be sustained. Logically the 'easiest' families will reach this point first, leaving the 'harder cases' behind. We have no evidence that the remaining 'harder' 98.3% of families will ever reach the exit criteria. Were the 90 families easier to re-programme? At referral 80% of the 692 families selected for the projects had some enforcement action recorded against them but for the 90 family sample this was only 51%. The exit sample is biased. The results tell us nothing about the future fate of the 1000 odd remaining families in the 53 projects. To leave out these facts in presenting positive project claims to the public and media amounts to intellectual fraud. This is not a new phenomenon in government reporting of FIP results over the last nine years. Given the cost of these projects and the probably unlawful detriments suffered by vulnerable families the continuation of FIPs is a national scandal.

A second key issue, even if the improvement results were meaningful for the bulk family population, is the question of sustainability. In fact the 90 families were evaluated only months, and certainly less than a year, after exiting the projects. The 'early outcome' results tell us nothing about the medium or long term fate of these families. There are some indicators however. We noted above that 'ASB risk factors'played a major role in targeting families. If these risk factors had been eliminated or significantly reduced by FIP interventions it would provide evidence for sustainability. In fact by project exit 80% of the families still had active risk factors. Logically if these families were being seen for the first time they would still be candidates for FIP recruitment. FIPEO admits

'FIP families by their very nature tend to have deep rooted and complex problems which can take time to reveal themselves let alone start to be resolved'

We noted the very high frequency of mental health and disability problems in the families with 69% of adults suffering from serious depression and 47% of children having ADHD / autistic spectrum disorders and 25% of families having one or more disabled members. Despite this we found that only 11% had received psychotherapy / counseling. FIPEO confirms that very little changed in underlying mental health / disability problems. The same is true for economic status with only a small drop in worklessness from 79% to 74%. If underlying 'risk factors' were largely unchanged can we expect any improvements in behaviour to be sustained? We saw that FIPEO admits

'It is less clear whether these positive outcomes will be sustained in the long term'

'more work needs to be done to assess the degree to which outcomes are sustained in the longer term'

FIP evaluation reports, produced by three different teams, have been saying this for **nine years** yet no long term study of family outcomes has been done. The reason is clear : **what evidence there is strongly suggests that claimed short term improvements are NOT sustained and this single fact would totally undermine the FIP model. It also would also confirm that the FIP in practice is simply a political propaganda device.** The current evaluators, realising the weakness of their position, turned to the previous evaluations of the six prototype FIPs for support (5). Unfortunately they appear to have looked only at government headline claims for sustained improvement. However the 'Longer Term Outcomes' family evaluation again took place less than one year after project exit… hardly long term. More importantly we saw that at project exit it was claimed that 85% of families showed zero or greatly reduced ASB but within a year this figure had declined to ~35% of families. In less than a year behaviour had decayed seriously in 50% of families (4, 5). This evidence, contrary to the reporting of the government and the FIPEO team, demonstrates 'positive behaviour outcomes' are NOT sustained.

5.2.2   FIP Early Outcomes

On the basis of the above the modest early outcome claims tell us nothing about long term outcomes even for the atypical, 90 easiest families sample first to complete intervention. Nevertheless the early outcomes teach useful lessons. The primary supposed aims of the FIPs are significant reduction in ASB in the community, stabilisation of tenancies and improved prospects for children. At evaluation 65% of families had no reported ASB compared with 8% at the start. Thus 35% of families were still engaged in alleged ASB after intervention completion. However as we noted, ASB is committed by individuals. 56% of individuals had no reported ASB at referral versus 86% by project end. So ASB had significantly reduced in 30% of individuals. This is a modest result given the very small family sample size, the bias in the sample…these are the easiest families… and the strong evidence casting doubt on sustainability. However these results are based on qualitative measures. Since there is no quantitative data on numbers and severity of alleged ASB incidents at the start and finish of intervention we cannot say what the real impact of these changes was on the community …surely the real point. All we know is that for court related enforcements , which perhaps measure more serious ASB, ' there appeared to be very little change' according to the evaluators.

Eviction risk reduction is a second key target. The FIPEO summary claims that

'the risk of families being evicted had also reduced considerably'

   However we learned that 86% of the families were in secure / assured tenancies at referral versus 82% at exit evaluation. This hardly seems to indicate an improvement in housing stability to the author. We also noted that the threat of eviction is used to force families into cooperating with FIPs, somewhat muddying the issue of causation. Were tenancies at risk at referral because the local authorities wanted particular families in the FIPs for other reasons? We also noted evidence that rent arrears and poor council house upkeep rather than ASB, may have precipitated family targeting.

Improving children's educational and social prospects is the third target area…a target which must be welcomed by all. We are told that families with children reported for 'truancy / school exclusion / bad behaviour' fell from 52% to 24% at project end. However at the level of individual children things look rather different. 60% of 5-15 year olds did not have these problems at referral and 92% were not excluded from school. In fact for the 90 family sample only 6% were excluded. The 40% of children with school problems is not surprising given that 47% of children had ADHD / autistic spectrum disorders while we know that nationally of 9000 exclusions in 2005 / 6 ~6000 had a learning disability. We also know that 60% of Aspergers Syndrome children have been attacked at school according to NAS surveys. We noted evidence that most mainstream teachers are 'not equipped' to deal with special needs. We learned that FIP staff intervened in schools as 'positive advocates' for the children and their parents presumably explaining their medical and social problems and gaining better support for them e.g. against bullying. Did child behaviour improve or were school attitudes to family mental disorders improved? Perhaps the school interventions demonstrate what can be done with well targeted support.

However, sadly, the underlying risk factors in mental health for children and parents and their poverty had not changed significantly. We learned of difficulties in accessing mental health treatment for the families and that only 11% received professional psychotherapy / counseling. Nor can any improvement convincingly be attributed to parenting classes. While 79% of families had child discipline issues we found that only 18% of parents attended third party classes while 17% had FIP run classes (where concern was expressed about unqualified FIP staff).

5.3   GENERAL CONCLUSIONS

The problems with FIP ethos, design and operation first identified in the Dundee Family Project evaluation in 2000 (2) and seen again in the six FIP prototype evaluations (4,5) are still evident in FIPEO and in this review.

FIPs are supposed to combine 'assertive and persistent' challenges to ASB with 'intensive support' for the 'guilty' families. Unfortunately projects are run by local authorities or their proxies and local authority agencies such as housing and ASB teams take an enforcement and containment led approach. 80% of referrals in the current FIPs came from enforcement based agencies and only 3%, for example, from health care professionals. Families are recruited into FIPs under threat of eviction, loss of benefits and loss of children.

The central assumption of FIP design is that bad behaviour in families is 'caused' by 'poor parenting' which immediately focuses attention onto lone mothers with multiple sick children. A second recognised 'causal factor' is said to be deprivation which translates into extreme poverty, worklessness and reliance on state benefits. A third acknowledged factor is mental impairment although this does not appear to be recognised as a fundamental underlying cause of the other problems. These 'risk factors' as we have seen appear to dominate family targeting rather than severity of ASB or housing risk. Because of the family focus qualitative data on ASB at the family level is seen as appropriate but this greatly exaggerates actual, individual, ASB frequency and criminality. The same is true for legal enforcement data. In fact there is no quantitative data at all on scale or severity of ASB. In this way families can be labeled the 'most problematic'. However we have seen that the worst families are excluded in the selection process, indeed selectors look for the 'most cooperative' families.

The very high frequency of mental illness and disability among the families should trigger Home Office and Youth Justice Board guidances and DDA 2005 statutory safeguards for vulnerable people in the ASB process. In fact these requirements are not even mentioned in describing the referral / selection process in FIPEO. (They are mentioned in the six prototype FIP evaluation but only to point out that they are not applied properly, if at all). This widespread neglect of the requirements to make a psychiatric assessment before deciding ASB interventions for vulnerable people is discriminatory and may be unlawful. Psychiatric assessment is vital since involuntary, aberrant behaviours due to mental disorders are easily mislabeled as antisocial. Recall that in FIPEO 47% of children had ADHD / autistic disorders; in the six prototype FIPs 54% of children were SEN or attended special schools. It is also clear that many mentally impaired families selected for FIPs had been victims of prejudice and disability abuse in their communities. Nationally Mencap and Mind found that 80-90% of impaired families had been verbally or physically attacked by neighbours. This inappropriate targeting has now been condemned by the Sheffield University team who evaluated the six prototype FIPs for the government and who arguably have more experience of FIP evaluation than anyone else (8,9). Consider the above in the context of 'support' offered by the FIPs. Poverty, mental illness, learning disabilities and community prejudice will not be cured by 'parenting classes', particularly when the lone parent involved is also mentally impaired. FIPs supposedly offer 'intensive support' to combat underlying causes of ASB. However despite the very high levels of mental illness and disabilities in the families only 11% received professional psychotherapy / counseling.

Overall only 18% received arranged support on health issues. The FIPEO and earlier evaluations admit that dealing with ' deeply entrenched and complex problems' is not easy and concede that the FIPs led to very little change in the frequency of mental health problems. If underlying causes of ASB have not been eliminated we cannot expect even temporary improvements in family behaviour and stability to be sustained. All the FIP evaluations have recognised this and called for long term monitoring of families but after nine years and ~ 60 projects this has still not been done. Not only is longitudinal data absent but snapshot data collected for FIPs is partial and of poor quality despite repeated pleas by successive evaluation teams for proper data collection. What data there is strongly suggests that alleged improvements in family behaviour are NOT sustained.

If FIPs worked to produce long term improvements in family behaviour and prospects there might arguably be some pragmatic justification for the coercive targeting of mentally impaired children and adults who get into trouble. Given that there is no objective evidence that they do work ; that they fail to deliver much needed medical support ; that they brand the vulnerable as 'families from hell', so exposing them to further abuse in the community, what is the justification for continuing these FIPs? That this targeting of vulnerable families happens while ignoring official safeguards and statutory requirements specifically designed for their protection is a national scandal. Why does this happen? Could it be that now the ASBO is discredited the government has to do something to convince an unimpressed public that they are still being tough on ASBO yobs and families from hell? In conclusion, to coin a phrase, the public and our legislators should understand that

This is not just social engineering. This is voodoo social engineering

S4 REFERENCES

1. 'Family Intervention Projects: An Evaluation of Their Design, Setup & Early Outcomes'; National Centre For Social Research, 2008. www. dcsf.gov.uk/research/data/uploadfiles/ACF44F.pdf

2. 'Evaluation of The Dundee Family Project'; Glasgow University www. scotland.gov.uk/library3/housing/edfp-14.asp

3. 'The Dundee Family Project: A Commentary on The Government Evaluation Report'; D P Gregg January 2007. Widely circulated to MPs and disability groups.

4. 'ASB Intensive Family Support Projects – An Evaluation of Six Pioneering Projects'; Centre For Social Exclusion website, Sheffield Hallam University (see also 'ASB IFS Projects', Housing Research Summary No 230, 2006. Dept. For Communities and Local Government)

5. 'The Longer Term Outcomes For families Who Had Worked With Intensive Family Support Projects'; Dept. For Communities & Local Government ; www. communities.gov.uk/publications/housing/ Familysupportprojects (see also Housing Research Summary No 240 ,2008 , DfCLG)

6. 'Interim Review of the Government Evaluation Report on Six ASB FIPs D Gregg, March 2007.

7. 'Review of Claimed 'Longer Term Outcomes' From Six ASB Family Intervention projects'; D P Gregg, 2008.

8. 'Disabled People's Experiences of ASB and Harassment in Social Housing : A Critical Review' ; CEIR, Sheffield Hallam University, for the Disability Rights Commission, August 2007 ; See the DRC website or www. shu.ac.uk/research/ceir/DRC

9. 'Antisocial Behaviour and Disability In The UK' CEIR Sheffield Hallam University : People, Place & Policy Online 2007: 2/1, pp37-47

10. 'Success For FIPs-Initial Findings' ; Dept. for Children , Schools & Families. www. dcsf.gov.uk/pns/DisplayPN.cgi.pn_id=2008 _0145

11. ' Together : Tackling ASB, Article 1 : How do I tackle ASB when an individual has a disability or mental health condition?' www. together.gov/article.asp?aid=1905&qid=36

12. 'Youth Justice Board Guidance on ASB : Annex A ; Disability, Mental Health & Special Educational Needs' www. yjb.gov.uk/publications/resources/downloads

13. 'BIBIC Research on ASBOs and young people with learning difficulties and mental health problems'; British Institute for Brain Injured Children website, 2005.

30181631R00226

Printed in Great
Britain
by Amazon